ALSO BY WALTER J. BOYNE

NONFICTION
CLASH OF TITANS: WORLD WAR II AT SEA
SILVER WINGS
ART IN FLIGHT: THE SCULPTURE OF JOHN SAFER
CLASSIC AIRCRAFT
FLIGHT
THE POWER BEHIND THE WHEEL
THE SMITHSONIAN BOOK OF FLIGHT
THE LEADING EDGE
DE HAVILLAND DH-4: FROM FLAMING COFFIN TO LIVING LEGEND
MESSERSCHMITT ME 262—ARROW TO THE FUTURE
BOEING B-52: A DOCUMENTARY HISTORY
PHANTOMS IN COMBAT

FICTION
AIR FORCE EAGLES
EAGLES AT WAR
TROPHY FOR EAGLES
THE WILD BLUE with Steven L. Thompson

CLASH OF WINGS

WORLD WAR II IN THE AIR

WALTER J. BOYNE

A TOUCHSTONE BOOK
PUBLISHED BY SIMON & SCHUSTER

TOUCHSTONE
ROCKEFELLER CENTER
1230 AVENUE OF THE AMERICAS
NEW YORK, NEW YORK 10020

FIRST TOUCHSTONE EDITION 1997

TOUCHSTONE AND COLOPHON ARE REGISTERED TRADEMARKS
OF SIMON & SCHUSTER INC.

DESIGNED BY KAROLINA HARRIS
MANUFACTURED IN THE UNITED STATES OF AMERICA

10 9   8   7   6

THE LIBRARY OF CONGRESS HAS CATALOGED THE SIMON & SCHUSTER
EDITION AS FOLLOWS:
BOYNE, WALTER J.
CLASH OF WINGS : AIR POWER IN WORLD WAR II /
BY WALTER J. BOYNE
P.   CM.
INCLUDES BIBLIOGRAPHICAL REFERENCES AND INDEX.
1. WORLD WAR 1939–1945—AERIAL OPERATIONS. I. TITLE.
D785.B69 1994
940.54'4—DC20   93-46526 CIP
ISBN 0-671-79370-5
ISBN 0-684-83915-6 (PBK)

ACKNOWLEDGMENTS

In the preparation of this book, I consulted hundreds of sources and was continually amazed by the depth and breadth of coverage of the constituent elements of the great air campaigns of World War II, and by the continual improvement, over time, in the efforts of both amateur and professional historians.

It is especially rewarding to discover a new author, one who has a particular interest in a single facet of the war and who spends an enormous amount of time and effort to elucidate that facet for others.

There is a special group of historians in the United States and Great Britain that I would like to acknowledge, men and women who have devoted their lives to their avocation and who flourish in small, loosely knit organizations like the American Aviation Historical Society, or the Society of World War One Aero Historians, or any one of a dozen similar specialized groups. They do their labor for love of the subject and for concern for the truth, and all readers of aviation history should be grateful to them.

In the course of my career, it was my privilege to meet a number of the great figures of World War II, including Ira Eaker, James Doolittle, Curtis E. LeMay, Francis Gabreski, Chuck Yeager, Bud Mahurin, Stanford Tuck, Douglas Bader, Johnny Johnson, Adolf Galland, Johannes Steinhoff, Walter Krupinski, Pierre Closterman, Hans Knoke, Sakai Saburo, Hans von Ohain, Sir Frank Whittle, and many, many more. It has also been a privilege to meet hundreds of less well known figures, each of whom has a story to tell. From the many conversations and sometimes extensive correspondence with these doers of great deeds, I was able to form a better impression of the human side of the air war. I hope that this is conveyed in *Clash of Wings*.

I am indebted to Henry Snelling, who has spent hours struggling with my facts and my syntax; to Leo Opdycke, for his sometimes caustic but always constructive comments; to Pearlie Draughn, the star librarian of the Air Force Association, who is always helpful; to Murray Peden, Queen's Counsel, and a sterling Stirling pilot who is also a great writer; to Bob Bender, my patient editor; to Jacques de Spoelberch, my agent; and to my family, for putting up with me.

WALTER J. BOYNE
Ashburn, Virginia
August 18, 1993

This book is dedicated to the participants of the great air campaigns of World War II, those who flew, maintained, built, planned, or simply paid for the weapons that were used in that great conflict. A very few people, primarily the air leaders and the great aces, became well known during the war. They did so only as a result of the efforts of the millions more who labored anonymously, doing their very best, whether it was bucking rivets in an aircraft factory in California, chipping stones for runways in China, or servicing planes in all weathers and all climates. A debt of gratitude is owed to them all.

CONTENTS

Preface   11

Chapter One: The Bluff Is Called   15

Chapter Two: The Plunge into Reality   49

Chapter Three: Wings of the Rising Sun   94

Chapter Four: Hitler's Biggest Gamble   139

Chapter Five: The African Tutorial   166

Chapter Six: Germany's Third and Last Chance   189

Chapter Seven: The Biggest Battleground   207

Chapter Eight: The Cost of Incompetence   240

Chapter Nine: Round-the-Clock Bombing   282

Chapter Ten: Air Superiority Lost, Then Won   321

Chapter Eleven: True Airpower . . . At Last   358

Appendix 1: Aircraft Types   381

Appendix 2: Statistics on Major Aircraft   389

Selected Reading   393

Index   397

PREFACE

Clash of Wings is a wide-ranging survey of the great air campaigns of World War II, extending from the first bombs dropped in Poland to the atomic weapons exploded in Japan. It covers all theaters, from the frozen steppes of the Soviet Union to the nightmare heat of Pacific jungle fighting. In each theater, the principal focus is on the people doing the fighting, and it is important to note that the ordinary soldiers, sailors, and airmen fought with dignity and courage, irrespective of their country or their cause.

As each campaign is analyzed, note is taken of the technical developments of the time—new aircraft, new weapons, new tactics—and as each campaign progresses, the leadership is evaluated. From this, it soon becomes apparent that the Allies were as blessed as the Axis countries were cursed by the quality of their respective leaders. President Franklin D. Roosevelt made extremely good judgments in his early choice of leaders, who, for the most part, served him throughout the war. In a similar way, Prime Minister Winston S. Churchill eventually assembled a closely knit group who accommodated to his unique mercurial genius. In contrast, Adolf Hitler feared his generals and ignored his admirals, using them as mere office boys to execute his will, and, as events required, to blame for his mistakes. Mussolini, that cardboard Führer, was unable to manage his senior officers, who, in turn, were largely incapable of managing their troops.

In the Soviet Union, a startling situation occurred. After Stalin's purges had weakened his armed forces to the point of dissolution, the German invasion caused a spontaneous welling up of new, capable, patriotic leaders who served him well. In Japan, the military leadership was both hopelessly divided, army against navy, and incredibly shortsighted.

Thus it was that the democratic nations were ultimately able to make the best use of the newest weapon, airpower. For almost all of the twenty-one years immediately following the end of World War I, conscientious statesmen, politicians, newspaper editors, and the general public believed it not only possible, but probable, that the next war might be won in a few days by the terror bombing of helpless cities. Fleets of aircraft were to stream in to drop tons of bombs, making London or Paris uninhabitable; the frightened, demoralized populace would flee, demanding surrender from its government. Curiously enough, the leading air force officers in all countries knew that this was an impossible scenario, beyond the means of any air force—but, for reasons of policy and economics, they would not admit this.

Hitler was well aware of the limitations of his Luftwaffe even as he threatened its employment to bully his way through a series of bloodless conquests. Mussolini was less successful than his ally, but did use airpower to defeat Ethiopia and to annex Albania and, implicitly, to threaten England and France. Hitler's bellicose threats were made more credible by the horrors of the Spanish Civil War and by Japan's indiscriminate bombing of helpless Chinese cities.

Yet when World War II began on September 1, 1939, the Axis powers scrupulously refrained from terror bombing the western Allies. The Luftwaffe worked in perfect harmony with the German Army in destroying Poland, climaxing the effort with a sustained terror bombing of Warsaw. Raids on Paris and London were strictly forbidden, in part for fear of retaliation, but in larger measure because the necessary equipment was lacking. Germany chose instead to depend upon its magnificent army, suitably supported by the Luftwaffe, hoping to win a series of short wars that would leave it master of the Continent.

Thus the Second World War began as a series of land and sea campaigns in which airpower played a subordinate role, principally in the support of army operations. It became a gigantic training program for all of the combatants, both civil and military, particularly in regard to the air war. In the military, almost all of the ideas developed during World War I and afterward proved to be totally obsolete; new methods had to be learned in everything from combat formations to dropping bombs. On the civil side, a tremendous reappraisal had to be made about the amount of resources, material and human, that had to be applied to the air war effort. The most amazing aspect of the phenomena is how quickly military personnel and civilians, men and women, became sharp professionals, able to execute their tasks with a degree of skill and rigor unimagined before the war.

Year by year, as the war expanded the industrial efforts of the combatant nations, airpower became ever-more important, to the point that it became a necessary condition for victory in Europe in 1944, and the decisive element in the Pacific in 1945.

The success of the Allied air effort can be attributed to many causes, including relative national wealth, but there are two important factors that are often not recognized, the first of which was the early realization by the United States, England, and Russia of the gigantic scale of effort necessary to exercise airpower. Where before the war a first-line air force of two thousand aircraft was considered formidable, all three of the Allied nations ended the war with air forces numbering in the tens of thousands. The Axis powers started with a numerical (and qualitative) air superiority, but waited for too long even to begin to match the Allied production of aircraft, crews, and all the attendant equipment. By 1942, they had fallen hopelessly behind. Italy never developed a serious manufacturing capacity, and in Germany, despite almost miraculous industrial achievements by Albert Speer, the increase in aircraft production came two years too late. Japan did not begin to realize its own industrial capacity until 1943 when, again, it was already far too late.

The second vital factor was that the magnitude of the Allied effort was enhanced and expanded by its qualitative superiority. The governments of the democratic nations—and their Soviet ally—proved to be far more effective than the governments of the autocratic Axis nations, despite their reputation for monolithic organization and discipline. The Allies were consistently able to use their scientists to greater advantage in creating new weapons, cracking codes, or developing better means of production. The Germans did, later in the war, develop some new weapons that heralded the coming age of missiles, but these proved to be far too little and much too late.

The Italian prophet of airpower, Giulio Douhet, had published his seminal work *The Command of the Air* in 1921. He had adherents in every air force in the world; in the United States, Brigadier General Billy Mitchell tirelessly preached the coming of airpower. Yet despite the massive efforts on all sides, true airpower was not demonstrated until twenty-four years after Douhet's book was published—in the skies over Japan. By the spring of 1945, a potent combination of B-29s and incendiary bombs had evolved that could destroy the vulnerable Japanese cities. With absolute air superiority established, the B-29s had the capacity to effect the utter destruction of Japan's industrial base but still lacked the ability to destroy the will of the Japanese people to fight and die. It was deemed necessary to take the next step, one that no one had prophesied—the attainment of *absolute* airpower. This came about at Hiroshima and Nagasaki, where the combination of the B-29 and the atomic bomb at long last sapped the Japanese will to resist.

Between the first tentative efforts in Poland and the mushroom clouds over Japan, there were great struggles on many continents and every ocean. In Europe, Russia, and Africa, airpower was an essential but subordinate component of the massive land battles. In the Battle of the Atlantic, aircraft were again important, but not decisive. It was different in the Pacific, where the naval campaigns took on an entirely new character; the great fleet engagements for which admirals of all navies had practiced were subordinated to the new style of carrier warfare. The island-hopping ground war in the Pacific was far more dependent on airpower than were the campaigns in Europe.

By the end of the war, airpower had demonstrated its effectiveness and had cast its long shadow for the future. In the next half century, there would be many small wars in which tactical airpower was important, but, contrary to almost everyone's expectations, World War III did not occur. It was deterred because true airpower—arrived at so laboriously and at such great cost—had been given such a devastating demonstration in the skies over Japan.

1

THE BLUFF
IS CALLED

World War II began in the air at exactly 0434 hours, September 1, 1939, when three German Stuka dive-bombers burst through murky weather to attack two railroad bridges spanning the Vistula River near Dirschau, Poland. Their task was to destroy the detonating wires leading to the explosive charges mining the bridges, and thus prevent Polish engineers from blowing them up.

World War II effectively ended in the air at 1058, August 9, 1945, when a single Boeing B-29 broke out of murky weather to drop an atomic bomb on the city of Nagasaki. A few more raids were flown by other aircraft, but their effect was inconsequential in comparison to the Nagasaki holocaust, coming as it did three days after the first atomic bomb had been dropped on Hiroshima.

The difference in capability between the slow, angular Stuka, its very shape a swastika in the sky, and the beautiful silver B-29 cruising high over Japan is a perfect example of the expansion of airpower that took place in six years of war. The relatively small 250-kilogram bombs the Stukas used at Dirschau related directly to the past; the 23-kiloton yield of the "Fat Man" bomb used at Nagasaki cast a terrible shadow for the future.

Adolf Hitler could not contain the war he started, and as the fighting spread around the globe, it called upon the very best efforts of heroic aircrews, dedicated mechanics, and industrious men and women on the production lines. The ephemeral glamour of the air war was captured on film: a flight of "the few" taking off in Spitfires to repel the incoming Messerschmitts; Jimmy Doolittle hauling a protesting B-25 into the air from the *Hornet*'s deck in his famous first raid on Tokyo; a stairstep echelon of Dauntlesses, peeling off to sink Japanese carriers; or at the end, lonely pairs of Messerschmitt Me 262s, slipping through the clouds like gray-green sharks, still attacking even though the war is nearly over. The terrors of war are also recorded, mass horrors like the devastated cities of London, Dresden, or Tokyo, and poignant individual tragedies as well.

This history of the major air campaigns of World War II chronicles the changing concepts of airpower from the almost wistful projections of Billy Mitchell to the horrifying reality of nuclear devastation. When the war began, every country had a concept of airpower that was both simple and erroneous. All of the aerial combat experience of World War I, China and Spain in the 1930s, and a dozen other smaller wars had failed to yield a genuine understanding of the degree of effort that the achievement and exercise of true aerial supremacy required. It would take almost six years of desperate battle and an immense expenditure of lives and matériel before true airpower was defined in the skies over Japan.

THE IMAGE OF AIRPOWER

The air war was generally characterized by wasted effort and false starts rather than by effective strikes, and the cost in lives both in the air and on the ground was frightful. Yet, like time and distance, the camera lens filters out these unpleasant aspects, leaving behind the drama and the glory, as if each of the grinning young men flashing the thumbs-up signal came through unscathed.

The newsreel films also leave the impression that true strategic airpower was an inevitable event. It was not, despite the credence given to the prophets who defined strategic airpower as the ability of a nation to impose its will upon an enemy by an overwhelming bombing campaign. The advocates of strategic airpower painted an irresistible vision of a quick, surgical decision—the knockout blow—in a first strike by a few hundred aircraft that would paralyze the enemy's homeland by destroying essential industries and inducing panic in its populace. Neither the Italian Giulio Douhet nor the American Billy Mitchell was willing to admit just how inadequate the contemporary technology was to do what they sought. When they first made their prophecies, aircraft simply could not fly far enough with a sufficient bomb load, and could neither navigate nor drop bombs accurately enough to be decisive. It would be two decades before they could.

AIRPOWER BY PROPAGANDA

In the interval between the two world wars, the threat of airpower was overriding in the minds of the leading politicians. Death from the air became a political stalking horse, best exemplified by the ominous warnings of England's Prime Minister Stanley Baldwin. On November 10, 1932, Baldwin declaimed "that the bomber will always get through," and warned that unless bombers were banned, European civilization would be destroyed. No one bothered to make a value judgment of the real probability of a war with France—for it was French bombers that worried Baldwin—or of the bombers' limited capability. Baldwin's words became a dictum from which a mental picture grew of an avalanche of bombers leveling the cities and killing the populace with poison gas. No one questioned this outcome, nor did anyone analyze the puny capability of the Armée de l'Air at the time, consisting as it did of a handful of frightfully ugly biplanes that were able to carry only small bomb loads and were for the most part incapable of hitting even so large a target as London.

The politicians' fatuous preoccupation with the bombers' knockout blow is difficult to understand, for excepting only the V-2 rocket and the atomic bomb, every type of air action later experienced during World War II had been demonstrated extensively in the preceding twenty years. In the process, any military staff should have been able to quantify the limitations as well as the possibilities of airpower in terms of the amount of damage that could be rendered by the amount of bombs that could be delivered. No one bothered to do this, and in 1936, Britain and France so trembled at the thought of an air war with Germany that they violated the treaties of Versailles and Locarno by permitting the remilitarization of the Rhineland. At the time, the Germans possessed fewer than three hundred Junkers Ju 52/3m bombers, converted passenger transports that had just sufficient range to reach England from German airfields—but not while carrying a bomb load. (Germany also had virtually no aerial bombs on hand, a fact less likely to have been known.) Simple mathematics and a comparison with the bombing effects experienced in World War I would have shown that even if all the German bombers had been operational and were launched unopposed in the attack they could have made on Paris, their 1,000-pound loads of small bombs would have done little damage. Instead, impressive calculations were made imputing tremendous—and unwarranted—killing power to each ton of explosive (72 deaths per ton of bombs was long used as a benchmark), so that it seemed that the populations of London and Paris would be decimated by a German attack. The fallacious deaths-per-ton-of-bomb statistics were enhanced by the special horror of poison gas, which was widely assumed to have annihilating powers.

To be sure, the media added to the general apprehension with editorial cartoons depicting apocalyptic results of bombing raids; books and films like H. G. Wells's *The Shape of Things to Come* added to the public's fear. The resulting panicky mental set was a windfall for Germany's master propagandist, Dr. Joseph Goebbels. It permitted Germany and Italy to brandish their nonexistent airpower to blackmail French and English leaders into submission time after time, making a mockery of the League of Nations by their actions in Ethiopia, the Rhineland, Austria, and Czechoslovakia. To add to the irony, Adolf Hitler, after threatening the use of cataclysmic surprise bombing attacks as a means of "peacefully" attaining his ends, forbade such attacks as soon as war broke out. The general fear of airpower had been reinforced when, on the other side of the world, Japan's early exercise of airpower savaged China and humiliated the United States with the bombing of the USS *Panay*. The political decisions that led to Neville Chamberlain's nationally applauded policy of appeasement and to France's apathetic Maginot Line defensive strategy were made possible by an unreasoning fear of what contemporary airpower could do.

There were some very logical reasons why no one from the military stepped forward to counter the claims. The levels of English and French military preparedness were so abysmally low that the military welcomed any public support, generated for any reason, no matter how hysterical. Both countries had been exhausted by the War to End all Wars—Churchill was to speak poignantly of the faces of the young men he didn't see in Parliament, all dead in Flanders—and both were enervated by the worldwide depression.

Great Britain was hamstrung by the infamous "Ten-Year Rule," a budget-cutting device that is echoed in today's post–Cold War economic situation, which calls for the substitution of prototyping for production. Under the Ten-Year Rule, defense spending was based on the assumption that there would be no war in ten years, a concept intended not to stifle ideas but to avoid the cost of large-scale production of equipment that would become obsolete. If war suddenly appeared imminent, then armament production was to begin. Wickedly attractive from a budgetary standpoint, it was indefensible in terms of engineering and industrial planning. Worse, it was suicidal in regard to negotiation, and destructive to the industrial base. Even in those rather simple days, an aircraft took four years to move from specification to production, and an aircraft engine took from seven to ten years. The result was a Royal Air Force equipped at the time of the Munich crisis with only a few Hurricane and no Spitfire squadrons; its defense rested primarily on the Gloster Gladiator, a fixed-gear biplane that would not have appeared very much out of place on the western front in 1918. Chamberlain, whom historians have called arrogant in his ignorance, preferred to pursue his appeasement policy rather than risk a war.

The greatest irony is that in 1938 this tiny force would have been adequate for the defense of Britain against the puny Luftwaffe Germany could have employed. The essential difference was that England knew how weak it was and imputed a nonexistent strength to Germany. Germany knew that both were weak, but bluffed successfully.

Logically, Germany's situation should have been the worst of all. Weakened by the blockade, stripped of arms by the Armistice, denied new weapons by the Treaty of Versailles, wracked by political dissension and an inflation of hallucinatory proportions, it should have been unable to rearm. Instead, much of the turmoil worked to the German advantage. Old plants were gone, new ones had to be built; old companies were weakened and could be subverted by the delicious bait of subsidy, attracting the best and brightest of German engineering talent. Most of all, the country was fascinated with aviation, for although the Imperial Navy had funked it in the Great War, remaining in port for most of the war, and the Imperial Army was beaten in the field, the Imperial German Air Force had battled valiantly to the end, young tigers like Captain Hermann Göring defiantly wrecking their aircraft rather than surrendering them.

In all countries, the development of both strategic and tactical airpower was compromised by the failure of political and military leaders to make the necessary investments in research and development, training, equipment, and logistics. When the hard exigencies of war exposed these deficiencies, the same leaders substituted the bravery and blood of their young aircrews for intelligent planning and farsighted provisioning. The vaunted Luftwaffe is a notable case in point. Despite the monumental blunders of its leadership and a totally inadequate training and logistics base that resulted in terrible casualties, its dwindling crews remained relatively effective to the end, asking no quarter in a war long lost. Similarly, because there was no other way to strike at Germany, England poured vast resources into its Bomber Command, which was decimated in a bloody campaign in which indiscriminate area bombing fulfilled all of the horrors of air war yet fell just short of the exercise of true airpower.

When war came in 1939, strategic airpower was for a long time overshadowed by the early successes of tactical airpower—air-to-air combat, ground attack, and dive-bombing. Nazi Germany expanded its borders to include almost all of Western Europe and Africa on the strength of its tactical airpower, while Japan acquired a Pacific empire by the same means.

The staggering early Axis success contrasts strongly with the prolonged failure of strategic bombing by England, Germany, and, for many years, the United States. In the end, only the United States attained true strategic airpower, and this in the last months of the war, after the risky expenditure of billions of dollars and by virtue of the experience gained in three years of hard fighting.

Even Germany, whose propaganda made conquest and airpower virtually synonymous, had until 1943 no concept of either the numbers of aircraft it really required for the task, or of its inherent capacity to produce them. Even though aircraft had been produced in massive amounts during World War I, the pitifully small air forces maintained between the wars constrained the thinking of most planners. When the whirlwind expansion came just prior to and during World War II, the lessons that had been so painfully learned since 1914, including the subsequent conflicts in Spain, China, and Manchukuo (northeastern China, occupied by Japan), were for the most part wasted. In every air force, the leaders were overwhelmed by new people, new situations, and, inevitably, old mistakes, for most of the conclusions drawn from experience by the future belligerents were usually erroneous. Thus Germany, after initiating strategic aerial warfare with its bombing of England by Zeppelins and Gothas in World War I, elected not to develop a strategic air force for the next war. Instead, it cast airpower as the handmaiden of the army, based on the experience gained using ground-attack aircraft on the western front and in Spain. England, on the other hand, resented the German attacks bitterly and determined to have a strategic bombing capability. The Royal Air Force's ghastly casualty rate during ground attacks with its fighters led it to draw exactly the opposite conclusion from the Germans, and caused it to ignore almost completely the concept of army cooperation in the postwar years, so when World War II came, it lacked for more than three years an effective dive-bomber or ground-attack aircraft.

Between the two great wars, all nations, including France and the United States, spent a great deal of their small air force budgets on observation planes to be used in direct cooperation with their armies. France went further, and wasted millions of francs procuring multipurpose aircraft that were useless either as fighters or bombers and were derisively called "collective coffins" by their large crews.

There were other errors, shared by other nations. The Germans inferred from their experience in Spain that fast bombers did not need fighter escorts, and the Americans amplified this with the concept of the "self-defended" heavy bomber. Aircraft like the B-17 Flying Fortress were to be so heavily armed as to be able to fend off fighter attacks and make deep unescorted penetrations into hostile territory. And on one vital point, all nations found erroneous agreement: it was believed impossible to create a fighter with sufficient range to escort bombers to the target and at the same time have sufficient maneuverability to combat enemy interceptors.

The experience of the past was largely wasted during World War II. It was not until after 1943 that most of the Allied leaders had learned on the job and become truly expert in the exercise of airpower; some of their Axis counterparts had the same learning breakthroughs, but their insight was handicapped by political ineptitude as well as matériel shortages. The Soviet Union, a special case by virtue of its size and the makeup of its armed forces, was able virtually to ignore the strategic aspects of air war, while concentrating so effectively upon the development of tactical airpower that its strategic needs were served. The leaders of the U.S. air forces also made initial errors but, aware of the almost unlimited resources behind them, were able ultimately to exercise both strategic and tactical airpower on a scale never before contemplated.

THE ELUSIVE QUEST FOR AIR SUPERIORITY

Almost all commanders in World War II recognized the requirement for air superiority to permit successful ground operations. What they did not recognize was the amount of money, training, time, and personnel necessary to obtain air superiority. Most nations never made the necessary investment; the United States, for a variety of reasons, including its delayed entry into the war, the purchase of war matériel by the Allied Purchasing Commission, and its natural tendency to think along massive production lines, did understand the size of the challenge and made the necessary investment, which bore fruit from 1942 on.

In general terms, the Air Corps's Air War Planning Division I enabled the United States to be the first nation to make a reasonably accurate calculation of the size and weight of effort that would be required to achieve strategic results. All the great powers of the world, with the exception of the Soviet Union, planned on air forces that might have as many as 5,000 aircraft in total, broken down into a variety of types, so that when war began—as most knew surely that it would—the "front-line strength" would be a force of perhaps 800 bombers and 600 fighters ready for combat. This earnest but shortsighted view of the scale of air combat missed by 1,000 percent what was eventually required, and underlay most of the misapplication of airpower throughout the war.

But in 1938, Hitler had convinced the world that Germany possessed the greatest air force in history; unfortunately for the Fatherland, he had also convinced himself.

At the same time, England was frantically scrambling to rescue the Royal Air Force from years of neglect, buying new fighters and laying down the design for new heavy bombers. France, once the possessor of the most powerful air force in Europe, was in a desperate situation, having built the wrong kinds of aircraft at the wrong time, and having simultaneously allowed its aviation industrial base to erode. The United States was able to capitalize on the European emergency and sell aircraft to the Allies. The Soviet Union was quietly, secretly building a larger air force than anyone believed possible, while Japan was, in even greater secrecy, creating small but very proficient army and navy air forces.

Each nation's air force selected the kinds of aircraft it thought suited to its national strategy. Thus, in terms of the weapons of another era, in the East, Japan was preparing a javelin to thrust into the heart of American defenses. In the West, Germany and the Soviet Union were perfecting the short sword to use in cooperation with their great land armies. At the same time, Great Britain was fashioning an unwieldy club with which to defend itself and France. The United States was going for the longbow—the strategic bomber.

THE STORM GATHERS

In the fall of 1938, tension in Europe was higher than at any time since the guns had roared in August 1914, as Adolf Hitler proclaimed that he would no longer suffer the mistreatment of people of German descent in the Czech Sudetenland. His propagandists and fifth-column activity had stirred up the 3.5 million so-called Sudeten Germans with a demand of unity with Germany; the situation was as confused and as foreboding as the recent breakup of Yugoslavia.

Yet it was not ethnic cleansing that dictated Hitler's desire, but rather geography and logistics. After the annexation of Austria, the map was now an explicit Rorschach blot with Germany's wolf-head mouth clamped about Czechoslovakia. If the latter country were occupied, Germany would be perfectly positioned to deal first with Poland and then with Russia.

Militarily, Czechoslovakia was a much more difficult challenge than Austria had been. The Czechs had thirty-five divisions at a time when England had two, France seventy-six, and the Germans thirty-six. The Czech Army was well trained and superbly armed by the Skoda works, which also turned out excellent artillery, tanks, and armored cars. In the mountainous areas on the German frontier, Czech engineers had constructed a system of defenses that were considered by many to be superior to, if less sophisticated than, France's vaunted Maginot Line. One signal difference was the extraordinary depth of the fortification belt, which in some cases ran back almost as far as Prague. Inasmuch as the conventional wisdom of the time dictated at least a three-to-one superiority of attacker over defender, the Czechs could have withstood a German invasion for months, even though fortifications on the Austrian frontier were less developed.

The German military command knew that their country could not survive a war against the combined powers of Czechoslovakia, England, France, and Russia, all of whom would be supported by the United States. But Hitler maintained that the leaders of these countries did not have the stomach for war, and that they would back down in a crisis. In the event, his thirst for aggression was assuaged by the other European leaders, each for different reasons. "Appeasement" is now taken as a generic term; then, it was a specific name for Neville Chamberlain's proclaimed policy, one that led to his ultimate humiliation. France, terrified by the thought of war with Germany without England at its side, went along, in spite of the fact that its sixty-eight regular divisions could easily have brushed aside the five regular and four reserve German divisions then opposing it. The government of Poland was greatly romanticized after the war began, but in 1938 it was greedily seeking a taste of Hitler's pudding by agreeing to support Germany in exchange for the acquisition of Tesin, a Polish-speaking area in the north of Czechoslovakia. Admiral Miklós Horthy, the Hungarian dictator, was also hungry for Hungarian-speaking regions of Czechoslovakia.

The Czechs chose to give up when the Soviet Union informed President Eduard Benes that it would not honor its agreement to defend his country because France had reneged. Benes resigned on the following day. Italy's Duce, Benito Mussolini, immediately proposed a meeting in Munich for September 29. France and England were invited to attend; Czechoslovakia was excluded. It was the apex of Mussolini's career, a morsel of memory he would savor when he was stowed away as a German puppet in the north of Italy, before his brutal end at the hand of partisans.

The negotiations at Munich were patently unfair. By means of the wiretaps he had placed on the telephone lines at all the embassies, Hitler was fully informed of Chamberlain's resolve not to go to war. After a long day's negotiations over meaningless details, the wolf's jaws closed and France and England agreed to strip Czechoslovakia of the Sudetenland—where the 1,200 miles of defensive lines were constructed. Chamberlain acceded to every German request with a toothy eagerness, happy to see his appeasement policy working so well, anxious to fly home to England with a piece of paper he believed would mean "peace in our time."

The quick chain of Hitler's successes combined with a worsening economic situation to bring war closer in early 1939. The Führer's rearmament policy of many guns and ersatz butter had brought the German state beyond full employment to a labor shortage. It had also exhausted Germany's already meager stock of foreign exchange, despite the economic sleight of hand of the president of the Reichsbank, Dr. Hjalmar Schacht.

Hitler resolved to remedy these problems with the occupation of the remainder of Czechoslovakia in March 1939, a move that would add to the Reich a strong economy, an expert work force, 1,500 aircraft, and the equipment of the twenty-seven divisions the Czechs still had under arms. Playing upon divisive nationalism still rampant today, Hitler prepared his way by urging receptive Slovakian leaders to declare their independence. The alternative he held out was to be ceded to Hungary, still eager to acquire Czechoslovakian territory where ethnic Hungarians lived. The Slovaks accepted his offer, agreeing to subordinate their civil, military, and diplomatic matters to Hitler's control, including all German measures against the Jews. Abandoned by the West, Czechia, as it was then called, now had to turn to Hitler for protection against Communist uprisings; the remainder of the Czechoslovakian plum was ripe for picking.

Harvesttime came on March 15, 1939, when, after browbeating Czech President Emil Hácha to the point of collapse from a heart attack, Germany was "invited" to become Czechoslovakia's protector.

The victory superheated Hitler's ego, already inflated to monstrous proportions and continually stoked by the flattery of his sycophants. Chamberlain and Édouard Daladier, the prime ministers of England and France, respectively, had bowed to him and were now, in Hitler's words, mere worms that he could grind beneath his heel. It became a conceit with Hitler that the Munich Agreement annoyed him because it denied him the war he wanted. His wishes would not be denied in Poland.

BORN IN BATTLE

Like the Israeli Air Force some thirty years later, the Polskie Sily Powiertrzne (Polish Air Force) had been born in battle. Fostered by parent units formed in France and Russia in 1918 to battle the Germans, the Polish Air Force was formally established on November 14, 1918, in Warsaw, as what would become the nation of Poland began taking over the local remains of the Austro-Hungarian Empire. Over the next two years, using an exotic mixture of German, Austrian, French, English, Italian, and Russian equipment, the Polish Air Force was a significant factor in establishing Polish independence. During this long and bitter war, the Poles had to face resurgent German hostility in the west, Czech incursions in the southwest and repeated Bolshevik attacks in the Ukraine.

In April 1920, under the ardent revolutionary Józef Pilsudski, the Polish armies surged into the Ukraine, capturing Kiev on May 7. Operating in support, the Polish Air Force attacked enemy communications and troop concentrations and acted as liaison between Polish Army units. The Poles overreached themselves, and in August the Red forces struck back, driving all the way to the gates of Warsaw. On August 14, in what Polish historians would subsequently call "the miracle of the Vistula" and "the eighteenth decisive battle of the world," Polish forces, stiffened by the French, counterattacked and decisively defeated the Russian armies. The war ended officially on October 18, 1920.

The Russo-Polish conflict was very different from the trench warfare fought on the western front; the lines were very fluid, and aircraft were more important for maintaining contact with both the enemy and with friendly troops. One telling effect of this experience occurred in August 1929, when now Premier Pilsudski, head of Poland's militaristic, anti-Semitic regime, decreed that "aviation is to serve only for reconnaissance and only in this direction should it be used."

Pilsudski's unrealistic directive had been fought by two of Poland's great air leaders. The first was General Wlodzimierz Zagorski, who created an air force second only to that of France in Europe, capable of independent operations. He purchased the best equipment available and fostered an indigenous aircraft industry. Primarily because his success made him a threat, but also because some of his financial dealings were questioned, Zagorski was forced out in 1926. He was succeeded as Commander in Chief by Colonel, later Brigadier General, Ludomil Rayski, who would guide the Polish Air Force from 1926 to 1939. The popular Rayski emulated Hugh Trenchard of the Royal Air Force in setting up a sound foundation of air bases and training schools. Forced by circumstance to subordinate the air force completely to the army, it was said of Rayski that he built the Polish Air Force, but did not teach it to fight.

TIME AND TIDE

During the First World War, the combatant powers were able to meet threats by rapidly fielding new types of aircraft, sometimes taking as little as two or three months from design to combat operations. By the mid-1930s, reequipping an air force became a much lengthier process. It took four years or longer from design to production, and another two years to reequip and train operational units. During the latter period, strength usually declined as obsolete aircraft were surveyed and new aircraft experienced the usual break-in problems. Consequently, the timing of a decision to embark upon a new generation of aircraft was critical. France, for example, had made a disastrous mistake in building up its air force with early-1930s designs; when it finally committed to reequipment in the mid-thirties, it was too late. Germany had caught the wave exactly at the right time for World War II, having its units equipped and trained by the fall of 1939. England was about a year behind Germany in the reequipment process, a disadvantage when war broke out, but one that was turned to an advantage by the time of the critical period in the fall of 1940.

POLISH PREPARATIONS

Poland's timing was exquisitely bad. It began its most significant modernization program in 1931, and had one of the largest and best-equipped air forces in Europe by 1933, when things were relatively peaceful. When other European nations frantically began to rearm, Poland lapsed into a period of stagnation from which it never recovered.

Poland's air force was small in number and equipped with obsolete aircraft, but that was not Poland's greatest problem. Bad leadership in the clique of colonels at the top was. The heady victories against the Soviet Union in 1920 still intoxicated the planners, and all preparations for war envisioned another, similar contest, with a glorious victory going to Polish lancers. Germany was dismissed as an idle bluff, and the militant colonels made wagers on how long it would take to march to Berlin if war did come.

As the colonels boasted, Poland's air force slipped into chaos, with no doctrine and confused lines of command (the air force commander, Rayski, was subject to orders from six different civil and military authorities). Each element of the air force was subject to the whim of local commanders. Yet, when the time came, the Polish flyers would dive into the fray with the same futile gallantry as their cavalry comrades charged the tanks.

THE LUFTWAFFE GOES TO WAR

Hitler's contempt for the leaders of England and France made him confident that they would not go to war when he invaded Poland. He was intent on a limited war, eager to prepare his German troops for further conflict. Having been correct so often in the past, he believed that he would get exactly what he wanted: a swift war against Poland alone, victoriously concluded well within the limited capacity of the German economy to sustain.

Hitler's exaltation over Foreign Minister Joachim von Ribbentrop's diplomatic tour de force, the Nazi-Soviet Pact of August 23, 1939, was marred by England's intransigence, and he was further shaken by Mussolini's decision not to abide by the Italo-German "Pact of Steel." Yet he pressed on, launching the attack on Poland on September 1, 1939, trusting to blind luck that England would not honor its commitment to Poland any better than it had honored its commitment to Czechoslovakia. When, on September 3, he was told that England had declared war, he turned savagely on von Ribbentrop to ask, "What now?" Von Ribbentrop's response that he expected a similar declaration from France was not exactly soothing. In the background, Göring was heard to say, "If we lose this war, then God have mercy on us!"

MEN AND MACHINES

The greatest problem of the Luftwaffe, still masked at the time, was its deep-seated organizational disarray, due to the inveterate infighting of its leaders. The Commander in Chief of the Luftwaffe relied heavily on his deputy, General Erhard Milch; at the same time, he was jealous of Milch's abilities and feared his rising popularity. Milch, in turn, was dismayed at the way Generaloberst (Colonel General) Ernst Udet was mishandling his duties as head of the Technical Office. Udet was himself dismayed by his own incapacity, but Göring would not relieve him. The fourth actor in the dismal play of personalities was the young Generaloberst Hans Jeschonnek, the Chief of Staff of the Luftwaffe, who didn't get along with anyone. Immature, but a faithful worshiper of Hitler, Jeschonnek, like Udet and Göring, would commit suicide.

At the beginning of the war, the flaws in the top leadership were not yet apparent and were greatly offset by the traditional latitude allowed German troops in the field; operational proficiency overcame doctrinal and leadership handicaps. A similar mid-level sense of cooperation prevailed in industry, which often compensated for the errors forced on it from above; it was by capitalizing on this inherent common sense that Albert Speer was able to effect a massive increase in production a few years later.

The Luftwaffe outnumbered the Polish Air Force in total by a factor of two to one and in operational aircraft by a factor of over three to one. The difference was even greater in terms of quality of equipment and training. As a result of its latest reorganization, the Luftwaffe was divided into four major commands: Luftflotte (Air Fleet) 1, with headquarters in Berlin, serving northern and eastern Germany; Luftflotte 2, headquartered at Braunschweig, covering northwest Germany; Luftflotte 3, headquartered at Munich, covering southern and southwestern Germany; and Luftflotte 4, with headquarters in Vienna, and covering Austria and southeastern Germany. Luftflotte 1, under General (later Field Marshal) Albert Kesselring, and Luftflotte 4, under General Alexander Löhr, were assigned the task of supporting the Polish invasion, with nearly 1,600 aircraft between them.

Two better leaders could not have been chosen. "Smiling Albert" Kesselring, tired of the bickering with Milch, had resigned his position as Chief of the Luftwaffe General Staff to take a field command. Kesselring was amiable and even charming, but he was also a tough leader who made the most of his resources. Later in the war, as field marshal, he would conduct the German ground defense in Italy with such brilliance as to earn comparison with Wellington in the eyes of some historians.

Löhr had commanded the Austrian Air Force at the time of the Anschluss. A handsome man, with a neatly trimmed mustache, Löhr would attain the rank of colonel general and serve in most of the hot spots of the war. In one of the many minor ironies of the war, he never became a field marshal because his fellow Austrian, Adolf Hitler, distrusted Austrians! So, apparently, did the Yugoslavs, who hanged Löhr in 1947 for war crimes.

The two men had at their disposal the best-trained, best-equipped air force in the world, staffed by loyal patriots eager to go to war. The saying that Germany had an Imperial navy, a Prussian army, and a National Socialist air force was never more true than in September, 1939. Recalling that the Luftwaffe had been officially founded only four and a half years before, it is important to examine how it was equipped.

RIDING THE WAVE

The Luftwaffe put 897 bombers and 210 fighters into the field, along with auxiliary reconnaissance and transport planes. They mustered 648 Heinkel He 111, Dornier Do 17, and Junkers Ju 86 level bombers; 219 Junkers Ju 87 dive-bombers; and 30 Henschel Hs 123 attack planes. The 210 fighters were divided between Messerschmitt Bf 109s and 110s. The miscellaneous reconnaissance and transports included Junkers Ju 52s, which were also used to drop incendiary bombs near the end of the war.

It was a powerful, well-balanced force, numerically and qualitatively overwhelming. Excluding the Junkers Ju 52 transports, 90 percent of the German aircraft were less than three years old. In comparison, in today's United States Air Force, the average age of the B-52 bomber is about thirty years, while that of the average F-15 is about ten years; about 21 percent of the total USAF fleet is over twenty-four years old.

Following is a brief review of each of the major types to serve as a baseline for comparison with equipment later in the war.

FIGHTERS

One of the classic aircraft of all time, the Messerschmitt Bf 109 was also produced in greater quantity than any other fighter plane in history, more than 33,000 having been built from the first prototype in 1935 to the last one produced in Spain in 1957. Proposed by the Messerschmitt firm in response to a request by the Air Ministry, the original fighter was a development of the very successful Messerschmitt Bf 108 Taifun sports plane, which had debuted in 1934. A four-place aircraft with a performance comparable to the early Beech Bonanzas, the Bf 108 is still flown today.

The Messerschmitt design team created the smallest possible airframe into which the largest available engine could be fitted. The original prototype, the Bf 109 V1, had a 695-horsepower Rolls-Royce Kestrel engine installed temporarily, later replaced by a 610-horsepower Junkers Jumo 210A. A measure of the basic design's capacity for development can be seen in the fact that the last model, the Messerschmitt Bf 109K-4, had substantially the same airframe, suitably strengthened, but equipped with a 2,000-horsepower engine. At the time of its first flight at the end of May 1935, the German fighter was unquestionably the most advanced in the world, for the English Hawker Hurricane would not fly until November 6, 1935, and the Supermarine Spitfire not until March 5, 1936.

In their effort to reduce weight, the Messerschmitt engineers placed the landing-gear attachment points on the fuselage. This saved weight and facilitated production and repair—one could replace a wing on the 109 while it stood on its own gear—but it made ground handling tricky. Takeoff and landing accidents were common, and persist to this day with the few surviving 109 warbirds still flying. As many as 10 percent of the total of the Bf 109s were lost in such accidents, 1,500 occurring from 1939 to 1941 alone.

Although some C and D models were used, the majority of the single-engine fighters facing Poland were the Messerschmitt Bf 109Es, which had 1,050-horsepower Daimler-Benz DB 601A engines and carried two 7.9-mm MG 17 machine guns in the nose and two 20-mm MG FF cannon in the wings. With their hundred-mile-per-hour speed advantage over the Polish P.Z.L.'s, the Messerschmitts could enter and leave combat at their own discretion. After the first few days, fighter-against-fighter combat virtually ceased, and the 109s concentrated on ground attack, strafing retreating Polish units.

Professor Willy Messerschmitt had responded less than enthusiastically to Göring's requirement for the 109's teammate, the Bf 110. The latter was designed as a heavily armed *Zerstörer* (destroyer) able to clear the way for German bombers by defeating enemy interceptors over their own territories. Already persona non grata to Erhard Milch, Messerschmitt tried to please Göring even though he personally believed that the larger twin-engine fighter necessary for such a task would be a compromise, unable to do any job well. The Messerschmitt design team pressed on, and on May 12, 1936, Rudolf Opitz, a test pilot famous for his later work with rocket-powered fighters, made the first flight with the Bf 110.

The twin-engine Messerschmitts did well in Poland in both the bomber escort and ground-attack roles. As potent as the 110's heavy armament was—four 7.9-mm and two 20-mm cannons firing forward and two 7.9-mm machine guns on a flexible mount in the rear—it had some difficulty bringing the slow but agile P.Z.L. fighters to combat, and it was decided early on that new air-combat tactics would have to be developed. Still, it appeared initially that Göring had been right in insisting on the 110's development.

BOMBERS

All four of the multiengine German bombers employed in the Polish campaign first appeared to the public as civil passenger transports. Of the four, the Heinkel He 111 was by far the most important in the Polish campaign and subsequently, for the circumstances of war forced it to continue as frontline equipment for years after it had become obsolete. The He 111A made its first flight on February 24, 1935, an elegant streamlined aircraft with elliptical wings and superb handling characteristics; with its speed of 217 mph, it was faster than the Luftwaffe's biplane fighters. A 2,200-pound bomb load was stowed vertically, in contrast to the American practice of horizontal stowage.

The He 111B proved itself in Spain, and there were a continuing series of design improvements. By September 1, 1939, the Luftwaffe had 808 of the type on hand, mostly He 111P models with engines of 1,100 horsepower and a top speed of 247 mph. The aircraft performed well offensively during the Polish campaign, but the 78 lost to enemy action revealed a glaring fault in defensive armament. The five hand-held 7.9 mm machine guns were totally inadequate, and the basic design of the aircraft did not lend itself to significant improvement. The defect would have tragic consequences for the crews of the He 111 a few months later in the Battle of Britain, and, indeed, for the rest of the war, for the plane fought on to the very end.

The Junkers Ju 86 flew for the first time on November 4, 1934. Production Ju 86s were initially powered with Junkers Jumo 205C diesel engines, which proved to be unsuitable. While diesels could run indefinitely at a standard power setting, the frequent changes of power required in combat rendered them unreliable.

The most elegant of the German bombers, and the fastest at 255 mph, was the Dornier Do 17 "Flying Pencil," which was never seriously intended to be a commercial transport although the factory said it could carry six passengers and express mail. Playing out their role in the hoax, Lufthansa experts refused it for commercial use on the grounds that the passengers' seating would have been too cramped (of course, they had not yet seen a jetliner's tourist class seat).

Long before the rejection, the Reich Air Ministry had begun tests of it as a bomber, fitted with standard Luftwaffe equipment. When war began, 319 were available for combat. The first Dornier Do 17s swept across the Polish border forty-five minutes after the war started, attacking railway bridges, airfields, troop concentrations, and ammunition dumps. Despite the delicate appearance of its slender fuselage, the Do 17 was very robust, able to make diving attacks at 370-mph speeds, making it less vulnerable to ground or air attack.

The final German multiengine bomber, the Junkers Ju 52 trimotor, was a progressive development of a design going back to the 1919 Junkers F 13. It had been recognized as obsolete as a bomber in Spain but, after all aerial opposition had been suppressed, was pressed into service dropping incendiaries on the forlorn defenders of Warsaw. As a transport, the Ju 52 would serve to the last day of the war and beyond.

THE STUKA—THE "SMART" WEAPON

The evil angular lines of the Junkers Ju 87 Stuka became notorious in the early months of the war, and like so many other German warplanes, it was destined to soldier on long after it should have been retired. The Stuka was beloved by its crews for its ruggedness and by ground forces for its pinpoint accuracy. Able to deliver its bombs with precision on targets as small as tanks and pillboxes, it was, in a larger sense, a "smart weapon," the guidance system in this case being the brains of the pilots behind the stick.

Oddly enough, its excellent performance in the Polish campaign would cause great harm to the Luftwaffe through the influence it had on some of the more feckless leaders of the Luftwaffe like Generaloberst Udet and Generalfeldmarschall Göring. Impressed by the Stuka's accuracy, these men reasoned that since level bombing was known to be very inaccurate, it would take hundreds of ordinary long range-bombers to get the same results that dive-bombers could achieve. In their naive enthusiasm, they discounted the greater size and complexity of the long-range bombers and insisted that they, too, have a dive-bombing capability. This mindless goal, ludicrous in the eyes of both the German manufacturers and the operational pilots of the Luftwaffe, resulted in performance degradation and monumental delays for the desperately needed Junkers Ju 88, and contributed to the outright failure of others, including the Messerschmitt Me 210, the Arado Ar 240, and the four-engine Heinkel He 177.

The Luftwaffe deployed only 219 Ju 87s in the Polish campaign, with astonishing effect in reality and on morale. The very first mission of the war was executed by a flight of three Ju 87B-1s, led by Oberleutnant (First Lieutenant) Bruno Dilley, who took off at 0426 on September 1 to attack the approaches to the Dirschau bridges spanning the Vistula River and to destroy the wires leading from the detonators to the explosives with which the Poles had mined the bridges. The attack went off eleven minutes before the official German jump-off time, and was successful, although the Poles were later able to repair the damage and blow up one of the bridges.

The Stukas were from that moment on continually engaged in attacking airfields, bridges, roads, artillery installations, and troop concentrations, peeling off in waves to put their aerial artillery precisely where and when needed. On Udet's suggestion (although some credit the idea to Hitler himself), the Stukas were fitted with wind-driven sirens, called the "trumpets of Jericho," the sound of which had a shattering effect on the already demoralized Polish soldiers. (Similar devices were used informally by the USAF as late as the Korean War.)

COMBAT IN POLAND

Poland elected to deploy its forces—800,000 poorly equipped troops in six armies—to defend both strategically and politically important areas, a task beyond its capacity, and one that set it up perfectly for the one-two punch that Germany had prepared. The Germans, led by General Walther von Brauchitsch (Hitler was not yet interfering in operational matters), disposed of sixty divisions with 1.25 million men. The Polish countryside, flat and dry in the summer heat, was perfect for tank operations.

In their optimism, the Poles thought that their resistance did not have to be prolonged, that the French would spring into action on the western front, crushing the few German divisions left there. The French had also promised immediately to begin shuttle-bombing Germany, flying from French bases to land in Poland, rearming and flying back. None of this materialized, as France settled back into an almost catatonic condition that would characterize the "phony war" in the west.

Contrary to most reports, the Luftwaffe did not catch the Polish Air Force on the ground during the first few days of battle. By August 26, when signs of the German attack were unmistakable, all Polish combat units were transferred to forty-three operational "campaign" airfields that had been prepared in secret. These were stocked with enough food, ammunition, and other supplies to last for up to ten days, while the main operational bases were relegated to acting as decoys for Luftwaffe attacks.

Given the speed advantage of the German bombers over the P.Z.L. fighters, interception was a difficult task, partially solved by a ground observer system, located in sixteen sectors and deployed in three concentric rings around Warsaw. Polish pilots sat in the cockpits of their P.Z.L. fighters, engines ready to start. When an enemy formation was reported by the outermost ring of observers, the fighters were scrambled in the direction and to the altitude reported. Additional information from the ground observers (Poland had no radar sets) was relayed as the fighters closed to the attack.

Fog and low clouds obscured Warsaw early on September 1, but the air action was still sharp and deadly. The first German formations of about a hundred aircraft—Heinkel and Dornier bombers, escorted by Messerschmitt Bf 110s—were intercepted at 0800, and in the ensuing battle, the German bombers jettisoned their bomb loads. An afternoon raid, in greater strength, with Bf 109 escorts, was similarly disrupted.

As in every phase of the war, right down to the bitter end, there were occasional instances when personal bravery illuminated the dark process. As the Luftwaffe formations droned in, the ground observer net alerted the Pursuit Brigade, and fifty Polish fighters lifted off, making contact ten minutes later. Lieutenant Aleksander Gabszewicz peered through the gull wings of his P.Z.L. P.11, charged his four machine guns and dove to attack a Heinkel He 111. Hit by his first bursts, the Heinkel pulled out of formation and, in the enthusiasm of the chase, Gabszewicz pursued it, firing until it crashed. It was the first German plane shot down in the looming battle of Warsaw.

The results of the first day's battles were to be typical for the whole war, with inflated claims on both sides and charges of parachuting pilots being machine gunned by the enemy. The morale of the Polish Air Force pilots was high, for they felt they had been able to compensate for their handicaps in numbers and equipment; they claimed fourteen victories against ten losses. Surprisingly, the Poles concluded that the twin-engine Messerschmitt Bf 110 was a tougher opponent than the 109.

In the uneven contest, the Luftwaffe was following the doctrine it had developed after the Spanish Civil War. The priorities were:

1. Destruction of the Polish Air Force and its support structure.
2. Support of the ground forces.
3. Attacks against military installations and armament industries in Warsaw.

In Poland, these principles were strengthened by a decision to focus all effort on a specific task before proceeding to the next objective. The theory of Blitzkrieg, lightning war, involved the elimination of obstacles—artillery batteries, field fortifications, armor concentrations—one by one, so that the German panzers could sweep forward. As long as her enemies were alone and unprepared for the new style of warfare, the concept worked beautifully for Germany.

Based on his mastery of close air support in Spain, General Wolfram von Richthofen, an eight-victory ace in the First World War, and a cousin of Manfred, the famous Red Baron, had been given a special assignment as *Fliegerführer zur besonderen Verwendung*, or "air commander for special purposes." Von Richthofen organized four Special Air Detachments, equipped with armored cars having the proper radios with the correct frequencies, and sent them forward with the panzers of General Walter von Reichenau's Tenth Army. As the army troops were not yet familiar with von Richthofen's methods, they didn't call for as many strikes as the general knew were required. There were also the inevitable pitfalls of inexperience—using the wrong channels, not having the correct codes, and most important, not understanding what was possible for support aircraft to do.

Like his more famous cousin, also a man of direct action, von Richthofen flew himself in a Fieseler Fi 156 Storch liaison plane right into the heart of the battle zone, personally picking out targets and calling in strikes. On his first mission, his plane was riddled with bullets from ground fire, and he made it back to German lines with fuel streaming from his punctured tank.

The P.Z.L. P.11 fighters were nimble and able to outmaneuver the Messerschmitts in dogfights, but the Germans soon refused to play their game, either attacking with hit-and-run tactics, or simply outspeeding the Polish defenders to attack other targets.

On the ground, the rapid advance of the tanks overran many of the Polish satellite airfields, and, in the heat of battle, the Poles began shuttling their aircraft to new airfields farther east. The inevitable confusion—spare parts, fuel, and supplies were frequently at the wrong field—resulted in a severe loss in utilization. There were also many accidents as the Polish Air Force's strength ebbed. As an indication of the level of misunderstanding, the Polish Air Force had thirty-one of their best Los bombers at the training base at Brzesc; for some reason, these were never committed to battle, although they would have almost doubled the medium bomber force.

The Polish Army was capable of one final riposte as the tragedy unfolded. On September 9, the army group deployed near Poznan (the one that had been earmarked to lead the assault on Berlin) found itself poised on the northern flank of the fast-moving German Army Group South, commanded by General Gerd von Rundstedt. The 170,000 Poles, organized into four infantry divisions and two cavalry brigades, flung themselves on the Germans and for a while threatened to break through the tautly stretched German lines, cutting off the Tenth Army.

But it was the Tenth Army that von Richthofen's Special Air Detachments were serving. An avalanche of Stukas blunted the Polish attack. The Stukas were complemented by forty Henschel Hs 123s of Major Spielvogel's II(Schlact)/LG2, an operational test unit that was investigating ground-attack methods, basing their work on the methods that were so successful in Spain.

The Luftwaffe mounted almost 1,700 sorties against the Polish troops threatening the German flanks. One characteristic of the Hs 123 was that at a certain rpm setting, its engine had a sound like a battery of machine guns; like the Stukas' sirens, the noise made the attacks seem intensely personal against ground troops, each soldier feeling as if he were the individual target; the noise also had a terrifying effect on horse-drawn transport. Most of the Polish troops had never been under attack by air before, and between the noise and the casualties, a general panic ensued. In the time gained by the Luftwaffe, the German ground forces regrouped and then decimated the Poznan army group.

By September 14, Warsaw was surrounded. On September 17, the Soviet Union, contending that the Polish government no longer existed, streamed across the borders to the lines of demarcation previously agreed upon by Hitler and Stalin, lines that some units of the German Army had already passed, for their existence had not been disclosed even to the army commanders.

The Poles reeled under the attack, but Warsaw continued to resist. More than 100,000 troops were manning the defenses, along
with a sizable artillery force that kept the German infantry and armor at bay. The city had been turned into a fortress, and its com-
mandant would not even receive the German ultimatum for its
surrender. Von Richthofen assembled his air forces, and on September 25 began the first terror-bombing attacks of the European
war. Unopposed by the Polish Air Force, and with only minor antiaircraft fire to contend with, German bombers methodically
cruised over the helpless city, dropping almost 600 tons of explosives, about 15 percent of them incendiaries. At the same time, the
German artillery ringing the city poured in an avalanche of shells.
The next day an infantry assault began; twenty-four hours later,
Warsaw surrendered. The Polish Air Force had fought bravely, but
it had lost 83 percent of its aircraft, 30 percent of its flying personnel, and 22 percent of its ground staff in a little more than two
weeks of fighting. In their attack, the Germans had used 60 percent
of their available bombs and most of their fuel reserves, although
this expenditure was offset to a degree by captured Polish matériel.

Hitler had taken a calculated risk when he began the Polish campaign, stripping his western-front strength down to thirty divisions, only twelve of them first-rate. Praised as the best army in the
world for twenty years, France's 110 divisions were augmented by
400,000 troops of the British Expeditionary Force. As the war in
Poland unfolded well for Germany, some divisions and bombers
were sent back to the west.

They were not needed. The phony war was on; after the French
had made a tentative entry and quick withdrawal from German territory, the two sides settled down to watch the war go by, avoiding
anything that might precipitate a major action. In Great Britain,
when the issue of bombing the Ruhr was raised, prominent members of Parliament objected to the idea because it involved "destruction of private property." Intoxicated with his victory and
pleased with his armed forces, on September 27, Hitler informed
his generals of his decision to begin the war against France at the
end of November.

In an address to the Reichstag, Hitler offered Great Britain
peace, but on terms that anyone but himself and his ill-informed
advisors would have known were unacceptable. His offer ignored,
Hitler began to assert himself more and more; when his generals
told him the weather in November would be unsuitable, he re-

minded them of his own years in France, and assured them that fighting would be possible until February or March. At the time, he was not contemplating a total victory in the west, intending only to seize the Low Countries and northern France as a base of operations against England.

The Polish campaign burnished the National Socialist spirit of the Luftwaffe, not least because losses had been high, with an 18 percent attrition over the three-week campaign. Of the 1,600 aircraft deployed, some 285 were lost to all causes, along with 239 crewmen. In a country where dueling scars, medals, and wound stripes were so highly prized, this blooding was seen as confirmation of the Luftwaffe's fighting qualities. And the Luftwaffe's successes had indeed been spectacular, particularly because so much had been improvised. Although it had been standard practice in peacetime maneuvers to move from field to field and to operate under relatively primitive conditions, the rapid progress in Poland completely outstripped the Luftwaffe's logistic capacity. The Luftwaffe's efforts were also impaired by a myopic policy that limited the production of spare parts on the assumption that aircraft down for repair would be temporarily abandoned, to be replaced by entirely new aircraft. Fortunately for Germany, in the fire of battle the Luftwaffe's "blackbirds," the black-overall-clad mechanics, worked miracles to keep aircraft in commission. They would continue to do so, unsung and unappreciated, right to the very end of a long and difficult war.

Within the success some hazards lurked. The campaign confirmed the Luftwaffe's belief that the doctrine developed in Spain was perfectly correct, even though there were troubling signs. The most significant one was the prevailing difficulty in communications between ground and air elements, which sometimes didn't exist at all. Ground and air troops did not yet have the close teamwork in cooperating against enemy forces that only practice could bring.

The most dangerous hazard of all was the conclusion drawn that the aircraft in service were fully adequate in both performance and number. It was a disastrous assumption, imponderable when one considers that the next enemies, England and France, were many times more powerful than Poland.

Once again the facts of life contradicted Nazi Germany's image as an efficient organization heeding its leader. Hitler had long before anticipated the need for vastly greater numbers of aircraft, calling in October 1938 for a 500 percent increase in aircraft production. His order had been ignored by both industry and his own Air Ministry officials in a way that would have been impossible in a "soft democracy" like the United States. There, when just a month later, in November 1938, President Roosevelt called for 50,000 aircraft annually, everyone sought to comply. But in Germany, the industrial experts proved to their own satisfaction that Hitler's goals could not be reached. They claimed that, even if accomplished, such a program would wreck the German economy; in any event, as a final argument, they proved that the fuel requirements for such an air force were impossible to fulfill. Thus it was that in the winter of 1939, the German factories continued on a virtual peacetime basis, working one shift for five or six days a week, and producing at the rate of less than 700 aircraft per month. Content with its performance in Poland, certain that it could handle the west, perhaps traitorously ill served by its intelligence sources, the Luftwaffe High Command was blissfully unaware that English aircraft production had already exceeded Germany's and was growing from day to day.

THE EMERGENCE OF HITLER AS MILITARY GAMBLER

Hitler's series of diplomatic gambles saw the Rhineland, Austria, Czechoslovakia, and the Lithuanian city of Memel drop into his hand. Although he refrained from second-guessing his commanders while observing the German forces in Poland, he now began to insert himself more into military planning, displaying a combination of talents that intimidated his generals. He had a flair for recognizing the unusual option or the simple solution to a complex problem, an insight that probably stemmed from his practical experience as a *front soldat* in World War I. And in the manner of latter-day U.S. Department of Defense technocrats, he won arguments on the basis of his prodigious memory for detail.

Adverse weather kept the Luftwaffe grounded, preventing Hitler from opening his attack in the west during the winter of 1939. During the enforced delay, Hitler rejected his army's rather pedestrian reprise of the World War I Schlieffen plan, and instead backed the plan of General Fritz Erich von Manstein, which coincided with one he had begun to articulate to his closest staff members in late October. Von Manstein's ideas were more in line with his own spontaneous style, calling for a shift of emphasis from the north to the center, and thrusting the panzers through the "impassable" Ardennes to race to the Channel coast.

But before this major test of arms, Hitler was to accede to the requests of Grossadmiral Erich Raeder and his own intuition for a quick campaign in Denmark and Norway. Here Hitler's gambling spirit, his willingness to risk both his small navy and important elements of his air force, would pay off—although at great cost to the navy.

THE WAR IN THE NORTH

In the short, intense war in Scandinavia, the Germans distinguished themselves on land and in the air, while taking a terrible drubbing at sea. For their part, the Allies disgraced themselves with an outrageous display of military and political dilettantism in which they made mistake after mistake before, during, and after the fighting. In the coldest terms, a well-trained, experienced German Army and Air Force outthought and outfought the British and Norwegians, while a brave but less-skillful Germany Navy was unable to cope with either British ships or Norwegian land batteries.

In the campaign, the Luftwaffe would bring itself to a peak of operational efficiency in preparation for the coming war in the west, demonstrating new techniques that had been talked about for years but never proven before in battle, including the use of airborne forces to seize strategic targets and hold them until ground forces arrived. The Luftwaffe demonstrated an exceptional ability to improvise in the field as it adapted to changing circumstances, taking advantage of the opportunities that the Allies presented on an almost continuous basis.

The war in Scandinavia was characterized by long distances, bad weather, terrible logistic problems, and bizarre political problems. Great Britain's First Sea Lord, Winston Churchill, had long advocated mining Norwegian waters to impede the flow of iron ore to Germany, and saw the invasion of Finland by the Soviet Union on November 30, 1939, as justification to seize Norway. Outnumbered ten to one, the Finns cut off the ill-trained, ill-equipped Soviet forces in the dense forests and slaughtered them. In a world dismayed by the repeated victories of the autocratic states, Finland's resistance was more than a tonic, it was a heady champagne.

The Soviet Union's military performance was perceived by England, France, and Germany as being ineffective, reinforcing Hitler's opinion that he would only have to "kick in the door to have the whole rotten house come crashing down."

In France and England, public indignation mounted over the brutal Soviet invasion, and pressure built to intervene. So perfervid was the Allied desire to help Finland that Churchill advocated breaking off diplomatic relations with the Soviet Union and bombing Russian oil fields at Baku—this at a time when the English were not bombing Germany. The Allies then asked Norway and Sweden for permission to send troops through their countries to aid Finland. Both nations refused, for they were enjoying a tremendous prosperity from their business dealings with Germany. The issue was rendered moot by a Soviet offensive that opened on February 1. Using forty-five infantry divisions and twelve armored groups, Soviet forces overwhelmed Finland, which sued for an armistice on March 12. The Finns had lost 25,000 out of 200,000 combatants, the Russians more than 200,000 dead, and the Finnish surrender removed for the public the most palatable reason for the Allies to invade Norway. In Germany, Hitler ordered preparations to begin on December 14, 1939, for his own invasion of Norway, reserving the exact date for later.

The *Altmark* incident on February 16, 1940, proved to be the final catalyst for both sides. A 15,000-ton supply ship for the scuttled pocket battleship *Graf Spee*, the *Altmark* had made its way to Norwegian waters with 299 English prisoners from sunken merchant ships on board. Churchill gave orders to the British destroyer *Cossack* to rescue those prisoners, even if it meant firing on Norwegian ships to do so. The *Cossack* forced its way past Norwegian gunboats, boarded the *Altmark* and rescued the crew members.

Hitler was shocked by this gross breach of neutrality by someone other than himself, and determined to speed up the invasion of Norway as an independent operation, in advance of the attack on the western front. It thus transpired that French and British soldiers were boarding ships to invade Norway to save it from the Germans at the same time that German soldiers were boarding ships and aircraft to save Norway from the Allies.

There were significant symptomatic differences in the methods employed. The Allies began a colonial-style operation, stationing individual battalions of troops at various points and ignoring the requirement for air superiority. Even after weeks of planning, their logistics efforts were terribly flawed, with equipment vital for winter warfare being forgotten. In contrast, the more experienced Germans moved swiftly and efficiently, boarding ships, massing troops, and preparing their fleet of aircraft to secure the primary objectives: the airfields. Once the airfields were secured, Luftwaffe units poured in to gain air superiority.

On April 1, the Allies decided to begin mining Norwegian waters one week later. On April 3, the German troop transports, disguised as coal freighters, sailed for Narvik. They were the first of a fleet of merchant vessels and warships crowded with troops and equipment that would sail in the next few days. Despite reports on German troop movements and on the sailings, Allied intelligence so misinterpreted German intentions that on April 4 the British Prime Minister, Neville Chamberlain, gleefully assured Parliament that Hitler had "missed the boat" on Norway. The phrase would come to haunt him, for, far from missing the boat, Hitler had already unleashed his juggernaut. On the eighth, Allied mining operations began, a flagrant violation of Norway's neutrality and a propaganda gift Germany quickly capitalized on; now the German invasion could be presented as a magically quick riposte to the Allied infringement.

From the start, Hitler had insisted on secrecy for Operation Weser, unaware (as he would be for the remainder of his life) that the British had cracked the "uncrackable" Enigma cypher machines, and a few of his enemies at the very top knew exactly what his plans were. Yet the knowledge did the Allies little good, as the scope of the cryptographic coup was so great that Great Britain did not yet know how to handle the information it received. Fearing that a too-widespread release would compromise the breakthrough, the information was not disseminated to the commanders. (In one of the little-known coincidences of the war, the RAF's own encrypting system, known as Typex, stemmed from the same Enigma Chiffriermaschinen patents that were developed into the German Enigma system.)

Hitler was still able to pick good commanders and trust them, and had given direction of the operation to a veteran of World War I fighting in Finland, General Nikolaus von Falkenhorst. The initial

Luftwaffe effort was under Generalleutnant Hans Geisler's Fliegerkorps X, normally headquartered in Hamburg. Later, Göring would send General Erhard Milch to command Luftflotte 5 from Oslo, in a move that both acceded to Milch's desire for an operational command—and distanced him from Berlin, where his increasing influence made Göring uncomfortable.

The Führer was fully aware that he was risking his small fleet, and he knew that the British could land troops with impunity anywhere along the thousand-mile coastline. Ignoring the odds against him, Hitler expected the elements of surprise and purposefulness to offset the deficiency in numbers—and he counted on the Luftwaffe. It did not fail him.

Operation Weser began just after 0500 hours on April 9, 1940, with attacks on both Denmark and Norway. Timing was critical, for the seaborne forces—troops stowed away on destroyers, merchant ships, and even smaller vessels—had to arrive at each of their destinations simultaneously, even though they were hundreds of miles apart. The Luftwaffe timing was less demanding, although more precise navigation was required. The forces available were marginal, for the Luftwaffe had allocated only 1,098 aircraft to the campaign, of which 557 were transports, 342 long-range bombers, 39 dive-bombers, 102 fighters, and 58 miscellaneous types.

Ships landed troops over a wide front, including Oslo, Kristiansand, Bergen, Trondheim, and Narvik as the Luftwaffe parachute troops seized vital points. They were soon followed by a serious airborne reinforcement and supply campaign. This had never been done before, and Hitler's willingness to chance the vagaries of Norwegian weather, the British Navy, and the valor of the defenders indicates courage and foresight surpassing that of his commanders.

Denmark fell on the first day. A minelayer and an icebreaker steamed into Copenhagen harbor, German battle flags illuminated by searchlights, to land troops who marched to the Amalienborg Palace. The worst bloodshed occurred when King Christian X's palace guards unslung their normally ceremonial rifles and fired at the German troops, only to be quickly shot down. Although King Christian X ordered that resistance cease, sporadic fighting continued and Messerschmitt Bf 110s strafed Danish airports, destroying more than a dozen aircraft without any losses. By evening, Denmark was secured.

In Norway, the parachute troops seized the main airfields almost immediately and soon the droning Junkers Ju 52/3m transports came in to off-load troops. As soon as the airfield perimeters were secured, flights of German bombers and fighters came in to begin operations, to be serviced by maintenance crews flown in on the second wave of transports. Yet even amid the drama, there was time for comedy. The huge four-engine Junkers G 38 transport, the *von Hindenburg*, was dispatched to Norway with a military band to celebrate the capture of the airport and to play the music for the triumphal march into Oslo. Built in 1929 as a tentative step toward a flying-wing aircraft, the G 38 was slow and ponderous, but it somehow managed to land at Oslo's Fornebu airport in advance of the airborne troops, so that the apprehensive band members had to stay peacefully on board until the paratroopers arrived.

The Norwegian resistance increased during the day. At Oslo, seven Gloster Gladiators repeatedly attacked the incoming German aircraft at terrible odds, flights of two diving down to engage as many as seventy aircraft at a time, and scoring a few victories. As the Germans seized one airfield after another, the Gladiators had to land on emergency strips in the countryside, where their ground crews rallied to refuel and rearm them. A memorable incident worthy of a Steven Spielberg film occurred at the Vaernes airfield near Trondheim, where a heavy snow had blanketed the runway, preventing takeoffs. A Lapp herdsman solved the problem when he brought three thousand white reindeer to trample the snow down, enabling the Norwegians to continue operations.

The Gladiator was a symbol of the discrepancy in airpower between England and Germany. Great Britain's last biplane fighter would serve nobly against great odds from Norway to Malta to the Far East, but it didn't belong in the same sky with the Messerschmitts.

King Haakon VII eluded German capture and spurred the resistance of the 50,000 Norwegian reservists, who continued to fight stubbornly for weeks. The British and French also reacted with unaccustomed vigor, as if they were glad the phony war was ending and they could at last come to grips with the Germans. The RAF sent bombers and reconnaissance planes from Scotland. One Bristol Blenheim from No. 254 Squadron, piloted by Sergeant C. R. Rose, made a brilliant attack on Stavanger, destroying one Bf 110 in the air, one Junker Ju 52 on the airfield, and a Heinkel He 59 floatplane in the harbor. At Bergen, fifteen Fleet Air Arm Blackburn Skuas, the most advanced dive-bomber in British service, attacked the previously damaged German light cruiser *Königsberg*, tied up at a wharf. Three hits and two near misses caused the vessel to capsize and sink, the first, but far from the last, large warship to be sunk by air attack in World War II. But in the manner typical of the first years of the war, it was too little and too late.

The English committed their aircraft carriers to the battle, including the *Furious*, the *Glorious*, and the *Ark Royal*. The low level of the Allied planning and staff work was best illustrated by the fiasco at Lake Lesjeskog, eighty miles southeast of Trondheim. Eighteen Gladiators of 263 Squadron were launched from the *Glorious* on April 24, 1940, to operate from the lake. When they arrived, they found an 1,800 foot runway scraped into the snow-covered surface, but little in the way of supplies. Batteries (to the British, accumulators) for the starting carts had been sent without the acid to activate them, there was little ammunition, and there were only a few mechanics.

After a night on the frozen lake, only two Gladiators were able to takeoff before the Germans attacked, bombing and strafing almost at leisure for more than eight hours. At day's end, only five Gladiators survived.

The greatest Allied naval success came at Narvik, which was beyond the range of German airpower. In two sharp actions, nine German merchant ships and nine destroyers were sunk, at a cost of two British destroyers. And it was at Narvik that the Allies made their major effort to hold on in Norway. Some 12,000 Allied troops were poured in during the last weeks of April, driving the Germans from the city and giving Hitler a crisis of nerves. Yet the German troops held on in the outskirts, and when the long-awaited battle for France opened on May 10, the Allies abandoned Norway.

The carrier *Glorious* would figure in another, even sadder event after the evacuation from Narvik in June. Eight Gladiators and ten Hurricanes had flown from the airfields near Narvik to land on the deck of the *Glorious*, although the Hurricanes were not supposed to be able to do so. As the *Glorious* steamed south toward Scotland, she was intercepted and sunk by the pocket battleship *Scharnhorst*. More than 1,400 were drowned, including all but two of the pilots who had escaped from Narvik.

Even before the battle in Scandinavia was concluded, Germany had already begun operations on the western front. Hitler had won the Battle of Norway, yet it may have been the biggest mistake of his life. If the Führer had surreptitiously given enough aid to keep Fin-

land fighting, it is not inconceivable that France and England
would have gone to war with the Soviet Union in the spring of 1940,
an event that would have completely turned world politics around,
and had the incalculable consequences of a conflict in which Germany and England fought each other while each fought the Soviet
Union. It was not to be; instead, there erupted the Battle of France.

2

THE PLUNGE
INTO REALITY

The air campaigns of the phony war, the Battle of France, and the Battle of Britain are all inextricably linked. For the Germans, it was a time of self-realization as the various components of the Luftwaffe and the army gained experience and worked more closely together. In the meantime, the British worked frantically to improve their situation; they were still saddled by procurement and training errors of the past, but were edging to a new level of proficiency. The French remained unable to cope.

THE FRENCH AIR FORCE AND THE DRÔLE DE GUERRE

Before the invasion of Scandinavia, a bemused world watched what the French called the *drôle de guerre*, the Germans the *Sitzkrieg*, and the English the phony war. Alienated by the prospect of another bloodletting like World War I, the detached Allies sat placidly behind their vaunted defenses, blue- and khaki-clad mice mesmerized by the field-gray German snake swallowing up eastern and northern Europe.

In those first eight months, there had been little attrition of the Allies' air forces except for the losses in Norway. The French were unable to take advantage of the time to reequip with new aircraft and to raise training standards to an acceptable level, for they were impaled upon the cusp of their rearmament process. When the war started, the French had possessed only 232 modern single-seat fighters (138 Morane 406s and 94 Curtiss Hawks) and only 8 modern bombers—5 LeO 45s and 3 Potez 633s. Even when French production lines began at last to deliver relatively large quantities of new aircraft, the undermanned, overorganized Armée de l'Air was unable to deal with them, and hundreds of aircraft that might have made a difference in the coming battle were grounded because they lacked essential equipment. By an almost convulsive effort in the late spring, French units had 637 fighters available on May 10, 1940, only to dilute their effectiveness by spreading them in small units throughout the country. Between May 10 and June 15, a further 851 new aircraft were accepted but never reached frontline units because they came from the factories without radios or guns.

The Armée de l'Air was also handicapped by its labyrinthine organizational structure. Incredibly, the air force's administrative doctrine for command and control was based on the *1870* Bouchard report on how to organize and administer the army. The late 1930s had been marked by a series of hasty revisions, including one immediately after war broke out. Each revision complicated the chain of command. Even worse, the changes destroyed all continuity between peacetime experience and wartime practice; the net result was the organizational fragmentation of the air force, with individual units placed under the control of different land armies. When combat came, each commander saved his air units for his own army's needs, amplifying the already significant French quantitative inferiority. The French doctrine fit perfectly into German plans.

Even though some units and many individuals of the Armée de l'Air would fight bravely against the Germans, the combination of inferior aircraft, inadequate training, and improper doctrine created a pervasive morale problem. In his remarkable autobiography, *Combat and Command*, Marshal of the Royal Air Force Sholto Douglas tells of the bitter defeatism he found at every level within the French Air Force. On June 3, 1940, at the height of the crisis, Douglas flew to the airfield at Villacoublay, just outside Paris, to discuss the urgent French appeals for more RAF fighter squadrons. Despite the importance of his visit, and their own self-interest in it, the French sent no one to meet him.

The Germans greeted him, however, making their only large-scale raid on Paris just after he arrived; he crouched in a slit trench looking at more than fifty French fighters sitting idle on the ramp, a half a dozen of which were destroyed. When the Germans left, he was taken to the officers' club, where he found all of the French pilots at lunch—utterly indifferent to the raid that had just taken place.

Their attitude was perhaps understandable. After years of tight budgets and confusion, they were being asked to fight an opponent who was obviously better equipped and better led. The famous aviator-writer Antoine de Saint-Exupéry expressed the problem of French morale poignantly. A reconnaissance pilot in the Escadre de Reconnaissance 33 (GR II/33), Saint-Exupéry had flown the best planes the French Air Force had to offer, the Potez 63.11 and the Bloch MB.174. In the last paragraph of his acclaimed *Flight to Arras,* he wrote, "Tomorrow, in the eyes of bystanders, we would be the defeated. The defeated have no right to speak."

THE ROYAL AIR FORCE PREPARES

The Royal Air Force would be as badly mauled as the French Air Force in the Battle of France, but it would never once consider itself defeated, and its right to speak would be beautifully articulated by Winston Churchill in the coming months.

Under the Chief of Air Staff, Air Chief Marshal Sir Cyril Newall, a man about whom historians unfairly wax unenthusiastic, the RAF had used the phony war to steadily build up its strength, with old squadrons eagerly trading their Gladiators for Hurricanes and Spitfires, and eighteen new units forming to give Fighter Command its prescribed fifty-three squadrons. (Six squadrons would soon be subtracted from the total: four Blenheim units being transferred to Coastal Command, and two Gladiator units being sent to the Air Component of the British Expeditionary Force in France.) The buildup came from the very hide of both the RAF and the Fleet Air Arm, but it gave many a young pilot discontented with flying bombers the chance to get into fighters.

Meantime, aircraft production was increasing steadily and, unlike the French program, was soon exceeding expectations. In April 1940, the plan had called for 1,256 aircraft, of which only 1,081 had been produced; by August of the same year, 1,310 were called for and 1,601 built. Much praise has been given Maxwell Aitken, Lord Beaverbrook, for raising production levels, but his influence actually came later, after his appointment in May 1940. The increases through the first part of 1940 may be attributed to the foresight of Wilfred Freeman in establishing the shadow factories, and to the goodwill and determination of the British workers. It was not a time of "I'm all right, Jack" labor.

In January 1940, England set up the British Air Force in France Command, with 416 aircraft, under Air Marshal Sir Arthur "Ugly" Barratt. The Advanced Air Striking Force (AASF) was to serve the needs of the entire Allied front, throwing its ten squadrons of Battles and Blenheims at natural bottlenecks like bridges and road intersections. The Air Component was dedicated to support of the British Expeditionary Force, with five squadrons of Westland Lysanders for army cooperation and short-range reconnaissance, four squadrons of Blenheims for long-range reconnaissance (i.e., as far distant as the Rhine River), and six squadrons of Hurricanes for protection flights.

Bomber Command added seven squadrons of Blenheims and two of the heavier Armstrong Whitworth Whitleys for night operations to the pot, against the strong reservations of its commander, Air Chief Marshal Sir Charles Portal, who felt, correctly, that the Blenheims would be slaughtered by enemy fighters swarming at the point of the advance.

The Hurricanes were the only aircraft adequate to meet the Germans, despite their several handicaps. The fixed-pitch wooden propellers, little different from those used on World War I fighters, limited the Hurricane's speed, rate of climb, and ceiling. The effectiveness of the powerful eight-gun armament was reduced because the armament manuals called for their fire to intersect at a range of 400 yards, too long a distance for the typical fighter pilot to be able to score effectively. These deficiencies were amplified by the traditional RAF tactics of three-plane "Vic" formations and textbook line-astern attacks (called by the Luftwaffe *die Idiotenreihe*—the row of idiots—because it made the bombers' defense task easier), which were simply not warworthy. Modern variable-pitch three-blade propellers came as soon as the factories could supply them, but it would take the long, bitter experience of both the Battle of France and the Battle of Britain to get the guns' range of intersection reduced to 250 yards and to have attack tactics revised.

The RAF had more than 160 of the handsome Fairey Battles in France. With its retractable gear, canopy and in-line Merlin engine, the low-wing Battle looked modern, but was obsolete with its 210 mph sea-level top speed and hopelessly inadequate armament of a single .303 Browning machine gun firing forward and a Vickers K machine gun firing aft. Four 250-pound bombs could be carried internally, with a further 500 pounds on external racks. Slow and vulnerable, the Battle lacked both armor and self-sealing tanks. The RAF, recalling the slaughter of low-flying fighters in World War I, reflexively avoided developing either dive-bombers or assault aircraft, and was left with the anachronistic Battle.

The Bristol Blenheim bombers were faster at 266 mph, but deficient in armament and armor and no match for the Messerschmitts. Designed by Captain Frank Barnwell—who had also designed the brilliant Bristol fighter of World War I—the Blenheim, like the Battle, was to cost the lives of many RAF crew members in the German Blitzkrieg.

The fourth plane employed in numbers in France was the Westland Lysander, a large, high-wing aircraft of unconventional beauty. It was far too slow and unwieldy to use in combat as an army cooperation aircraft and was quickly withdrawn from the fray. Later in the war, its low speed and ability to land in short fields at night would make it invaluable for clandestine operations behind enemy lines.

The Bomber Command's contribution, the Whitley, was an aircraft ugly enough to have flown with the French Air Force, but despite its lack of aesthetic appeal, the Whitley was the RAF's workhorse in the first years of the war. By May 1940, experience had already shown that it would not survive in daylight combat with Messerschmitts, and the Whitley was confined to night attacks.

FALL GELB—OPERATION YELLOW

On the eve of the Blitzkrieg, the matériel losses the Germans had suffered in Poland and Norway had not yet been made up entirely; the Luftwaffe had possessed 1,002 operational bombers on March 30, but only 841 three months later. And although the efficient training scheme that Milch had insisted on establishing was generating 15,000 aircrew members per year from more than a hundred flying schools, many experienced leaders had been lost. Yet, day by day, new aircraft and crews were trained and ready to fight. The war in the west was to be fought over limited distances against a demoralized enemy, and thus was perfectly suited to German equipment and doctrine.

The Germans were so confident of success that they committed two major errors, both of which would have crucial importance later. First, the High Command implicitly ratified the decision made at the end of the Polish campaign that the Luftwaffe was armed with the appropriate numbers and types of aircraft. Then, in February 1940, Field Marshal Göring decreed that all work was to stop on aviation projects that would not be finished in time to be used in the war, which had the direct and dire effect of suspending work on the Junkers Jumo jet engines and on the Messerschmitt Me 262 jet airframe.

Nonetheless, just six months after Hitler's original November date for the offensive in the west, the *drôle de guerre* became most unfunny on May 10, 1940. With both army and Luftwaffe at the absolute peak of their form, the Nazi Blitzkrieg was unleashed on Luxembourg, Belgium, the Netherlands, and France. The attack adhered to Hitler's own ideas, particularly in regard to the airborne forces, and it would be launched in what the world would come to know as "Hitler weather"—perfect for air warfare.

The German onslaught did not come without warning; even if Dutch officials had not been warned by both British intelligence and the *Italians* of the date of the attack, the signs of the buildup were evident in terms of the sounds of troop movements and the rise in radio traffic. And yet surprise was still achieved, particularly in the airborne masterstrokes that Hitler had instigated.

The Germans had reorganized the Luftwaffe, subordinating all air operations to Luftflotten 2 and 3. Generaloberst Kesselring, with Luftflotte 2, had control of the northern area of the front, working with General Fedor von Bock's Army Group B. Generaloberst Hugo Sperrle, who looked like a Hollywood stereotype of a brutal Prussian officer, was to cover the main operations of Army Group A under Generaloberst Gerd von Rundstedt, the archetype of the best of Prussian officers. Sperrle also covered Army Group C, in the quiet sector to the south, commanded by General Wilhelm von Leeb.

The Luftwaffe focused on the new assault with intensity; of the 4,500 first-line aircraft available to them, the Germans mustered some 4,050 aircraft, including 1,300 long-range bombers, 380 dive-bombers, 860 Messerschmitt Bf 109s, 250 Messerschmitt Bf 110s, 640 reconnaissance planes, 475 transports, and 45 gliders. On the ground, Germany had 136 divisions, opposed to the 135 of the Allies. The Germans fielded 2,700 tanks of very uneven quality (many of the better ones were from Czech stores) against 3,000 enemy tanks, some of which were far superior technically. The trump card was the Luftwaffe, the largest and the finest air force ever assembled for a single campaign.

MAY 10, 1940—BLITZKRIEG IN THE WEST

At first light on May 10 (the day that Hitler's nemesis, Winston Churchill, became Prime Minister of England), German armored columns cut through three neutral countries—Belgium, Holland, and Luxembourg. Airborne attacks were under way on key fortresses and airfields as the Luftwaffe struck at more than seventy air bases as well as at rail and other communication links. Early reports claimed almost 400 aircraft destroyed on the ground; actual losses were perhaps half that number, but the damage to morale was tremendous. The Germans attacked with élan, the Dorniers and Heinkels coming in so low that many were damaged by fragments from their own bombs. Messerschmitt Bf 110s followed up in strafing attacks concentrating on fuel supplies and aircraft in the open.

Hitler, very aware that it was *his* strategic plan that was being tested, was nervous about protecting the flanks of von Rundstedt's Army Group A in the center, which was to make the surprise attack through the Ardennes. In the south, von Rundstedt's flank was covered by von Leeb's Army Group C, which was to simulate a frontal assault on the Maginot Line to tie down French forces from the Swiss to the Belgian borders. The northern flank, where the Germans expected the bulk of the dangerous French and British mobile forces to be concentrated, was far more vulnerable.

The fabled Maginot Line extended only from Switzerland to Belgium; the great gap from there to the English Channel was to be protected by Allied forces. The Allies' Plan D called for French and English armies to rush forward to form a solid front along the Dyle River, massing behind the twenty-two divisions of the Belgian Army.

These were theoretically to make a four-day fighting retreat and assume a position in the center. The movements required for Plan D were too elaborate and time-consuming, especially for the ill-trained, badly equipped, and poorly led French and English divisions, whose unit commanders were hamstrung by an unwieldy chain of command. As events unfolded, the Luftwaffe allowed the Allied armies to move forward unhampered, deliberately not attacking the transportation systems funneling the Allies into the bag.

To spring the trap, key bridges had to be captured and the formidable line of Belgian forts had to be pierced, while at the same time Dutch forces had to be sealed off in Holland. Hitler ordered paratroops to seize the airfields and bridges, specifically directing that the key to the Belgian defense, Fort Eben-Emael, be taken by specially trained gliderborne troops.

The details of the assault were planned by General Kurt Student and Major Heinrich Trettner, his Chief of Operations Staff. Student, a fighter-squadron commander in the First World War, had enjoyed a meteoric career, first establishing the technical schools that brought professionalism to the Luftwaffe and then heading the German center for testing airplanes and equipment at Rechlin. As a reward, in 1937 he was given command of Fliegerdivision 7 (7th Air Division), and tasked with creating a paratroop force.

Most of the senior German commanders, even "Smiling Albert" Kesselring, considered the airborne attack in Holland to be extraordinarily risky, for it was to be undertaken before air superiority had been obtained. To prepare the way, the Germans sent in 75 Heinkel He 111s from Kampfgeschwader (KG) 4 (a Kampfgeschwader is roughly equivalent to a U.S. wing), and another 28 from KG 126; KG 30 employed 34 of the new Junkers Ju 88s, while KG 1 sent 28 Junkers Ju 87s. The black-crossed bombers fanned out to attack Schiphol, Waalhaven, Bergen, De Kooy, and Ypenburg airfields, as well as Rotterdam and The Hague. Even though more than half of the Royal Netherlands Air Force was destroyed on the ground, the German failure to provide a fighter escort would cost them heavily.

An hour later, Student's airborne assault began, with 200 Ju 52s dropping paratroopers to seize the bridges at Moerdijk and Dordrecht, and to attempt the takeover of the government facilities at The Hague. The paratroopers were followed by another 200 Ju 52s landing troops to secure the airfields and other key points. The airborne operations were successful everywhere except at The Hague, where tough Dutch soldiers overcame the Germans in a bloody firefight.

For the first time in history, newsreel cameramen captured a new method of attack as it occurred. The images of paratroopers diving one after another out the door of the lumbering Ju 52s, their parachutes snapping open to drift white against the early-morning sky, were seen around the world as another example of Germany's invincible power. Yet the force was perilously small; Student had only 4,000 paratroopers at his disposal, along with a 12,000-man light-infantry division carried in the transports. Student led from the front, flying in with the 22nd Division and actively commanding on the ground. He soon realized that German ground forces were not going to arrive as soon as planned, and he adapted his tactics to hold the key points until they did. On May 14, after the troops had arrived, he was severely wounded in the head by a sniper's bullet in Rotterdam, knocking him out of action for eight months. Simultaneously with the first paratroop drops, a dozen antique Heinkel He 59 floatplanes made a daring landing in the Nieuwe Maas River to capture a key bridge at Rotterdam.

Despite losing more than half of the aircraft on the ground, the Netherlands Luchtaartafdeling (Army Air Service) responded furiously, launching their pretty little Fokker D XXI fighters against the lumbering Ju 52 and, when they could break through the escorting Messerschmitts, slaughtering them.

As in all wars, minor triumphs emerged among major tragedies. A tiny group of Dutch patriots had taken advantage of a unique situation to recapture the airfield at Ypenburg, then waited in ambush as sixteen troop-filled Junkers Ju 52 transports came in to land. The Dutch systematically destroyed fifteen of the transports with machine-gun fire, then captured the sixteenth, intending to fly to England in it. Just as they were about to board, a dozen Hurricanes from 32 Squadron appeared over the field; instantly, they peeled off, dove down and destroyed the Junker—and with it the Dutch patriots' plans.

Claiming fifty-five air victories, the Dutch fought valiantly for three more days, with increasingly fewer successes against ever higher losses. Even at the end of the first day's fighting, more than one weary Dutch pilot landed, only to find that his air base now belonged to the Germans.

The Royal Air Force entered the fight early in the morning with

six Hurricane squadrons, joined on the following day by three
more from England. Blenheim bombers and fighters of the Advanced Air Striking Force concentrated on the Ju 52 transports.
The RAF claimed thirteen Ju 52s destroyed, all but one on the
ground, but ten Blenheims were shot down, mostly by Messerschmitt Bf 110s. It was the start of a Trenchard-like pattern of reckless, doomed bravery that persisted until Dunkirk.

At the same time as the attack on Holland, the invasion of Belgium opened with what many believe to have been the single most
brilliantly executed battle of the war, the capture of Fort Eben-
Emael by a small elite force of gliderborne troops.

Unlike many of the nineteenth-century fortresses in Europe,
Eben-Emael was utterly modern, having been completed in 1935.
Located just north of Liège, it was a totally self-contained complex
of concrete and steel burrowed into a cliff that rose more than a
hundred feet above the Albert Canal. Theoretically an impregnable
position, it prohibited entrance from the southerly projection of
the Netherlands known as the Maastricht Appendix, a fifteen-mile-
wide strip between Germany and Belgium. Eben-Emael was considered impervious to bombs or shells, and its numerous gun
batteries had an unimpeded field of fire that promised to hold off a
land assault indefinitely.

Student expanded his planning to include the capture of the
Kanne, Veldwezelt, and Vroenhoven bridges over the Albert Canal,
in addition to Eben-Emael. A special unit was formed from the 1st
Parachute Regiment and designated Sturmgruppe (Assault Group)
Koch, for its commander; extensive training went on in deepest secrecy. At 0430 hours on May 10, 82 aircraft took off from the outskirts of Cologne—41 trimotor Junkers Ju 52 tow-planes and 41
Deutschen Forschungsinstitut für Segelflug DFS 230A gliders belonging to Luftlandegeschwader 1. A flying Trojan horse that could
deposit its troops silently within the enemy camp, the DFS 230A
was another true revolution in warfare. Towed through the early
morning at a snail-like 112 mph, each of the gliders carried a pilot
and up to nine fully armed paratroops.

Eleven gliders were assigned the task of taking Eben-Emael, and
they slipped in to land directly on top of, or near, the fortress. Seventy-eight German parachute engineers, led by a Lieutenant
Witzig, disembarked. The specially trained sappers raced over the
top of the fortress, using a brand-new, top-secret explosive to spike

guns and jam turrets, all the while throwing grenades and shooting
through the embrasures. The intense fighting lasted until the next
day, with the handful of Germans striving to contain the 1,200 Belgian defenders inside and to keep them from firing on the German
Army advancing across the canal. Stukas were called in, but the
Belgian defenders did not surrender until German ground forces
reached the fort. The bridges fell on May 11 as well, after similar
bitter fighting. In later assessments, the Germans were to rank the
fighting quality of their opponents in this early stage of the battle in
this order: Belgian, Dutch, British, and French.

The Allied Plan D of the Second World War was as ill-fated as
Plan 17 had been in August 1914. During the first two days of the
offensive, the Allies carried out their advance to the Dyle River
front, where their mobile divisions became deeply involved and unable to move when it was at last discovered that the dynamic attacks on Holland and Belgium were but a diversion for the
knockout blow being delivered by von Rundstedt's Army Group A
in the center.

There the Germans raced forward on a narrow front only fifty
miles wide, the Stukas rolling in constantly as flying artillery, the
1,800 tanks of the seven panzer divisions of Army Group A bursting through the Ardennes. By May 12, having roughly shoved aside
some second-class French divisions, they found themselves near
Sedan, the site of the fateful battle in September 1870, when
Napoleon III surrendered to the Prussians.

The coordination of the Luftwaffe and the ground forces was
still not as good as desired. Radio communications were often a
hopeless muddle, and the clearly defined bomb lines had become
meaningless with the ever-swifter advance of the panzers. Supply
problems loomed large, as the Luftwaffe ground staff struggled to
get bombs and fuel to the advance airfields not only for the aircraft,
but to bring shells and fuel to the tank columns. So crucial was the
petrol situation that gasoline was drained from the tanks of each
landing aircraft, leaving just enough for their return flights.

Yet the air-ground effort came together after May 12, as General
"Hurrying Heinz" Guderian's XIX Panzer Corps coiled to spring
across the Meuse River. Guderian's "brutal Prussian" image, conveyed by his official photos, belied his maverick mentality; he was
a compassionate man who could understand the sufferings of his
enemy.

Guderian's armor was spearheaded by General Erwin Rommel's 7th Panzer Division, which first crept across the Meuse to establish a narrow bridgehead, little more than one hundred yards wide. After a prematurely stopped counterattack, French artillery began bombarding German positions. It was answered by a high-level bombing attack from Dorniers, followed by an eight-hour Stuka bombardment. When the German troops of the 1st, 2nd, and 10th Panzer Assault Units started across in their rubber boats, still under French fire, the Stukas shifted their tactics, bombing the Allied reinforcements coming up and protecting the flanks of the extended German panzer columns, just as the U.S. Army Air Forces would do for General Patton only four years later. A decisive element was the use of ultra-high-frequency (UHF) radios by Luftwaffe operators who were installed in tanks and who communicated directly with the Stukas. It was the last link in an important chain that would enable the Germans to cross the Meuse swiftly and in great force.

The French were bewildered by both the axis and the speed of the German attack in the center. Each time they regrouped to engage the Germans with artillery fire, they were subjected first to level bombing from Dorniers and Heinkels, and then to the mind-numbing attack of the Stukas. The Stukas' combination of noise and accuracy unnerved the French defenders; soldiers staggered out of shelters impervious to the 250-kilogram bombs the Stukas carried, no longer able to endure the constant shock waves. The Stukas of Fliegerkorps VIII, commanded by General Wolfram von Richthofen, flew eight or nine sorties a day, pressing air and ground crews to the limits and creating a level of havoc that surprised even the Germans. Within hours, the slow fighting retreat of the French X Corps turned into a rout. The minor bridgehead was quickly expanded, and by May 14, German tanks were across the Meuse, beginning the breakthrough of the French defenses. Guderian's troops were set to pry France open like a knife slipped into the shell of an oyster.

They were little impeded by the Allied air campaign, still not recovered from its initial slow start on the morning of May 10. "Ugly" Barratt, still unaware of the threat in the center, delayed until noon, then ordered four flights of eight Fairey Battles each to attack troops moving through Luxembourg. It was a last resort; of the thirty-two Battles flung into the teeth of the German flak, thirteen were shot down and almost all the rest were severely damaged, an indication of what was to come. The true cost of saving money on aircraft procurement became abundantly clear—the Battles were not battleworthy, yet they had to be used, even at the sacrifice of their crews. The Belgian Air Force made their own dismal discovery about the Battle when six out of nine were shot down the same day in an attempt to bomb the Veldwezelt Bridge.

The pattern would repeat itself with bewildering frequency over the next ten days; with consummate bravery, the Allies threw their inadequate aircraft at the surging German columns, only to be decimated by the dense German flak. The Battles and Blenheims that made it through the torrid antiaircraft fire were pounced on by roving Messerschmitts. When the French committed the best of their new aircraft—sleek, twin-engine Breguet 693s and LeO 451s—they were slaughtered in the same brutal way.

The Allied fighters did better, particularly because the Germans were not providing escorts for their bombers. Near Sedan on May 12, six French Curtiss Hawks caught a formation of Junkers Ju 87s and shot down eleven without any losses. In fighter-against-fighter attack, both the British Hurricanes and French Hawks acquitted themselves well, but they lacked centralized control and were too few in number. As each day passed, the Germans moved from air superiority toward air supremacy. In this, they were aided by the collapse of the French maintenance scheme. In-commission rates hovered around 40 percent, in large part because of the inchoate, paperwork-ridden supply systems.

In their delaying action in the north, the German forces compressed the Allies into an ever-smaller area. On May 14, a confusion in orders led to the German terror bombing of Rotterdam; the world seized upon it as the realization of Douhetian horror, the massacre of 30,000 civilians; later investigation showed that about 980 had died. The Germans had attempted to halt the attack, but failed because of the same poor communications that continued to plague their air operations. Yet the shock of the bombing caused the Dutch to surrender the next day, even as Guderian's forces raced for the Channel.

On May 16, the total bankruptcy of the French command was revealed. In Paris, Churchill asked the French Commander in Chief, General Maurice Gamelin, "Where is the strategic reserve?"—to which Gamelin replied, "Aucune" (There is none).

It was a catastrophic announcement, for the entire concept of the Maginot Line had been to build up a vast reserve force to throw into the battle. It did not exist, and France was lost.

Gamelin and Foreign Minister Paul Reynaud begged Churchill for more fighter squadrons to "stop the tanks." Knowing full well that the Royal Air Force could not afford it, Churchill agreed to ask that a total of ten more squadrons be allocated to the Battle of France.

On the same day, unknown to the world, a tenacious commander in England, Fighter Command's Air Chief Marshal Hugh Dowding, wrote a letter to the Under Secretary of State at the Air Ministry that would have profound effects and which in fact would ensure victory in the coming Battle of Britain. Dowding was just past the point at which he would normally have retired and was widely regarded as both eccentric and passé. But his letter laid out the true military circumstances in terms so clear that no one could mistake them. Pleading against sending any more fighters to France, Dowding said that 52 fighter squadrons were essential to the defense of the British Isles; he now had only 36. After requesting to be informed exactly what level of strength was to be left to him, he said:

"I believe that, if an adequate fighter force is kept in this country, if the fleet remains in being, and if Home Forces are suitably organized to resist invasion, we should be able to carry on the war single-handed for some time, if not indefinitely. But if the Home Defence Force is drained away in desperate attempts to remedy the situation in France, defeat in France will involve the final, complete and irremediable defeat of this country."

Thus Dowding, in no uncertain terms, held his political superior's feet to the fire of his realistic assessment. If Hitler, or even Göring, had permitted a German Dowding to advise him in an equally straightforward manner, Germany might well not have lost the war.

By May 20, Allied air resistance was crumbling, with the most effective effort coming from RAF squadrons operating out of England. In France, the Air Component was reduced to sending flights of three to five aircraft to deal with wave after wave of German bombers; most pilots flew four or five missions a day. The Advanced Air Striking Force had almost ceased activity, unable to sustain mission loss rates of 40 to 50 percent and more. In contrast, the Luftwaffe was free to interdict Allied troop movements at will, and still able to assist in the ground battle as needed.

THE VICTORY INSIDE THE DELIVERANCE

With their flanks exposed by the imminent surrender of the Belgians in the north and the failure of the promised attack by the newly formed French Sixth Army from the south, the British Expeditionary Force (BEF) made a fighting withdrawal to Dunkirk. Their ultimate deliverance derived from Hitler's decision on May 26 to accept von Rundstedt's request that the German armored columns not try to cut the British off from the sea; von Rundstedt was concerned about the armor bogging down and not being available for a counterstroke from the remaining French armies in the south. Hermann Göring leaped at the opportunity, promising Hitler that his Luftwaffe would halt the evacuation and finish off the remainder of the BEF and the French First Army by air attack with far greater severity than the army would have done.

The Luftwaffe, its strength already reduced by more than half by the relentless pace of the advance through France, was scarcely allowed to pause and catch its breath before attempting its new task at Dunkirk. There, for the first time in the war, the German Air Force was prevented from carrying out its mission. The Royal Air Force defeated the Luftwaffe over Dunkirk.

OPERATION DYNAMO

Prompted by a May 20 decision by Churchill to assemble an armada of small ships suitable for cross-Channel operations, the British Admiralty began its evacuation operations at 1857 hours on May 26 with the hope of rescuing as many as 100,000 French and English troops from Dunkirk. In the next eight days, 850 ships of all types, ranging from small personal sailboats to destroyers, evacuated 338,000 men, including 112,000 French and Belgian soldiers. The troops of the French First Army fought valiantly to the end to maintain the defensive perimeter. (Evacuations from other ports raised the total to 558,000, the difference between life and death to England.)

Dunkirk was like a lens for the RAF, focusing its activities for the first time on a single place and a single battle. Dowding's Fighter Command flew 287 sorties on the first day, operating sixteen squadrons at full strength over the beaches. Aircraft took off every fifty minutes to patrol; the distance from their airfields to Dunkirk meant they had only fifteen or twenty minutes on station, so there were long gaps in the coverage that the men crouching in the sands below bitterly resented.

The aircraft from England cooperated with Hurricanes still flying from a forward strip near Rouen. To this was added the strength of the Coastal Command, which contributed its own Blenheims and Lockheed Hudsons as well as the awkward-appearing but effective Blackburn Skuas and Rocs borrowed from the Fleet Air Arm. To the Germans, the intensity of the RAF's assault came as a surprise—a debriefing sheet for a Dornier Do 17 squadron comments that "the British pilots attacked with the fury of maniacs."

For once, the roles were reversed for the Luftwaffe. While it still had numerical superiority, with 300 bombers and 550 fighters, it had for the first time no qualitative advantage. Worse, the advance had been so swift there had not been time to prepare forward airstrips. The Messerschmitts were operating from fields used in the offensive and had even less "time over target" than did the RAF fighters flying from England. Nazi bombers were still based in Germany, and the long en-route times reduced their effectiveness. The RAF's intervention kept many German bombers from reaching the beaches, and the explosive effect of their bombs was diminished when they burrowed into the soft sand of the beaches.

The RAF's ace in the hole was the Spitfire, which proved to be a rude surprise to the enemy. German intelligence had reported that the Bf 109 was a far superior fighter; in fact, the two planes were very close in performance, the Spitfire having an edge in maneuverability and top speed, the Messerschmitt being better in both climb and dive. In the final analysis, a victory in a fight would depend upon the skill of the pilot. The 109s had an advantage in that their fuel-injected Daimler-Benz engines permitted them to push over in a dive, saving precious seconds. The Merlin engines of the Spitfires and Hurricanes, otherwise so admirable, were fitted with carburetors; when pushed into a dive, pulling negative G forces, the engines promptly quit.

The fighting was intense for the whole period, but the Luftwaffe, long used to having things its own way, had only two great days. On May 27, it punished the RAF in the air and caused tremendous casualties on the ground, destroying troops and ships. Then again, on June 1, the Stukas sank three destroyers and two big transports.

Gradually, the advantage shifted to the defenders, even though this was not understood by the soldiers and sailors on the ground who bitterly asked, "Where is the bloody RAF?" Even months later in England, it was not unusual for soldiers to jeer at airmen.

That it was doing more than its share was proven in the losses. In nine days of battle, the RAF flew 3,561 sorties and lost a total of 177 aircraft, compared to the Luftwaffe's 240. Even more than gaining the greater number of air victories, the RAF had permitted the evacuation; it had won the victory in the deliverance.

LAST INNINGS IN FRANCE

The ground war unfolded relentlessly as the Germans both drove for the Channel and arched around behind the Maginot Line to trap the French armies that had fought so valiantly there. The air war continued with undiminished fury, despite the fact that both sides were extended to their very limits. But the most crucial battle was one of words between the French and British governments. In the heat of battle, two governments that had totally neglected the development of the dive-bomber now turned in desperation to the fighter plane to stem the flow of German tanks. Neither side dared admit what it knew full well—that the small-caliber machine guns of the Hurricane were inadequate to stop even the German light tanks. With no other possible solutions in hand, the French Prime Minister demanded that more and more British fighter squadrons be sent to France. It was almost impossible for Churchill to refuse the request, for England could not exhort France to continue the battle while refusing to send all the fighters it could.

Churchill wanted to keep the French in the war, fighting with their fleet and from North Africa; near the end of the battle, he went so far as to propose a political union of the two countries, with common citizenship. The French cabinet rejected the idea, voting instead for capitulation. Despite this, with an eye on how history would be written, Churchill still called for more Hurricanes to be sent to France. Even at the end, when he knew that the RAF could no longer have an effect, and even though he knew that Hurricanes were being lost at a rate of twenty-five per day while the factories were delivering only four a day as replacements, Churchill still felt that the sacrifice should be made so that the French could not say they were abandoned. He made a very close call, one that came dangerously near to causing the loss of the subsequent Battle of Britain.

With the beaches at Dunkirk empty and the ports of England clogged with disheartened survivors, there was only one important leader in Germany who saw the opportunity of the century: General Erhard Milch. Milch recommended to Göring that England should be invaded immediately, with whatever the Luftwaffe and the navy could throw together. It was a gamble, but he was certain that the British were so disorganized that even a few divisions put ashore would make the difference. The idea was too radical for leaders of a campaign intended originally only to occupy northern France. Now, intoxicated by success, but still not quite believing it, Hitler chose to crush France completely, ordering his troops to turn and attack the French positions along the Somme.

The disorganized, disheartened French Army apathetically waited for the blow. The Armée de l'Air had almost ceased to exist, and by early June 1940, the RAF in France was down to eighteen serviceable aircraft. Despite Dowding's warnings, two more Hurricane squadrons were assigned to Barratt's Advanced Air Striking Force, with four more flying into France to undertake missions and then to return to England. Italy added to the pressure by declaring war on the Allies on June 10, 1940.

Turning to the father-figure leadership of the hero of Verdun, Marshal Henri Philippe Pétain, France surrendered to Germany on June 20, in the forest of Compiègne, in the same railway car in which Germany had surrendered to France on November 11, 1918.

Informed that France had surrendered, Air Chief Marshal Dowding said simply: "Thank God, we're now alone"; he no longer had to worry about his Hurricane squadrons being bled off to die in France.

A THIRTY-DAY GIFT FROM GOD

Immediately after the surrender, Hitler went on a week's vacation, touring the area he'd fought in during World War I with some old friends. His euphoria was understandable. A man who had risen only to a rank equivalent to an American private first class in the First World War, he had amassed the army and created the *strategy* to conquer all of Europe. From Norway to Spain, from Belgium to

Russia, Nazi Germany was in control, and he had received word from "reliable sources" that there was an active fascist movement in England ready to make peace. Hitler was certain now that England would accept his reasonable peace terms, put to them in his speech to the Reichstag on July 19, almost a month after the French surrender.

In that month, Dowding exerted every effort to bring the RAF back up to strength. The Royal Air Force was badly bruised, having lost 950 aircraft, including 386 Hurricanes and 67 Spitfires. The pilot shortage was even more critical, for some 435 British pilots had been lost—killed, missing, or prisoners of war. Another eighty British pilots died over Dunkirk. Fighter Command was authorized to have 1,456 pilots; it had only 1,094 on strength. Dowding ransacked the Fleet Air Arm, Bomber Command, and Coastal Command for pilots to replace those lost in France.

In the meantime, the Luftwaffe was also trying to recover from its 28 percent loss in strength since the fighting began with the invasion of Norway. The greatest losses had been among the Junkers Ju 52 transports—213 destroyed from all causes out of 531 employed. Far too many of these had been taken from the various training bases, and cost not only the aircraft but also the most experienced flight instructors.

Coincidentally, the aggregate losses of Messerschmitt Bf 110s, bombers, and dive-bombers also ran to 30 percent—110 of 367 of the twin-engine fighters, 122 of 417 Junkers Ju 87 dive-bombers, and 521 of 1,758 bombers. The single-engine Messerschmitt Bf 109s fared best, with 257 out of 1,369 being lost—"only" 19 percent. There were also 488 aircraft damaged, bringing the grand total of destroyed and damaged to 1,916, or 36 percent of the force.

These were shattering figures, but the magnitude of the loss was not reflected in any letup of Luftwaffe activity. New aircrews were brought forward, new airplanes flowed from the factories, and the entire air force prepared to move forward to new airfields from which to undertake the Battle of Britain.

THE BATTLE OF BRITAIN

There were four great battles in World War II upon which the tide of history turned—the battles of Britain, Midway, El Alamein, and Stalingrad. Of these, two were truly revolutions in warfare, while two were classic examples of matériel-driven land battles.

El Alamein and Stalingrad were of the latter type—enormous land armies locked in battle, the issue decided by the weight of men and metal—hundreds of thousands of troops, thousands of tanks, guns, and aircraft. In both battles, the Allies were able to build up a much-greater strength in all arms, and over time were the inevitable victors. The greater strength lay with the Axis powers at both the Battle of Britain and the ferocious sea engagement at Midway; both battles were revolutions and very different in character. At Midway, two great navies fought what proved to be the decisive battle of the war without any exchange of fire between surface vessels. It was entirely an air battle between carrier forces. As in the Battle of Britain, the winning Allied side was outnumbered but had superior intelligence and better leaders. Midway was a sharp, short battle; the main engagement itself lasted only four days. The Battle of Britain was far more protracted, beginning in July with dilatory strikes against Channel shipping, building sharply with attacks intended to destroy the RAF, changing tenor with the bombing of London, and then finally petering out in late October in a series of night raids that were known by both sides to be increasingly ineffective. Just as the security of the United States Navy had been won by a handful of pilots breaking the back of the Japanese carrier force at Midway, so the defense of England rested on a relative handful of pilots, "the few" Churchill would so movingly cite a few months later.

The odds seemed very long. Hitler's armed forces had achieved their triumphs through carefully planned operations executed with precision and panache. His General Staff was formidable and his intelligence forces were considered to be ubiquitous, sinister, and effective. And standing above all was Hitler's own cunning expertise, which so far had not failed him in peace or war.

In contrast, England was led by Winston Churchill, a sixty-six-year-old man who had been repudiated by his country for much of his adult life as a reckless, romantic adventurer, the author of Gallipoli. England still possessed the greatest navy in the world, but its army was in shambles, with only two divisions ready to fight, and with most of its equipment now being inventoried by its new owners, the German Army.

Great Britain's refusal to surrender confounded Hitler, who persisted in a love-hate relationship with his Anglo-Saxon enemy. With genuine reluctance, he ordered his commanders to begin planning two operations simultaneously. The first was an air campaign to bring England to its knees; once this was done, Hitler magnanimously would guarantee a portion of the English empire. If the air attack failed, then England was to be invaded in Operation Sea Lion.

Hitler knew that air superiority had to be established before he could invade, and on August 1, 1940, issued a directive that put the destruction of the Royal Air Force as the first priority. Hitler added that *after* achieving air superiority, harbors and food supplies were to be attacked. Third priority was to be given to attacks on merchant ships and warships. After this came the support of German naval operations of an unspecified nature, but presumably sorties by German capital ships. Almost as an afterthought, he added to this fourth priority that the Luftwaffe must remain "battleworthy" for Operation Sea Lion. This was a crucial element, for as difficult as it was to undertake the strategic efforts required for the defeat of the RAF, it was impossible for the Luftwaffe simultaneously to provide tactical support of an invasion. Hitler specifically reserved the right to order revenge raids for himself.

The Luftwaffe staff provided detailed planning that called for the elimination of the RAF by defeating the fighter forces located to the south of a line between London and Gloucester; then the air offensive was to be extended northward by stages to finish the job. This effort was to be supported by day and night bombing raids against the British aircraft industry. After this, the Luftwaffe was to blockade Great Britain by attacking shipping and ports.

Flushed with their recent victories, the Germans gave the operation a Wagnerian flourish, naming it *Adlerangriff* (Attack of the Eagles), with the beginning day for the attack to be *Adlertag* (Eagle Day). Ironically, there was more of an element of Greek tragedy than of Wagnerian opera for the Germans, for their plans happened to be exactly the emergency the British had spent years preparing for. As a result, the contest in 1940 has some of the overtones of an early Alec Guinness film comedy, in which ingenious amateurs (the RAF) manage to defeat an overwhelmingly powerful adversary (the Luftwaffe) with clever tricks.

In reality the British won because they had a handful of people in every area—aircraft design, armament, radar, ground observer corps, training, operations—who were clever and farseeing, and more than ready to reap the benefit of a German plan custom-made to be beaten by the British preparations.

Still, it was a much closer-run race than Waterloo; the Germans might have won if they had had the least bit of luck in planning, in equipment, or in leadership. The hard-pressed Luftwaffe crews, tired and strained after a solid year's campaigning, conducted themselves with honor and courage. Had they been left to their own devices, they just might have overwhelmed the RAF in a fight to the finish.

But it was not to be, for a host of reasons, some of which stemmed from egotistic personalities at the top—men like Göring and Hitler who, unable to defer gratification of their hunger for a quick victory, shifted objectives at crucial moments. There were flaws within the German planning and psyche. The Germans had capable air commanders in Generalfeldmarschall Albert Kesselring (Luftflotte 2), stationed in Belgium and northern France, and Generalfeldmarschall Sperrle (Luftflotte 3), stationed in Normandy and Brittany. Both had been promoted to the exalted rank of field marshal in the shower of advancements Hitler had ladled out on June 19. Despite their rank, however, they were severely handicapped by the chain of command which led back to a weak chief of staff, Generaloberst Hans Jeschonnek, through the capricious Göring to Hitler.

What no one on the German side perceived was that the air war was going to be won by *fighters* and not by bombers. If the German fighters did not clear the way for the bombers by destroying the RAF, the bombers would not "always get through"; worse, they would be destroyed in such numbers as to make invasion impossible.

Air Chief Marshal Hugh "Stuffy" Dowding, a man not greatly loved by his superiors, was only grudgingly asked to stay on just before his scheduled retirement. Unlike many on either side of the Channel, Dowding was not fighting for decorations, promotion, or for an ideology. All of his planning, and now all of his fighting, was geared to one purpose: to repel the invasion by keeping a fighter force in being. His goal was not to destroy the German fighters but to maintain enough strength to savage the bombers *before* they dropped their bombs on English targets. This was an important distinction, one that was later criticized within the Royal Air Force itself, where an ultimately persuasive faction thought that the principal aim should be to down the greatest number of bombers whether they got through to their targets or not.

Dowding divided the country into first three, and later, in July 1940, four, defensive zones; the principal barrier to German attack was No. 11 Group, commanded by Air Vice Marshal Keith Park and positioned directly across the Channel from the Luftwaffe's fields in France. Park was a hands-on commander who, clad in an immaculate white flying suit, flew his own Hurricane to drop in unexpectedly on any one of his twenty-plus squadrons of fighters, of which he had six of Spitfires, fourteen of Hurricanes, and two of Blenheims.

In a considerably larger area to the north was Park's archrival, and ultimately Dowding's nemesis, Air Vice Marshal Trafford Leigh-Mallory with No. 12 Group's fourteen squadrons—five each of Spitfires and Hurricanes, and two each of Defiants and Blenheims. Leigh-Mallory's primary task was to defend the Midlands area; the secondary role was to provide reinforcement to 11 Group when required. It was serving in this tactical reserve capacity that grated upon Leigh-Mallory and his firebrand wing commanders, including the irrepressible Douglas Bader, and which would fuel the flames of later controversy.

No. 13 Group was positioned well north of Manchester, commanded by Air Vice Marshal Richard Saul, with nine squadrons of Hurricanes, three of Spitfires, and one each of Defiants and Blenheims. Saul's mission was to defeat attacks from Luftflotte 5, operating out of Norway and commanded by one of the most astute personnel men in the Luftwaffe, Generaloberst Hans-Jürgen Stumpf. To ease congestion, the fourth group, No. 10, was created later with four squadrons of Spitfires, three of Hurricanes, and one each of Gloster Gladiator biplanes and Blenheims. It was located to the southeast of No. 11, and commanded by Air Vice Marshal Sir Christopher Brand. The defense of England was old hat to Brand, a South African who had shot down six enemy planes during World War I, including a Gotha over London.

Dowding's headquarters at Bentley Priory was the central nervous system of Fighter Command; there would be no counterpart to it on the German side for years. Signals were passed from both radar stations and the Observer Corps to the filter room and the operations room, where Dowding himself often presided, personally making the crucial decisions on how many aircraft were to be launched. From Bentley Priory were issued the orders that went to the sector stations, and from there to the airfields. Newsreels and films have made familiar the tense scenes of young soldiers, men and women, fitted with earphones and armed with magnet poles like croupier sticks, pushing the numbered counters that showed both attacking and defending formations. It was a marvelously complex operation that functioned with efficiency.

The distance between the center of No. 11 Group and the center of No. 12 Group was only about 150 miles, sufficient to provide both a difference in tactics and a bone of contention. Because 11 Group was so close to the enemy, its squadrons did not have time to climb to altitude and assemble in large formations. The additional distance gave 12 Group time to do so, and thus arose the famous "big wing versus little wing" controversy, in which Leigh-Mallory insisted that the correct tactic was to assemble a large number of aircraft to attack the enemy formations, even if it meant that the German bombers would be able to drop their lethal loads on their assigned targets. Dowding and Park objected, both from the point of view of humanity—they wanted to abort the bombers' attacks whenever possible—and from practical considerations. As in so many bureaucratic feuds, the arguments about tactics really masked a disagreement among strong personalities—and the desire for the glory of combat.

COMPARATIVE STRENGTHS

The massive German territorial expansion was affecting the Luftwaffe, the sheer space to be covered necessarily diluting its strength. Whereas 4,050 airplanes had been mustered to throw into the Battle of France, the Luftwaffe could deploy only 2,550 serviceable aircraft against England—998 bombers, 261 dive-bombers, 224 Messerschmitt Bf 110s, 805 Messerschmitt Bf 109s, and 262 other types, including 231 reconnaissance planes and 31 obsolete attack aircraft. Against this well-trained force, the RAF could, in the second week of August 1940, muster 704 operational fighters, of which 620 were Hurricanes and Spitfires. The remainder were Gladiators and Blenheims, and these could have only a minor effect upon the outcome. Despite this diminution of strength, there was no major effort by the Germans to accelerate aircraft production—

it was business as usual, even while the British were making gains in production every month.

In previous campaigns, the mix of aircraft had been perfect; short-range fighters able to operate from strips close to the front, backed up by medium bombers and the morale-shattering Stukas. The 30-to-120-mile stretch of water separating England from the Continent rendered this same mix inadequate. The Germans desperately needed long-range fighters and heavy, four-engine bombers capable of carrying a large bomb load, and none were available.

Heretofore, the Luftwaffe had always been focused on its preplanned targets, fighting an enemy that obligingly elected to defend itself at every point. This permitted the Luftwaffe's concentrated forces to penetrate wherever it wished. Now the situation was changed. The Luftwaffe spread its effort over a variety of targets, only to find itself impaled upon the sword of a very focused enemy—the RAF. The difference was radar, which today would be called a "force multiplier."

The Germans were familiar with radar, having had it under development since 1934; they had already erected Freya radars on the coast of France. The difference was in employment. The Germans used their radars in their primal role, to detect ship traffic, not to control their fighters or bombers. Equally inexplicable was their inability to guess, for many weeks, exactly what the RAF was doing. Even after radio intercepts revealed that RAF squadrons were being directed to engage the German formations with great accuracy, Luftwaffe intelligence drew precisely the wrong conclusions, assuming that rigid control from the ground would tie the RAF to individual ground stations, and thus translate to immobility in the air. From this they deduced that "the assembly of strong fighter forces at determined points and at short notice is not to be expected."

The exact opposite was true. In simple terms, the expert use of radar, in concert with the usually disciplined response of Fighter Command and the efforts of the Observer Corps, won the Battle of Britain for England. (The qualification "usually disciplined" is made because Leigh-Mallory's 12 Group sometimes disregarded the controller to enter the fight on its own terms.) By using radar, Dowding's system could assign exactly the number of fighters deemed suitable to meet each incoming German raid. Although time did not always permit the radar to get the fighters from 11

Group to the best position and altitude, it did ensure that few sorties were wasted and that German feints were largely ignored. After the first few weeks, the RAF often chose not to scramble to engage intruding fighters—they were in the bomber-killing business, and Dowding saw to it that they stuck to their trade.

Not much had changed in the lineup of RAF aircraft, but most of the Hurricanes and Spitfires had been retrofitted with de Havilland constant-speed propellers, vastly improving their performance. The Spitfire's ceiling was increased by a critically important 7,000 feet, and its maneuverability and its takeoff and landing performance were greatly improved. The Hurricane's performance was similarly enhanced, particularly in maneuvering at altitude.

Even though attention was centered on Spitfires and Hurricanes, England pressed on with other, sometimes desperate, measures. The hopelessly inadequate Boulton-Paul Defiant continued to be produced at the rate of twelve per week. The Defiant was a misbegotten idea, a Hurricane-like fighter equipped with a four-gun turret and no forward-firing guns, intended to sail past enemy aircraft like a ship of the line, loosing broadsides. Another wild plan, code-named Banquet, called for equipping de Havilland Tiger Moth trainers with bomb racks to carry eight 20-pound bombs. The Tiger Moths were 80-mph biplanes, and would themselves have been a banquet for German flak gunners, but the idea was symbolic of England's gutty defiance and comparable to issuing pikes to the Home Guard.

Although the composition of the RAF's squadrons had remained essentially the same, there was a significant change in venue. Instead of flying from improvised fields in France, or flying across the Channel to fight over Dunkirk, the fighter squadrons were operating from their home bases, fighting for their native soil. If an RAF pilot was forced to bail out, he could use the efficient British railway system to be back at his home base in time for the next mission. For the Luftwaffe, bailout meant capture.

The Luftwaffe's most important aircraft, the Messerschmitt Bf 109E, had a maximum range of 410 miles under optimum conditions. Under combat conditions, with fuel expended in the weaving coverage over bombers, the 109E could just reach inside the English shoreline. In raw terms, this meant thirty minutes over, twenty minutes in combat, and thirty minutes back, and on its return flight the 109 pilot had to cross the chill English Channel with his red low-fuel-warning light flickering, causing the German pilots to joke about *Kanalkrank*—Channel sickness. From the two main areas of German bases in France, the fighters could reach about 125 miles, covering either the bases nearest the Channel, or parts of London.

The Messerschmitt's lack of range epitomizes the Luftwaffe's inadequate planning for the Battle of Britain. The German Condor Legion had used droppable auxiliary fuel tanks years before in the Spanish Civil War. Sixty-six-imperial-gallon plywood jettisonable tanks had been manufactured in quantity for the 109 before the offensive in the west, but they tended to leak badly and were considered a fire hazard by the pilots. None were used in the Battle of Britain, nor was there any massive effort to supply more suitable tanks after the battle began, even though auxiliary tanks were fitted to the Stukas.

Less important, but after all the buildup a greater disappointment, was the failure of the *Zerstörer* concept. The twin-engine Messerschmitt Bf 110s proved to be a total failure as a long-range fighter. Not only could they not escort bombers and survive, but they themselves had to be escorted by 109s. Similarly, the terror of European skies, the Junkers Ju 87, had a brief period of continued success in attacks on convoys in the Channel and in the initial incursions over England, but soon proved unable to survive over England; the plane's slow speed made it difficult to escort and it was impossible to protect in its dive.

German and British historians have different views on the dates for the Battle of Britain, as well as different views on its conduct and outcome. In general terms, however, the Luftwaffe's efforts over England extended from the end of the fighting in France to the beginning of the fighting in Russia. The most intense fighting was during the period from July 10 to October 31, 1940, and these are the dates generally given to the Battle of Britain by RAF historians, who have further divided the campaign into phases. Each of these phases can be characterized by the battles that raged on selected days.

PHASE ONE—JULY 10 TO AUGUST 7

The German attack built up slowly, beginning with pinprick attacks on England at night, sixty or seventy aircraft ranging over a variety of targets. The bombing was as ineffective as the defenses—

there were still no radar-equipped night fighters, and the Luftwaffe's losses of one or two planes per day were usually due to non-combat causes. There were also many mine-laying raids. Fliegerkorps VIII, von Richthofen's crack Stuka unit, which had provided flying artillery support for the panzer divisions, and Fliegerkorps II, commanded by Göring's close personal friend since World War I days, Generaloberst Bruno Lörzer, were given two assignments: to gain air superiority and to close the Channel to all English shipping by day. To accomplish the task, they had about 75 Dornier Do 17 bombers, 60 Stukas, and 200 fighters. Gradually stepping up their activity, the Germans sank 40,000 tons of shipping in the month beginning July 10. Protecting the shipping was difficult for the RAF, because Dowding husbanded his forces by keeping escort patrols small, and because the radar warning times were often insufficient.

To gain battle experience, the RAF reacted to selected German intrusions by protecting and turning back flights of Messerschmitt Bf 109s taunting English defenses. Many RAF units were still flying in the standard arrowhead Vic formation, using one of five standardized "Fighting Area Attack" methods to engage, the aerial equivalent of using Marquis of Queensberry rules in a bare-knuckle barroom fight. Gradually, squadron by squadron, the RAF adopted the standard four-plane German *Schwarm*, calling it the "finger four" formation.

The initial fighting was a learning process as the Germans probed and the RAF responded; losses were moderate on both sides, although claims were not, sometimes by a factor of four to one. The exaggerations were understandable; in the heat of battle, more than one pilot fired at an aircraft; if it was destroyed, everyone who had fired naturally claimed it. Because the Germans knew their fuel-injection engines gave them a diving advantage, a Luftwaffe pilot would push over to disengage in a full-power dive that sent black smoke from his engine exhausts in a billowing stream that easily convinced a keyed-up RAF opponent that the 109 was going down in flames. Postwar assessments indicate that the Luftwaffe lost 192 aircraft, the RAF 70 during Phase One. Many more were damaged on both sides, some to be repaired, some to be "reduced to produce."

One important element surfaced during this period, the chilling fact that the Luftwaffe had a far more efficient air-sea rescue ser-

vice than the RAF. White-painted Heinkel He 59 floatplanes
marked with red crosses did an excellent job fishing both German
and RAF pilots from the Channel. They were, however, also providing intelligence to the Luftwaffe on British shipping, and on July
14, Great Britain announced that ambulance aircraft would be
fired on if they flew into operational areas. In the meantime, the
RAF scrambled to set up a comparable air-sea rescue operation.

At the end of the first phase, both sides had reason to be satisfied
with their efforts. The Royal Air Force had learned a great deal and
had grown moderately in strength, adding five squadrons to its totals, four of them comprised of Czech and Polish pilots. The Luftwaffe, meantime, girded its loins to undertake Adlerangriff.

Hitler, having created eighteen field marshals in his July 19
avalanche of promotions, had also established the preeminent rank
of *Reichsmarschall* for Göring. In his first order of the day in his exalted new rank, with typical bombast, Göring sent the following
message on August 8: "From Reichsmarschall Göring to all units of
Luftflotte 2, 3, and 5. Operation Adler. Within a short period you
will wipe the British Air Force from the sky. Heil Hitler."

PHASE TWO—AUGUST 8 TO AUGUST 23

Weather had delayed the scheduled August 10 Adlertag, and the attack was reset for August 13. August 12 was dedicated to what
could have been the most important Luftwaffe attack of the war—
raids on British airfields and radar stations. If German intelligence
had been adequate, they would have known how important these
were to English defenses and persisted.

The Luftwaffe crews performed like the professionals they were,
the attacks being well coordinated, with heavily escorted groups of
bombers and dive-bombers putting Manston airfield out of action,
and damaging the forward airfields at Hawkinge and Lympne.

The raids on the radar stations were made by Erprobungsgruppe
210, a special German fighter-bomber test unit, with two *Staffeln*
(squadrons) of Messerschmitt Bf 110s and one of Bf 109s, commanded by Hauptmann (Captain) Walter Rubensdörffer. Rubensdörffer was a hard taskmaster, insisting on absolute adherence to
orders and to the tactics he prescribed. Erpro 210 fighters used the
standard Revi gunsight to make diving attacks at an angle up to 45

degrees, at airspeeds from 300 to 400 mph, which made them very elusive targets. The 109s could carry four 110-pound bombs or a single 551-pound bomb, while the 110s carried two 551-pound bombs. Both used terrain-following techniques to mask their approach to the radar stations, then climbed to altitude for the run-in. On August 12, Rubensdörffer led sixteen Bf 110s in an attack on four of the Chain Home radar stations at Dover, Dunkirk (near Dover), Pevensey, and Rye. Three of the four stations were badly damaged; the fourth, at Pevensey, was more stoutly constructed and survived almost intact.

These attacks disrupted the radar network temporarily, masking a raid on Portsmouth by 100 Junkers Ju 88s of Kampfgeschwader 51, the Edelweissgeschwader, escorted by 140 single- and twin-engine Messerschmitts. Fifteen of the Ju 88s, led by KG 51's commander, Oberst (Colonel) Dr. Fisser, smashed the Ventnor Chain Home station on the Isle of Wight with exceptionally accurate bombing. Coming off the target, Fisser and nine of his squadron mates were intercepted and shot down by two squadrons of Spitfires, but for a desperate moment they had rendered England's radar system vulnerable. Because of this and a follow-up attack, the Ventnor Chain Home station was out of action for eleven critical days. The British concealed this and other damage from the Germans, scrambling frantically to get their stations back on the air and supplementing them with mobile units and reports from the Observer Corps.

Adlertag began as scheduled on August 13, but Göring himself recalled Luftflotte 2 because of bad weather. The Luftwaffe still managed to fly 1,485 sorties. The Germans lost 39 aircraft, many of them Stukas, while the RAF lost 15. Day by day, the Battle of Britain was turning into an aerial Verdun, which happened to be the only winning strategy for the Luftwaffe. Deluded by the Chief of the Luftwaffe Military Intelligence Branch Colonel Josef "Beppo" Schmid's optimistic reports, which took Luftwaffe victory claims at face value while at the same time underestimating English production by 50 percent, Göring and his commanders assumed that they had whittled the RAF down to less than 500 Hurricanes and Spitfires. There were actually more than 750 on hand, and their numbers were building daily. Keeping enough pilots on hand was Dowding's main problem, and would continue to be.

On Wednesday, August 14, the Luftwaffe relaxed slightly, sending slightly under five hundred sorties against southeastern England. Both sides gathered strength for August 15.

BLACK THURSDAY

The weather that had seemed to conspire against Göring now turned fair; on August 15, the Luftwaffe planned to saturate the English defenses with raids from all quarters, attacking airfields and forcing the RAF fighters into the air to be destroyed.

Beginning just before 1100 hours, the telltale signals of incoming aircraft were relayed from the Chain Home radars, whose coverage did not reach deeply within the Continental coast, but picked up the aircraft as they climbed to altitude and assembled in formation.

The first waves, Stukas escorted by fighters, struck at Hawkinge and Lympne, both forward airfields for the Hurricanes operating out of Biggin Hill. Lympne, a few miles east of Hawkinge, was almost always on the Luftwaffe's hit list. Just before noon, attention shifted dramatically to the usually quiet north as Luftflotte 5 launched an attack, the Germans assuming that the British defenses in the north had been denuded to feed the struggle in the south. They were quite wrong, for Dowding, against the advice of most of his subordinates, stoutly believed in rotating squadrons out of the line of battle when they became fatigued, and the airfields in 13 Group's area were stocked with veteran units eager to get a crack at the enemy.

A "decoy" force of 17 Heinkel He 59 seaplanes flew on a track toward Edinburgh in the north, then retired. The feint was intended to draw RAF fighters up early, and away from the area of the main attack by a force of 65 Heinkel He 111s, with 20 Messerschmitt Bf 110 escorts from Stavanger, Norway. The German bombers drifted north to virtually follow the track of the seaplanes, which now served as a beacon for the incoming raid. Spitfires and Hurricanes of four squadrons fell on the formations, shooting down eight bombers and seven fighters, without any losses. An interesting sidenote was the *Zerstörer* tactics; as soon as attacked, the Bf 110s assumed the defensive Lufbery circle from World War I, while the Heinkels jettisoned their bombs and fled.

One hundred miles to the south, a force of fifty Junkers Ju 88s of Kampfgeschwader 30 was dispatched from Aalborg, Denmark, without fighter escort and straight into the guns of the Spitfires of 616 Squadron. The Ju 88s of KG 30 were made of sterner stuff than their brothers to the north, for despite the loss of six aircraft they pressed on to bomb the airfield at Driffield, Yorkshire, destroying ten bombers on the ground. It was the first and last daylight raid by Luftflotte 5—it was clear that bombers could not operate over England without escort by Messerschmitt Bf 109s—and the 109s didn't have the range to fly from Norway or Denmark.

The markers on the plotting board at Bentley Priory were now moving in the south, where in the course of the afternoon and evening a continuous pattern of raids developed, some with as many as 150 aircraft. The attacks persisted through the night, a force of seventy Heinkels splitting up to hit nine different cities.

The British claimed more than 180 German aircraft shot down; actual losses were 75, still enough to shake Luftwaffe morale. But it was costly for Fighter Command as well, with 34 aircraft downed and 17 pilots killed. Göring should have been proud of his men; they had flown 1,786 sorties, about a third of them by bombers, and many of them had pressed their attacks resolutely. With its superior numbers, the Luftwaffe was in a position to wear the RAF down by attrition, for the battle was like a chess game in which Germany, one pawn ahead, could win by ruthlessly trading pieces until the end.

Göring did not have the temperament for a battle of attrition, his ego demanding that the RAF be torn from the skies in a few days, with only a few German losses. In his pique, he attributed the Luftwaffe's casualties not to British fighters or radar, but instead to a lack of fighting spirit in his pilots, a leitmotif he would sound throughout the battle.

But Göring also drew some correct conclusions, allowing only one officer to fly in an aircraft, not allowing Luftflotte 5 to attack from the north, and forbidding Stukas and Bf 110s to operate without a three-to-one escort of 109s. He also made two monumental blunders, based on his own incompetence and the shamefully bad intelligence support provided him.

In the first, believing that the attacks on the radar sites had not been productive, Göring removed them from the target list. Had the attacks been repeated, day after day, the radar sites would have been destroyed and Fighter Command would have had to commit to battle under far less advantageous circumstances, so that the Luftwaffe could probably have worn it into the ground.

Göring's second bad decision was to weaken his fighter force by insisting that the Messerschmitt Bf 109s fly very close escort to the bombers, depriving them of their great advantages of altitude and speed. The Americans would later make the same tactical mistake.

Göring also went on to ruthlessly cull out older commanders, even those like Theo Osterkamp, a thirty-two-victory ace from the First World War who was flying regular missions over England and had the temerity to insist that the RAF was not yet defeated. Göring then brought forward younger pilots to command the units, not entirely a bad idea, when you could call upon young Werner Mölders or Adolf Galland. Unfortunately, there were precious few Mölders or Gallands in the Luftwaffe, or in any other air force.

The second phase of the Battle of Britain turned into a weary struggle as the RAF rose again, day after day, to meet the German invaders. German intelligence analyzed each day's victory claims and estimated the strength of the RAF ever lower, from 400 to 300 operational fighters. The Luftwaffe was obviously near a great victory; the only impediment seemed to be its continuing high loss rate. The feeling was communicated to the frontline units. They were accustomed to victory, and if their own losses were high, then the RAF's losses must necessarily be higher.

The RAF was indeed hurt; by the end of the second phase of the battle, it had lost 175 aircraft, and even though about fifty new pilots joined Fighter Command each week, pilot reserves were dwindling. When a new pilot joined the fray, he was usually a handicap; only after flying four or five missions did he begin to pull his weight. The Luftwaffe losses were greater: 403 planes, about half of which were fighters.

PHASE THREE—AUGUST 24 TO SEPTEMBER 6

The fact that Hitler really intended to invade England once air superiority was established is borne out by the change of tactics in Phase Three. Where Göring once had predicted that it would take four days to destroy the RAF, the Germans now realized that they were in fact running out of time to undertake an invasion before the winter weather struck. To accelerate the process of destroying Fighter Command, Göring now made his best decision so far, ordering heavy attacks on airfields in the extreme south and southeastern parts of England, with the intent of either forcing the RAF into the air to be shot down or destroying it on the ground. Luft-flotte 3's single-seat fighters were transferred to the Luftflotte 2 area in the Pas de Calais. In effect, the Reichsmarschall was maximizing the utility of his 109s by giving them the shortest distance to fly to get into combat. The weight of his attack and the effectiveness of the 109s were diluted by the requirement for close escort; even though the Luftwaffe still had more than 900 bombers on strength, they never appeared at once, coming instead in waves of as few as 60 and as many as 400. A typical formation might have 250 bombers.

It was hard, brutal work, more reminiscent of street fighting in an embattled city than the "clean combat in the blue" writers liked to romance about. The Germans sent very heavy escorts, often several fighter *Geschwaders* to a single bomber group, as the Luftwaffe pressed its attack on Biggin Hill, Hornchurch, Tangmere, and other airfields. During the mere two weeks of this hard-fought third phase, 269 new and repaired Hurricanes and Spitfires found their way to the British squadrons—which had lost 295 planes destroyed and another 171 damaged. Worse, the RAF was losing pilots, killed or injured at the rate of 120 a week, while replacing them at less than half that number. Dowding's policy of rotating squadrons out of combat when they became too fatigued was no longer possible. Previously, squadrons were able to stay in the line for five or six weeks; now all the squadrons were tired, as the loss rate bled their strength down in ten days. The Luftwaffe had lost 361 aircraft, and by September 6 there were signs that it was shifting its emphasis; Dowding warned that heavier attacks were to be expected on the fighter-aircraft factories.

PHASE FOUR—SEPTEMBER 7 TO 30

The most ferocious German attacks bridged the period between August 15 and September 15, wearing the RAF thin, yet, notwithstanding Winston Churchill's dramatic account to the contrary, the RAF never reached a point at which it had no aircraft or pilots in reserve. Whenever a squadron needed replacement aircraft, they were immediately delivered. Still, the RAF was trending toward defeat; its greatest daily loss came on August 31, when 39 fighters were lost in combat, 14 of the pilots killed. Had the Germans persisted at the same level of intensity for only three more weeks, they would have established air superiority.

But the Germans were hurt badly as well; no *Staffel* was immune to the continuing losses, and Göring's biting criticisms undermined morale. Unknown to anyone, the course of the battle had inadvertently been decided on the night of August 24. German bombers sent to strike Rochester got lost and by mistake dropped their bombs on London—the first since the last Gotha raid on May 19, 1918. Churchill, waiting for just such an excuse, had Bomber Command on twelve-hour notice to retaliate if bombs hit London. When they did, the RAF dispatched 81 bombers—Whitleys, Wellingtons, and Hampdens, all twin-engine aircraft—to Berlin.

Angered at this British effrontery, on September 2, 1940, Hitler ordered reprisal raids on London, shifting the focus of the attack from destroying Fighter Command. The Luftwaffe obeyed on September 7, using new tactics. Almost 1,000 aircraft, nearly 350 of them bombers, bored in at high altitudes, above 16,000 feet. As Stanley Baldwin had predicted so many years before, the bombers did get through, killing more than 300 people and injuring slightly fewer than 1,350. That night, the Germans came back 300 strong to attack the burning city again. The cost of the day's activity was heavy—34 German aircraft were shot down compared with 28 RAF fighters—but it forced the Luftwaffe to shift to night attacks, the beginning of what Londoners called the "Blitz."

Despite the bitter battles, optimistic German intelligence reports continued to foster the idea that the RAF was only four or five days from total collapse, and Hitler persisted in talking about beginning Operation Sea Lion, the invasion of Great Britain. Yet like a winded runner nearing the end of a marathon, the Luftwaffe was now pacing its attacks; there was now only light activity on the day following a heavy raid as the mechanics patched damaged aircraft and the crews sought some rest.

September 15 now replaced Adlertag in German thinking as the day that the RAF would finally be broken. Once again the issue of scale intervened; the Germans were pinning their hopes on the effect of sorties by only 277 bombers in three separate waves. (Eighteen fighter-bombers also attacked Southampton.) The RAF reacted in strength, shooting down 35 bombers—a 12 percent attrition rate—and 20 fighters. The results were so disappointing that Hitler postponed Sea Lion indefinitely, and the Luftwaffe began to concentrate on night raids on London. Daytime attacks were still made but were confined to the faster Junkers Ju 88s and fighters.

London suffered greatly during the Blitz, but Churchill, Dowding, and the other leaders realized that the Battle of Britain had been won, that the invasion could not come until the next year, if at all.

PHASE FIVE—OCTOBER 1–31

The nature of German attacks changed in the final phase. During the day, the Luftwaffe kept the British radars busy with feints, fighter sweeps, and sudden raids by small groups of fighter-bombers sent in to attack from high altitudes. The technique was difficult for the RAF to combat because radar warning times were so limited, but the danger was not nearly so great—the fighter-bombers could only drop small loads of bombs, and these inaccurately.

The Germans turned to the darkness for safety. Although they developed better equipment than the British for navigation and bombing at night, the crews were not proficient, and would, once more, have to learn on the job. For its part, the RAF had no suitable night fighter, and London was destined to take far greater punishment at night than had been inflicted by day. But England's strength grew every day, and the island that was once ripe for plucking could no longer be invaded.

EFFECTS

Great Britain now celebrates Battle of Britain Day on September 15 each year; it was the first, and most essential, victory England won in World War II. In the process of the battle, Germany lost 1,733 aircraft and almost 3,000 aircrew members and did not dare to risk its fleet or its armies across the Channel. RAF's Fighter Command lost 1,017 aircraft and 537 pilots; another 248 aircraft and almost 1,000 crew members were lost by Bomber Command and Coastal Command. England was saved from invasion, and Hitler made his fatal turn to the east, where his aircraft losses would be in the tens of thousands, his casualties in the millions. Great Britain won the admiration of the world; pilots from fourteen nations had flown in the RAF against the Luftwaffe, including ten from America, three of whom gave their lives. As the battle was going on, a great training system was growing up around the world, the British Commonwealth Air Training Plan.

Yet the margin of victory had been small. Germany might have won except for a bewildering set of circumstances that worked to the British advantage. On the English side, a number of decisions made years before by some prescient thinkers allowed the combination of eight-gun fighters, sufficient pilots, and a radar network, complete with Observers Corps. The Germans made grievous errors, including an almost casual changing of objectives that must have had Clausewitz turning in his grave. Had the Luftwaffe been allowed to fight to the bitter end to eradicate the RAF, it might have done so. But both Göring and Hitler lacked the tenacity that Churchill had in such great measure; they were used to winning quickly and without much pain—they ordered the attack to be shifted to the cities, and so lost all chance of winning. And against the German vacillation there remained, like a sharp stone in a boot, the hardy, undeviating Dowding.

In truth, the difference was that while Churchill had Dowding, Hitler had Göring. Curiously, after the defeat, Hitler continued to value Göring, allowing him to live an imperial lifestyle, while Dowding was sacked less than two weeks after the Battle of Britain ended, replaced by Air Marshal Sholto Douglas. (The big-wing advocates had won; Keith Park was given a lesser command, while Leigh-Mallory took over 11 Group.) Dowding received no recognition upon relinquishing command of Fighter Command, nor upon his subsequent retirement. He did not protest, but he was deeply pained to think that his work was not valued. Six months later, he was ennobled, becoming Lord Dowding of Bentley Priory—it was scarcely enough for a man who had so brilliantly led those few to whom so many owed so much. He was never made a Marshal of the Royal Air Force, the RAF's highest rank, as he so richly deserved.

LESSER CAMPAIGNS

In the eight months between the nominal end of the Battle of Britain on October 31, 1940, and Germany's invasion of the Soviet Union on June 22, 1941, the war expanded uncontrollably into half-a-dozen minor theaters. In many of these, the air campaigns were less critical than those of the previous year and were often waged by obsolete aircraft.

Yet these campaigns revealed a major flaw in the thinking of the German High Command: its inability to comprehend the difference in the amount of time an air force spent in battle, compared to that spent by the army or the fleet. In an army operation, individual divisions might be in sharp actions for several weeks, but were then replaced by fresh units. Ships of the fleet came to battle only rarely; even submarines on patrol were inactive much of the time. But from the start, the Luftwaffe was committed every day that weather permitted; even when there were no land campaigns, it remained heavily engaged. And, equally important, ordinary noncombat flying of military aircraft was hazardous, particularly in the ill-disciplined Luftwaffe, which had a higher accident rate than other air forces. Ironically, the very mobility of the Luftwaffe, which made it so valuable to the Wehrmacht, also eroded its strength.

The impact of the constant battle on strength and training was somewhat masked by the influx of new equipment and new personnel, but this in turn made it difficult for Luftwaffe units to maintain cohesiveness. The attrition rate of leaders was high, as it was with ordinary pilots, a situation exacerbated by the inevitable process of promotions to other units. The statistical result was an ever-lowering standard of experience and training. The ground crews—the hardworking "blackbirds"—usually stayed with their assigned units for longer periods, but even here the pressure of combat took its toll.

After months of straining its resources to the utmost, and after nearly wearing the Royal Air Force down, the Luftwaffe was gradually assigned to other tasks. With the exception of the so-called "Night Blitz," antishipping strikes, and the assault on Crete, these were once again primarily Continental operations, Blitzkrieg tactics in close support of thrusting army columns. The Luftwaffe performed brilliantly again and again, far better than its top leadership warranted. Unfortunately for the Germans, the period of apparently brilliant successes was marred by the failure of the High Command to invest more resources in areas where decisive victories might have been gained at relatively little cost: the North Atlantic (to be dealt with in a later chapter), Malta, and North Africa. The Luftwaffe leadership also failed completely to realize how much the continual bloodletting was weakening the German Air Force, at a time when it would soon be asked to destroy Germany's most powerful enemy, the Soviet Union.

THE NIGHT BLITZ: OCTOBER 1940 TO MAY 1941

Reichsmarschall Hermann Göring did not—could not—admit that the Battle of Britain was over, despite the undeniable evidence of losses that forced him to first alter, then break off, the daylight battles. He had continually shifted the focus of his attack, with only one constant factor: serious Luftwaffe losses. As the weather deteriorated from early October 1940 on, Göring switched from daylight operations to night raids against London, a task for which the Luftwaffe had the equipment but not the training. Few of its squadrons had the necessary experts in navigation and bomb dropping for night work, and many of the pilots were not sufficiently proficient to execute night landings in bad weather on the ill-prepared fields from which most units operated. Inevitably, the already-high accident rate went up.

The disappointment in level-bombing accuracy in Spain had led the Luftwaffe to experiment with a series of bad-weather navigation and blind-bombing techniques that were much-advanced over anything England possessed. These included the Knickebein (crooked-leg) method, in which a pilot was guided on course by a continuous tone heard through his headset. This used the Lorenz system, which created a solid tone by using overlapping dot and dash signals like those of American instrument radio ranges of the time. The pilot flew the beam until another radio transmitted an intersecting signal that sounded a different tone, the cue to drop the bombs. Unfortunately for the Germans, the English had discovered the Knickebein equipment (used with a standard Empfänger Blind 1 blind-landing instrument) in a crashed Heinkel He 111 and put Professor R. V. Jones and his little band of boffins to work on the problem. Jones played a key role in British scientific intelligence, becoming its director in 1944. They quickly detected how the system operated and what its frequencies were, and then devised electronic countermeasures to "bend the beam," winning one of the early battles in the nascent electronics war with the Germans.

The Germans responded to British jamming with progressively

more sophisticated equipment—X-Gerat and Y-Gerat—that well-trained crews could use as pathfinders. But the generally low crew proficiency with such equipment, combined with the primitive British electronic warfare efforts, forced the Luftwaffe to rely mainly on moonlit nights to navigate and bomb.

Although it seemed horrendous at the time, the scale of the German bombing effort was small compared to that meted out by the Allies later in the war. On an average evening, 200 bombers would attack, over a relatively extended period; on peak nights, with multiple sorties, the number might be increased by 50 percent. By November, Göring made yet another shift in the campaign Schwerpunkt, ordering his elite Kampfgeschwaders 100 and 26 to lead the way in bombing English industrial centers. KG 100 led an attack by 469 bombers on the city of Coventry, using the X-Gerat as a pathfinder, while KG 26 used Y-Gerat against the Rolls-Royce engine works at Hillington. The results were so successful that the term "to Coventrize" entered the lexicon of bombing to signify mass destruction. Later in the month, 700 aircraft attacked Birmingham, but without the same level of destruction. The heaviest raid on London was made on May 10, 1941, a year to the day after the opening of the brilliant offensive in the west. The Luftwaffe flew multiple sorties to send 550 aircraft over London, dropping 708 tons of bombs and 86,700 incendiary bombs.

All the while, England kept building the Royal Air Force; by spring, Fighter Command had almost doubled its strength. The new Bristol Beaufighter night fighter entered service with the first crude airborne intercept radars. These were swiftly developed, however, and their crews became adept in their use; during the heavy German raids on May 19, 1941, Beaufighters shot down 24 of the enemy bombers, compared to only 2 by antiaircraft guns.

And then the Blitz was over, except for nuisance raids, as the Luftwaffe stole east like a thief in the night for the showdown with Russia. Perhaps the greatest effect of the Blitz was the bloodthirsty desire for revenge it inspired in the British. Bomber Command began its inexorable buildup, with the first of the big four-engine bombers, the Short Stirling, making its first raid in February 1941. It would be followed by an ever-growing fleet of Handley Page Halifaxes and Avro Lancasters that would rain terror on all the major German cities and most of the minor ones.

DIVERSION TO THE SOUTH

In a contest of egos reminiscent of the Charlie Chaplin film *The Great Dictator*, Benito Mussolini surprised, upstaged, and outraged Adolf Hitler on October 28, 1940, by invading Greece. Mussolini, intoxicated perhaps by the cautious fifty-mile advance his troops had made from Libya into the Western Desert of Egypt, expected to occupy Greece quickly, his son-in-law, Foreign Minister Count Galeazzo Ciano, having promised him that bribes to corrupt Greek officials would pave the way for the Italian troops. (To give some small credit, Ciano and two of Mussolini's sons, Vittorio and Bruno, flew in combat in Spain, Africa, and Greece.)

Unfortunately for the Italians, no one had told the Greeks about the plan, and they promptly drove the invaders back into Albania. (Signs quickly appeared on the French-Italian border, saying GREEK SOLDIERS STOP HERE—THIS IS FRENCH TERRITORY.) The Italians, who had begun the invasion with seven of their best divisions arrayed against three under-strength Greek divisions, poured more men and equipment in, building up to a sixteen-division force. The Greeks were able to mobilize only thirteen divisions, but they were far better motivated.

In the air, the odds were greater; the Regia Aeronautica had 463 aircraft to commit to the campaign, including 92 reasonably modern low-wing monoplanes (80 Fiat G.50 and 12 Macchi-Castoldi MC.200s), and 93 of the Fiat biplane fighters that had done well in Spain. The bulk of the bomber force was composed of the excellent Savoia-Marchetti SM.79s, with a backup of SM.81s.

In opposition, the Greek Air Force had an eclectic collection of 150 aircraft, the most numerous of which were 36 P.Z.L. P.24 fighters imported from Poland. The rest of the force consisted of a very mixed bag of English Bristol Blenheims, Fairey Battles (12 each), French Marcel Bloch MB.151s and Potez 63s, and an assortment of obsolete observation planes from France, Germany, and England. These managed to more than hold their own until the arrival of Royal Air Force units in November.

Things got progressively worse for the Italians, as they fought their war not as a part of an Axis, but in parallel with the Germans. In Albania, they were barely holding the line against the Greek attacks, although the fighting had begun to exhaust the Greek forces. On November 11, 1940, at Taranto, in a single stroke, the Royal Navy wrested supremacy in the Mediterranean from the Italian

Navy. The English launched a classic torpedo plane attack that served as a model for the Japanese in planning their attack on Pearl Harbor. Ancient Fairey Swordfish torpedo planes from the carrier HMS *Illustrious* burst into the harbor in two waves, sinking the battleship *Duilio* and two smaller vessels, and badly damaging the battleships *Cavour* and *Littorio*. Then on December 10, in Egypt, 31,000 British soldiers routed more than 200,000 Italian troops, capturing 38,000, and vast amounts of supplies, at a cost of 624 dead, wounded, and missing. There was no lack of bravery on the part of the Italian soldier; there was a complete lack of leadership in the Italian officers' corps. Most Italian officers were against the war, against the Germans, and against exerting themselves. The situation was perhaps typified in the system of rations, by which officers ate sumptuously every night at candlelit tables, attended by servants, while the troops starved in the field on ancient tins of sardines.

SUCCESS IN THE BALKANS

Hitler had counted on Italy to maintain peace in the Balkans and thus secure his southern flank. Now everything had to be revised, including a month-long delay of Operation Barbarossa, the invasion of Russia, so that the prestige of the Axis could be restored and Germany's southern flank made secure.

In preparing for Operation Barbarossa, Germany had used its usual heavy-handed diplomatic efforts in the Balkans, where Rumania, Bulgaria, and Hungary were already committed to Hitler's cause. Yugoslavia was forced to join the Axis alliance on March 25, when Prince Regent Paul acceded to the pressure. Hitler had not anticipated the reaction and was incensed when a coup by anti-German elements of the Yugoslav Army overthrew Prince Paul and formed a new government. The Führer demanded that his army immediately undertake Operation Marita, the attack on both Yugoslavia and Greece, thus saving Italy and securing his southern flank—but delaying his invasion of Russia by a fateful month.

The Luftwaffe was able once again to achieve demoralizing success bombing civilian targets. On April 6, it launched a two-day assault—Operation Punishment—on Belgrade, which had been declared an open city. The intensive attacks, which used an optimum mixture of high explosives and incendiaries to maximize the number of fires, spread terror through the city and killed 17,000 civilians. The bombing was accompanied by a multipronged armored thrust that showed the German Army at its most professional, using mountain passes to thrust around the million-man Yugoslav Army, then destroying it in detail. At the same time, German forces crashed into Greece from Bulgaria, shattering the Greek resistance and hurling the recently arrived British troops back. By April 27, it was over, the campaign ending in another Dunkirk for the British, with 43,000 troops being rescued, but leaving all the heavy supplies behind.

The swift, and to the Allies, demoralizing, German successes were only possible because of the extraordinary flexibility of the Luftwaffe, which, as soon as war was eminent, moved almost 1,000 aircraft into the area from distances as far as 1,000 miles away. Once into their newly established bases, the Luftwaffe was operationally ready within a few days.

The air war in Greece had been fairly even before the arrival of the Germans. The RAF had established dominance over the Italian Air Force early on, even though it was operating with only four squadrons of obsolete Gladiators from inadequate airfields with a minimum of equipment and maintenance facilities. These were soon supplemented with Hurricane and Blenheim squadrons, drawn at great cost from North Africa. This initial English contribution may have produced one of the highest-scoring but least-known of the British aces, Flight Lieutenant Marmaduke St. John "Pat" Pattle. Pattle arrived with the Gladiators of No. 80 Squadron, and eventually ran up a victory total of 28 Axis planes, with many more unconfirmed. One of Pattle's biggest days came later, on February 28, 1941, when No. 33 and No. 80 Squadrons shot down 27 Italian aircraft. Pattle, flying a Hurricane, scored five victories in two separate dogfights. Later in the year, on April 20, 1941, Pattle scored a triple victory before being shot down himself. Curiously, despite the desperate need for British heroes, Pattle's exploits were not well covered in the press, and he only began to receive the recognition due him several years after the war.

PARATROOPERS OVER CRETE

The speed of their success in the Balkans had surprised even the Germans, and the man who had planned the assault on Fort Eben-

Emael now called for a parachute invasion of Crete. Generaloberst Kurt Student, recovered from his wounds and eager for more glory now commanded Fliegerkorps XI (Parachute and Airborne Troops). Student, believing Malta to be too tough to tackle, persuaded Göring that Crete would be useful as a base for attacking Cyprus and ultimately the Suez Canal. Göring obtained Hitler's permission, without even consulting the German Army High Command—this was to be strictly a Luftwaffe affair, one that would recover its glory.

The invasion of Crete was much more ambitious than the airborne attacks in Norway and Holland; there a few hundred paratroopers had quickly been backed up first by airborne troops and subsequently by ground forces. In Crete, there would be no ground forces to count on.

After extensive delays getting his men and matériel together, Student opened the invasion of Crete on May 20, 1941, with attacks by von Richthofen's Fliegerkorps VIII to destroy Allied aircraft on the ground. The Germans quickly gained air superiority, not only in the airspace above Crete, but over the sea approaches, denying the British the possibility of reinforcement. Even so, the resistance of the 42,000 Allied troops, disorganized as they were by the precipitous retreat from Greece, was far tougher than anticipated and came close to defeating the Germans. Unfortunately, the Allied defenders were so accustomed to German victories that they assumed that their triumphs had been local, and that the Germans must have been victorious elsewhere.

Student was dismayed by the first reports of the German setbacks. In desperation, his pride at stake, he poured troops in by Junkers Ju 52s and gliders; many were shot out of the air by the intense antiaircraft fire, while others simply crash-landed on the still unsecured airfield at Maleme. These carried the 100th Mountain Rifle Regiment, crack troops who seized control of the airfield. The next day's airlift was more conventional, and a troop buildup began that eventually pushed the Allied troops toward the sea. England found itself facing another evacuation.

It was a Pyrrhic victory for Student, however. Although the British lost 17,325 killed, wounded, and prisoners, the Germans had suffered the loss of 5,670 of their elite troops. Aircraft losses were not high except for the Junkers Ju 52 transports, of which 170 were destroyed or damaged. Even though Crete proved to be of immense strategic value, the casualties shocked both Student and

Hitler. There would never again be a German airborne operation of comparable scale.

The successes in the Balkans reestablished the prestige the Luftwaffe lost in the Battle of Britain. Once again the Luftwaffe's mix of aircraft had been correct for a Continental campaign, even one across the difficult terrain of the Balkans. Before Crete was finished, Luftwaffe units were already redeploying to fields adjacent to the borders of the Soviet Union.

3

WINGS OF
THE RISING SUN

While the Luftwaffe was gathering its strength for its great leap forward into the Russian abyss, the Japanese military air forces were preparing for their own grand design, one that exceeded in everything but their expectations all that had gone before.

Japanese aviation had its basis in myth, for the country's founders, the very Sons of Heaven themselves, were supposed to have descended to Japan in a Sky Ship. The growth of military aviation was rather more prosaic, a microcosm of the general industrial growth pattern of the nation—i.e., the assiduous duplication of foreign technology while establishing an indigenous industry. An early example was the army's purchase of its first balloon from France, which resulted in the production of the Japanese kite balloons used against Russia in the attacks on Port Arthur.

It was not until 1910 that two Japanese Army captains, Tokugawa Yoshitoshi and Hino Kumazo, learned to fly, in France and Germany, respectively. Each brought back samples of their training aircraft, a Henri Farman from France and a Grade from Germany. Hino was apparently something of a nonconformist, but Tokugawa became the father of Japanese military aviation, designing and flying aircraft modified from foreign designs, and establishing a training program for pilots. The Japanese Navy received its aerial inspiration from an American source, when New York's W. B. Atwater demonstrated a Curtiss hydroplane on May 11, 1912, in Tokyo. Atwater was a consummate salesman. Besides making three flights, including the first water takeoff ever made in the Orient, he carried a Japanese naval officer with him and dropped a message to the Minister of the Navy. The result was the sale of four Curtiss Triads, standard Curtiss pushers equipped with a watertight flying boat hull and a simple retractable gear. From this slight beginning grew the naval air force that twenty-nine years later would strike at Pearl Harbor.

Two distinct and enduring patterns were thus established at the very beginning of Japanese military aviation. The first was a rivalry between the army and navy air forces. The second was an unapologetic exploitation of foreign technology. The Imperial Japanese Navy sent six officers to France and the United States to learn to fly. During the fall of 1914, the navy employed its first seaplane tender, the *Wakamiya Maru*, in operations against the German fortress at Tsingtao, using four Maurice Farman seaplanes. On board was a young officer, Onishi Takijiro, who would one war later foster the Kamikaze Corps.

A British aviation mission arrived at the navy's invitation, and the former chief designer at the Sopwith Aviation Company, Herbert Smith, stayed on at Mitsubishi to develop a series of aircraft. Many of these served on the first purpose-built aircraft carrier to enter service, the *Hosho*, launched in November 1921. (Ironically, the *Hosho* would be the only one of Japan's aircraft carriers to survive World War II.)

In response, the Japanese Army in 1918 purchased a number of World War I French aircraft and invited a sixty-three-man French instructor's mission to the country, headed by Colonel Jacques Faure to mold the Army Air Force's initial tactical organization.

The Japanese learned quickly and in 1932 began the formation of many of the successful design teams that would create the aircraft used with such devastating effect during World War II. The degree of Japanese success in producing its own designs is typified by the Mitsubishi Type 96 bomber (later designated G3M2 and called Nell under the Allied code-name system) with which the navy made the first transoceanic bombing raids on August 14, 1937. The Kanoya Kokutai (a kokutai—naval air corps—was a unit of up to about 150 aircraft) used this modern twin-engine bomber to fly a 1,250-mile overwater flight from Formosa to attack targets at Hangchow and Kwangteh in China, a mission beyond the capabilities of any other operational bomber in the world at the time. The durability of the design was demonstrated four years later, when G3M2s were largely responsible for the sinking of HMS *Repulse* and HMS *Prince of Wales* off Malaya, in a naval action that shocked the world.

Like its Axis partner Germany, Japan managed to catch the tide of aircraft modernization at exactly the right time for its own initial purposes. In a brilliant three-year period, from 1935 to 1938, Japan created the specifications for the majority of the aircraft with which it would take on the Western powers. Japan's excellent security combined with Western disdain for Asian designs to keep them an almost total secret before Pearl Harbor. Even when the facts came from highly reputable sources like Claire Chennault, then supervising the Chinese Air Force, the reports were discounted. Later, the evident capability and longevity of Japanese aircraft, all of which remained in battle until the end of the war, made at least their Allied code names—Zero, Betty, and so on—familiar to almost everyone in the West. (The Allied code-name system came into being when the Allies realized they had no ready way to identify Japanese aircraft, being unfamiliar with the language, the manufacturers, and the difficult Japanese nomenclature. The system was started by Captain Frank T. McCoy, Jr., and his two-man staff, Corporal Joseph Grattan and Technical Sergeant Francis Williams. As a Tennessean, McCoy selected hillbilly names like Zeke, Nate, and Rufe, because they were short, distinctive, and easily remembered. The system worked well, and continued until the end of the war.)

It's interesting to compare the most famous of the Japanese aircraft with their contemporaries and to determine how they achieved their design goals. The Japanese Navy stressed maneuverability and long range in its fighters, and long range and bomb load in its bombers. Speed was an important consideration, but the requirements for the other characteristics were paramount.

The Aichi D3A (Val) dive-bomber first flew in January 1938, and was an all-metal, low-wing monoplane powered by an 840-horsepower Nakajima Kikari nine-cylinder air-cooled radial engine. Top speed was 240 mph at 9,845 feet altitude; range was 915 miles. The Val carried one 551-pound bomb under the fuselage and two 132-pound bombs under the wings.

The Val compared very favorably with the Douglas SBD Dauntless dive-bomber, which first flew on May 1, 1940, a design of the late Ed Heinemann, a versatile genius who was a specialist in creating lightweight warplanes. Both aircraft had two small-caliber machine guns firing forward and one aft; both were pleasant to fly and easy to maintain. The Dauntless was stronger and heavier.

Engines were the weak point of Japanese aircraft design because of a shortage of materials, inferior lubricants, and inadequate quality control. When a captured U.S. North American P-51 Mustang was tested by the Japanese later in the war, they were dumbfounded that the Merlin engine did not leak oil in copious quantities, as all its Japanese counterparts did.

One hundred twenty-six Aichi D3A1s took part in the attack on Pearl Harbor, scored heavily in the battles in the Indian Sea, served everywhere in the Pacific, and were finally put to use as kamikaze aircraft at war's end.

Another second-generation indigenous aircraft, the Mitsubishi G4M1 Betty first flew on October 23, 1939. It was the medium bomber with which Japan went to war, and in which the surrender parties went to Iwo Jima. A handsome, if somewhat rotund, aircraft, powered by two 1,530-horsepower Mitsubishi radial engines, with a top speed of 266 mph, it had the phenomenal range of 3,256 miles. Quite maneuverable for an aircraft of its size and weight, the Betty was, save for its limited bomb load of 1,765 pounds, an ideal bomber—but only under conditions of Japanese air superiority. When faced with strong opposition, or when forced to attack heavily defended targets, the Betty was very vulnerable. Early models had been deliberately designed without armor or fire-resistant fuel tanks to save weight so that the desired range specification could be met; this rendered them so susceptible to gunfire that their crews ruefully nicknamed them the "Flying Lighters" for their propensity to burst into flame.

The North American B-25 Mitchell was an American counterpart to the G4M. First flown on August 19, 1940, it was heavier, faster, and carried more bombs—but for shorter distances. With a 3,000-pound bomb load, it could reach only 1,500 miles, but that was enough for the Pacific's island-hopping campaign. The Mitchell was much more strongly built than the Betty, with adequate armor and self-sealing fuel tanks. Although the G4M was more heavily armed than most Japanese bombers, with four 7.7-mm machine guns and a 20-mm cannon, it could not compare to the Mitchell, which was fitted over time with a variety of armament packages ranging from two power-operated turrets, each with two .50-inch machine guns, to a solid nose with eight forward-firing .50-inch machine guns; some later models packed twelve .50-inch machine guns and a 75-mm cannon.

As a final comparison, the Mitsubishi A6M Zero was by far the most famous Japanese fighter. It was built in greater quantities and served longer and in more theaters than any other Japanese warplane. The A6M2 models that spearheaded the attacks on Pearl Harbor and the Philippines had a maximum speed of 331 mph. Fully loaded, it weighed only 5,313 pounds; Allied pilots were as shocked by the agility of the Zero in the Second World War as their forerunners had been by the maneuverability of the Fokker Triplane in the First. Early in the war, it was not uncommon for Japanese pilots to flaunt their skill by performing aerobatics during the course of a dogfight, not unlike a football player spiking a ball after a touchdown. (Later it was learned that, at least on some occasions, the aerobatics were actually combat signals, used because the Japanese aircraft radios were so unreliable.)

The Zero had a surprisingly heavy armament, with two 7.7-mm machine guns in the upper fuselage decking, and two wing-mounted 20-mm cannon. The combination of light weight and heavy armament encapsulated the Japanese offensive mentality, which took as a given that its aircraft were there to do the shooting, not to be shot at.

The Zero's two most famous opponents early in the war were the Curtiss P-40 Warhawk and the Grumman F4F Wildcat. The P-40 (called Tomahawk or Kittyhawk in its British versions) weighed 1,000 pounds more when empty than the Zero did when loaded, but it was slightly faster at 352 mph, and far more stoutly built. The Wildcat was a little heavier than the Zero, just about as fast, but not nearly so maneuverable. It was tremendously strong, giving birth to the nickname "the Ironworks" for the Grumman Aircraft Corporation. Both the P-40 and the Wildcat developed tactics by which their heavy .50-inch machine guns could chop the lighter A6M to pieces, for to dogfight with the Zero was suicidal, a lesson it took little time to learn.

The fortunes of war soon forced the Japanese to revise their thinking and begin to design heavier and more stoutly built aircraft, just as they belatedly realized they had to accelerate production. The equipment timing tide was now against them, however, and despite magnificent efforts on the part of their engineers and

production personnel, they were able to build only limited numbers of the new aircraft, while continuing to pump the old standbys
off the production line. Japan found itself in this position—"behind the power curve," in aviation parlance—because it had shared
Germany's limited vision of the scale' of airpower necessary in a
global conflict. Both the Japanese Army and Navy air forces had
extensive combat experience, the former in Manchukuo against the
Russians, the latter in China. Both were convinced that the aircraft
they had evolved were correct for their mission, and preferred the
concept of relatively small, i.e., *affordable*, air forces, manned by
the most expert crews available.

The excellence of the Japanese aviators was obtained at bitter human cost in training and in combat. All Japanese military training
was based on a brutal dehumanizing process that turned recruits
first into automatons and then into predatory killers who regarded
their adversaries as racially inferior and hence subject to any mal-
treatment, including mass murder. The training for air force pro-
grams was no less severe, resulting in a very small, elite force of
aggressive, superbly conditioned pilots, but at a profligate cost in
wasted personnel and matériel. In the prewar years, the washout
rate was so high it kept graduation numbers down to a few hundred
pilots annually. The system also inhibited individual initiative, a key
factor later when the loss of the leader in a dogfight would throw a
Japanese unit into confusion. When the pressures of war forced an
expansion of the system, the base was too small to accommodate to
it, and the Japanese, like the Germans, were forced to reduce training standards far below that of Allied pilots. Ultimately, young men
barely able to get an airplane off the ground would be sent on one-
way kamikaze missions, scarcely more than animated autopilots.

Japan erred in assuming that it could economize on airpower because it would always control the scale of the fighting. Like Germany, it learned to its sorrow that there is nothing more expensive
than a second-best air force. Japan's aircraft production figures reflected its priorities. Total Japanese aircraft production rose from
just over 1,500 in 1937 to 4,467 in 1939. Then, despite the increase
in world tension and the growing certainty of war with the United
States, Japanese aircraft production leveled off, with 4,768 and
5,088 produced in 1940 and 1941, respectively. In 1941, the United
States was just warming up its assembly lines as it produced almost
20,000 aircraft.

STALEMATES IN PARALLEL, DECISIONS IN REVERSE

During 1941, the two major Axis powers, Germany and Japan, would weigh their respective military situations, consider their options, and then execute diametrically opposed strategies. Germany, stalemated by the Battle of Britain, saw Russia as a relatively easy opponent, the solution to its problems. A victory over Russia would provide the means for a victory over England. Japan, stalemated by China's enormous size, knew from bitter experience in Manchuria that Russia would be too difficult an opponent, even when it was at war with Germany. Incomprehensibly, Japan turned instead to attack the British Empire, the United States, and the not-inconsiderable forces of the Netherlands East Indies.

This decision symbolized the difference in outlook between the Allied and Axis powers. The United States and England realized that if Germany was defeated, victory against Japan was assured, while the defeat of Japan might not assure the defeat of Germany. Japan, despite Germany's urging, never understood that a victory over Russia might lead to victory over, or at least a negotiated settlement with, the United States and England.

There were considerable differences in the goals of Japan and Germany, the latter intending to knock Russia out of the war in six weeks and then organize all of the resources of the European Continent to subdue Great Britain. Japan had a much fuzzier strategy. The United States had responded to Japan's aggression in China and Indochina with a series of economic sanctions, first stopping steel shipments, then freezing Japanese assets, and finally, in concert with the British Empire and the Dutch in Indonesia, placing a virtual embargo on oil shipments. Japan, already economically drained by the war in China, correctly saw this as a knife held to its throat; it had only two years of oil in reserve, and could not let its supplies fall below this level without irreparably weakening its naval power. Therefore, it determined to act. Having already coerced the Vichy government into letting it acquire the dismantled French empire in Indochina, Japan sought to include Siam, Burma, the Dutch East Indies, the Philippines, and a bulwark of islands that would extend from the Aleutians to the Solomon Islands, a defensive framework of unsinkable aircraft carriers. Then, its oil supplies secure and the resources of the conquered territory exploited in the Greater East Asia Co-Prosperity Sphere, the Japanese fleet could defend its new empire until Great Britain and the United States were willing to negotiate a peace.

Unfortunately for both Germany and Japan, their strategies were based more on hope than on hard military intelligence, on arrogance rather than on an understanding of the determined nature of their enemies. The result was a tragedy for the world.

JAPAN DECIDES FOR WAR

The Japanese Navy was originally quite conservative, its war games based on luring the U.S. fleet to home waters, whittling down its strength en route by submarine action. The climax of the games was always a great fleet showdown, in which the Japanese battleships would sink the enemy. This scenario became the gospel of Japanese naval strategy.

In contrast, the Japanese Army was radical, demanding expansion in China, and, from 1937 on, embroiled in the war with China on an ever-increasing scale. This involvement eventually translated to supreme political power when General Tojo Hideki became Prime Minister on October 17, 1941. One result of this was that the conservative attitude of the Japanese Navy was gradually diluted by interservice rivalry. As tensions rose with the sinking of the USS *Panay* in December 1937, the navy came to want its own war, in which it would sail south to oust the colonial powers from their holdings.

One of the greatest minds in the Japanese Navy, Admiral Yamamoto Isoroku, remained conservative; his foreign travels and two stays in the United States convinced him that Japan could not win against the Anglo-Saxon powers. Yet Yamamoto was a patriotic Japanese who believed as his colleagues did that Japan had earned its place in the sun, and that the time had come for Japanese leadership—that is, hegemony—in Asia.

After the First World War, Yamamoto had become fascinated by airpower and led a crusade to build aircraft carriers and procure the best in naval aircraft. So great was the respect in which he was held that the Japanese Parliament approved the creation of a separate fleet of aircraft carriers in addition to the traditional battle fleet of battleships, cruisers, and destroyers. And, by a twist of politics and fate, in 1939 Yamamoto was named Commander in Chief of the Combined Fleet—i.e., both the carriers and the battle fleet.

A veteran of the sneak attack on the Russian fleet at Port Arthur in 1904, Yamamoto felt that if there must be war, it had to start with a similar attack on the American fleet at Pearl Harbor. (Yamamoto had lost two fingers in the 1904–5 war. Notoriously fond of geisha girls, Yamamoto often received a manicure as part of an evening's entertainment. The price for a manicure was 100 sen; Yamamoto, who had only eight fingers, received a discount, hence his nickname, "Eighty-sen.")

The admiral had no illusions about the ultimate results of his action; he wrote that if ordered to fight, "I shall run wild for the first six months or a year, but I have utterly no confidence for the second or third year." But it must be remembered amid the almost universal postwar Yamamoto hagiography, the admiral did not oppose the war with one-thousandth the vigor with which he advocated the plan on Pearl Harbor he was to develop. Had he thrown his undeniable weight and reputation against the war into the scales with similar intensity, had he resigned, or had he spoken directly to the Emperor against the war, it might have been prevented.

Instead, he prosecuted his idea with all his considerable energy and intelligence, seeking the help of the most competent staff officers, and then forcefully selling his idea to the Japanese Imperial Naval General Staff. Like any good manager, he selected key people to flesh out his basic plan. The first was Rear Admiral Onishi Takijiro, a veteran pilot and a hardworking, intelligent commander who would be certain to analyze the basic plan to scout out possible pitfalls. Onishi, in turn, sought the advice of two of the most experienced and highly thought of aviators in the Japanese Navy, Commander Maeda Kosei, an expert on torpedo bombing, and Commander Genda Minoru, who was, in his way, the Japanese Navy's Billy Mitchell when it came to conceptualizing airpower. Genda had been an assistant air attaché in London in 1939 and 1940, and had also studied the British attack on Taranto, in southern Italy. An ardent advocate of the all-out attack, he would recommend the occupation of Hawaii, not merely its bombing.

Yamamoto saw to it that he was placed in command of his operation and began to gather the ships, the planes, and most especially the leaders with which to undertake it. Like a good commander, Yamamoto acceded to many of the changes Genda had proposed, for example the use of fighters, dive-bombers, level bombers, and torpedo planes, instead of just torpedo planes in the attack. He stopped short of invasion, however, and insisted that the U.S. aircraft carriers, battleships, and cruisers were the principal targets, along with land-based airpower installations; key elements like fuel storage and port facilities were relegated to target-of-opportunity status. With the American fleet destroyed, the flank of the operations to the southeast would be protected—for a while.

To be sure that the same success was obtained at Pearl Harbor that the British had achieved at Taranto, Commander Genda created new techniques for launching torpedoes and at the same time dramatically improved level-bombing results. Elaborate torpedo tests were held in Kagoshima Bay, which resembled Pearl Harbor in some essential respects, and with modification of the torpedo with wooden stabilizing fins and alteration of delivery techniques, the Japanese planners found that accurate hits could be made at a rate of over 80 percent. (The idea of wooden fins had been copied from English experiments, relayed to Japan by naval attachés.)

Just as Yamamoto had reached down deep into the navy ranks to select Genda as his planner, so did Genda reach to obtain the best leaders. Overall command for the air strike was given to Lieutenant Commander Fuchida Mitsuo, a longtime friend and Naval Academy classmate. Fuchida naturally followed the same process, picking outstanding leaders for each of the components—fighters, level bombers, torpedo bombers, and dive-bombers. These men and their units would train arduously, honing their skills while still unaware of what their target would be.

At this point, everything in the Japanese Naval Air Force was working optimally, exactly as had been planned. A relatively small force, equipped with the best aircraft available for the task, and manned by the most skilled pilots, would undertake the riskiest military operation in Japanese history.

THE ATTACK BEGINS

Japan opened the war with an immensely complex war plan that included the Southern Operation—the thrust toward Malaya and the Dutch East Indies, the acquisition of Guam and Wake islands and the invasion of the Philippines; all of these depended upon a successful attack on Pearl Harbor.

The timetable on a diplomatic solution had run out on November 26, 1941, when the Carrier Task Force sailed from Hitakappu

Bay in the Kurils, under the command of Admiral Nagumo Chuichi. Nagumo was short and stocky, well liked by his fellow officers, and admired by his men. A battleship admiral, totally inexperienced in air operations, he was given the task because he was senior, even though he was unalterably opposed to the operation even after ordered to conduct it, concerned that his navy was throwing away twenty years of planning to risk everything on a single attack.

None of Nagumo's pessimism could be found at the operational level; the pilots were eager to make the attack, concerned only about doing well so that Japan would achieve a great victory. Some of the veterans had 2,000 hours of flying time, much of it in combat—the average number of flying hours was 800, extraordinary for the period. Those American opponents who would get airborne would average less than half this amount.

The thirty-one-ship fleet was powerful enough to inspire optimism, consisting as it did of six aircraft carriers—the brand new *Shokaku* and *Zuikaku*, which had been rushed to completion, and which could carry 74 aircraft and steam at 34 knots; the *Akagi* and *Kaga*, the slower, oft-rebuilt workhorses of the fleet, which could carry 70 aircraft; and the light carriers *Hiryu* and *Soryu*, which could carry 53 aircraft each. The Carrier Task Force was screened by two pre–World War I battleships, the 29,330-ton *Hiei* and *Kirishima*, and three cruisers—the *Abukama*, the *Chikuma*, and the *Tone*. A miscellaneous support group of destroyers and tankers completed the array.

Luck was with the Japanese; they cloaked their ships in a storm front as they steamed far north of the regular shipping lanes, avoiding a chance meeting with a vessel of foreign registry that might have blown their cover. The Americans, with a single invaluable exception, would not have similar good fortune.

AWARE BUT UNREADY

The United States forces in Hawaii were more powerful than is popularly believed. They were handicapped by a divided command and an innocence about war, not understanding how rigorously prepared a nation had to be when faced with a serious enemy like Japan.

Like their Japanese counterparts, American Army and Navy

commanders in Hawaii had often war-gamed a carrierborne attack on the islands. American intelligence had made huge strides in cracking the Japanese codes and was aware that a crisis was building. The Japanese maintained excellent radio discipline as Nagumo's fleet sortied, and kept up an elaborate radio spoof to mask the departure of the ships, but naval intelligence in Hawaii knew that two carrier groups had not been heard from for more than two weeks—an ominous lapse of contact.

In Washington, President Franklin Roosevelt, his Secretary of State, Cordell Hull, and his military advisors all knew that war was probable, even as they went through the charade of negotiating with the Japanese special ambassadors. They expected the initial blows to fall upon the Philippines and Malaya, based on their knowledge of the location of most of the units of the Japanese fleet. Their thinking might have been clouded by a recent shift in basic strategy, which called for the forward placement of heavy bomber units in the Philippines, to deter if possible, but to destroy if necessary, any Japanese aggression. The aircraft to be used were the very early model B-17s, of which the United States still had only a handful, and for which effective tactics had yet to be developed.

The essential problem facing Roosevelt and his staff was knowing precisely when or how the Japanese would strike. The Japanese diplomatic code had been broken by Colonel William F. Friedman and his team in the summer of 1940, but there was an inevitable time lag in first deciphering the code and then translating it into English; the Japanese were also very wily in their transmissions, using poetic allusions and other indirect means of conveying content.

The inability to exploit fully the cryptographic coup was fatally compounded by the universal failure to use the available resources to the best advantage to anticipate the attack. If the available Boeing B-17s and the Consolidated PBY's in Hawaii had flown a constant 360-degree patrol around the islands, the Japanese fleet would have been discovered far from its launch point. The patrol planes were not used to the limits of their capability, nor were the truck-mounted SCR-270-B radar sets. (Five radars were operational, at Kaawa, Opana, Kawailoa, Fort Shafter, and Koko Head.) The failure to take these apparently obvious precautions stemmed in large part from the undeniable element of "business as usual" in the U.S. military establishment, a phrase that had special meaning in Hawaii, where life was easy, particularly on weekends.

An overwhelming disbelief at all levels that the Japanese would attack Pearl Harbor extended to the navy and army commanders, respectively Admiral Husband E. Kimmel and Lieutenant General Walter C. Short. Both men were highly respected officers who failed in their assigned tasks and were relieved of their commands immediately after the attack. Neither officer had all the information that was available provided to them, but the disaster happened on their watch, and they had to take the blame. Subsequent congressional hysteria resulted in their being charged with "dereliction of duty," a patently unfair assertion. Although they were cleared in the long run, there is no doubt that both men made too many mistakes and failed utterly in their estimate of the situation, remaining in a training mode even as war was about to begin. Most of all, however, they failed because they did not exert themselves and their men as Yamamoto exerted himself and his men. Other U.S. commanders learned from the incident; rarely throughout the war would there again be a lack of effort.

The American air forces in Hawaii included 231 army and 250 navy and Marine aircraft. Of the army aircraft, about one half were relatively modern: twelve Boeing B-17Ds, twelve Douglas A-20As, twelve Curtiss P-40Cs, and 87 P-40Bs. Among the remainder were 18 Douglas B-18s, essentially a bomber version of the Douglas DC-2; 39 Curtiss P-36As and 14 of the Boeing P-26 Peashooters, fun to fly but hopelessly obsolete. The rest included a variety of obsolete observation, training, and attack planes. The composition of the force became academic when the Japanese destroyed most of them on the ground.

The one stroke of fortune that graced the United States on the eve of Pearl Harbor was that Japan's primary target, the aircraft carriers USS *Enterprise* and USS *Lexington*, had sailed, taking with them the muscle of the navy's fighting force. (A third carrier of the Pacific fleet, the USS *Saratoga*, operated out of San Diego.) The *Enterprise* was returning after ferrying a squadron of Marine fighters to Wake Island. The *Lexington* had departed for Midway Island on December 5. Of the 250 navy and Marine aircraft in Hawaii, most were the Consolidated PBY-3 and PBY-5 patrol boats. These were newly arrived, and many were down for maintenance, as there were not enough spare parts and "cannibalization" was frowned on.

The Marines of Marine Air Group 21 had 10 Grumman F4F-3 Wildcats and 23 Douglas SBD-1 and SBD-2 Dauntless dive-bombers, as well as 32 other miscellaneous aircraft. Most of these would be destroyed.

NIITAKA YAMA NI NABORE

The fateful order *Niitaka Yama Ni Nabore* (Climb Mount Niitaka) was given to Nagumo's force on December 2. Formosa's Mount Niitaka, the tallest mountain in the Japanese empire, was symbolic of the difficulty of the attack. Nagumo, fretting with anxiety to the extent that he unnerved some of his subordinates, maneuvered his task force to its launch position 200 miles north of Oahu. Although he knew that the aircraft carriers were gone, he believed the eight battleships and nine cruisers reported to be at anchor were a worthy target.

At precisely 0600 on December 7, the Japanese 1st Attack Force of 183 aircraft began taking off, young Japanese warriors in their war-tailored flying machines hurtling down the pitching carrier decks, carrying with them the dreams of the nation, the seamen cheering, the officers doffing their caps in stiff, precise movements that betrayed only the emotion of patriotism. Curling up like wisps of smoke, the attack formations assembled in thirty minutes; 39 of the fighters remained over the carriers as a defense. Forty-two Zero fighters were assigned the task of securing air superiority and strafing targets of opportunity. Of the bombers, 52 were Aichi Val dive-bombers and 89 were Nakajima B5N Kates.

The Kate was by far the most advanced torpedo plane in the world at the time, two generations beyond the English Swordfish, and vastly better than its American counterpart, the Douglas TBD Devastator. A low-wing, all-metal monoplane, it was sleek and powerful-looking, truly an aerial samurai sword.

Of the 89 Kates dispatched, 49 were intended for use as level bombers, carrying 1,800-pound armor-piercing bombs that the Japanese had ingeniously converted from 16-inch battleship shells. The other 40 Kates carried the superb Japanese 1,764-pound torpedoes, better than any other in the world, modified for use in Pearl Harbor's shallow waters.

The first radar sighting came at 0613 by the Koko Head and Fort Shafter units; then at 0645, radar stations at Kaawa, Opana, and Kawailoa all picked up targets heading south, just 135 miles from Oahu. The plots were relayed to the Central Information Center, a temporary room built on top of a warehouse at Fort Shafter, an amateur imitation of the operations room at Bentley Priory in England. In charge of the center was Lieutenant Kermit Tyler, a pursuit pilot whose only previous experience with radar had been a four-hour shift a few days before. By 0700, according to schedule, all the radar stations began shutting down; only the Opana station continued to operate, trying to gain some needed training.

At the same time the three stations picked up the first wave, the 2nd Attack Force of 168 planes began taking off: 78 Val dive-bombers, 54 Kate horizontal bombers, and 36 Zeros.

Although the Japanese pilots were too keyed up to be aware of it, and their American opponents would be too busy and too angry to notice, it was a beautiful aggregation of aircraft. Unlike Japanese uniforms, austere and bereft of decoration, Japanese planes early in the war were quite colorful. Commander Fuchida's silver Nakajima B5N2 had the usual bright red *Hinomaru* circle insignia ("meatball" to the Americans) on the top and bottom of both wings and the fuselage sides, but also sported an empennage striped with equal-width bands of bright yellow and red. The elegant Zero fighters accompanying him were an overall silvery gray with a matte-black cowling. Each carrier had identifying colors; the fighters from the *Akagi* had a single *Hinomaru*-red stripe around the aft section of the fuselage, while those from the *Kaga* had two red stripes. The *Soryu* and the *Hiryu* used one and two stripes of blue, respectively, while the *Shokaku* and the *Zuikaku* used the same arrangement in white. Against the bright blue Pacific sky, they made an ominously pretty picture.

At 0702, the single operating army radar station at Opana picked up large formations of aircraft coming in and reported them again to Tyler. The young lieutenant assumed that it was either navy aircraft returning from the carriers, or the flight of Boeing B-17Es due in that morning. He adhered to normal practice and dismissed the warning, not realizing until he got a call from Wheeler Field after 0800 that an attack was under way.

The first wave formed into attack formations just north of Kahuku Point; both formations skirted the western coast of the island before turning inbound over Haleiwa. The dive-bombers, under Lieutenant Commander Takahashi Kakuichi, headed east, where 25 Vals from the *Zuikaku*, led by Lieutenant Sakamoto Akira, dropped their 550-pound bombs on Wheeler Field. It was a fine target, for the U.S. Army had obligingly drawn its aircraft into tidy rows, in compliance with repeated warnings about the possibility of sabotage. The fighter leader, Lieutenant Commander Itaya Shigeru, realized almost immediately that they had achieved complete surprise and ordered his Zeros down to strafe.

Takahashi took the remaining 26 Vals south to attack Hickam Field and Ford Island, following the preplanned tactics of splitting up and diving from different directions. At the same time, 26 Vals from the *Shokaku* attacked Ford Island, decimating the acres of patrol and scout planes drawn up there.

Genda's rigorous training paid off as the Kate torpedo planes bored in on Battleship Row from the east to get torpedo strikes on the *Arizona* and the *West Virginia*. In a coordinated attack from the west, other Kates torpedoed the battleships *Utah, Oklahoma, California,* and *Nevada* and two cruisers, the *Raleigh* and the *Helena*.

The Japanese continued their attack as the pandemonium below turned into a combination of terror, hysteria, and sporadic return fire even as the now-world-famous radio message, "Air raid, Pearl Harbor. This is not a drill!" sang out. The Zeros systematically strafed targets of opportunity, their pilots overjoyed when a squadron of 18 Douglas SBD-2s sent ahead from the *Enterprise* obligingly blundered into the scene. The Zeros shot down six of the Dauntlesses, and a seventh fell victim to navy antiaircraft, which was now firing, understandably enough, at anything that flew.

As the black smoke roiled upward from targets all over the island, the B-17s the radar had assumed were inbound now came onto the scene, unarmed and unaware. Like hunters unexpectedly flushing a covey, the Zeros converged on the B-17s. The Boeings proved to be tougher targets than the SBDs, with only one shot down while three were badly damaged.

After the torpedo bombers slanted their weapons into the water, the new configuration and technique letting the torpedoes run at about thirty-three feet below the surface, they exited the area. As they left, 49 level bombers came in, each Kate carrying a single 1,700-pound bomb. Four bombs struck the already wounded *Arizona*, detonating the forward magazine and breaking the ship in half. The hard months of training paid off with uncanny precision as hits were also scored on the *West Virginia*, the *Tennessee*, the *California*, and the *Maryland*. America's battleship fleet was already crippled, so that the flank of the Southern Operation that Yamamoto had worried so much about was secure before 1000 hours, December 7, 1941.

While the ships settled forty feet to the floor of Pearl Harbor, the Japanese attacked land targets of opportunity, dive-bombers going for hangars and other permanent facilities while the Zeros concentrated on strafing parked aircraft. American resistance was so disorganized that only one Zero was shot down by antiaircraft fire.

American pilots, some still dressed in evening clothes, drove to a small auxiliary field at Haleiwa, where the 47th Pursuit Squadron had not yet been hit. At 0815, five young lieutenants began a series of sorties that would last until 1000, landing and refueling, taking whatever aircraft was ready to go, either Curtiss P-40s or P-36s. Although there was no briefing, and certainly no air control from the ground, the pilots had no problem finding the enemy. In the course of two sorties, Second Lieutenant George S. Welch scored four victories; he would get twelve more in the next two years, all of them multiple kills, two, three, or four at a time. Lieutenant Kenneth M. Taylor scored twice before returning to Wheeler to rearm. On his next takeoff, he was wounded by an attacking fighter but went on to fly his sortie, damaging one bomber.

The 2nd Attack Force struck at 0850, flying down the east side of Oahu to curve in to attack the same targets. This time 78 Vals repeated the attack on Ford Island ships and Pearl Harbor before switching their attention to Hickam Field and the Marine base at Ewa. Lieutenant Commander Shimazaki Shigekazu, flying from the *Zuikaku*, split his 54 Kates into three groups of 18 each. The first 18 struck Kaneohe Naval Air Station, while 27 attacked Hickam Field and 9 proceeded to work Ford Island over again.

This time the ground defenses were fully prepared and shot down 14 Vals. At Pearl Harbor, the *Pennsylvania*, in drydock and previously unscathed, was struck by a single 551-pound bomb, while three destroyers were damaged. (The appearance of the Japanese from a southerly heading was important later; ignoring all of the radar reports, the Americans searched to the south for the Japanese carriers, which were making full speed away to the north.)

By 1000, all the surviving Japanese aircraft but one had departed. Commander Fuchida coolly circled over Oahu in his Kate, estimating the damage, becoming convinced that another strike was not only feasible but necessary.

No American would have thought so, for the damage was catastrophic. Five battleships were sunk, two beyond hope of salvage even in the shallow water of Pearl Harbor. Three other battleships, three cruisers, and three destroyers were badly damaged, along with a number of smaller vessels. At least 188 aircraft were destroyed, with another 100 badly damaged. Casualties were very high—2,403 killed and 1,178 wounded. The Japanese lost 29 planes, 5 midget submarines, and 1 fleet submarine.

As each Japanese aircraft returned to its carrier, it was greeted by an exultant crew. Then intelligence officers began an interrogation, trying to assess the damage done, the losses suffered. Admiral Nagumo consulted both Fuchida and Genda; the former wanted to return to knock out the island fuel installations, while Genda pressed for a search for the missing carriers, even if it meant staying in the area for days. In the end, Nagumo elected to withdraw, content with the damage he had inflicted, unwilling to risk his fleet to a counterattack.

EFFECT

Tactically, the Japanese attack on Pearl Harbor was a brilliant military maneuver, carefully planned and perfectly executed, achieving almost all that could have been achieved given that the primary targets, the carriers, were not in port. At the same time, it shielded the massive thrust being undertaken to the south. In strategic terms, it was fatal to the empire, for it embarked Japan upon a war it could never hope to win.

The net effect of the attack upon the United States was positive, transforming the country, removing any indecision about entering the war and silencing those isolationists and members of America First who wanted to keep the United States out of war at any price.

Curiously, the direction the war would take was now given an aberrational spin by Adolf Hitler, who broke precedent by honoring his pact with Japan. Hitler declared war on the United States on December 11, 1941. Had he not done so—and there was every reason not to do so—the American public would have insisted that the war with Japan be given first priority; it is doubtful that Congress would have authorized a declaration of war on Germany immediately, or even for months to come, given the long series of humiliations Japan would inflict upon the country. Although the ultimate outcome of the war would probably have been the same, there would have been changes that might have affected the course of history. Given the facile duplicity of Stalin and Hitler, it is not inconceivable that they would have arrived at a temporary peace in mid-1942, which would have permitted Germany to concentrate on the North African campaign and strengthen its defenses in Western

Europe, while avoiding the bloodletting of the eastern front. It would have had, in addition, at least another two years to perfect the jet fighter and the V-1 and V-2 weapons.

THE WILD RUN BEGINS

The Japanese air attack on the Philippines, while less well reported at the time, was far more effective than the attack on Pearl Harbor, for it established an air superiority that made the outcome of the concurrent invasion inevitable.

The American response at Hawaii had been amateur, and led to the relief of the commanders on the spot; the response in the Philippines had been so irresponsible as to approach criminal negligence, yet General Douglas MacArthur, by force of circumstances, emerged as one of the great martyrs of his time. His later conduct of the war justified his reputation, but in the Philippines, on December 8, 1941 (the Philippines were on the other side of the International Date Line), his inaction and lack of preparation were inexcusable. A commercial Manila radio station had broadcast the news of the attack on Hawaii at 0330 local time (0830, December 7, in Hawaii) and all American military units were placed on the alert.

Although the main force of the Imperial Japanese Naval Air Force had been held up on Formosa by ground fog (just as the Luftwaffe had been prevented from bombing Warsaw on the first morning of the war), the Japanese undertook a series of attacks on the Philippines early in the morning, any one of which should have been enough to jar MacArthur into an offensive response. The first occurred at dawn, when thirteen Nakajima Kates and five Mitsubishi A5M Claude fighters from the *Ryujo* (a light 10,600-ton carrier that would be sunk eight months later by U.S. aircraft) bombed and strafed the naval base at Davao on southern Mindanao. Two Consolidated Catalina flying boats were destroyed, but antiaircraft fire succeeded in knocking down one of the bombers. So careful were Japanese preparations that a destroyer was on hand to rescue the crew members from the Kate. This attack elicited no action from MacArthur's headquarters, nor did another, smaller attack three hours later.

At the Imperial Japanese Army Air Force airfields in Formosa, the fog had lifted earlier due to the difference in surrounding terrain. The army launched 25 Kawasaki Ki-48 Lilys against northern

Luzon, hitting the Tuguegarao airfield at 0700; the Lilys were twin-engine light bombers that had distinguished themselves bombing the Chinese forces against little aerial opposition. Inspired by the Russian Tupolev SB-2 bombers, and resembling the American Martin Maryland, the Lily had a top speed of about 300 mph but carried only about 800 pounds of bomb. At the same time as the raid on Tuguegarao, another formation of 18 Mitsubishi Ki-21 Sallys hit the resort town of Baguio in the center of the island. The Sally was a medium bomber with a top speed of 268 mph and a 1,650-pound bomb load.

At the same time the *Ryujo*'s planes were beating up Davao, the U.S. Far Eastern Air Force's commander, Major General Lewis Hyde Brereton, a hard-bitten veteran of air combat in World War I, was at General MacArthur's headquarters at Fort Santiago. Brereton was requesting permission to launch his 35 B-17s against Formosa as soon as possible. After the war, General MacArthur denied that Brereton had made any such request, even though army records clearly indicate that he had. MacArthur's Chief of Staff, Brigadier General Richard K. Sutherland, later maintained that the decision to keep the bombers on the ground had been Brereton's alone. The precise truth will probably never be known, but Brereton's version is the most compatible with the actual events. It is also consistent with the army doctrine of the time, and with Rainbow 5, the recently revised basic war plan to be used in the event of attack. Given that the B-17s were vulnerable on the ground, and that their only value was in an offensive mode, it seems reasonable to conclude that Brereton would have requested to launch the B-17s.

For whatever reason, the Americans booted away their opportunity in confusion just as luck smiled once again on the Japanese. The fog had lifted over Formosa, and tidy formations of bombers and fighters, the latter equipped with large long-range jettisonable fuel tanks that would have made German pilots envious, arrived at Clark Field at the moment when a huge assembly of American bombers and fighters was being refueled. Some of these were returning from patrol, their fuel low; others were being readied for missions. Their presence resulted in a target the Japanese could scarcely believe, for they were acutely conscious that surprise had been lost, and expected tough opposition.

Yet their attack went off as smoothly as that of Pearl Harbor, the only difference being that the aircraft had come from Formosa rather than from aircraft carriers, and included twin-engine bombers—26 Mitsubishi G3M Nells from the 1st Kokutai and 27 G4M Bettys from the Takao Kokutai. With them were 36 Mitsubishi A6M Zeros, and it would be the latter that would do the most damage, dropping down to strafe the densely parked aircraft.

Once again it was war waged in a pattern as stylized as a Kabuki play, the Japanese dictating the size and composition of the attack, the enemy below passively enacting the victim's role. This time there were only indifferent results from the high-altitude level bombing, but hard and certain execution in air-to-air and air-to-ground fighting. By day's end, the U.S. Far Eastern Air Force had been gutted, with about 60 fighters destroyed, 47 of them on the ground. Twelve B-17s had been destroyed and 2 damaged; a further 30 aircraft of miscellaneous types were wiped out. Confidence was eroded as the Japanese delivered attacks on the radar stations and communication centers. It has never been determined if these were simply lucky hits on vital targets of opportunity, or if the Japanese were attacking predetermined targets.

The next day, bad weather on Formosa provided a day of rest for the Americans to recoup their losses. The confusion and panic inherent in the situation was portrayed in five tragic accidents in which four Curtiss P-40s and a B-17 were lost. Despite everything, a fighting spirit prevailed amid the chaos and a total of fifteen B-17s were readied for a dawn attack on Formosa on December 10. However, word came from Lieutenant Grant Mahoney, one of the great unsung heroes of the war, that the Japanese were landing troops at two points in the north of Luzon, and the B-17s were dispatched to bomb the invasion fleet. Unknown to the Americans, the Imperial Japanese Army Air Force already had fighters operating out of the small island of Bataan, which had been secretly seized on December 8. These aircraft, Nakajima Ki-27 Nates, were not as modern as the Zeros, and had difficulty engaging the Fortresses at altitude. The Fortresses dropped 100-pound bombs on the Japanese invasion fleet without doing much damage, and both Curtiss P-40Es and Seversky P-35s strafed the vessels.

The Severskys had originally been sold to Sweden, but 60 were requisitioned by the United States in October 1940, and of these, 48 were sent to the Philippines as P-35As. Although it was the first cantilever monoplane with retractable gear to be ordered for the air corps, the P-35 was a transitional airplane, having neither the armor nor the armament required for combat. Its greatest contribution to the war effort was that it led to the development of the Republic P-47 Thunderbolt.

Prior to the attack, the strength of the air forces of the two powers was relatively even in numbers and, to a lesser extent, in quality. The Japanese attacked with 398 aircraft, 243 from the navy and 155 from the army. Of these, 186 were fighters and 135 bombers. The most important fighter was the Zero, clearly superior to any American aircraft it would meet, but there were also the Nates and Claudes, which were inferior to the American P-40s, but superior to the P-35s.

Despite the prevailing disorder on the American side, Lieutenant Joseph H. Moore, commander of the 20th Pursuit Squadron, led his unit into the air while the attack was going on. Five of his aircraft had been destroyed in strafing attacks, and five more were caught by bombs during takeoff, but Moore, with three others, attacked the Zeros. Lieutenant Randall B. Keator hit a flight of four and shot one down, the first American victory in the Philippines; he followed this a few moments later with another. Moore himself got two others in a long, low-level dogfight in which his obsolescent Curtiss P-40B was at a great disadvantage. P-35s of the 34th Pursuit Squadron also engaged, and Lieutenant Ben Brown shot down a Zero, the first of three he would get in the course of the Philippine campaign.

From the debacle, other heroes emerged. Third Pursuit Squadron's Lieutenant Mahoney, who would finish the war an ace and a lieutenant colonel, shot down a Zero over Iba, while Lieutenant Jack Donalson of the 21st Squadron got two more over Del Carmen; by April 1942, he, too, would become an ace.

The individual victories were not enough to stem the Japanese, who systematically attacked all the airfields, including the remote sites where a handful of aircraft had been dispersed. American strikes were soon limited to reconnaissance sorties, or carefully selected strikes against particularly dangerous targets. By December 16, a decision was made to send the remaining B-17s south to Australia, for later use, and on December 31, most of the last of the American fighter pilots were evacuated, no longer having aircraft to fly. The Japanese had established total air superiority, and their ground and naval forces moved accordingly.

In the months prior to the war, General MacArthur had announced that he would defend all of the Philippines, crushing any invasion on the beaches. He commanded a nominal force of 120,000 troops, most of them untrained, ill-armed militia, stiffened with about 30,000 regular American troops and Filipino scouts. Faced by the landing of 107,000 troops of the Japanese Fourteenth Army at three different invasion points, the harsh reality of combat against unequal odds forced him to change his original defense plans. The American and Filipino forces dropped back to defend Bataan, a twenty-five-mile-long, twenty-mile-wide peninsula, using the island fortress of Corregidor as a base command post.

MacArthur had pinned his hope on an immediate American relief expedition and had stockpiled the peninsula with food, ammunition, and hospitals sufficient for a six-month defense. Unfortunately, the planning had been done on the basis of a holding force of 43,000; in actuality, more than 100,000 people, military and civilian, were crowded into the area and were immediately on short rations. The peninsula was also a playground for malarial mosquitoes, and both armies were soon afflicted, the Japanese more than the Americans, for the enemy medical system was, and would remain, primitive.

The United States desperately needed heroes to offset the continuing flow of bad news, as the Japanese scored victory after victory. Manila was declared an open city, while the Americans on Bataan clung to the cruel chimera of the a U.S. relief expedition. Lieutenant Boyd "Buzz" Wagner, commanding officer of the 20th Pursuit Squadron, provided some relief of his own. On December 13, returning from a reconnaissance sortie, he encountered four Japanese Ki-27 fighters near their Aparri airfield, shooting them down and strafing others on the field. On December 16, he got another, to become the first USAAF ace. In April 1942, as a lieutenant colonel flying Bell P-39s, he shot down three more aircraft to become for a while the Fifth Air Force's top ace. Wagner, a handsome man with an Errol Flynn mustache and a fifty-mission crush hat, was perfect for press releases, and his victories helped boost morale. He was to lose his life in an aircraft accident in the United States in 1943.

Another more famous hero was B-17 pilot Captain Colin Purdie Kelly, Jr. On December 10, Captain Kelly dropped three 600-pound bombs from 22,000 feet on what was believed to be a battleship of the *Haruna* class. Leaving the ship dead in the water, with black smoke pouring out, Kelly's B-17 was attacked by two enemy fighters and set on fire. Kelly ordered his crew to bail out; before he could leave, the aircraft exploded and he was killed. Kelly was awarded the Distinguished Service Cross for his action, and the American press fed upon the incident, claiming that the *Haruna* was sunk, even though the actual target, the cruiser *Ashigara*, was not badly damaged.

The defenders of Bataan held on until April 9, 1942, unaware that the Japanese forces facing them were almost exhausted and would not have been able to resist a counterattack. The Japanese then concentrated a fierce artillery bombardment on the 15,000 troops crowding the island fortress of Corregidor, sometimes pounding the fortress with 16,000 shells a day, until it surrendered to an invasion force on May 6, 1942. General Jonathan Wainwright, placed in command after MacArthur had been ordered to evacuate to Australia, was forced to order a general surrender throughout the Philippines. Thirty-thousand American and 100,000 Filipino troops laid down their arms in the most bitter defeat in American history, made worse by the subsequent Japanese brutality exercised in the Bataan death march and the prison camps.

THE OTHER THRUST

As badly as the Americans felt about the Philippines, the battle there had been far longer and tougher than the opposition to the rest of the Japanese thrust to the southeast, and the ugliness of the surrender in no way corresponded to the utter humiliation of the British Empire in the rapid fall of Malaya and Singapore. In this operation, airpower was not a significant factor after the devastating blow to British prestige when the battleship *Prince of Wales* and the battle cruiser *Repulse* were sunk. Both ships were easy prey to the 26 land-based G4M1s of the Kanoya Kokutai and 60 G3M2s of the Mihoro and Genzan kokutais. Here once again the high standards of Japanese training proved themselves, for although the two British warships had no air cover, they were magnificently armed with antiaircraft guns, and they responded to the attack with high-speed evasive maneuvers. Nonetheless, the Japanese level bombers struck with devastating accuracy, followed by multiple coordinated attacks by torpedo planes. Fourteen torpedoes hit the *Repulse* and seven the

Prince of Wales. Within two hours, both ships were sunk, at the cost of only three Japanese aircraft.

British air opposition in Malaya was weak and quickly brushed aside; Japanese high-level bombers systematically attacked the fortress of Singapore, and dive-bombers were brought in to quell any British counterattacks.

For eighty years, the English had assumed Singapore could only be attacked from the sea, and equipped it with guns that would out-range and sink the heaviest battleships afloat. Built at a cost of £60 million, an unimaginable sum for the period, the fortress had all its guns pointing out to sea, situated to fight a fleet that never came. The undefended jungle to the north proved to be as impenetrable to the Japanese as the Ardennes had been to the Germans. Contrary to popular opinion, the Japanese army at the time was not taught specialized jungle tactics. Instead, it learned from on-the-job train-ing as it filtered down the Malay Peninsula, bypassing the small British contingent's road blocks and using airpower to overcome any genuine strong points. Curiously, there were ample British air-fields in the peninsula, but just as the harbor had no fleet, the fields had few planes. Those that were there, except for a handful of Hur-ricanes, were totally inadequate.

As the Japanese flowed down the Malay Peninsula, they gathered an aura of invincibility. On February 15, 1942, the 70,000-man gar-rison of Singapore surrendered, a triumph of the greatest magni-tude for the Japanese, who had put only 35,000 men into combat in the theater and who had already lost 3,500 killed and 6,000 wounded. If the British had resisted to the last man and the last car-tridge, as Winston Churchill had ordered them to do, the Japanese would have been halted, for they had completely outrun their sup-plies. Yet the Japanese commander, the wily General Yamashita To-moyuki, bluffed the British into the greatest, most humiliating defeat in their history. The British suffered 138,700 casualties in the campaign, mostly prisoners, many of whom would die in Japanese labor camps.

The rest of the Japanese thrust went in the same way—quick eradication of opposing airpower followed by a relentless push by ground forces. By May 20, 1942, Japan had conquered the Philip-pines, Malaya, the Dutch East Indies, and Burma. They had seized Wake Island, Guam, and a host of smaller islands. In all, some 20 million square miles of territory had been added to the Japanese empire. Yamamoto had indeed run wild, far faster than his most optimistic schedule, and his country settled into a euphoria called by more sober Japanese "the victory disease." In a country where militaristic propaganda was unremitting, these serial victories intoxicated not only the populace and the armed forces but the very leaders themselves, men who should have known better. The effect was similar to the euphoric malaise that gripped the German conquerors after the victory in the west—time was wasted, and leaders at all levels began to focus on celebrations and honors rather than on the next victory.

THE MARCH TO MIDWAY

During the first six months of 1942, the Allied air effort in the Pacific would be borne by two widely disparate elements. The first was carried out in China by Claire Chennault's famous Flying Tigers, the American Volunteer Group that first entered combat on December 20, 1941, inflicting heavy losses on Japanese bombers attempting to bomb Kunming. Equipped with obsolete Curtiss P-40s (technically Model H81-3As, and in fact Tomahawk IIs diverted from a British contract), and manned by volunteers released from active duty with regular U.S. forces, the AVG relied on Chennault's tactics and a primitive but effective early-warning system to defeat the Japanese.

Chennault, the renegade champion of fighter aviation in the Army Air Corps, a man thrust out of the service because he was too insistent on ideas running counter to the popular wisdom, was wise in the ways of the Japanese. He trained his pilots always to use two-plane elements in hit-and-run tactics that capitalized on the P-40's advantage in level-flight speed and its vastly superior diving capability. The P-40s were strongly built, and their heavy firepower blew the fragile Japanese bombers into pieces.

During their short span of existence, the Flying Tigers claimed 296 victories and lost about 50 airplanes and 9 pilots. In a manner becoming relentlessly popular, later historians have scanned the surviving records, fifty years after the fact, and asserted that the Japanese lost only about 100 aircraft to the AVG. The numbers are meaningless—what is important is the lift that Chennault and his men gave to Allied morale at a time when there was nothing but bad news to be found on every front. And when the AVG was dissolved and many of its members absorbed into the United States

Army Air Forces on July 4, 1942, a tradition of flying, fighting, and winning had been firmly established.

A similar boost to morale occurred on April 18, 1942, when Lieutenant Colonel James H. Doolittle led a strike of sixteen modified North American B-25B Mitchells on Japan. In a daring maneuver that risked the invaluable aircraft carrier *Hornet*, Doolittle took off six hundred miles from the Japanese coast, to strike targets in Kobe, Osaka, Nagoya, Tokyo, and Yokohama. Doolittle knew full well that it was only a token raid, for each B-25 carried only three 500-pound high-explosive demolition bombs and one 500-pound incendiary cluster. It was not enough to do much damage, but more than enough to severely shake Japanese morale while raising America's.

The raid achieved total surprise, and although no B-25s were shot down in the raid, all the airplanes were subsequently lost. The bases in China originally planned as landing sites were unavailable, and fifteen crews had to bail out or crash land. One aircraft made it to Vladivostok, where the Russians interned it and the crew. Three crew members were killed in the crash landings, and another eight were captured by the Japanese, then tortured and interrogated. Of these, three men were executed "as examples." Of the remaining five, one died in prison, and the other four survived the war, to begin, with the other veterans of the raid, a series of classic anniversary celebrations each April 18.

Doolittle knew how little damage had been done and was convinced that he would be brought home and court-martialed for his failure. Instead, his achievement was recognized for the moral tonic that it was. He was given the Medal of Honor and promoted to brigadier general.

His attack had another unforeseen and far-reaching effect, for it had become obvious that the U.S. fleet was still a threat and must be destroyed, turning the Japanese away from the concept of an attack on the Soviet Union. This led directly to the decisive engagement of the Pacific war, the Battle of Midway. Yamamoto planned the new assault, building up to it with two important but lesser battles.

CEYLON AND THE BATTLE OF THE CORAL SEA

Yamamoto knew that aggressive action was necessary both to keep the British and American fleets off balance, and especially to keep them from joining forces in a combined action. He assigned Nagumo, the reluctant victor of Pearl Harbor, the task of smashing the British fleet in the Indian Ocean with a surprise raid on the naval base at Trincomalee in Ceylon (now Sri Lanka). Nagumo took five aircraft carriers, three battleships, six cruisers, and twenty destroyers into the fray, expecting to find Admiral Sir James Somerville's fleet of five battleships (mostly obsolete), three aircraft carriers, seven cruisers, and sixteen destroyers in port. The code breakers let Somerville know the Japanese were coming, and he moved his warships out of the harbor and his aircraft into the air.

The Japanese attacked on April 1, 1942, and although no major engagement ensued, the aircraft carrier *Hermes* and two British heavy cruisers, *Cornwall* and *Dorsetshire*, were sunk by dive-bombers. Somerville determined that Nagumo's fleet was superior and elected to take evasive action. The most important aspect of the battle was a passive one: the astute British reaction should have tipped Yamamoto that his naval cypher was broken. It did not, and he continued the elaborate orchestration of what he hoped would be the decisive battle.

A preliminary step to the Midway adventure occurred just over one month later, from May 6 to 8, in the Battle of the Coral Sea, the first battle ever between aircraft carriers. The Japanese plan was typically complex and depended upon a nonexistent security, for their signals were being intercepted and interpreted by the Allies.

As a part of the overall thrust to the east, Yamamoto had decided to take Port Moresby in New Guinea as a base for an attack on Australia, and Tulagi in the Solomons as a staging base for further operations. Determined to contest the Japanese advance on Port Moresby, the British and Americans reacted, putting together a fleet consisting of a mixed American-Australian cruiser squadron of seven vessels, and the two American aircraft carriers *Lexington* and *Yorktown*, under the command of Rear Admiral Frank J. Fletcher.

Fleet Admiral Chester W. Nimitz was a quiet, gentle man who drove himself hard and smoothed the way for others to cooperate by replacing less aggressive officers with fierce fighting admirals like William F. "Bull" Halsey and Raymond Spruance. Nimitz also supported Fletcher, whose reputation had sagged with the fall of Wake Island. Nimitz sent the three men charging against Japanese island bases, counterattacking with the only weapon he had, the three carriers *Enterprise*, *Lexington*, and *Yorktown*. The damage was not decisive, but the effect on American morale was, for it was filled with incidents like Lieutenant Edward "Butch" O'Hare's winning the Medal of Honor for shooting down five Japanese Kates in a single engagement.

SCRATCH ONE FLAT TOP

With many of his ships needing repair and refitting after four grueling months at sea, Admiral Yamamoto dispatched the Japanese Fourth Fleet, commanded by Vice Admiral Inouye Shigeyoshi to cover the Port Moresby–Tulagi operation. Once again the Japanese split their forces, sending one element through the Bismarck Sea to Port Moresby and a second to the southern Solomons to the base at Tulagi. A third force was to defeat any ships attempting to contest the invasion at Tulagi, then depart and raid Australian air bases.

Admiral Nimitz determined to take whatever risks were necessary to give the Japanese a bloody nose, sending his two carrier groups, Task Force 17, with the *Yorktown* under Fletcher, and Task Force 11, with the *Lexington* under Rear Admiral Aubrey W. Fitch. As a mark of his confidence, Nimitz gave Fletcher overall command, despite rumors of his being too cautious, rumors validated all too swiftly off Guadalcanal in the months to come.

After some initial strikes on Tulagi by aircraft from the *Yorktown*, the results of which were vastly overrated by exuberant crew members, both fleets played blind man's bluff, missing opportunities to strike the other. The preliminaries to the Battle of the Coral Sea opened on May 5 and continued through the May 6—the bitter day that Corregidor surrendered. Scout planes from both fleets located each other, the opening jabs in what would become a slugfest between airplanes; it was a historic event, the world's first aircraft carrier battle in which no surface ship would see an enemy vessel.

The first Japanese large-scale attack on May 7, 1942, turned out to be a colossal mistake; the scouts had misidentified the USS *Neosho* as an aircraft carrier, accompanied by a cruiser. The *Neosho* was an oiler, and the "cruiser" was the destroyer *Sims*, but when the massive Japanese air detachment arrived—36 Vals, 24 Kates, and 36 Zeros—its commander, Lieutenant Commander Takahashi Kakuichi, elected to attack anyway. (Takahashi had led the attack on Wheeler Field six months before.) While the Japanese were sinking the *Neosho* and the *Sims*, a corresponding misidentification had sent Douglas Dauntlesses and Devastators from both the *Lexington* and the *Yorktown* to a point near Misima Island. From his 15,000-foot altitude, Commander Weldon L. "Ham" Hamilton spotted wakes, calling out his sighting to Lieutenant Commander Robert Dixon, who was leading *Lexington*'s Scouting Two's Dauntlesses. Quite by chance they had found the carrier *Shoho*, her varnished wood deck gleaming yellow in the sun. The American attack began at 1100 with a dive from 10,000 feet by three SBDs, the first time a Dauntless would attack an enemy carrier. The *Shoho* defended itself fiercely, steaming in wild maneuvers while the escorting cruisers put up a barrage of antiaircraft fire.

The *Shoho* managed to avoid more than superficial damage until "Ham" Hamilton put a bomb through her flight deck, destroying her steering. Four more bombs and several torpedoes then followed before the *Lexington* aircraft were finished, leaving *Shoho* burning for the *Yorktown* attack force, which arrived fifteen minutes later. It was an easier target now, still under way at 20 knots, but no longer able to put up the same volume of antiaircraft fire. The *Yorktown*'s pilots put more bombs into it, and the *Shoho* slid under the waves, the first of many Japanese carriers to do so. An immortal radio call went out, one that was picked up immediately by the media and made a symbol of a new stage in the war. Lieutenant Commander Dixon exuberantly radioed: "Scratch one flat-top! Dixon to Carrier. Scratch one flat-top."

In the lull after the first sharp battle, the two opposing fleet commanders, Rear Admiral Hara Chuichi of the relatively inexperienced Japanese Carrier Division 5 and Fletcher with Task Force 17, hesitated, reluctant to send out aircraft on a search-and-destroy mission only then to be discovered themselves either during the launch or the recovery phase. Hara reacted first and, late on May 7, launched an attack with 27 torpedo planes and level bombers. They ran into Fletcher's Combat Air Patrol, however, and in the ensuing dogfight lost 7 planes compared to 3 for the Americans, the Japanese bombers jettisoning their loads into the sea. But these were tenacious veterans, and they knew the importance of precisely fixing the enemy's position; they circled the *Yorktown* amid the storm of antiaircraft fire and coolly radioed back her position.

Fourteen of the surviving Japanese planes were lost at sea on the way back to their ship. All the horror and the loneliness of war is accentuated by forgotten incidents like this, 14 planes going down at sea, each carrying three frightened men to anonymous graves.

The next day, both fleets were brought under observation by 0815; the Americans got off the first strike force, launching 75 aircraft by a 0915. The *Shokaku* and the *Zuikaku* were 175 miles away, lurking in an undercast, but the former was caught in a clear patch by both SBDs and Devastators, which were working without fighter cover. Nine of the Devastators dropped torpedoes—all nine malfunctioned, signaling a fleetwide malady of depth controls and exploders that would not be cleared up for months. Fifteen dive-bombers flashed through the combat air patrol and the antiaircraft barrage, scoring three hits that left the *Shokaku* burning.

Hara had launched 69 aircraft almost simultaneously with the *Yorktown*, and by 1100 had begun a devastating attack on the *Lexington*. Unlike the ill-coordinated American attack on the *Shokaku*, the Japanese pilots worked well together, their torpedo planes streaming in from all quadrants while the dive-bombers poured down from above, as regularly spaced as the steps of an escalator.

Two torpedoes into the *Lexington*'s port side allowed water to pour in, setting up a list and inhibiting her maneuverability so that three more torpedoes and many bombs could be delivered. The Aichi Vals peeled off at 17,500 feet and dove down like arrows to pull out at 2,500 feet, almost unable to miss. In the distance, the *Yorktown* was blasted by an 800-pound bomb that penetrated four decks and killed or wounded 66 crew members; despite the damage and the billowing smoke, flight operations went on.

In the immediate aftermath, both sides claimed victory. In a brilliant show of damage control, the listing *Lexington* was righted by shifting oil ballast, and air operations were resumed. But as she began to creep back toward repairs at Pearl Harbor, a massive aviation fuel explosion gutted the ship. Even as it continued at 25 knots, and aircraft were recovered, the fire soon raged out of control. The *Lexington*'s captain, Frederick C. Sherman, reluctantly gave the order to abandon ship. The "*Lady Lex*" would not sink, however, until an American destroyer, the USS *Phelps*, delivered the coup de grâce with five torpedoes.

In terms strictly of matériel, the Japanese had won a slight advantage. They had sunk one destroyer, one oiler, damaged one carrier, and sunk the 36,000-ton *Lexington*. The Americans had sunk the 11,262-ton *Shoho*, one destroyer, and several smaller vessels. The *Yorktown* was far less severely damaged than the *Shokaku* and returned to service in time for the next battle. The Japanese had lost

99 aircraft compared to 77 for the Americans, including those sunk with the *Lexington*.

Strategically, however, the Japanese thrust to Port Moresby was stopped in its tracks. This should have made Yamamoto pause and reflect, for in two recent battles, the Allies had been well prepared and, in the Coral Sea, very offensive-minded, fighting the Japanese on equal terms rather than just reacting defensively. Instead, he continued preparations for the most far-reaching and elaborate operation in Japanese naval history, one dwarfing the attacks that opened the war.

JAPANESE FORCES AND STRATEGY FOR THE MIDWAY OPERATION

In a curious way, Yamamoto's victory at Pearl Harbor laid the grounds for his defeat at Midway. Having had his battleships destroyed, Admiral Chester Nimitz made a virtue of necessity and created the Carrier Task Force, sharpening its claws in some trial runs and then positioning it perfectly for a riposte.

The Japanese admiral had admonished others about the "victory disease" and then succumbed himself, for he regarded the Coral Sea battle as a victory and accepted the repulse at Port Moresby as something that could easily be rectified. His intention was to establish a barricade of islands in an arc ranging from Kiska in the Aleutians through Midway, Wake, the Marshalls, the Gilberts, Guadalcanal, and Port Moresby. From this defensive line, he would operate long-range patrol planes to monitor the American fleet and deny American submarines refueling ports.

And most of all, he would force Nimitz to fight; he would bring the U.S. Pacific Fleet to battle and destroy it. Midway, 1,300 miles northwest of Pearl Harbor and regarded as "Hawaii's sentinel," was, in short, bait for an overly elaborate trap. There were many miscalculations involved, the worst of which was the Japanese still believing that the Japanese codes were secure; almost as bad was their thinking that Nimitz had to be lured to fight, especially when the soft-spoken Nimitz had his fist cocked and ready to let fly.

Yamamoto mustered the following forces:

- The Advance Expeditionary Force, consisting of four groups of submarines, which were to be posted north and south of Frigate Shoals, thus cordoning off Hawaii. In the

event, the submarines arrived on station after the American
forces had passed.

• The Carrier Striking Force, consisting of the *Soryu*, the
Kaga, the *Akagi*, and the *Hiryu* and commanded by Admiral
Nagumo; all four ships had been at Pearl Harbor, and if the
Battle of the Coral Sea had not intervened, they would have
been joined by the *Shokaku* and the *Zuikaku*.

• The Military Occupation Force—troop transports
screened by two battleships, a light carrier, and seven cruisers.
This force was to place troops ashore on Midway.

• The extraordinary Main Body, which had seven battleships, including the *Yamato*, Yamamoto's palatial flagship
and the largest and most powerful warship afloat, dwarfing
even the German *Tirpitz* or the new American *Idaho* class. Yamamoto lived so well on his flagship (too well, some said) that
it was referred to as the *Yamato Palace* by officers serving on
less luxurious ships. The Main Body was subdivided into
those under Admiral Yamamoto's personal command (three
large battleships and a light carrier) and the Aleutian Support
(or Screening) Force, which had four battleships and two light
cruisers.

• The Northern Area Force, which was subdivided into the
2nd Mobile Force, with two carriers and two heavy cruisers,
and the Occupation Forces for Adak, Attu, and Kiska in the
Aleutians.

In all, there were 165 ships in the vast endeavor, which had a
complicated plan and a demanding timetable to follow. The 2nd
Mobile Force was intended to open the battle with an overwhelming bombardment of Dutch Harbor on Unalaska Island on June 3
to confuse the Americans and cover the occupation of Adak, Attu,
and Kiska. The northernmost part of the operation indicates more
clearly than anything the total dependence of the Japanese upon
good security, for the elaborate feint was virtually meaningless if
Nimitz didn't take the bait.

The Carrier Striking Force was to smash Midway Island's defenses, then defeat the American Pacific Fleet, which was expected
to steam to Midway's aid. Yamamoto would then personally lead
the Main Body's heavy battleships to finish off any survivors of the
air attack.

The Military Occupation Force in the meantime was to have seized Midway Island and converted it into a Japanese air base. And, lurking halfway between Midway and the Aleutians, ready to fight any American naval forces that came either way, was the Aleutian Support Force.

Neither Clausewitz, Nelson, nor Togo would have approved of such a wide and almost pointless dispersal of forces. Yamamoto commanded the largest fleet ever assembled in the Pacific to that date, yet he dissipated it so that the U.S. fleet might defeat it in detail. He was also very ill, afflicted with a parasitic infection believed to have been caused by worms from eating sushi. His spirits were low, and one must wonder if, in the solitude of his well-furnished cabin on the *Yamato*, the knowledgeable Yamamoto ever thought of Napoleon at Waterloo, stricken with hemorrhoids.

AMERICAN FORCES AND STRATEGY FOR THE DEFENSE OF MIDWAY

Nimitz and his staff did not have complete information on the Japanese intentions, but they had enough to take immediate countermeasures, including the reinforcement of Midway Island and the incredibly swift return of the *Yorktown* to combat. The battered carrier reached Hawaii at midafternoon on May 27, 1942, with an estimated three months required to get her battleworthy. She left the drydock at 1100 on May 29, still with hundreds of workmen on board, and sailed on May 31 at 0900.

Nimitz also disposed of two other carriers from Halsey's Task Force 16, the *Enterprise* and the *Hornet*; the three carriers would make up the Carrier Striking Force under Fletcher, who also commanded Task Force 17 with the *Yorktown*. On board his ships he had 77 Grumman F4Fs, 112 Douglas SBDs, and 42 Douglas Devastators.

Halsey was ill, so Nimitz replaced him with Rear Admiral Raymond A. Spruance, a recognized cruiser expert to whom Fletcher would wisely, modestly, and courageously turn over the conduct of the air battle when the *Yorktown* was hit.

In addition to the carriers, Fletcher had 6 cruisers, 9 destroyers, and 19 submarines. Nimitz estimated that this Pacific Fleet would face up to 4 battleships, 5 carriers, 9 heavy cruisers, 5 light cruisers, 24 destroyers, and 25 submarines.

But Nimitz counted on both tactical and strategic advantages. Tactically, he had Midway itself, not only unsinkable, but a magnet for Japanese bombs, diverting them from the Pacific Fleet. Midway had a powerful air force for the time, with 32 PBYs for patrol duty, and 6 newly arrived Grumman TBFs, the same sort of plane a young Ensign George Bush would fly later, as part of VT-8 ("VT" was the Navy designation for "Torpedo Squadron"). The 2nd Marine Air Wing had two units: VMF-221 had 20 Brewster F2A Buffaloes and 7 Grumman F4F Wildcats, and VSMB-241 had 11 obsolete Vought SB2U-3 Vindicators and 16 SBD-2s. There was also a detachment of the Seventh Army Air Force, with 19 B-17s and 4 Martin B-26 Marauders, outfitted to carry torpedoes. Midway also had two good search radars, far better than those on the carriers.

Strategically, Nimitz had the drop on Yamamoto by his better intelligence services, and he was operating at shorter ranges from his main base. Nimitz in fact had inverted the old Japanese war plan, luring Japan's fleet out to be whittled down.

The Marine Corps garrison was reinforced, raising the total to 2,000 troops. By June 4, Nimitz had 105 aircraft on Midway, along with 141 officers and 2,886 men. He now positioned his carriers just outside the range of expected Japanese reconnaissance until the last, vital moment.

THE BATTLE OF MIDWAY

The elaborate, intensive Japanese feint at Dutch Harbor took place as scheduled on June 3 without inflicting much damage, and without perturbing Nimitz—he had enough to handle near Midway. Strategically, the attack was a fizzle, tactically almost a nonevent. The first American riposte came from Midway when the 431st Bombardment Squadron sent nine B-17Es, the latest off the Boeing production line, into battle. Led by Lieutenant Colonel Walter C. Sweeney (later a four-star general and commander of the Tactical Air Command), they caught the transport force 570 miles west of Midway, dropping thirty-six 600-pound demolition bombs but scoring no hits. High-altitude bombing of rapidly moving ships was never going to be easy. Four Consolidated PBYs, acting in the unlikely role of torpedo planes, attacked the transports early on the

A projection of American prewar airpower in the Philippines during the age of innocence. Two flights of Boeing P-26 Peashooters pass over Philippine cadets and their Stearman trainers. Obsolete well before 1941, the Philippine Air Force used the P-26s with valor against the Japanese. (*Air Force Association Photo*)

The architects of German airpower at ceremonies for the *Graf Zeppelin*, Germany's sole aircraft carrier, launched in December 1938. Generalfeldmarschall Hermann Göring is speaking; to his right is Generaladmiral Erich Raeder. On the right, standing behind the Führer, Adolf Hitler, is the man most responsible for the Luftwaffe's early successes, Generaloberst Erhard Milch. The *Graf Zeppelin* was never completed. (*Air Force Association Photo*)

The last Hawker Hurricane of the more than 14,000 built. Less famous than the Spitfire, it was the most important RAF fighter in the Battle of Britain. (*Author's Photo*)

The first American ace of World War II, Pilot Officer William R. Dunn, in the cockpit of his Spitfire. Serving in the RAF, Dunn scored the first victory for the Eagle Squadron; twenty years later he fought again in Vietnam. (*Air Force Association Photo*)

A line-up of Polish P.Z.L. Los bombers in service with the X Bomber Squadron of the 1st Air Regiment on the eve of World War II. The double-wheel bogie of the landing gear is interesting, and most unusual for the period. (*Courtesy of Andrezej Glass, the Wojskowy Institute of History, Warsaw*)

American industry benefited from French and English purchases of warplanes. Famous test pilot Sam Shannon is shown here on the wing of a Martin Maryland, prior to delivery to the French Air Force. (*Author's Photo*)

Orders for aircraft came in so rapidly that plants could not be built fast enough; here Lightning I's for the RAF are assembled outside the Lockheed Burbank plant. In the background, the invaluable Hudson patrol bomber may be seen. (*Warren Bodie Photo*)

German airpower had already made itself felt in Europe; here paratroopers fall from the trusty Junkers Ju 52/3m transport. (*Musée de l'Air et de l'Espace Photo*)

Great things were expected of the radical Bell P-39, shown here on prewar maneuvers; unfortunately, it was purchased without a supercharger, which rendered it worthless as a high-altitude fighter. It did serve well as a ground-attack plane, particularly in Russia. (*Warren Bodie Photo*)

A Boeing B-17E over Guadalcanal. The Japanese respected even the early-model Fortresses, one official journal commenting that the B-17's speed made it "essentially a four-engine fighter." (*Air Force Association Photo*)

Grumman Wildcats of the Cactus Air Force on Guadalcanal; the stubby little F4F was not as maneuverable as the Zero but was much more rugged. When flown with the proper tactics, including the Thach weave, two Wildcats could take on several Zeros. (*Courtesy Dennis Franks, Marine Corps History Office*)

Marine Captain (later Governor) Joe Foss lovingly pats the cowling of his personal F4F, in which he shot down 26 Japanese aircraft in 63 days, equaling Captain Eddie Rickenbacker's World War I record. (*Air Force Association Photo*)

By 1943, the strength of American aviation was making itself felt around the world, and there was a sufficient margin to let crews come home to sell war bonds. Here the future Chief of Staff of the United States Air Force, Brigadier General Hoyt Vandenberg, greets veterans of the Ploesti raid. (*Air Force Association Photo*)

Jimmy Doolittle had struck a blow for morale with his 1942 raid on Tokyo; expecting to be court-martialed for what he considered its failure, he was instead promoted to brigadier general and given the Medal of Honor. He's shown here with his wife Jo, President Franklin D. Roosevelt, Army Air Forces Commander General Hap Arnold, and Army Chief of Staff General George C. Marshall. (*Air Force Association Photo*)

The bombing raids in Europe became increasingly costly; the B-24s, although fast and long-ranged, flew at lower altitudes and were considered more vulnerable than the B-17s. This Liberator, hit over Vienna, broke in two shortly after this photo was taken. Most of the crew were seen to bail out. (*Air Force Association Photo*)

The remains of Doolittle's B-25 after his bailout "somewhere in China." (*Air Force Association Photo*)

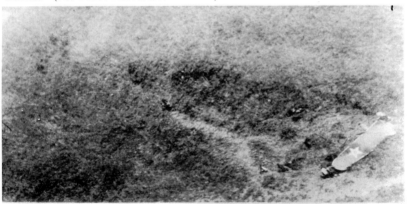

The Martin B-26 medium bomber gained an early reputation as a pilot killer, but actually had the lowest loss rate for any bomber in combat. (*Air Force Association Photo*)

The war in the North African desert proved to be a training ground for the American Air Force, which cut its teeth on first-rate German and Italian opposition. This captured Macchi-Castoldi MC.202 was one of the best Italian fighters. Fortunately for the Allies, they were produced in relatively small numbers. (*Howard Levy Photo*)

The German invasion of the Soviet Union was initially a walkover for the Luftwaffe. Aircraft like the infamous Junkers Ju 87 were no longer suitable for combat in the West but were effective on the eastern front. This Ju 87 has been modified with a 37-mm cannon for tank killing. (*Air Force Association Photo*)

Initially, Soviet fighters, pilots, and tactics were no match for the Luftwaffe; somehow the Soviet Union managed to absorb the initial losses and turn out quantities of new planes like this Yak-3, which almost matched the Messerschmitt Bf 109 in quality and soon outstripped it in quantity. (*Air Force Association Photo*)

Stalin called the Ilyushin Il-2 Shturmovik "bread and air" for his Russian forces. The Germans hated the aircraft, which was difficult to shoot down and had tremendous tank-killing power. (*Author's Photo*)

In the Pacific, after the recovery from the shock of Pearl Harbor, massive efforts were made to keep China in the war. "Flying the Hump" became a billion-dollar enterprise, and the Curtiss C-46, after initial teething problems, turned into a workhorse. (*Air Force Association Photo*)

Supplying China was a difficult task; everything, including fuel for return trips, had to be flown in to airfields constructed painfully and patiently by an infinite amount of Chinese labor, one rock at a time. (*Air Force Association Photo*)

(LEFT) Two of the great personalities of the war—Frank Whittle, who invented the jet engine used by England and later the United States, and Donald Douglas, founder of the Douglas Aircraft Company. (*Air Force Association Photo*)

(BELOW) On the other side of the ocean, a similar photo, taken two years earlier, just after the first flight of a German jet, the Heinkel He 178, on August 27, 1939. A young Hans von Ohain toasts his colleagues, with manufacturer Ernst Heinkel seated at his right. (*Author's Photo*)

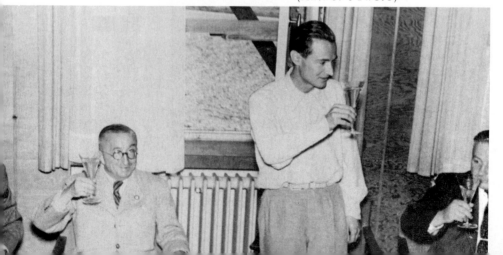

The best British bomber of the war, the Avro Lancaster; it was rugged, fast, carried a huge bomb load, and was relatively maneuverable. (*Author's Photo*)

The German night-fighter force was unprepared when war began; it grew sophisticated rapidly, and in the Battle of Berlin achieved air superiority over the British. Here a tired Luftwaffe crew begins to debrief, even as their Junkers Ju 88 is fueled for the next mission. (*Author's Photo*)

The USAAF learned rapidly, too, and grew in strength. On January 25, 1944, Francis S. Gabreski (right) scored his eleventh victory and was promoted to lieutenant colonel. (*Air Force Association Photo*)

The Germans had achieved air superiority over Europe in the fall of 1943; in the spring of 1944, the arrival in quantity of the North American P-51 long-range escort fighter reversed the situation. (*Warren Bodie Photo*)

The Messerschmitt Bf 109 remained in production throughout the war—and after, in other countries. Equal to any fighter in the world in 1939, it gradually lost its edge, but even at war's end was a strong opponent in the hands of a good pilot. (*Author's Photo*)

Enemy aircraft, like this Focke-Wulf Fw 190 captured in North Africa and carrying U.S. insignia, were carefully evaluated to determine their strengths and weaknesses. The Fw 190 was generally easier to fly than the Bf 109, but it did not perform as well at altitude. (*Warren Bodie Photo*)

The Focke-Wulf developed over time, and the Fw 190-D9, with a Junkers Jumo 213 engine, was one of the best fighters of the war. (*Author's Photo*)

Colonel Ernst Udet, 62-victory ace in the First World War, consummate aerobatic pilot, and the man who did the most to ruin the Luftwaffe. Pushed into a position he did not want and knew he could not fill, Udet's lack of management skill was disastrous for the development of Luftwaffe weaponry. He commited suicide in despair. (*Air Force Association Photo*)

Ryan PT-23 trainers in formation. The United States and Great Britain enjoyed the luxury of virtually unlimited training resources, with good weather, abundant fuel, and thousands of training planes, turning out tens of thousands of pilots. In Germany, the weather was often bad, the fuel shortage impossible, and a cadet's formation mate might turn out to be a Mustang looking for a kill. (*Courtesy William Wagner*)

The Douglas Dauntless was not a spectacular performer, yet it was in the right place at the right time and at Midway decisively reversed the direction of the war. John Northrop, Ed Heinemann, and Donald Douglas all played roles in its creation and production. (*Author's Photo*)

When a Japanese Zero was finally captured and analyzed, it was revealed for what it was: an excellent, original aircraft that achieved its maneuverability and long range by the sacrifice of structural strength and safety equipment. (*Author's Photo*)

The Japanese learned from experience and improved their fighters but were never able to build them in the necessary quantities. This Kawasaki Ki-61 Tony was the only Japanese fighter powered by a liquid-cooled engine. (*Author's Collection*)

The Nakajima Ki-44 Shoki (Tojo) was a fast, heavily armed fighter that reversed the Zero formula, sacrificing maneuverability for structural strength and speed. It had inherent vices that kept noncombat losses high but was effective against American bombers, including the B-29. (*Warren Bodie Photo*)

The Kawanishi H8K Emily was probably the best patrol bomber of the war; on its first combat sortie, it returned to raid Honolulu on the night of March 4–5, 1942. Heavily armed, it was considered difficult to shoot down—an exception being made in this case. (*Author's Photo*)

As the carrier air war grew in intensity, so did American airpower grow in strength. But not all American aircraft were immediate winners. The Curtiss SB2C Helldiver had a long and agonizing teething period and was never regarded with the affection accorded the Dauntless. (*Author's Photo*)

Admiral Marc Mitscher in a characteristic pose; he was considered by many to be the most able carrier admiral of the war. (*C. V. Glines Photo*)

Sometimes the expressions say it all. Here Lieutenant Generals Carl "Tooey" Spaatz, George Patton, and Jimmy Doolittle chat, Spaatz with a characteristically skeptical look. To Doolittle's left, Major General Hoyt Vandenberg listens to Brigadier General O. P. "Opie" Weyland. Spaatz and Doolittle did not always get along. (*Air Force Association Photo*)

next morning and placed one torpedo in an escorting tanker, the *Akebono Maru*.

June 4 would be much different. The Japanese Navy was very familiar with the Pacific's weather, and had used the nasty cold shelter of clouds to approach its launch point, 240 miles northwest of Midway, just as it had used clouds to hide its approach to Pearl Harbor. At the same time, Fletcher's Task Force 17 was steaming southwest, to arrive 202 miles north of Midway, within striking distance of Nagumo's fleet, ready to launch at 0430.

Nagumo, unaware of the presence of Fletcher's ships, struck first at Midway, Lieutenant Commander Tomonaga Joichi, commander of the *Hiryu*'s air unit, leading the force of 108 airplanes. The *Hiryu* and the *Soryu* launched 36 Kates while the *Akagi* and the *Kaga* sent 36 Vals. Each carrier provided Zeros as protective cover.

Unknown to the Japanese, a patrolling Consolidated PBY had spotted two of the carriers and radioed their position to Midway. The report was heard on the *Yorktown* as well, and Fletcher ordered Spruance to attack, intending to follow up as soon as he'd recovered his dive-bombers, which were on patrol.

Aircraft erupted from the Midway runway, some to save themselves from attack, others to defend the island. Marine Major Floyd B. Parks, leading the Brewster Buffaloes and the Grumman Wildcats, was surprised to see the Zeros *below* the incoming bombers. The Marine fighters dove to the attack, getting six bombers before being brutally cut up by the faster, more maneuverable Zeros. A surviving American pilot—one of the few—said that the Brewsters seemed to be tied to a post while the Zeros made passes at them. Within minutes, fifteen of the Marine fighters had been shot down, their pilots lost, and another seven planes were damaged.

At Midway, the Japanese bombers destroyed some buildings and oil tanks, but it was hardly a decisive effort, and it was obvious that a second attack was imperative.

The first strike on the Japanese came from the Midway-based torpedo planes, six Grumman TBF Avengers, led by Lieutenant Langdon K. Fieberling, and four Martin Marauders of the 69th Bombardment Squadron (Medium), led by Captain James F. Collins, Jr. Most of the attacking torpedo planes were hit before they got into a position to launch; those torpedoes that were dropped didn't run true; there were no hits. At about the same time, Colonel Sweeney led fourteen B-17Es into the battle, dropping bombs from 20,000 feet and claiming hits that subsequently were discounted.

DENOUEMENT AT MIDWAY

Two unrelated but parallel events determined the outcome of the Battle of Midway, and with it the war. Nimitz's cryptographers had given him the information necessary to enable him to position the American fleet like a cocked pistol pointed at the Japanese intruders. The first event would remove the pistol's safety; the second would pull the trigger.

Around 0430, Nagumo dispatched seven reconnaissance planes, six Aichi E13A1s from his cruisers and a single Nakajima E8N2 from the *Haruna*. The Aichi was a handsome twin-float monoplane, code-named by the Americans "Jake," and carried a pilot and two crew members at a 120-mph cruising speed with an endurance of up to fifteen hours. The fourth Jake to be launched from the cruiser *Tone*, flown by Lieutenant Amari Hiroshi, was supposed to search the exact area where Fletcher's task force lurked. A catapult malfunction delayed its launch for more than thirty minutes. When the Jake finally reached its search point and located the American fleet, at 0728, the message it sent back didn't indicate a carrier. Fifty-two minutes later, it signaled, "One apparent carrier sighted to the rear of the enemy." The warning was too late and the pistol's safety was off.

At 0925, Lieutenant Clarence "Wade" McClusky, an ex–fighter pilot just learning the dive-bomber trade, was leading Dauntlesses from both the *Yorktown* and the *Enterprise* on a disappointing search. He had flown the requisite time on a course of 240 degrees to reach the place where the Japanese fleet was supposed to be, and found only empty sea. Ignoring his dwindling fuel supply, he elected to fly on in the same direction for another ten minutes. Without authorization, but in the spirit of the engagement, he then turned to the right, to the northwest (he could equally well have turned left; if he had, the battle would have been quite different). Twenty minutes later, at 0955, his fuel reserves gone, he caught sight of the Japanese destroyer *Arashi* steaming toward the Japanese fleet. McClusky knew that pursuing the attack meant that any of his aircraft that survived the attack would have to ditch in the sea. He never hesitated, turning to follow the destroyer, his flight of 32 SBDs now the finger curled around the American trigger.

NAGUMO GUTS IT OUT

Two great nations had spent years readying their powerful fleets to do battle; when at last the fighting started, it would resolve down to anxious hours preparing to launch an attack, but just terrifying minutes enduring them. Once launched, the attack force was out of the hands of the shipboard commander, who could only wait for radio reports of the action. When the planes returned and were recovered, they would be rearmed and refueled—and vulnerable. At the height of the battle, the adversaries would be attacking each other almost simultaneously.

Admiral Nagumo was standing by, with 93 aircraft armed to strike at any U.S. carriers that appeared. When Lieutenant Commander Tomonaga radioed back that a second strike would be necessary at Midway as a prelude to the invasion, Nagumo, that reluctant warrior, made a fatal decision. At 0715, he ordered his 93 strike aircraft to unload their antishipping weapons and to rearm with bombs suitable for attacking Midway. He knew that his ships would never be more vulnerable than when the aircraft ordnance was changed. In the meantime, he kept the carrier decks clear for aircraft returning from the attack on Midway.

When the belated signal discovering the American fleet came in from the *Tone*'s scout plane, pandemonium broke out on the Japanese carriers as the aircraft were now forced to change their armament *again*. Kates were shuttled down on the elevators, where sweating crew members swapped bombs for torpedoes. The pressure of the moment prevented the normal cautious handling of the bombs; instead of being trundled to safe storage, they were left on the floor, adding to the explosive potential of high-octane gasoline.

More aircraft from Midway appeared. Sixteen Marine SBD dive-bombers of VSMB-241, led by Major Lofton R. Henderson, made an ineffective attack, losing eight planes in the process to the Zeros that flashed through the formations like barracudas through a school of fish. There were so many American targets that the enemy fighters conserved their ammunition, firing a few sighting rounds with their machine guns before unleashing their 20-mm cannons. Henderson was hit hard, and gallantly kept directing his squadron even after he had been set afire and was diving toward the water. He would have both a destroyer and the immortal Henderson Field on Guadalcanal named for him.

The last planes from Midway were Major Benjamin W. Norris's eleven obsolescent Vought Vindicators of VSMB-241, which attacked the *Haruna*. Neither the SBDs nor the Vindicators did much damage, but they had kept the Japanese carriers twisting and turning, unable to recover the planes coming back from the attack on Midway, many of which crashed into the sea.

The consistent success of his fleet in evading the American attackers heartened Nagumo when at 0835 he was able to begin recovering some of his planes. It appeared that his luck was holding.

But an hour and thirty-three minutes before, Admiral Spruance had gambled on an all-out attack, ordering the *Enterprise* to send 33 SBD Dauntless dive-bombers, 14 TBD Devastators, and 10 Wildcats, and the *Hornet* to send 35 Dauntlesses, 15 Devastators, and 10 Wildcats. It was a desperate decision—the Japanese ships were 155 miles away, and the admiral's aircraft had an average radius of action of no more than 175 miles; if the position of the enemy ships was wrong, or if his planes got engaged in combat, they wouldn't make it back to the carriers.

Fletcher had to recover aircraft, and this delayed launching from the *Yorktown* for two hours. He then sent off only part of his force—17 Dauntlesses, 12 Devastators, and 6 Wildcats. Only two Japanese carriers had been located—he had to have a reserve in the event the other two were found.

By 0917, Nagumo had recovered all his remaining aircraft, and turned to launch a strike against the American fleet. His decks were littered with aircraft still rearming and refueling, but his good fortune seemed to continue as his turn took him out of the path of one formation of 35 Dauntlesses, which missed sighting the carriers. Eight minutes later, Nagumo's fleet experienced the modern equivalent of the Charge of the Light Brigade when it came under attack from "Torpedo 8," VT-8. Eight Douglas Devastators, led by Lieutenant Commander John Waldron and without fighter escort, headed for the *Soryu*. The Devastators, scarcely able to make 100 knots (115 mph) when carrying a torpedo, flew into a whirlwind of antiaircraft fire, through which Japanese Zeros slashed to attack them. One by one, they were shot down, only one plane getting close enough to drop its torpedo, and that without effect. The pilot who dropped, Ensign George "Tex" Gay, was also the sole survivor. Gay floated in the middle of the Japanese fleet throughout the day's battle in the best, if wettest, seat in the house, and was picked up by a PBY the next afternoon. Gay was cool under fire; his aircraft damaged, his gunner killed, he was hit in the arm by a 7.7-mm machine-gun bullet. He pulled it out and stuck it in his mouth for safekeeping. After the war, Gay became an airline captain and a gifted inspirational speaker.

Five minutes after VT-8's charge to destruction, VT-6, led by the veteran Lieutenant Commander Eugene Lindsey, attacked from the *Enterprise*; 10 of 14 Devastators were shot down before they had a chance to drop, Lindsey's among them. Those that dropped missed.

The torpedo-plane disaster was played out to its fullest at 1000, when Lieutenant Commander Lance Massey led the *Yorktown*'s VT-3 against the *Soryu*. Once again flak and the Zero fighters intervened, and 10 Devastators were shot down, Massey going down in flames. Ensign Wesley Osmus, a Devastator pilot from VT-3, was not as fortunate as George Gay had been. Osmus bailed out of his stricken TBD and was rescued by the Japanese. On board the destroyer *Arashi*, the one McClusky had followed to find the carriers, he was tortured to get information on the disposition of the American fleet, then executed and his body dumped overboard.

The Americans had launched 41 TBDs and lost 35 without registering a single hit, a perfect testimony to the high cost of second-rate weapons. Unwittingly, however, they served a noble purpose, for the Japanese ships had to maneuver to avoid them and were unable to launch any defensive fighters or to attack American carriers. When the dive-bombers came, the Zeros were down on the deck, devastating the Devastators.

At 1001, twenty-five minutes into his unplanned, intuitive diversion to the northwest, Wade McClusky spotted through his binoculars the Japanese carriers steaming in diamond formation, and without hesitation pulled the trigger of Nimitz's pistol. First, he reported the position of the enemy fleet to the *Enterprise*, then at 1022 dove on the *Kaga*, while five other Dauntlesses attacked the *Akagi*, Nagumo's flagship. It was far from a textbook attack; McClusky should have gone for the farther ship, and too many planes were diving at the *Kaga*, but in the end it didn't matter.

Diving the Dauntless was more businesslike than exhilarating. The Dauntlesses flew in three divisions of two-plane sections, stepped down from the leader. The SBD pilot retarded the throttle, raised the nose slightly above the horizon, and reached down with his right hand to pull the diamond-shaped handle that deployed the dive brakes and the landing flaps. He then half-rolled, the glint of the sun on the canopy flashing a warning signal to the enemy below. The Dauntless assumed a 70-degree dive—which looks like straight down to the pilot—and picked up a speed of about 240 knots. From 15,000 feet, the pilot had about forty seconds to align his aircraft with the path of the ship, kill any wind drift, peer into his three-power telescopic sight (which often fogged over), and put the crosshairs on the yellow deck below, all the while keeping the ball in the gunsight (not unlike the ball in the turn-and-bank instrument) centered. In the back, the gunner, facing the rear, would be clinging to his twin 50-inch machine guns, ready to ward off any intruding Zeros.

In the forty-second, six-mile-a-minute dive, the pilot would keep his sights on the target, his right hand caressing the stick, his feet light on the rudder pedals, his left hand resting on the drafty cockpit coaming as if it were the side window of a Model A Ford. Between 2,500 and 1,500 feet above the sea, the pilot reached with his right hand to release the bomb (there was also a "pickle switch" on the stick to drop), retracted the dive flaps, and pulled back hard on the stick to begin a six-G pullout, jinking away from antiaircraft fire, hoping to avoid any Zeros.

On the bridge of the *Akagi*, Admiral Nagumo looked up to see his worst nightmare: a waterfall of American planes diving from 15,000 feet, spaced five seconds apart, and growing larger until the 500- and 1,000-pound bombs detached from their bellies to home directly down on his precious carriers. McClusky's bomb missed the 38,200 ton *Kaga* (the name in Japanese means "Increased Joy") and so did those of his two wingmen, but there were other SBDs behind. Lieutenant Wilmer Earl Gallaher put a 500-pounder into the tightly packed planes parked aft on the deck in a welter of high-octane gasoline, bombs, and torpedoes. (Gallaher's SBD had been parked forward, with less room to take off, so he carried a 500-pound bomb instead of the 1,000-pound size.) The bomb pierced the deck, setting off a series of secondary explosions in its passing. Later it was reported that Gallaher had looked back and said to himself, "*Arizona*, I remember you." Two more bombs struck forward, near the huge white-rimmed *Hinomaru* insignia; within seconds a raging fire fed by fumes, high-octane fuel, and exploding ammunition was storming through the ship. The Japanese damage-control parties battled the flames for three hours, unable to reach 800 men trapped below decks; all went down with the ship.

Lieutenant Dick Best, with four other SBDs, had been elbowed out of the way by McClusky's impetuous attack on the *Kaga*; seconds later, he rolled in on the *Akagi*, which was steaming straight ahead and not putting up any antiaircraft fire. Best's 1,000-pound bomb went through the flight deck amidships, and his wingmen scored two more hits aft among the parked planes. The *Akagi*, as the *Lexington* and the *Kaga* had been, was devastated with internal explosions and fires. On board the *Akagi*, this time on the receiving end, were the two architects of the Pearl Harbor attack, Genda Minoru and Fuchida Mitsuo, the latter recuperating from an appendectomy. They saw more than a ship going up in flames—it was their world.

Almost simultaneously with McClusky's dive, *Yorktown*'s Dauntlesses arrived, with VB-3 led by Lieutenant Commander Maxwell Leslie. Their target was the *Soryu*, which had just completed readying an attack group with fuel and bombs, and was turning into the wind to launch them. VB-3's Dauntlesses split up to attack from three different directions, and placed three 1,000-pound bombs spaced evenly along the deck—forward, amidships, and aft. The *Soryu* exploded into flames; twenty minutes later, its crew abandoned it. A damage-control party came back on board and tried to effect a tow, but around two in the afternoon, the refurbished and tenacious U.S. submarine *Nautilus* placed three torpedoes into its side. The gallant *Soryu* sank almost seven hours later, more than 700 of her crew sinking with her.

Yamamoto, out of touch 500 miles away from the battle aboard the *Yamato*, had not been aware of Nagumo's Japanese fire drill in twice ordering changes in his aircraft's ordnance loads. The distance had provided a filter of optimism; when he heard the signal from the *Tone*'s scout plane about the American carrier, he was pleased, for it meant the American fleet was being brought to battle, as per his plan. Minutes later, he received a message stating, "ATTACKED BY ENEMY LAND-BASED AND CARRIER-BASED PLANES. *KAGA, SORYU*, AND *AKAGI* ABLAZE." Ominously, the message wasn't from Nagumo, on the *Akagi*, but from the cruiser *Tone*. Yamamoto could not know that Nagumo had been forced to squeeze through an open port in the *Akagi*'s bridge, then crawl down a rope line, fighting his way through flames to transfer his flag to the light cruiser *Nagara*. The *Akagi* continued to float for hours and was finally sunk by torpedoes from the Japanese destroyer *Nowaki*.

In the heat of the battle, no one was as yet assured of the outcome. On board the *Hiryu*, 110 miles northwest of the *Yorktown*, was the tough, pugnacious Admiral Yamaguchi Tamon, the man most widely rumored to be in line to succeed Yamamoto if that awful need ever arose. At 1100, Yamaguchi launched a flight of eighteen Vals and six Zeros. At 1150, when Leslie and the remainder of VB-6 were entering the landing circle, the *Yorktown* radioed that an attack was imminent.

The twelve Wildcats of the Combat Air Patrol, the carrier's fighter defense, hit the Japanese, but seven Vals got through, three scoring direct hits that left the *Yorktown* dead in the water and burning fiercely. The aircraft that were about to recover on board now went to the *Enterprise*. Many would run out of fuel and would ditch beside American ships.

Yamaguchi launched another strike, ten Kates and six Zeros, the numbers themselves reflecting the degree to which Japanese naval airpower had been humbled. The *Yorktown*'s damage-control parties had been doing good work; the magazines were flooded, carbon dioxide had kept the gasoline from exploding, and the vessel was under way again, making 15 knots and with all fires extinguished. The Wildcats of the Combat Air Patrol were effective, shooting down five Kates, but two torpedoes hit the *Yorktown* and she was once again dead in the water, rudder jammed and listing at a sickening 26-degree angle.

But now it was the *Hiryu*'s turn. Just as the Kates were in their last torpedo runs on the *Yorktown*, VS-6, Scouting Six from the *Enterprise*, sighted the *Hiryu*. An attack force was immediately mobilized on the *Enterprise*, with Earl Gallaher, still excited over his accurate hit on the *Akagi*, selected to lead a scratch force into battle. VB-6 and VS-6 had only 11 SBDs available, but VB-3 had recovered on the *Enterprise* when the *Yorktown* was hit and had 14 ready. Of the 25 dive-bombers in the attack, 14 had 500-pound bombs and 11 had 1,000-pounders.

The endless day took on yet another dimension as Gallaher and 23 other Dauntlesses launched at 1530. Unknown to them, 11 more SBDs from Midway had landed on the *Hornet*, and within thirty minutes, an additional 16 aircraft were enroute to the *Hiryu*. The dive-bomber pilots had learned something from the ill-coordinated battle earlier in the day; too many planes had attacked the *Akagi*, even after she was mortally damaged. This time they planned for

Gallaher to take out the *Hiryu*, while the others attacked the battleships reported sailing with her. They were pardonably overconfident.

The weakness of the Japanese was now evident; instead of the usual hornet's nest of fighters, Gallaher lead his formation unmolested into a textbook attack from the sun. By the time the six Zeros that were on patrol reached the SBDs, they were already diving.

Below, the *Hiryu* began a belated turn, enough to put Gallaher's bomb off to the side. The fourteen VB-3 aircraft heading for the battleships saw Gallaher miss, and swiftly turned around to dive on the *Hiryu*. Now the half-dozen Zeros concentrated on the diving SBDs, while the *Hiryu*, only 17,300 tons, but fast and well equipped with antiaircraft guns, fought desperately to escape.

The *Hiryu* almost made it, evading the bombs of most of the aircraft, but three bombs from the last few SBDs crashed through her yellow deck. Yamaguchi watched with dismay but without surprise; before he'd left for the battle, he had told his wife, "We're going to a place where the enemy's expecting us—I may not get back this time."

Like all of her sister ships, the *Hiryu*'s own exploding bombs and torpedoes hastened her end. Yamaguchi toasted his men with a beaker of water and stayed to go down with his ship. The dramatic gesture became a little overdrawn as the *Hiryu*, like the *Akagi*, stayed afloat even though it was a burned-out hulk, and even after the Japanese destroyer *Makigumo*, acting on Yamaguchi's direct orders, fired two torpedoes into it.

At 0255 on June 5, Yamamoto gave the order for his still huge fleet to withdraw, abandoning the Midway operation. Turning to his officers, he said, "I'll apologize to the Emperor myself."

AFTERMATH

Buoyed by their victory, but anxious to make it even more decisive, the U.S. fleet turned to the pursuit of the enemy. The unlucky Japanese cruisers *Mikuma* and *Mogami* had collided in a hasty turn away from the United States submarine *Tambor*. The two cruisers fell behind and were spotted by a Catalina on patrol from Midway. On June 6, the *Enterprise* and the *Hornet* launched an attack, sinking *Mikuma* and severely damaging the *Mogami*.

Yamamoto's prediction had come true; he had run wild for seven months instead of six, and he knew that the first Japanese naval defeat in 350 years had turned the tide against his homeland. In the space of just a few minutes on June 4, 1942, at that point the most bitter day in Japanese military history, a handful of obsolete Douglas dive-bombers sank four aircraft carriers, won the Battle of Midway, reversed the course of the Pacific war, brought an almost hysterical wave of enthusiasm to the United States, destroyed the best of Japan's naval aviators, and cured its leaders of the victory disease forever.

4

HITLER'S
BIGGEST GAMBLE

The Japanese aerial sword was broken on the hard Midway shield in a single sharp engagement. Only a few hundred aircraft were involved in combat on either side and the issue was resolved within a four-day period in a relatively small area.

In agonizing contrast, the German aerial sword was ground to the hilt against the Russian armed forces, in an engagement that spanned forty-seven months, involved tens of thousands of aircraft, and hundreds of thousands of square miles of territory.

German expectations were high in June 1941 when the Luftwaffe finished the most massive of its many redeployments, covertly pulling resources from all over Europe to be poised along the borders of the Soviet Union. By a combination of excellent staff work, good (but not perfect) security, and Stalin's almost wistful desire that war would not break out, the Germans were able to begin the war with massive victories that seemed to affirm that their Blitzkrieg doctrine, the close cooperation of dedicated Luftwaffe units with the thrusting panzer divisions, was indeed the correct one.

One factor stands out about German performance throughout the war, and especially in Russia: at the operational levels, once out of the rank atmosphere of Hitler's headquarters and Göring's imperial palaces, the German military was characterized by selfless cooperation, not only within an individual service, but among the services. It was almost as if the men doing the fighting resented the futility of the disputes at higher headquarters and agreed to overcome them with goodwill and cooperation.

SOVIET LEADERSHIP

The VVS (*Voyenno-vozdushnye sily*) as the Soviet air force was called, like all of Russia's armed forces, had suffered Stalin's paranoid series of purges that not only deprived the air force of an astonishing 75 percent of its leadership, but paralyzed remaining leaders with a legitimate fear that any action that did not conform explicitly to orders might lead to a firing squad. The military purge had begun in May 1937 (some say as a result of an elaborate German plot), when Marshal Mikhail Tukhachevski was arrested, given a mock trial, and executed. An endless stream of executions expanded like a wicked chain-letter scheme, as the purge of friends or suspected friends of Tukhachevski was followed by a purge of *their* friends and associates, and on and on. Neither past heroism nor demonstrated devotion to the party was considered. Where Hitler had humiliated his Wehrmacht leaders into retirement, or bribed them, Stalin obtained control of the armed forces by a simpler method: he killed most of them and terrified the rest.

The reign of terror reached deep down within the air force, taking all corps and military district air commanders, most of the next level, the divisional and brigade commanders, and even one-half of the regimental commanders. Nor did the madness stop with the military; it ravaged the Soviet aviation industry, doing even more damage there, for there was a much smaller pool to draw on to replace the victims. Everyone was suspect, from chiefs of design bureaus down to workers in the factories. If an experimental aircraft didn't meet its design goals, or if it crashed during testing, sabotage was proclaimed and the bureau designers imprisoned, including such stellar figures as A. N. Tupolev and K. A. Kalinin. If the same standards had been applied to the United States, we would have lost chief executives at Boeing, Northrop, Curtiss, Douglas, and every other facility.

More than half the senior officers and a great percentage of the junior officers were killed, and their deaths left those who survived justifiably terrified. The fear extended even into flying training, where pilots were reluctant to fly because they might have an accident and be accused of sabotage.

Despite all the difficulties, the Soviet aviation industry and the VVS responded to Germany's desperate assault of June 1941 with a vigor that no one could have anticipated, with new leaders emerging from the ranks with a Russian concept of airpower. This process was simplified because the VVS became entirely a subsidiary arm of the ground forces, dedicated almost exclusively to close air support. Nonetheless, the proficiency of both industry and the Soviet Air Force was revealed over the years, building sharply after 1943 and continuing to grow until the breakup of the Soviet Union in 1991.

SOVIET ORGANIZATION

When war broke out, the VVS was divided into the following components:

- The Long-range Air Force of the High Command, with five corps and two separate divisions, employing bombers and transports.
- "Fronts" for each military district with fighter and short-range-bomber divisions. Each division had three regiments, and each regiment had about 60 aircraft.
- A newly conceived composite division of fighters, bombers, and ground-attack aircraft for each land army.
- The Military Service Air Force, essentially equivalent to the observation units in other armies, and used for communications and liaison.
- The Naval Air Service, which had over 2,500 aircraft and was divided among four fleets: Baltic, Black Sea, Northern, and Pacific.

The organization was a conventional one, reflecting the role of the VVS as a substitute for, or a component of, the artillery. It might have served the Soviet Union in an offensive campaign in which it maintained the initiative. In the face of the German onslaught, however, the inferior Soviet communication networks rendered the organization first cumbersome, then terminally flawed.

SOVIET EQUIPMENT

The VVS *almost* caught the tide of equipment change perfectly; had it had another six months before the German invasion, the course of war might have turned sooner. One inadvertent result of the purges had been the establishment of new leaders of design bureaus to replace those who had become politically suspect, and these bureaus produced a series of new aircraft whose names would become familiar to two generations of western observers: Mikoyan, Ilyushin, Gurevich, Yakovlev, and Lavochkin.

For the most part, however, the 4,000 fighters and bombers stationed at airfields within reach of the Luftwaffe were familiar obsolete types like the Polikarpov I-15 and I-16 and Tupolev SB-2s. In the first half of 1941, the first of the new and still not very satisfactory fighters appeared, including 335 Yak-1s, 322 LaGG-3s and 1,289 MiG-3s. Modern though these fighters were—low-wing monoplanes with retractable gear and enclosed cockpits—none were equivalent to the Messerschmitt Bf 109Fs opposing them. The MiG-3, despite having won the Stalin Prize for its designers, was considered dangerous to fly by Soviet pilots. Of the three, the Yak-1 and LaGG-3 would lend themselves best to development, becoming within two years equal to anything the Germans had to offer. Some 30,000 Yakovlev fighters were built, almost the same as the total number of Messerschmitt Bf 109s.

The airplane that Stalin proclaimed was as vital as air or bread to the Soviet Army was the Iluyshin Il-2, the famous Shturmovik (ground-attack) close-support aircraft. Termed *Schwarz Tod* (Black Death) by the Germans, only 249 Il-2s had been delivered by June 1941. Despite the disruptions to production, 1,293 more were delivered by the end of the year. Ultimately, 36,163 (plus 4,966 of the Il-10 all-metal derivative) would be built, more than any other warplane in history.

The Il-2 (originally a two-seater, but converted at Stalin's demand into a single-seater) was similar in size, shape, and weight to the infamous Fairey Battles, but far different in structure, performance—and results. The Il-2 was built as a single armored unit from the cockpit forward, both engine and pilot being well protected. The rear of the fuselage was of wooden monocoque construction, while the wings were all metal. Early models were armed with two 7.62-mm machine guns and two 20-mm cannon; the Shturmovik could also carry eight rocket projectiles or up to 1,321 pounds of bombs.

The only new bomber in use by the VVS at the time of the invasion was the Petlyakov Pe-2. A twin-engine attack plane/dive-bomber of uncommonly elegant design, some 458 had been built before June 1941, but few were in service.

In general, the Soviet Union had achieved virtual parity with Germany in the performance of its major aircraft types, and was gearing up for a much higher level of production. Reports of this from responsible German leaders like Werner Baumbach were discounted by the indefatigably incompetent Colonel Josef "Beppo" Schmid, chief of Luftwaffe intelligence. Schmid's analyses of information on the production and fighting capacities of both England and the Soviet Union were disastrously optimistic.

OPERATION BARBAROSSA

German code names tended to give away the nature of the operation; Hitler had grandly titled the invasion of the Soviet Union Operation Barbarossa, after the great Red Beard, Frederick I, who had marched to the Holy Land in the eleventh century. Operation Barbarossa was Hitler's own great crusade to achieve lebensraum, the territorial expansion in the east that realized the ideology expressed so forcefully in *Mein Kampf*. He planned a six-week campaign to destroy the Soviet armies with the tried and proven Blitzkrieg techniques, after which there would be a leisurely follow-up to prepare once again for an attack on Great Britain.

Hitler's forces were massive; more than 3 million men in 162 divisions, including 200,000 from satellite nations. The Luftwaffe had deployed 2,770 first-line aircraft available out of its 4,300 total. The force makeup was similar to previous campaigns:

Single-engine fighters	830
Twin-engine fighters	90
Dive-bombers	310
Long-range bombers	775
Long-range reconnaissance aircraft	340
Tactical reconnaissance aircraft	370
Coastal aircraft	55
Total	2,770

Although the basic types of aircraft remained the same, most were the latest model. Thus the fighter units had the Messerschmitt Bf 109F-2, perhaps the best of the entire long 109 series, while the bomber *Staffeln* were equipped primarily with Junkers Ju 88As (about 500) with the remainder Heinkel 111Hs. There were also a sizable contingent of obsolete aircraft, including the aging Junkers Ju 87 Stuka, but once air superiority was achieved, even these could operate with impunity.

Three *Luftflotten* (air fleets) were arrayed against the Soviet Union, grouped to provide the maximum support for the thrust of the ground forces. Luftflotte 1, under Generaloberst Alfred Keller, had responsibility to support Army Group North in its drive through the Baltic states. Luftflotte 2, under Generalfeldmarschall Albert Kesselring, had both the largest territory and the most resources; it was to support Army Group Center whose first objective was Smolensk. Luftflotte 4, under Generaloberst Alexander Löhr, supported Army Group South, which covered the area south of the Pripet Marshes to the Rumanian border.

The vast area to be attacked and the disposition of the Russian forces posed a problem to the Germans. Oberst Theo Rowehl's special reconnaissance unit had conducted almost five-hundred long-range flights, illegally pinpointing most of the major Russian airfields and many of the minor ones. One German aircraft had crashed near Rovno on April 15, 1941; despite the fact that it was obviously a reconnaissance plane, complete with cameras and exposed film, the Soviets did not protest. Stalin, hypnotized by the Germans, seemed to be trying to will that there would be no war.

Early in the morning on June 22, 1941, thirty bombers, drawn from three experienced *Kampfgeschwaders*, crossed the Russian frontier at high altitude to avoid detection, and then dropped down on ten selected Soviet airfields just as dawn broke. The aircraft were a mixed bag—ten Ju 88As from KG 3, ten Dornier Do 17Zs from KG 2, and ten Heinkel He 111s from KG 53. The Soviet bases were completely unprepared for an attack, the aircraft drawn up in long rows, wing to wing, as inviting to the veteran German bombardiers as Wheeler Field had been to Fuchida's pilots.

When dawn broke, the first wave of aircraft was joined by hundreds more aircraft doing level bombing and strafing on sixty-six Russian airfields. Even the Luftwaffe's greatest booster, Hermann Göring, could not believe the results. Eighteen hundred and eleven

Soviet aircraft were destroyed the first day, all but 322 on the ground. The Germans lost 32 planes. The next four days' scores showed not that Soviet defenses were stiffening but that they were running out of airplanes, for the tallies were 800, 557, 351, and 300. By October 5, the Red Army Air Force had lost more than 5,000 aircraft.

Ironically, it was Stalin, with his legendary paranoia about treason and sabotage, who was the agent of this mass destruction. *He* had received full information on the German overflights, had been warned by the British that an attack was imminent, and had even been given the exact date of the attack by Richard Sorge, his infamous spy in Tokyo. Yet until the very end, when there was no longer time to react, he suppressed all attempts at readiness, hoping somehow to buy more time from the Germans. The Russian frontier forces were surprised, despite a last-minute warning from Marshal Semion Timoshenko. As the bombs rained down and the tanks raced forward, plaintive Russian radio calls asked for instructions in the clear, just as they had done twenty-seven years before at Tannenberg. The senior staffs didn't believe the messages and sent back sharp reprimands for not using the proper codes.

The Soviet communication system was in shambles, but the bombers of the VVS were ordered to undertake strikes against the German forces pouring across the border. It was here that the purges exacted a second toll, for the inexperienced Soviet pilots flew in tight formations, maintaining the same course and altitude despite both enemy fighters and enemy flak. They were shot down in droves, often without ever getting near the target: von Richthofen considered their tactics so bad that he termed the slaughter "infanticide." The situation was so desperate that the Soviet bombers were sent not only without fighter escort, but even without gunners—just a poor pilot more terrified of the firing squad than of the Luftwaffe.

Thus began the killing that would allow the greatest aces of the Luftwaffe to run up victory scores of hundreds of aircraft, totals that were believed to be fabrications until they were validated after the war. In air-to-air battles there was, for the most part, simply no contest. The majority of the Soviet fighters were the stubby little I-16s that had just managed to survive against the early-model Messerschmitts in Spain; against the 109F, they had no chance at all. Most Russian pilots were inexperienced, their tactics poor and their leadership nonexistent. There were a few seasoned veterans who could make the most of their I-16s and score victories, and there were others who had recourse to the World War I ramming tactic called *taran*.

In the meantime, dozens of German pilots began scoring victories at an unbelievable rate. Werner Mölders was the first ace in history to crack the 100-victory mark, and was promptly promoted to *General der Jagdflieger* as a result. It was but the start; by war's end, the record had been lifted to an astounding 352 by Major Erich Hartmann. There were 107 German aces with more than 100 victories by 1945, 15 with more than 200, and 2 with more than 300—Hartmann and Major Gerhard Barkhorn. One reason for the victories was the superior skill and extraordinary courage of the German pilots; a second cause, more sinister, was that the Germans had no rotation policy for their airmen—they flew until they were killed. Curiously, the greatest World War II combat ace was not a fighter pilot. The champion was Colonel Hans-Ulrich Rudel, a Stuka pilot who destroyed 519 Soviet tanks, was shot down more than thirty times, and was the sole recipient of Germany's highest decoration, the Gold Oak Leaves with Swords and Diamonds to the Knights Cross of the Iron Cross. Rudel flew 2,530 missions, many after having his right leg blown off by flak—and survived the war.

With air superiority temporarily achieved, the German ground advance went like clockwork, the Stukas leapfrogging forward to remove any nests of resistance to the German tanks. In a departure from previous practice, one that was to prove increasingly uneconomic over the next four years, level bombers such as the He 111, Ju 88, and Dornier Do 17 were used as ground-support aircraft, bombing and strafing at low levels, and suffering high casualties from antiaircraft guns as a result.

The German forces pressed on in great slicing maneuvers that enveloped whole groups of Soviet armies at a speed that seemed to confirm American estimates that the Germans would win over the Soviets in three months: Minsk fell in mid-July, with 290,000 prisoners; Smolensk a week later, with another 100,000; in September, the Kiev pocket yielded another 665,000; while in October, another 650,000 were captured at Vyazma. (Numbers are numbing; it should not be forgotten that few prisoners on either side survived captivity.)

Even the most ardent anti-Hitlerites, such as the Chief of the General Staff, General Franz Halder, were swept away by the events, Halder recording in his diary that the campaign had been won in the first two weeks of battle. Yet there was a discordant note in the same diary; Halder wrote that for every dozen Soviet divisions destroyed, another dozen materialized as if from thin air. The German intelligence system had estimated that the Soviet Army might contain 200 divisions, but by August, they had already identified 360, and more were coming every day. Some came in civilian clothes, some without rifles, but they came and were killed, and still more came.

The slaughter continued in the air as the Luftwaffe ground crews demonstrated their proficiency at using advance airfields to support the bombers and fighters. Dive-bomber pilots routinely flew from dawn to dusk, flying a dozen sorties a day in missions that were fifteen minutes over, bomb and strafe, then fifteen minutes back, to rearm for another attack with their engines running. Yet the incredible mobility of the Luftwaffe was also a sign of its weakness; like a too-small blanket, pulling it to one sector of the front merely uncovered another sector. Units that had stormed forward to Smolensk in July were switched to the Leningrad front in August, then down to Kiev in September. It was a brilliant use of matériel, but it cost the Luftwaffe heavily; short on spare parts, damaged aircraft often had to be left behind because of the sudden moves. As a result, unit strength declined almost equally from combat attrition and from maintenance problems. Field Marshal Milch personally toured the fields in August, dismayed at the waste. He returned and organized flying squads of mechanics to move from unit to unit, cannibalizing some aircraft to repair others, and raiding the bulging spare-parts stocks to confiscate those that army-wise mechanics had put away for a rainy day.

In the midst of the chaos, the Russians had pulled off an industrial miracle, moving more than 1,500 industrial facilities of the aviation industry almost brick by brick to new locations in the Urals, the 10 million members of the work force riding on freight trains with the equipment. The conditions were subhuman, but within days of arrival at the new locations, aircraft were again coming down production lines that were now safely out of reach of German bombers. Aircraft production fell by more than 30 percent during the move, but within ninety days had increased above previous levels. It was some time before the quality matched previous levels, but the airplanes were coming.

The Russians traded space for time, not because it was their strategy—on the contrary, Stalin had demanded that every front be held at all costs—but because the Germans forced it on them. As time passed, the German penetration spread out, becoming deeper and wider along all three main axes of attack before waning from a lack of supplies. The resulting delay coincided with Hitler's vacillation about what to do next. After waiting for six critical weeks, from mid-August until October 1, 1941, Hitler finally ordered an all-out attack on the prize he could probably have won in August: Moscow.

The Luftwaffe had gathered 1,320 aircraft in Luftflotte 2, under Kesselring's command. The experienced German air-land team surged forward as two panzer armies tore the Red Army apart so effectively that all communication with Moscow was lost. The appropriateness of the code name Operation Typhoon was confirmed in two ways, first by the rapidity of the initial advance and then by the November weather, which bogged the offensive down in torrential rains that turned the Russian trails (they could not be called roads, having no prepared surface or drainage system) into a sea of mud impassable to wheeled vehicles. Difficulties in supply and Hitler's greediness to conquer even more territory than originally had been planned combined to bring the massive campaign to a halt. At the end of November, there were already 3 million Russian and 800,000 German casualties, the latter a staggering number that put the war in a new perspective for the Germans. Their previous victories had been relatively inexpensive, the triumph in France costing only 155,000 casualties. Because the Red soldiers fought on when surrounded, the percentage of deaths was exceptionally high among junior officers. Yet when Hitler was alerted to this loss of his lieutenants, he replied, "Why, that's what the young gentlemen are there for." His cavalier attitude was typical of a regime that demanded everything from the individual for the state.

The demands of the Mediterranean suddenly forced Hitler into a major blunder. To meet Rommel's requirements, he transferred Luftflotte 2, including the hardworking, effective Fliegerkorps II, to Sicily. The timing could not have been worse, depriving the German Army in front of Moscow of the airpower it so desperately needed—and arriving too late for Rommel to use to counter the British attack in North Africa.

The situation was compounded when the worst winter in twenty years intervened, in concert with a hundred fresh Russian divisions under the command of Marshal Georgi K. Zhukov. The German offensive reached to within nineteen miles of Moscow before feebly dying in its tracks. Russian aerial strength grew; the VVS flew 51,300 sorties in the defense of Moscow, 45,000 of them in ground attack, five times the number the Luftwaffe had been able to put up. In these attacks, the Ilyushin Il-2 Shturmoviks became ever-more numerous, heralding the time when it would be the scourge of the German panzer divisions. A massive Russian counteroffensive began on December 5, extending more than 560 miles along a front from Yelets to Kalinin.

The German Air Force watched its strength dwindle in a nightmare of shortages and malfunctions. Of 100,000 Luftwaffe vehicles in Russia, less than 15 percent were operational. The combat aircraft, standing hangarless in open fields and cold-soaked for days in subzero weather, could be started only by desperate means, which extended to building an open fire under the engine. The few units that had heaters and blowers to warm engines were forced to use them instead to free mechanics' hands frozen to their tools. The one bright spot was that Erhard Milch had at least seen to it that the Luftwaffe personnel had winter clothes, something totally overlooked by the German Army logistics experts.

A pattern of inevitable decline emerged, one that would become more and more defined as the war progressed. Luftwaffe strength in Russia dropped to 500 operational planes, while the VVS had more than 1,000 aircraft operating from better fields on the Moscow front alone. The Soviet Air Force, well used to cold weather, continued to function; for the first time, VVS aircraft could operate with impunity, supporting the advance of the ground forces and keeping the relatively few German sorties from reaching their targets.

The Soviets attacked all along the front through January and February 1942, securing gains of up to 150 miles. Hitler had assumed personal command of the army, ordering every unit to stand fast or die in "hedgehog" positions at key communication points. The cruel tactic was the only correct one for the circumstances; if the Germans had started to retreat, the Russians would have cut them to pieces. The front did hold and Hitler took the practical success of his order as confirmation of his skill and fortitude as a warlord. He continued to apply the "no retreat" rule to every situation for the rest of the war.

The disaster in front of Moscow had one positive side effect for the Germans; it was finally apparent even to Hitler that the number of aircraft being produced for the Luftwaffe was insufficient. Although the fighting on the other two fronts—England and the Mediterranean—had been limited thus far, it still was a drain on total resources. Erhard Milch had already started a vigorous expansion program that rationalized the German aviation industry, changing it from a series of small factories manufacturing complete aircraft into a system in which "rings" of smaller factories manufactured components to be fed to three huge factories. Milch's system was marvelously effective—as long as the Germans retained air superiority over Europe. When the Allied bombers came in 1943, it had to be totally revised.

Early in February 1942, an event occurred that would forecast the decisive battle of the war. For the first time, Soviet armies encircled and trapped a German army corps; six divisions and a number of pickup units, 100,000 men in all, were surrounded at Demyansk, trapped on the open plains in temperatures that dropped to −50°F.

A massive airlift program began under the direction of Colonel Fritz Morzik, who agreed to airlift 300 tons of supplies a day to Demyansk if he were provided with a daily average of 150 serviceable Junkers Ju 52s and all the related equipment to keep them flying.

Despite Russian opposition, the Demyansk airlift succeeded, at the cost of 265 transports lost—more than half the annual production of the Ju 52 at that time. Morzik kept six German divisions alive and fighting for three months, until May 20, 1942, when they were at last relieved by ground forces. He did not quite reach his 300-ton quota—the daily average was 276 tons—but it was a magnificent effort, one that created a precedent that would be employed at Stalingrad with disastrous consequences.

THE 1942 SUMMER OFFENSIVE

While the spring thaw immobilized even the Russians, Hitler decided to let his center rest on the defensive, make a smaller-scale attack on Leningrad, and concentrate most of his forces for an attack to the south, where he hoped to gain control of Soviet oil fields and obtain the oil he needed so desperately.

German personnel losses had been enormous, approaching 50 percent of the entire invasion force; the panzer divisions, which had begun the war with 3,350 tanks, had lost more than that number, and received fewer than 1,000 replacements. Other vehicle losses were so bad that mechanized divisions were no longer mobile. In the course of the war, the Wehrmacht turned again to horses, using more than 3 million. The 162 army divisions deployed in Russia were divisions in name only, some having only two or three battalions. Only eight were ready for offensive operations.

Through intensive production effort, shifting resources from other fronts, and incorporating 51 divisions from satellite countries, the German Army built up strength to launch its attack on the Caucasus. It was an impossible task for the means Hitler had in hand; his senior advisors recommended a pullback, Generalfeldmarschall von Rundstedt suggesting the original starting line in Poland as a sensible defensive point.

Relatively speaking, the Luftwaffe was in better shape than the army, having built up its maximum strength to 2,750 aircraft, about the same as before the invasion, and comprised of basically the same types. The disposition was different, however, with 1,500 assigned to Luftflotte 4 in the south, 600 in the long central front, and 575 in the north. Hitler continued to leave the operations of the Luftwaffe alone. Although he knew how many shells of what caliber were available to every army division and controlled the movements of units down to battalion level, he allowed the Luftwaffe commanders to run their own show after he had selected the objectives.

For almost two months, it appeared that Hitler might be right after all. Sevastopol fell, with 150,000 prisoners, and the panzers plunged unimpeded across the fields of grain, moving in great scissors movements that gobbled up thousands of square miles of territory—but very few Russians. The Soviet Army had learned from its preceding campaigns, and now pulled back when necessary. Hitler put an optimistic interpretation on the low prisoner count: the Russian Army was disintegrating, it had no more men to lose. As a direct result, he pulled forces out to reinforce the Leningrad front, and even sent some to France.

The Luftwaffe again wreaked havoc with the VVS, almost like the early days of the invasion. There was a substantial change in air operations, with more emphasis placed on long-range bombers attacking Russian formations behind the lines rather than close air support.

But in a repetition of his mistakes of the previous year, Hitler became greedy, expanding the original southern thrust to split into three directions: east to Stalingrad, west to the Black Sea, and south to Baku on the Caspian. As the offensive sped across the monotonous steppe, he became intoxicated by his apparent success and intervened more deeply into operations. Not content with being Chief of State, Commander in Chief of the Armed Forces, and Commander in Chief of the Army, he assumed command of Army Group A, tasked with reaching the Caspian Sea.

In the meantime, Army Group B began the attack on Stalingrad on August 10. Resistance stiffened quickly, as it became apparent that the Russians were going to make a stand, and the Luftwaffe began concentrating aircraft in the sector, building to a strength of 1,000.

STALINGRAD

Although the African and the bombing campaigns will be covered in subsequent chapters, it must be noted here that the Russian war was not conducted in a vacuum, for the intensive activity in the west, at sea, and in the Mediterranean theater decisively affected what happened to Barbarossa in 1942, as in 1941. Even as matériel was drained off to assist in the struggle in Tunisia, there came an even more urgent requirement: Stalingrad.

Standing astride the Volga River, Stalingrad (today known again as Volgograd), a city of 500,000, was a major railroad center and had huge tank and armament factories. Sited almost as a natural fortress, its valley-sundered hills lifted from the featureless plains to the west to give the defenders plenty of cover. After the burnt-out wooden outskirts of the city had been penetrated, the Wehrmacht entered a *Blade Runner* world of broken brick factories where bitter hand-to-hand battles were fought not for a mile of land, but for a room, a store yard, in a basement-to-basement struggle that the Germans called *Rattenkrieg*—the "war of the rats." Even though the Germans initially outnumbered the defenders three to one, and possessed far more armor and artillery, the Soviets simply would not give up, and, by enduring, triumphed. Marshal Zhukov, who had saved Moscow, kept the number of Russians within Stalingrad at an absolute minimum, all the while readying vast resources for a massive counterattack. His German counterpart, General Friedrich von Paulus, played directly into Zhukov's hands, abrading his army against the rough barricades by frontal tactics that included sending in infantry in front of the tanks to draw fire and reveal the Soviet positions.

In the earliest stages, the standard Luftwaffe ground-attack tactics worked well; eventually, there were few identifiable targets to hit, one clump of rubble resembling another, and the Soviet troops scampering between them like malevolent mice. The Luftwaffe might have made a difference if it had been employed in its most profitable role, the interdiction of the Soviet supply lines, especially the ferries that crept across the Volga day and night, crowded with troops and supplies. Unfortunately, German tactics had become standardized, while the Russians were still innovating.

From early August on, all available Luftwaffe elements had been fully employed in the battle for Stalingrad, flying thousands of sorties. By October 30, 1942, the Junkers Ju 52s of the Luftwaffe fleet had already flown 21,500 sorties, carrying 43,000 tons of troops, fuel, and equipment.

NOVEMBER 19, 1942

As Marshal Zhukov lured the German Sixth Army ever deeper within the city of Stalingrad, he saw that the weakest link in the enemy front was the northern sector, held by the Rumanian Army. Against them, Zhukov concentrated 500,000 infantry troops, 230 regiments of artillery, 900 T-34 tanks (the best in the world), and 115 regiments of "Stalin's Organs," the terrifying Katyusha rocket batteries.

For the first time since the start of the summer offensive, the VVS obtained numerical superiority over the Luftwaffe—1,500 planes against 1,200. Many of the Soviet aircraft were obsolete, but more than 60 percent of them were the hard-hitting Shturmoviks and two of the most important fighters, the Lavochkin La-5 and the Yakovlev Yak-9. Though both were faster, more maneuverable, and possessed a greater rate of climb than the Messerschmitt, the Yak-

9 was the more significant advance and was manufactured in greater numbers than the La-5. Both designs were simple and straightforward, and the conventional wood and steel-tubing construction made them easy to maintain in the rough environment of the Russian front.

The stress of war had made Stalin realistic enough to tolerate suggestions, and he permitted the introduction of the Il-2m3, an improved version of the Shturmovik, reverting to a two-seat design. The new model proved to be a costly surprise to the Germans, who for a brief period continued to make tail attacks against it, unaware of the stinger in the rear cockpit. Flying in close defensive formation, the rear gunners made the new Il-2 much tougher to shoot down.

When Operation Uranus, the Soviet counterattack, began on November 19, the massive Soviet forces brushed the Rumanians aside and swept south, while one day later a southern pincer swept first west and then north. Within five days, the Germans were entombed in Stalingrad. Hitler immediately proclaimed it to be a fortress; Göring, ever eager to please, pledged that his Luftwaffe could deliver the 750 tons per day of supplies necessary for the army to fight.

This was almost three times the amount delivered to Demyansk under far less difficult conditions. Sober reality soon forced the target down to 300 tons per day, just enough to maintain the trapped armies, but not enough to sustain them in combat. The reaction of senior officers of both the army and the Luftwaffe was that it was an impossible task, and von Richthofen, the respected victor in so many campaigns, flatly stated that it couldn't be done. It was agreed that the only correct course was for the Sixth Army, under Generaloberst von Paulus, to fight its way west to meet a German relief force. Hitler rejected the suggestion: having said the city was captured, he would not give it up. He undoubtedly considered the situation a reprise of the crisis before Moscow—his will had prevailed then, and he knew it would prevail now. (The relief force under von Manstein fought its way to within thirty-five miles of the pocket in December. If von Paulus had marched west, they would have met. Von Paulus, as stupid as he was ambitious, refused.)

With the crash-program technique that was now customary, 850 transport aircraft were assembled for the relief effort. Junkers Ju 52s, the redoubtable "Tante [Aunt] Ju's," formed the bulk of the fleet, but there were also 180 Heinkel He 111s—badly needed for bombing duties—and a ragtag collection of Focke-Wulf Condors, Heinkel He 177s, Junkers Ju 86s and 90s, and anything else that could fly. Perhaps more significant than the numbers and types of aircraft available was what was missing on the ground for an adequate aerial supply mission: practically everything. There were no adequate landing fields, normal approach lights, radio facilities, matériel handling equipment, repair facilities, trucks, hand carts, storage bins—nothing, in short, necessary to handle matériel once it was flown in.

THE VVS COMES OF AGE

But there was bad weather in plenty, an ever-increasing quantity of Soviet antiaircraft guns, and more and better Soviet aircraft. Even more important, the VVS had been drastically reorganized by General A. A. Novikov, a man propelled by his talent rather than by his political beliefs. The era of the purge was over—at least temporarily.

In April 1942, Novikov had invoked a new concept of thirteen (ultimately seventeen) mobile "air armies," each controlled by an air commander who could work with any army commander to whose front he was assigned. The air armies were composite forces and consisted of about 1,000 aircraft in fighter, bomber, ground-attack, and reconnaissance regiments, along with smaller ancillary units for training and night bombing. In a way, it was a vast expansion of the von Richthofen flying circus of the First World War, for each air army was outfitted with sufficient trucks, depots, repair organizations, and other components necessary for sustained independent operation.

Behind these mobile air armies was the Stavka (Headquarters, Supreme High Command) Reserve Air Corps, which by the end of the war was numerically almost as large as the combined total of the air armies in equipment. The Reserve Air Corps brought new aircraft and aircrews to a central area for training and subsequent dispatch to combat units.

The Luftwaffe offensive action over Stalingrad served the unintended function of training the VVS. As more and more Soviet aircraft were dedicated to the theater, the VVS pilots became adept at countering German tactics. Important decisions were made about improving equipment, including deciding—at last—that in the future, all aircraft should have radios. As the VVS learned, the Luftwaffe was worn down, as much by the harsh operating conditions on the open steppe as from combat.

The Soviets presumed from the start that the Germans would attempt to airlift supplies to their troops, and planned for an "aerial blockade." A series of concentric circles was drawn about the German forces. The first (outer) circle defined the periphery of the encirclement, over which the German transports would first have to fly. Two entire air armies, the Eighth and Seventeenth were dedicated to intercepting incoming aircraft. The second circle circumscribed the trapped Germans. The area between the first and second circles was divided into five sectors, each one with airfields for bombers and fighters. Inside the second circle was an antiaircraft zone that could put up a veritable curtain of antiaircraft fire.

The Luftwaffe turned to its impossible task with its usual vigor. Fighters, stationed both outside the cauldron and within it, daily contested with the VVS for air superiority not over a country or a front, but instead over the narrow corridor through which the transports flew once the airlift began on November 25.

From staging areas farther west, the transports stopped at Morozovskaya airport, 115 miles from Stalingrad, or Tatsinskaya, 135 miles distant. There they were serviced, loaded, and dispatched for a flight down to Pitomnik airfield, one of four within the German pocket, which was about 50 miles in diameter.

Under ideal conditions, with perfect weather and no Soviet air opposition, the Germans might have been able to supply 250 to 300 tons per day. Unfortunately, the weather went from bad to worse, with subzero temperatures and visibility reduced to nothing by driving snow. Planes and crews were incapacitated at both the takeoff and landing points and the airfields became strewn with wrecked aircraft, each one a hazard to the next to land. Soviet fighters looked upon the slow Ju 52s as cold meat, and even the Shturmoviks turned from tank busting to hunting transports. When the Soviets captured the airfields at Tatsinskaya and Morozovskaya in late December, the daily tonnage slipped down to about a 100-ton average. In late January, the last air strips inside the pockets were lost, and the Germans were forced to air-drop supplies, which landed in Soviet lines as often as in their own. (Bureaucracies function in crises even worse than they do in ordinary times; some of the supplies dropped included condoms, fish meal, and other totally useless items at a time when starving soldiers would go out under sniper fire to scavenge the flesh of a dead horse.) On February 3, the day after the last pocket of German soldiers surrendered, only 7 tons were dropped. Overall, the Luftwaffe had managed to average about 113 tons per day, far short of the minimum required—and pledged.

Throughout the battle, the VVS grew increasingly aggressive, harassing the long lines of transports despite their fighter escorts, and striking out to attack the German takeoff points. On January 9, 1943, the Soviet Air Force made a surprise attack two-hundred miles from Stalingrad, deep behind German lines, on the makeshift airfield at Salsk, where 150 Ju 52s were based. A flight of seven Il-2s commanded by I. P. Baktin dropped out of the overcast to bomb and strafe at their leisure, destroying 70 aircraft. In another instance of individual heroism, Colonel I. D. Podgorny led 18 aircraft of the 235th Fighter Air Division in an attack on a formation of 16 Ju 52s, shooting down 15. The VVS fought by night and day; Po-2s droned endlessly over the lines, dropping small bombs, while as many as 40 of the excellent Petlyakov Pe-2 bombers attacked larger targets.

The VVS overwhelmed the Luftwaffe, flying 35,929 missions from November 19, 1942 to February 2, 1943, 80 percent of them in support of ground forces. The Luftwaffe could manage only about half that number. The tide of the air war had turned irrevocably in terms of equipment, numbers, and even training. Since the German invasion on June 22, 1941, and despite the massive dislocation from the loss of its territory, the Soviet Union had built 41,000 aircraft and trained 131,000 aircrew members. In addition, the VVS had caught the tide of technical change in the midst of the war, for the aircraft flowing from the factories were all new types, to use with the new tactics it was learning from the Germans.

The Luftwaffe would still be capable of great feats, but it could no longer be decisive, for it had trained a larger enemy too well. There would still be brilliant victories and wonderful examples of individual bravery and skill among the German pilots, but these would not be enough.

The Germans in Stalingrad surrendered on January 31, 1943. Of the 284,000 men in the pocket, almost 160,000 had died in the miserable cold and filth of the city, while a fortunate 34,000 wounded had been evacuated by air. Sixty thousand had been captured during the encirclement, and another 91,000 surrendered with the city, including 24 generals and Generalfeldmarschall von Paulus, the first German field marshal ever to be captured. Of the 151,000 captives, perhaps 5,000 returned to Germany at the end of the war. When other German, Italian, Rumanian, and Hungarian losses are included, the casualty figure rises to over 540,000.

The Luftwaffe's losses were proportionately high. Although the Russians claimed 3,000 victories, the German tables show that 495 transports were lost, including 269 of the Ju 52 and 169 Heinkel He 111s. Almost 200 fighters were also destroyed. The Luftwaffe was now in the position of a hemorrhaging patient sustained only by the continuous infusion of new blood. Its strength was continually maintained and sometimes even increased by new planes and new crews, but the new crews died within days of their arrival, sometimes before they had even unpacked or their names and faces had become familiar to their comrades. The iron core of veterans became more expert even as they became smaller in number. These "old stagers" had more combat experience than flyers in any air force in World War II, surviving because they were good—and lucky.

The losses do not reflect the Continent-wide dislocation of the Luftwaffe caused by the efforts made to relieve Stalingrad—the accidents en route to staging areas, the disruption of training, the dissipation of fuel supplies and other resources. So great were these side effects that the Luftwaffe was actually able to rebound after Stalingrad had fallen; when the great wound of the airlift was at last closed, strength could be redirected elsewhere, and the patient seemed to gain new life.

THE LONG DOWNHILL SLOPE TO BERLIN

For all essential purposes, the air war in Russia was decided; there would be twenty-seven months' more hard fighting, but the issue was no longer in doubt. For the rest of the war, the Luftwaffe and the VVS retained their essential ground-support role, the latter possessing far greater means with which to carry it out. And although the diminishing Luftwaffe retained its élan and proficiency, the vast VVS grew better every day, learning from the

Germans and developing its own specialized techniques.

That the Luftwaffe continued to do as well as it did was due to men like General Wolfram von Richthofen, who proved to be far more important in the Second World War than the famous Red Baron had been in the first. Having opposed the Stalingrad supply operation from the start, von Richthofen took the opportunity to re-organize his forces. Now commanding Luftflotte 4, von Richthofen established a unified command over the entire southern front. He ruthlessly weeded out weak units, sending the personnel back to the Reich for refitting but keeping their aircraft behind for the remain-ing units, and in doing so, revitalizing the Luftwaffe. In January 1943, as Stalingrad edged toward surrender, the Luftwaffe could put up only 350 sorties a day. By March, it was averaging 1,000 per day in support of the amazing German land offensive that began on Feb-ruary 21. This offensive, which saw the recapture of Kharkov and Belgorod, cities the Russians had not expected to lose again, was led by General von Manstein. It was perhaps the most brilliant German campaign of the war, given the recent defeat at Stalingrad and the staggering Russian numerical superiority.

It was also the last time that the classic German Blitzkrieg tactics would work, embellished as they were by a new technique, the in-terdiction of Soviet railways far behind the Russian lines. Von Richthofen, who received a well-deserved promotion to field mar-shal in February 1943, displayed a maestro's skill as he concen-trated his forces to coordinate with von Manstein's attacks, switching them from point to point with great flexibility. Von Manstein was so grateful for his air support that he later character-ized von Richthofen as the most outstanding officer the Luftwaffe had produced.

Kharkov was the last great German victory. From this point on, the Luftwaffe mode of operation was changed irrevocably. From having the initiative, and doing what it *wished* to do offensively, it was forced into a defensive posture, doing what it *had* to do—i.e., provide army support. From this once unthinkable position, the sit-uation continued to degenerate, until the Luftwaffe was in a posi-tion to do only what it *could* do—that is, those actions which its limited strength still permitted. Among these were the flurry of night air raids on Russian industrial centers, undertaken gladly by the humbled bomber crews because such raids were so much easier than flying against England, or engaging in close air support. By

late 1944, the situation had deteriorated to the point that the Luftwaffe could no longer win even local air superiority at a minor
point, even when it concentrated its available forces. The Russian
enemy had become too strong and too skilled. One of its primary
training grounds was the campaign in the Kuban.

STALEMATE IN THE KUBAN

The following month, the Nazi future was painted in bleak colors
in the Kuban Peninsula of the North Caucasus. The relatively ob-
scure but important battle ran from April 17 through June 7, 1943,
on a scale comparable to the Tunisian fighting, and ended in a stalemate on the ground. In the air, the Russians demonstrated for the
first time a parity with the Luftwaffe in terms of aircraft performance, tactics, and individual pilot ability. Given the growing numerical disparity between the two air forces, this could only mean
disaster for Germany.

The Russians deployed 800 aircraft, most of which were the new
generation of Soviet fighters, but for the first time including sizable
numbers of Lend-Lease aircraft—Douglas A-20 bombers, and Bell
Airacobra and Supermarine Spitfire fighters. (By this time, Russia
had received more than 3,000 planes, 2,400 tanks, and 80,000
trucks via Lend-Lease.)

The VVS demonstrated its new skills over the Kuban. A leading
Russian ace, A. I. Pokryshkin, the Werner Mölders of the VVS,
adapted the German two- and four-plane *Rotte* and *Schwarm* formations as the Russian *para* and *zveno*. He insisted on tight discipline and on closing to short range for firing, and introduced
vertical maneuvering into the Russian tactics. Pokryshkin, who
would finish the war as a colonel with 59 victories, second only to
Ivan Kozhedub's 62, scored 20 of them while flying his American-
built Bell P-39 in the Kuban campaign.

In the end, pressures on both sides from other fronts resulted in
the stabilization of the ground situation, but not before 2,800 Russian and 800 German aircraft had been destroyed in air battles. The
3.5-to-1 ratio was not immediately recognized as a Pyrrhic victory,
in part because the Luftwaffe was experiencing a substantial
growth in numbers for the first time in the war. Thanks to Milch's
reorganization of the aviation industry, which also included a

switch in priority from bombers to fighters, there had been a remarkable rise in production in Germany. By June 1943, the Luftwaffe reached its peak strength of the war, 6,000 aircraft, but the
ever-heavier bombardment of the Reich, the crisis in the Mediterranean, and the increasing concern about the coming Allied invasion in France meant that only 2,500 aircraft could be allocated to
the Russian front, and of these, only 600 were fighters. In 1942, the
Germans produced 15,409 aircraft for use on three fronts, while the
Russians produced 25,240 for one front, and had the benefit of substantial reinforcements via Lend-Lease. The disparity would grow
in 1943 and each succeeding year.

THE LONG SHOT AT KURSK

Like a losing poker player who has no choice except to play the final hand, Hitler allowed himself to undertake a last great offensive,
Operation Citadel, one that his generals advised against, and about
which he himself felt doubtful. In one of the major ironies of the
war, it was Hitler, the compulsive gambler, whose nerve failed
when the going got tough.

The 1942 Russian winter offensive had resulted in a huge salient
in the German lines around Kursk, a small city three hundred miles
south of Moscow. Although his resources were limited, Hitler
knew, in the words of one of his staff members, that "he held a wolf
by the ears." He realized that he must retain the initiative and score
a last great victory before the Russian buildup in strength inevitably swamped him.

Hitler determined upon a spoiling attack that would pinch off
the huge Kursk salient, 100 miles wide and 150 miles long, and perhaps preempt the Russian summer offensive. Unlike the summer offensives of 1941 and 1942, which were intended to be war-winning,
removal of the Kursk salient was a modest attempt to shorten the
front lines and savage a large concentration of Russian armies.

The attack was long-delayed, first for weather and then because
Hitler wanted to wait for more Panther tanks, upon which he
placed so much hope. Security was bad, compromised both by Ultra interceptions and by a spy ring within the German High Command. As a result, the Russians had time to prepare eight
concentric rings of defenses. They were eager to have the Germans

wear themselves down upon it, and then counterattack. Within the eight rings, the Russians concentrated nine field armies, 20,000 artillery pieces, and 920 Katyushas, the multiple-rocket projectors with a scream as demoralizing as their explosives. The areas in front of and between the fortifications were the most intensively mined terrain in history—more than 4,000 mines per square mile. The Soviet Air Force had almost 2,900 planes as the battle opened, more than 1,000 of them fighters, and 940 Shturmoviks, many the latest model equipped with a tail gunner and two 37-mm cannon.

By drawing from other sectors of the front and from the west, the Luftwaffe had built up a surprising strength, concentrating 70 percent of the aircraft in the east on the battle, more than 2,000 aircraft. Because of the demands in the Mediterranean and over Europe, only 600 of these were fighters, a deficiency that would loom large later in the battle. There was a leavening of the more modern types, including Focke-Wulf Fw 190Fs and Henschel Hs 129s, the latter the best German attempt to create a Shturmovik.

The twin-engine Hs 129 was first flown in September 1939 and developed at a desultory pace over the next several years. Its 700-horsepower French Gnôme-Rhône engines were unreliable, and it was only 20 mph faster than the Junkers Ju 87 it was intended to replace, but far less maneuverable. Heavily armored, it packed a 30-mm cannon deadly to armored vehicles. It is perhaps indicative of the relative state of the air forces of the western Allies and the VVS that the Hs 129 was a failure in North Africa, prey to both the harsh climate and U.S. and British fighters.

The first day was almost like the happy hunting days when Barbarossa began, the Luftwaffe winning its battle by a tremendous margin. Just before the attack began on July 5, the Russians sent in 400 aircraft in an attempted spoiling attack on German air bases. Alerted by radar, German fighters were scrambled to slaughter the incoming Russians, shooting down 132 in just a few hours. At the end of the first day, 432 Russian planes were claimed versus a loss of 173, mostly bombers, by the Luftwaffe, which had launched 4,298 sorties.

German tanks made good progress from the south, backed up by strong close air support. One stellar performance was by First Lieutenant Hans-Ulrich Rudel, flying an experimental model of what would become the Ju 87G Stuka. Taken directly from the test unit, and armed with two 37-mm Flak 18 cannon in detachable pods under the wings, Rudel killed 12 T-34s in one day. A call was sent back to the test group to bring all modified aircraft to the front, to form a *Panzerjäger Staffel*, an elite antitank unit.

There were corresponding victories on the Russian side, for the latest Shturmoviks decimated the panzer divisions with "circle of death" tactics. The "Ilyushas," as the Russians called them, would set up a pattern over a German tank column, circling so that the attack was delivered against the thin skins at the rear, and making pass after pass until the tanks were all destroyed or their ammunition was gone. It was here that the German fighter shortage was felt; there were not enough to break through the screen of escorting Yak-9s and La-5s to hit the Shturmoviks.

On the ground, the fighting was as intense as the *Rattenkrieg* of Stalingrad, but conducted in the open air of the steppe. The German panzers, which were used in the past as rapiers, slashing behind enemy lines, were now employed as chisels to chip away at the dense Russian defenses. The Soviet forces made good use of the minefields, siting groups of as many as ten antitank guns to fire in salvos at individual tanks, bleeding German strength before they could reach the opposing Russian tanks.

By nightfall on July 11, it seemed that with another convulsive effort the Germans might link up, trapping the Russians and essentially breaking the entire eastern front open for exploitation. But on the next day, the 600 German tanks ready to break out were met by the same number of Soviet tanks. For eight long hours, the greatest tank battle in history was fought, each side aided by its ground-attack planes. When evening fell, the Germans crept away from the battlefield.

At the crucial moment, Hitler was shaken by news of Allied progress in the invasion of Sicily (begun on July 10) and by word of a Russian offensive at Orel. Ordinarily, it was Hitler who urged his generals to persist, and they who advised retreat. Hitler once again ignored the advice of Field Marshal von Manstein, who before the battle had recommended its cancellation but who now felt that despite the losses on July 11 the Germans still had a chance for a decisive victory. Nervous, Hitler decided to cancel the offensive and pull his battered armor out.

It had been a titanic struggle, with 2 million men, 5,000 aircraft, and 6,000 tanks engaged. At Kursk, the prepared defenses, minefields, and armor held up the German panzers just as the vastly improved control of Shturmoviks and fighters by radio helped the VVS overpower the Luftwaffe. And at Kursk, it was obvious that the day of the Blitzkrieg was over for Germany—and just beginning for Russia.

THE LUFTWAFFE LICKS ITS WOUNDS

Despite the surge in production figurers, the Luftwaffe was clearly on the decline, in large part due to its inability to introduce new aircraft of improved performance to compensate for the growing numerical inferiority.

After Kursk, the Soviet Union never relaxed the pressure, pressing forward with a series of offensives, summer and winter, that kept the Germans entirely on the defensive. The extent of Soviet gains was conditioned by the length of their supply lines rather than by the degree of German resistance, for so great was the Russian superiority in every sphere that a breakthrough could be made on any front at any time.

Without any margin of reserve, the Luftwaffe was switched from point to point along the front to meet Soviet initiatives. Totally subordinated to the army's immediate emergency needs, it was unable to undertake more than close-support operations for tactical objectives. Until late 1944, the German Air Force could on special occasions rally to secure air superiority over a sector of a particular front for a short time, but the rapid growth in strength of the VVS prevented any extended domination. The Luftwaffe tried to reposition and reorganize its forces to defend against the Russian thrust toward the Rumanian oil fields. But even by drawing badly needed fighters from the defense of the Reich and from Italy, the Germans no longer had the means to oppose the VVS effectively.

By the time the Red tide rolled toward Berlin, it was protected by no less than 7,500 aircraft on that front alone, facing perhaps 400 Luftwaffe fighters. The VVS was in a position to employ airpower as the Russian Army had traditionally employed artillery and manpower, in massive quantities and without regard to losses.

A RETROSPECTIVE VIEW

A serious review of the German-Russian conflict reveals that there was little the Luftwaffe could have done differently to affect the outcome of the war. Hitler's reckless gamble in attacking the Soviet Union (later often defended by apologists as a necessary preemption of a coming Soviet surprise assault) embroiled his country in a war that could not be won, given his other commitments. The Luftwaffe performed its tactical role almost flawlessly throughout the war, even under the most difficult circumstances.

5

THE AFRICAN
TUTORIAL

RELEARNING THE LESSONS

The war in the Mediterranean raged for almost four years, from the initial British triumphs in Italian Somaliland, through the accordion-style combat in the North African desert, where the Afrika Korps and the British Desert Rats chased each other back and forth, until the end of the Mediterranean campaign in Italy. In this long and bitter combat, less remembered now than the western and eastern fronts in Europe, the Allied powers first ignored the lessons of airpower, then used them brilliantly for a brief period. They were then forgotten, before being finally revived, improved upon, and made standard.

It is difficult now to understand how the western powers could have observed the brilliant success of the German Army and Luftwaffe in combined operations and not attempted to emulate it. Yet it was not until mid-1942 that a formal attempt was made to coordinate army and air force activities as the Germans did. This is all the more mystifying in view of the fact that successful Allied coordination had been effected in East Africa in 1940, and in the western African desert in 1941.

Further, both General George C. Marshall and Winston Churchill had seen the need for well-coordinated close air support and demanded that action be taken. Air force leaders in the American Army had always been preoccupied with the strategic bomber, to the extent that they did not even create an official manual addressing the task of close air support until mid-1943, and even then, it was a most cursory one.

Churchill was even more farseeing in a memorandum he issued September 5, 1941, stating unequivocally that the old concept of expecting an air umbrella over frontline troops, particularly fast-moving columns, was a thing of the past, citing it as a "mischievous practice" in the application of airpower. He went on to define exactly the command relationships of the air and the ground commanders. The Air Officer Commander in Chief was to give the Military Commander in Chief (i.e., either army or navy) all possible aid, regardless of other attractive targets, for "Victory in battle amends all." The Military Commander in Chief was to specify the targets, and then the Air Officer Commander in Chief was to use his maximum force, in the most effective manner possible. Yet the Royal Air Force resisted these instructions, perhaps recalling the terrible losses in fighters while strafing trenches in World War I, as well as the more recent defeat of its Battles and Blenheims in France.

THE VAST AND PRICKLY MEDITERRANEAN THEATER

Benito Mussolini had proclaimed the Mediterranean Sea to be Italy's "Mare Nostrum" and, given Italy's geographic position and his long and vocal backing of airpower, it should indeed have been Italy's private sea. The Mediterranean instead became a vast sink into which Axis resources were endlessly poured.

The importance of the Mediterranean area was evident to leaders of all the warring nations. Churchill would have preferred to fight the entire war there, pecking around its periphery to reach "the soft underbelly" of Europe and thus avoiding an invasion that would for the third time place the British Army in combat with the Germans in France. Hitler placed less importance on the area, although he did have grandiose ideas for using Egypt as a jumping-off place for an invasion of the Middle East. After this, he envisioned two important linkups. The first would be with his own troops, driving down through the Caucasus, and the second, with Japanese troops in India. Had he been willing to put in the same amount of resources early in the war (when there was a chance of winning in North Africa) as he did later (when the war there was irrevocably lost), he might actually have succeeded.

In sheer size, the Mediterranean theater exceeded the Russian front, extending 2,200 miles in length from Gibraltar to the Suez

Canal, and averaging about 500 miles in width. And despite the image of palm trees and wave-lapped shores, it could be in its own way as inhospitable as Russia, with long seasons of blazing heat and sandstorms instead of cold and driving snow.

The two theaters had many things in common. One, rather unexpectedly, was "General Mud," for the torrential rains in Africa could turn the ground into muddy swamps that halted even tracked vehicles and were more difficult to traverse than the muddy Russian earth. Another similarity was the dependence upon tenuous supply lines. In Russia, the German lifeline was the railroad, subject to constant guerrilla attacks and so supplemented to the maximum degree possible by airlift. In North Africa, Germany depended upon ships rather than trains, and used cargo aircraft to an even greater degree than in Russia. From the Ultra intercepts, the Allies knew exactly when the Axis convoys would sail, their routes and their cargoes, and used their superior airpower to pick them off, concentrating on ships carrying the most vital cargo.

Air combat was initiated by the Italians, who made the first of many attacks on Malta on June 11, 1940, immediately after their "stab in the back" declaration of war. Two months later, on September 13, 1940, the Italians also made the first ground assault, a very tentative invasion of Egypt. Fighting in the Mediterranean went on through a long series of battles, many of them conducted several times on the same sites, until the final German surrender in Italy on April 29, 1945.

The air campaigns in the Mediterranean varied in intensity over time, and during the early period of the struggle, the balance of airpower, like the ground war, shifted from one side to the other on a regular basis. Later, after the proper tactics were developed, the Allied air forces overpowered the enemy to the degree that the Luftwaffe virtually wrote off the Italian theater as impossible to defend. Curiously, this taught another lesson: a bitter and often successful defensive battle can be fought without any airpower at all, if the ground commander is willing to take the losses involved. In Italy, later in the war, and subsequently in France and Germany, the German Army showed that it could put up a determined struggle in the face of overwhelming airpower—but at a tremendous cost in lives, and without any prospect of winning more than time.

The size of the theater and and the length of the long war there requires that each air campaign be dealt with separately, although many were concurrent. The often-unappreciated Italian Air Force needs to be examined first.

THE ITALIAN AIR FORCE

Mussolini had used the Regia Aeronautica as a fascist showpiece, a symbol of his progressive thinking. In the late 1920s and early 1930s, his backing enabled his flyers to set many records. In 1933, the brilliant airman and independent thinker General Italo Balbo led a formation flight of twenty-four twin-hull Savoia-Marchetti SM.55 flying boats from Orbetello to Chicago, creating a tide of goodwill for Italy—and probably sealing his own fate, for it was not wise to become too popular in a fascist state. (The mass flights gave rise early in the war to the term "Balbo" for a large formation of aircraft—the more prosaic term "gaggle" later supplanted it.) In 1934, Lieutenant Francesco Agello flew a Macchi-Castoldi MC.72 at Lake Garda to set the still-standing piston-engine seaplane speed record of 440.6 mph. There were many other similar achievements that prepared the Regia Aeronautica, despite its limited numbers, to distinguish itself in battle.

Of its total strength of approximately 1,800 first-line aircraft, the Regia Aeronautica had 975 bombers, of which 594 were the fabric-covered Savoia-Marchetti SM.79 Sparvieros (Sparrow Hawks). Easily identified by its "humpback" fuselage and obsolete three-engine layout, the SM.79 had set no less than twenty-six records for speed and distance prior to the war, and had served with distinction in Spain. Its performance compared well with the Heinkel He 111 or the Bristol Blenheim, for it had a 270 mph top speed, and a range of 1,242 miles with a 2,755-pound bomb load. The wood and fabric construction made the aircraft vulnerable to small-caliber shellfire, and it flamed readily—the crews who flew it were brave indeed. Yet the pilots loved its maneuverability, and it was not difficult to maintain. While used variously as a level bomber and a close-support plane, the Sparviero was probably the best torpedo bomber of the war, in any air force. The Luftwaffe, normally somewhat haughty in its relations with its Axis partner, recognized the superiority of both Italian torpedoes and Italian tactics, and set up a school for their pilots at Grosseto on the west coast of Italy.

The Italian Air Force entered the war with obsolete fighters, most of which were the elegant Fiat CR.42 Falcos, the last biplane fighter to be manufactured by any belligerent in World War II. The biplane configuration lent itself to the natural talents of the Italian flyers, who excelled in aerobatics. In the opening battles of the war in East Africa, the Falcos fought well against South African Air Force Gloster Gladiators, Hawker Harts, and similar contemporary biplanes. The more experienced Italian pilots, many of them veterans of the Spanish Civil War, were dangerous opponents. The CR.42s were so maneuverable that the Hurricane pilots had to adopt the tactics used by German Messerschmitt pilots against them—avoiding dogfights and using dive-and-zoom attacks.

The early Italian monoplane fighters, the Fiat G.50 Freccia (Arrow) and the Macchi-Castoldi MC.200 Saetta (Thunderbolt), were delightful aircraft to fly, but lacked the CR.42s' maneuverability and the speed of opposing fighters. Despite its racing heritage, and its long experience with powerful engines (Fiat had built a 1,000-horsepower engine in 1923, and one of 2,800 horsepower in 1931), Italy had no powerful modern engine to place in its fighters. The basic excellence of both the Freccia and Saetta airframes were demonstrated later, when they were adapted to use the German Daimler-Benz DB 605A engine. The result was the Fiat G.55 Centauro (Centaur), considered by many to be the best Italian fighter of the war, and the sleek Macchi-Castoldi MC.202 Folgore (Lightning), which easily dominated the P-40s and Hurricanes in Africa. Later developments of these aircraft, the Macchi-Castoldi MC.205 and the Fiat G.56, although manufactured only in very small numbers, were equivalent in most respects to the Focke-Wulf Fw 190, or the North American Mustang.

All Italian fighters were handicapped by a lack of firepower, being equipped with few guns, and these of inferior performance. The early aircraft had only two nose-mounted 12.7-mm machine guns, while most later models added only a 7.7-mm machine gun in each wing.

Despite the otherwise excellent quality of their later-model aircraft, the Italian Air Force was deficient in quantity and serviceability. Only 1,500 of the Macchi-Castoldi MC.202s and 105 of the Fiat G.55s were delivered before Italy's capitulation in 1943. Despite Italy's long experience in Africa, the air force maintenance personnel failed to provide such rudimentary necessities as the tropical filters to keep delicate engines running. As a result, serviceability levels often fell to as low as 30 percent. Both of these faults—low production and poor serviceability—derived in part from the inherent elegance of the Italian designs. To make a contemporary automobile analogy in terms of mechanical complexity, difficulty of production, and maintenance, if the British Hurricane was a Ford, then the Macchi-Castoldi MC.202 was a Ferrari.

The human factor of the Italian Air Force mirrored that of the Italian Army and Navy: brave, capable, and even dashing leaders at the squadron level and below, but corrupt incompetence at the top, well illustrated by the Italian general who said that he enjoyed military life because of its comfortable pay and the assurance of excellent pasta daily. Undoubtedly, the fault lay with the imposition of a fascist, militarist regime on a people far too sensible to embrace it. The tragic result for the Regia Aeronautica was a total lack of foresight in everything from basic strategy to procurement, logistics, and training.

What was not lacking was courage in the cockpit. The Italian pilots flew hard and well under difficult circumstances, and distinguished themselves in many difficult battles in Africa, the Balkans, Russia, and over their homeland. Even after the surrender in September 1943, they fought on, some in the new fascist air arm sponsored by Germany, the Aeronautica Nazionale Repubblicana (ANR), others in the pro-Allied Italian CoBelligerent Air Force. (The decision to fight for one side or the other was rarely a personal political choice on the pilot's part, but rather depended on where his unit—or his family—happened to be at the time of the armistice.)

The Regia Aeronautica produced a number of heroes, one of the most highly regarded being Major Carlo Emanuele Buscaglia, who flew SM.79 torpedo planes with élan against the Allied convoys. (Buscaglia was listed as missing after a November 1942 raid on Bougie Harbor in Algeria. When the Germans permitted the creation of the Aeronautica Nazionale Repubblicana on October 10, 1943, a new torpodo bomber group, Gruppo Autonomo Aerosiluranti "Buscaglia" was named in his honor. Buscaglia then embarrassed the Fascists by emerging from a prisoner-of-war camp to join the Italian CoBelligerent Air Force, forcing a quick name change for the ANR unit.)

There were a significant number of Italian aces, although their scores are more difficult to confirm because of an unusual reluctance upon the part of the Regia Aeronautica, unlike Germany or the Allies, to glorify its aces. By drawing on several sources, it appears that Major Adriano Visconti and Captain Franco Lucchini were the leading aces, each with 26 victories. Lucchini had shot down 5 aircraft in Spain, and 21 more as a part of the Regia Aeronautica. Visconti scored 19 victories prior to the surrender, and 7 more afterward, flying for the ANR.

Despite a shortage of leaders and equipment, the Italian Air Force fought bravely, alone and in concert with the Luftwaffe, beginning with an assault on a tough little island.

MALTA

Of all the invasions of World War II, one of the most important was one that did not take place: the invasion of Malta, part of the British Commonwealth. Hitler twice toyed with the idea and twice turned it down. He was hesitant because the parachute assault on Crete had been terribly costly, and Malta's terrain was even less suitable for airborne landings than that of Crete. He also knew that he would have to depend upon the Italian fleet to follow up on an airborne invasion of Malta. Suspicious of the royalist leanings of the Italian Navy, he feared that it would run at the approach of the British fleet, leaving the Germans in the lurch. Finally, at a time when he was almost committed to approving the decision to invade, his then-favorite general, Erwin Rommel, seemed to make the need less urgent by his advance in Africa. (More of this later.) Yet Hitler and all his staff had but to look at a map to realize how important Malta was to the war in the Mediterranean.

Hitler was chagrined in June 1940 when Italy lost the chance for a successful surprise invasion of Malta by formally declaring war on France. Instead, Mussolini opted for a bombing campaign, and Malta's long siege began on June 11, 1940, when fifty-five Savoia-Marchetti SM.79 bombers and eighteen Macchi-Castoldi MC.200 fighters launched from bases in Sicily for an attack on dockyards and air bases.

FAITH, HOPE, AND CHARITY: LEGEND AND FACT

One of the great myths of the war was that three ancient Gloster Sea Gladiator biplanes, named *Faith*, *Hope*, and *Charity*, held out alone against the full might of Mussolini's air force. According to legend—or perhaps a clever propagandist's story—the defenders on Malta had quite by chance found four Sea Gladiators in packing crates. Three aircraft were quickly assembled, and were the only planes available on June 11, when the Italian Air Force attacked. According to the story, the three Sea Gladiators fought on alone for seventeen days until, on June 28, the first Hurricanes arrived to assist.

It's a wonderful story—and almost true. There were in fact eighteen Sea Gladiators in storage, of which six were assembled, the remainder being used for spare parts. Because they were so few, the Sea Gladiators were used with utmost discretion; rarely were there more than two in the air at any given time. No one can confirm that any of them actually bore a name at that time, much less Faith, Hope, or Charity. (The fuselage of one of the original aircraft, serial N.5520, is restored and on display at the National War Museum. It is named *Faith*, perhaps retroactively.)

But myth or legend, the saga of the Gladiators, and of all the many fighters that subsequently joined them, symbolizes the bulldog courage of the defenders of Malta, courage that would be called upon in full measure in the hard years that followed.

Malta had a brief respite in the autumn of 1940. The general glow of Axis optimism aroused expectations of peace following the fall of France, and the Italian attacks on Malta diminished. The Air Officer Commanding in Malta was Air Vice Marshal Hugh P. Lloyd, a dogged fighter of Churchillian stripe, who was determined not only to survive defensively, but to turn Malta into an offensive base. He had reinforced Malta with more Hurricanes and a few Fairey Fulmars. The latter were a lighter, cleaned-up, more heavily armed development of the infamous Battle, and oddly enough, proved to be quite effective as two-seat fleet fighter planes. Lloyd next brought in Martin Maryland reconnaissance planes, Vickers Wellington bombers and Short Sunderland flying boats, transforming the island into a formidable threat. The Wellingtons began attacking targets as far away as Tripoli and Albania, while the Marylands' vital reconnaissance role was highlighted on November 10, when a report was brought back that the Italians had five battleships, fourteen cruisers, and twenty-seven destroyers in the harbor at Taranto, set inside the heel of the Italian boot. The attack by Fleet Air Arm Fairey Swordfish torpedo planes off the aircraft carrier *Illustrious* set the pattern for Pearl Harbor.

Unable to cope with Lloyd's aggressive tactics, the Italians appealed to the Luftwaffe for help, and the veteran Fliegerkorps X, the most experienced antishipping unit in the world, was sent to Sicily, arriving in January 1941. Under the command of General Hans Ferdinand Geisler, Fliegerkorps X ultimately built to a strength of 330 aircraft, including 120 long-range bombers, 150 dive-bombers, 40 Messerschmitt Bf 110s, and 20 reconnaissance planes.

Fliegerkorps X had a threefold task. First, it was to neutralize Malta as a base for British air and naval forces and secure the Axis supply routes to North Africa. Then it was to interfere with British supply routes, closing the Sicilian straits to British shipping and halting supply convoys to Malta from Gibraltar. Finally, it was to support operations in North Africa.

Malta was totally dependent upon Great Britain for supplies, and any convoys approaching the island had to run a 600-mile gauntlet, at risk of attack at any moment by aircraft, U-boats, and even the MTBs, the motor torpedo boats used so effectively by both Italians and Germans. The German onslaught began with a dive-bombing attack on Force H, a huge convoy that included the aircraft carrier *Illustrious*. The first two Stuka *geschwaders* had arrived in Sicily on the morning of January 10; by noon both were attacking the convoy, slamming bombs into the deck of the *Illustrious*, which managed to creep into the Grand Harbor at Malta, beginning what became known as the "*Illustrious* blitz."

Of four attempts by convoys to resupply Malta from January through March, most were thwarted, and only 26,000 tons of supplies reached port. Then, for the next three months, nothing came through. The fighter force on Malta was replenished by flying land-based aircraft off carriers held just outside the range of Axis bombers. But the Germans were vigilant and would attack British aircraft almost as soon as they landed, hammering Malta every day, establishing air superiority and bombing docks and airfields repeatedly. Despite the fact that cover was almost impossible to find on the rocky island, the German bombing attack caused relatively few casualties. Yet it achieved what it set out to accomplish: the suppression of attacks on Axis shipping. The defending RAF units were hampered by the proximity of the island to the Sicilian airfields; by the time radar detected the enemy coming in, it was always too late to gain an altitude advantage. Losses were heavy, with the casualty rate running as high as 25 percent for sustained periods. Replacement pilots were thrust into battle without any chance at acclimatizing themselves to the conditions on Malta.

The hard times and scarcity of supplies brought out the best in British improvisational skills. Bristol Blenheim engines and propellers were adapted for use on the Gladiators, vastly improving their performance. When the tail-wheel tires of the Martin Maryland reconnaissance planes wore out, metal from shot-down enemy aircraft was melted and recast to create new tail-wheel hubs that could use Blenheim tires.

In April, German units began to withdraw, to begin preparing for the invasion of the Soviet Union, thus ending the second phase of the battle. The attack was resumed by the Regia Aeronautica, but at a far lower level of intensity. The greatest opportunity was gone, but the temptation to invade Malta would rise again with Operation Hercules, agreed upon by Hitler and Mussolini the following spring.

Supplying Rommel became a crisis in the fall of 1941; in October, 63 percent of all cargoes dispatched to North Africa were sunk. A decision was made to gain air and sea supremacy between southern Italy and Africa, and Field Marshal Kesselring assumed command of all German Air Force units in the Mediterranean. Further, his trusty Luftflotte 2 was brought from the Russian front, drastically weakening the Luftwaffe on the Moscow front. Kesselring's assault began during the last week of December and lasted through May, with sorties sometimes approaching 5,000 per month. The suppression of British attacks on Axis shipping enabled supplies to be built up for the ever-changing war in North Africa.

THE ACCORDION WAR IN THE WESTERN DESERT

Both the air and the ground campaigns in the Western Desert were unusual in the rapidity with which fortune shifted from one side to the other. The vast North African desert has been described as a tactician's paradise and a quartermaster's hell, for while the open, generally flat terrain lent itself to engagements as much like great naval battles as armored encounters, the long distances and the harsh climate made sustaining units in combat extraordinarily difficult. The series of five campaigns has also been described as a "battle of the airfields," for all but the final offensive operations were characterized by similar experiences with airpower. The airpower of the advancing army diminished as it had to use unprepared airfields, while that of the retreating army gained strength as the retreating forces fell back on prepared airfields.

The first British success in the Western Desert began on November 18, 1940, when Operation Compass, intended only as a large-scale raid, turned into an offensive that rolled the Italians all the way out of Libya. With a ragtag collection of aircraft—Hurricanes, Gladiators, Blenheims, and Lysanders—the RAF's aggressive tactics quickly established air superiority over the Regia Aeronautica while British tanks rumbled through the widely scattered Italian fortified camps.

Despite being vastly outnumbered, the Western Desert Force went forward, defeating the last of the Italian Army at the Battle of Beda Fomm on February 6, 1941. In the campaign, the British pushed on almost to Tripoli, capturing 130,000 prisoners, virtually all of the Italian armor and artillery and 20 generals. The British losses were 500 killed and 1,428 wounded or missing. The Regia Aeronautica lost 58 aircraft in combat and hundreds more captured on the ground. The RAF lost 26 aircraft to all causes.

Not pressing on for the extra few miles to Tripoli was a grave and costly error, for Hitler now sent General Erwin Rommel to command what soon became the famous Deutsches Afrika Korps. Two small-scale divisions, the 5th Light and the 15th Panzer, arrived in Tripoli in March. The Afrika Korps, benefiting from the concurrent heavy raids on Malta, was able to gather enough supplies for the first of Rommel's remarkable counteroffensives, which opened on March 31, 1941.

After the first few days, Rommel conducted his first campaign with almost no air support at all, all of the Axis landing fields being so muddy as to be unserviceable. His Air Command Africa faced an equally weak RAF composed of four squadrons: one each of Lysanders and Blenheim IVs and two of Hurricanes. The RAF was gradually augmented over time, but with difficulty, for the route for British reinforcements was as agonizing as the German route was hazardous. Aircraft traveling by ship, around the Cape of Good Hope and through the Red Sea to Egypt, took seventy days. A flying route was established from Takoradi, in West Africa, but even this was a 3,700-mile journey that exhausted the crews. Although 90 percent of the aircraft made it through, on arrival they required immediate overhaul from wear and tear.

A curious war-within-a-war developed, in which the Royal Air Force managed to maintain air superiority and launch many missions during Rommel's offensive, yet was unable to prevent the

Germans from using their expertise in air, armor, and antitank guns to pry open the British defenses.

The British Army was simply unable to cope with the Afrika Korps's slashing tactics, and it fell to the RAF to prevent the situation from turning into a complete rout. Where before the army had often asked "Where is the bloody RAF?" the RAF now wondered why the army wouldn't fight.

The RAF's new capability derived from two men, Air Chief Marshal Arthur W. Tedder and Air Vice Marshal Arthur "Mary" Coningham, whose typical prewar RAF nickname came from his New Zealand origins, home of the Maori people. Both were unusually capable officers.

Tedder, at the moment of his appointment as Air Officer Commander in Chief, Middle East on May 5, 1941, lacked the most important commodity in British service—the confidence of Winston Churchill. He nonetheless set to his work with vigor. Just fifty-one years old, a scholar and something of an artist, the pipe-smoking Tedder was unflappable. A sloppy dresser, totally informal, fond of practical jokes, and a friend of the enlisted troops, he was the antithesis of the stuffy image of a British flag officer.

And he knew how to get along, first and foremost with General Sir Claude Auchinleck, another sudden replacement, who was General Officer in Command of the Middle East. (Like Lincoln in the Civil War, Churchill was looking for a general who would fight and win, sacking commanders without remorse and without regard for past services. Auchinleck would do brilliant work, personally intervening on the battlefield to save the situation on two separate occasions, but, let down by his subordinates, he was fired in his turn.) Tedder worked equally well with the new commander of the Western Desert Air Force (WDAF), Coningham. Unfortunately, the talents of this trio were not matched by the commander of the newly named British Eighth Army, Lieutenant General Sir Alan Cunningham.

Churchill, fearing that a Russian collapse would free scores of German divisions for Africa, wanted an offensive as soon as possible to drive Rommel back and preempt the Afrika Korps's next drive. Both sides slowly built up supplies, Rommel's being curtailed by the incessant air activity from Malta, and the Eighth Army's slowed by the long distances involved.

This time Great Britain struck first, launching Operation Crusader on November 18, 1941, with overwhelming superiority in the air and on the ground. Coningham had been supplied with twenty-seven squadrons, sixteen of them fighters, and he took advantage of the bad weather, which immobilized the Luftwaffe on its ill-prepared forward bases. Within three days, complete air superiority had been established, and Eighth Army tanks were rolling forward. After some initial setbacks in battle with Rommel's tanks, the British rolled the Afrika Korps all the way back to El Agheila, where the Germans had started out eight months before.

Rommel was resilient and made grateful use of the respite given his supply lines by the renewed German assault on Malta. With a minimum resupply of tanks, he bounced back on January 21, 1942, destroying the strung-out, fuel-short British army units, recapturing much of Cyrenaica (the Italian colony in what is now Libya.) RAF fighter-bombers saved the day, even though handicapped by obsolete equipment. The fighter-bomber was of course faster than its light-bomber counterparts, but more important, its landing fields could be placed closer to the front, cutting down on the time between the request for ground support and its execution. With the best will in the world, Coningham could not get bombs on target from his Blenheims in less than two and a half to three hours, an eternity in the mobile warfare of the desert, while the Hurricanes were on the scene in thirty minutes or less.

Coningham's Hurricane I wasn't the perfect answer, however, because its eight .303 Browning machine guns were ineffective against tanks, as were the 40-pound bombs it carried. Further, the Hurricanes were vulnerable to the barrage fire of the excellent German flak, which was much more effective than British antiaircraft guns. However, the Hurricanes pointed the way for the Hurricane IIs, Typhoons, and Thunderbolts which, with their far-heavier armament loads, would devastate the enemy only a little while later.

After his first thrust, which carried him to a battle line running from Gazala to Bir Hacheim on February 4, Rommel halted to build up his forces. Opening the port at Benghazi gave Rommel extra supplies, which enabled him to thrust forward once again on May 26, beginning a triumphant march which, coming after the fall of Singapore and the arrival of the Japanese on the Indian border, seemed to confirm the end of the British Empire.

Using obsolete Blenheims, Tomahawks, and Hurricane I's, the Western Desert Air Force flew almost 14,000 sorties between February and May 1942, losing 300 aircraft to the heavily reinforced Axis forces. The Luftwaffe also had a trump card in the form of 120 of the excellent Messerschmitt Bf 109F fighters, which were clearly superior to anything the British had. The "Star of Africa," Captain Hans-Joachim Marseille of Jagdgeschwader 27, brought his victory total to 158 in the African campaign using the Bf 109F. A brilliant marksman (he averaged only fifteen rounds per victory), Marseille once scored 17 victories, all RAF fighters, in a single day. Ironically, it was a 109F that killed him, for he lost his life bailing out when his engine burst into flames. He was not yet twenty-three.

Rommel's new offensive stubbed its toe on the tough Free French defense of Bir Hacheim, where General Marie Pierre Koenig and his brigade held him up for nine vital days. Overhead, Coningham's Desert Air Force (DAF) battled it out with the Luftwaffe, each side making almost 1,500 sorties during the battle. For the first time, the two air forces were approximately equal in numbers, the DAF having about 600 aircraft against a German-Italian force of about 530.

On the ground, German tactics artfully combined both tanks and antitank guns to prevail over British armored forces. The Eighth Army had a three-to-one advantage in tanks, which were also superior in quality, but these were committed to the attack in small units that the Afrika Korps was able to defeat in detail. The excellent work of the Desert Air Force couldn't compensate for the ill-coordinated British efforts on the ground, and Rommel moved forward, this time capturing Tobruk on June 21, 1942, after a two-day assault. The defeat, a disaster second only to that at Singapore, caused Churchill deep anguish and raised questions about the fighting worth of the British Army. Here the Stukas were again at their most formidable, destroying British strongpoints with incredible accuracy. Rommel was far more pleased by the supplies he had captured in Tobruk (1,400 tons of fuel, 2,000 vehicles, and innumerable arms) than he was by his resultant promotion to field marshal. In his next advance, 80 percent of his vehicles would be British, creating a serious identification problem for RAF bombers.

Ironically, this windfall would ultimately prove his undoing. Hitler had earlier decided that if Tobruk were taken, it would not be necessary to capture Malta. The prospective Operation Hercules, the seaborne assault on the island, had always worried him, and he was glad to have an excuse not to undertake it. Yet Malta would now survive to rebuild itself, choking off the air and sea supply routes to become the instrument of Germany's ultimate defeat in Africa. Further, the British debacle would give Churchill further weapons in his argument against an invasion of France and for an invasion of North Africa in 1942.

A nearly exhausted Afrika Korps won another great victory over dispirited British forces at Mersa Matruh on June 27–28, and then drove on to fight the first battle of El Alamein, its strength reduced to forty tanks. The Luftwaffe, which had made intensive efforts during the battles at Tobruk and Bir Hacheim, was now exhausted, decimated both by attrition, the sheer wear and tear of intensive desert service, and a shortage of fuel. There were still 290 Luftwaffe aircraft available, but no matter how hard the "blackbirds" worked, they could not create spare parts out of the thin, hot desert air, nor pump aviation gas from the barren desert sand.

Rommel elected to fight at El Alamein with a vastly diminished air force. The Desert Air Force, in contrast, threw every aircraft it could gather from any theater into the fray, flying almost 5,500 sorties in the first week of the battle. Rommel could combat superior numbers of tanks on the ground, but his armor melted away in the air assault, and he was forced on the defensive, hundreds of miles from his supply depots, in the face of an enemy that grew stronger every day.

A waiting game then began that served the British better than the Germans, and illustrated again the importance of scale and focus. To the Germans, locked in battle on the eastern front with more than 360 Russian divisions, the eight or nine divisions of the British Eighth Army were small potatoes indeed. But Africa was the only place where British soldiers were engaged in fighting the Germans, and resources were drained from England and the Commonwealth to replenish the African forces. Churchill considered the theater so critical that he risked a breach of relations with Australia by committing Australian soldiers to Africa at a time when the Japanese were threatening to invade their mother country.

During the retreat, General Auchinleck had again taken direct control of the Eighth Army, saving it from destruction. This was not enough in Churchill's eyes, and Auchinleck was sacked, to be replaced by General Sir Harold Alexander as General Officer in Command. The Eighth Army also received a new commander, Lieutenant General Sir Bernard Montgomery.

August 1942 became the turning point in the Egyptian desert for the Afrika Korps. Somewhat surprisingly, given his ego and his irascible nature, Montgomery professed regard for airpower and placed cooperation with the Desert Air Force as his first order of priority, saying, "There are not two plans, Army and Air, but one plan, Army-Air." Unfortunately for future cooperation, when victory came, Montgomery would claim it as the army's alone.

THE BATTLE OF ALAM HALFA

Although often overshadowed by the Second Battle of El Alamein, the Battle of Alam Halfa was immensely significant for the air war, for it painted in bold strokes what was in store for Germany and made an indelible impression upon Field Marshal Rommel. When he later was given a command in France to resist the coming invasion, Rommel would base all his strategy on the assumption of overwhelming Allied airpower.

Alam Halfa was a key hill in the British defenses, and it was there that the Desert Fox made his last desperate attempt to win a decision in the Western Desert and march to Cairo. Like General Robert E. Lee in the Civil War, Rommel knew his inferiority in numbers and supply ruled out a successful defensive war, and yet he had an abiding faith in the offensive capability of his army. Like Lee, Rommel gambled one more time on an offensive, and like Lee, he lost, for this time he could not draw the English armor into his antitank-gun traps.

Much of the credit for his defeat goes to the intelligence provided the Allies via Ultra, which pinpointed his convoys, depriving him of as much as 80 percent of his supplies and 40 percent of his fuel. Ultra intelligence also revealed the date he intended to begin his offensive, August 30. Thus alerted, Coningham began a day-and-night bombing operation on August 21, securing almost complete command of the air with his twenty-two squadrons of fighters. By September 2, the Desert Air Force had dropped more than 1,000 tons of bombs in 3,500 sorties against tanks, trucks, and encampments, devastating the morale of Rommel's troops, who asked plaintively, "Where is the Luftwaffe?" Using American-built bombers—Martin Baltimores, Douglas Bostons, and a USAAF squadron of North American B-25 Mitchells—Coningham oppressed the beleaguered Germans with the regularity and the relentlessness of his attack. The German Stukas, once so formidable, now had to jettison their bombs to escape the swarming Allied fighters. In the meantime, Montgomery kept his army entirely on the defensive, not exposing his tanks to Rommel's counterstrokes.

It was a pivotal moment for the British Army. From this battle forward, it would never be denied air superiority by the Allied air forces. Further, its expertise in the art of close air support would continue to improve—with some embarrassing lapses, including the forthcoming Operation Torch, the invasion of North Africa.

THE SECOND BATTLE OF EL ALAMEIN

Rommel had shot his bolt and now could only withdraw—which Hitler forbade him to do. Montgomery, with a precision and a caution that would become legendary, built up massive amounts of artillery and tanks and an overwhelming superiority in airpower. With 1,263 Allied aircraft, versus 600 for the Axis, Coningham unleashed a blizzard of air attacks. The battle raged from October 23 through November 4; the Allies flew 11,586 sorties and lost 97 aircraft. The Axis flew 3,120 sorties and lost 24 planes, but the difference in the sortie rate doesn't begin to reflect the difference in effectiveness. In an offensive mode, the German Stuka-panzer combination was deadly, able to reach strongpoints and destroy them. It was far less useful defensively, when the enemy was mobile and operating beneath an absolute canopy of aircraft.

The Eighth Army broke Rommel, who, despite his losses, lack of air cover, and shortage of fuel and vehicles, conducted a masterly retreat. On the Allied side, Montgomery seemed paralyzed by his victory, unable to follow up in the famous Desert Rat style of the past. At the same time, his uncontrollable ego took over, and he took full credit for the victory over Rommel, beginning a breakdown in the previously warm relations with the air commanders, Tedder and Coningham. The latter two were so distressed by Montgomery's unwillingness to pursue Rommel aggressively that they set up improvised airfields far behind the retreating Afrika Korps, airlifted in the necessary fuel and ammunition, and conducted virtual guerrilla operations against the long lines of fleeing Axis vehicles.

Eventually, the Afrika Korps made it back to Tripoli, from where Rommel had started twice before. When the Allies began their Operation Torch, the battered remnants of the Afrika Korps were still able to wage a brilliant, largely overlooked campaign to secure the northern half of Tunisia for what Hitler called a bridgehead and the Allies would see as a gigantic trap. With Montgomery following slowly, and with Operation Torch maladroitly handled, Hitler began to funnel in supplies on a scale previously undreamed of, at a time when all but Hitler knew that it was too late.

THE INVASION OF NORTH AFRICA—OPERATION TORCH

The North African invasion, which had been hotly argued from the start, offers a wonderful illustration of the civilian control of the United States military. U.S. military officers, from Army Chief of Staff General George C. Marshall down, believed that the main thrust of both air and ground effort should have been against Europe. The Combined Chiefs of Staff, that wonderful innovation of British and American planning, also opposed the invasion. Yet President Roosevelt wanted to get American troops into combat as soon as possible, a desire Winston Churchill shared. The two leaders prevailed, and the biggest invasion operation in history to date took place on November 8, 1942. The Western Task Force, composed of 102 ships sailing from the United States, landed on the coast of Morocco from Safi through Casablanca to Mehdia. The site was selected partially to forestall a possible intervention by Spanish forces and partially to ensure that a "pure American" force went into battle. A Center Task Force, composed of American troops and British naval forces, landed near Oran, and an Eastern Task Force landed at Algiers. At Algiers, only 10,000 troops were American, the rest British. In each case, American troops were to be the first ashore, to assuage French sensibilities about "perfidious Albion."

The ensuing ground war was initially characterized by hesitance and timidity, of which Germany took full advantage. It immediately occupied the rest of France, simplifying its transport and shipping problems but adding to the immense territory it had to defend.

With the same élan it would show the next year in the occupation of Italy, Germany seized a defensible line in Tunisia and began pouring in equipment, aircraft, and manpower at a rate that made the perennially supply-starved Rommel bitter. A buildup of forces began that ultimately would include 250,000 soldiers—Rommel had fought at El Alamein with 54,000 Germans and about the same number of Italian troops. In addition, the latest weapons were shipped in, including some of the brand-new Tiger tanks.

In a curious aberration that can only be attributed to personality conflicts both within and between the RAF and the USAAF, none of the lessons on close air support, learned at such cost in the Western Desert, were applied during the opening stages of Operation Torch. Despite the demonstrated success of Tedder's techniques, he was not even consulted on the plans for Torch. Further, the physical separation of the headquarters prevented any effective cooperation between the 454 aircraft of the Eastern Air Command, headed by Air Marshal Sir William Welsh, and the 1,244 planes of the Western Air Command, headed by Major General James H. Doolittle.

The lack of cooperation between Allied air forces was matched by a lack of coordination between air and ground. The Germans took full advantage of the situation—after months of being hounded by the Desert Air Force, it was intoxicating for the German Air Force to rule the skies over Tunisia. Once again the Luftwaffe had air superiority, gained not through weight of numbers but instead through superior aircraft—the Allies still had nothing to match the Bf 109F and Bf 109G—and the use of hard-surface airfields.

Rommel had capitalized on Montgomery's timidity, keeping the Afrika Korps one jump ahead of the Eighth Army during the 1,700 mile retreat by the extensive use of minefields and antitank gun screens. By mid-February, the Germans were able to concentrate their forces in Tunisia. With their shortened supply lines and increased priority in the overall war effort, the Axis forces in North Africa gained strength and were even able to administer a drubbing to green American troops at the Battle of Kasserine Pass on February 14–15.

Two significant changes in command were about to occur. On the Axis side, Rommel went on sick leave, turning his command over to Colonel General Jürgen von Arnim. Overall command of Axis forces was given to the Italian General Giovanni Messe. On the Allied side, one of the outcomes of the Casablanca Conference in January was that Tedder was to become Air Officer Commanding of the Mediterranean Air Command. Under him, commanding the Allied air forces in northwest Africa, was U.S. Major General Carl Spaatz. The new arrangement followed RAF practice, in that Doolittle was given the Northwest African Strategic Air Force, Air Vice Marshal Sir Hugh Lloyd was given the Northwest African Coastal Air Force, and the old campaigner Coningham was given the Northwest African Tactical Air Force.

Tedder, Spaatz, and Coningham cooperated splendidly, the new arrangement sweeping away the old difficulties of personality and bureaucracy, and forecasting the harmonious operations of the next two years. Doolittle's Strategic Air Force had both American heavy bombers and British Wellingtons, while Coningham's Tactical Air Force employed the tactical aircraft of the American Twelfth Air Force, as well as Air Vice Marshal Harry Broadhurst's Desert Air Force. The almost instantaneous, and to some, miraculous, change in attitude and technique would have tremendous impact on the Battle of the Mareth Line, which began on March 20. The Mareth Line had been built by the French as a defense against Italian invasion from Libya, and consisted of old Beau Geste–style forts supplemented by tank obstacles, artillery emplacements, and strongpoints made up of antitank guns and tanks buried hull-down in the sand.

The Allied air forces heavily outnumbered the Axis forces and had added some important new aircraft to its inventory. Spitfires were now available to contest the Bf 109s, and the Hurricane IID made its appearance. The latter was equipped with two 40-mm cannon in underwing pods, which reduced its speed to below 300 miles per hour and impaired its maneuverability, but was deadly against tanks and other armored vehicles. A less well known but equally important factor in the success of Tedder's forces was the availability of large numbers of Douglas C-47s to carry supplies to the field. When in early January 1943 the Twelfth Air Force was so short on 500-pound bombs that operations were threatened with cancellation, the faithful "Gooney Bird" air transports were life-savers, bringing in each day the next day's missions' worth of bombs. Just as the German air transport force was being throttled into extinction, the Allied airlift capability was coming into its own. It would increase on a scale unimagined by any air force or army commander.

The Desert Air Force won the battle of the Mareth Line with a furious assault that began with level-bombing attacks, a "creeping barrage" that paralyzed enemy troops in their positions. This was followed by continuous flights of fighter-bombers that sought out German antitank teams and destroyed them. In just over two hours, 412 sorties by the Desert Air Force cracked open the Mareth Line so that armor could push through without difficulty.

From this point on, the fate of Axis troops in Tunisia was sealed. The Germans continued attempting to resupply on a lavish scale, but Allied bombers virtually sealed off Tunisian ports and picked off individual ships trying to sneak in. The Luftwaffe tried to pick up the slack by making 150 sorties a day in both the standard Junkers Ju 52s and the newer six-engine Messerschmitt Me 323 Gigants, a mammoth converted glider that could carry ten tons of fuel. Tedder's forces responded with an aerial assault that resulted in four separate massive victories, all under the code name Operation Flax.

On April 5, the Northwest African Air Forces destroyed 39 aircraft on the ground, shot down 27 more, and damaged another 67. The biggest dogfight took place over the Tunisian province of Cap Bon, where 26 P-38s intercepted a formation of 101 Luftwaffe aircraft escorting a convoy of a dozen ships. Sixteen of the enemy planes were shot down without Allied loss. Five days later, 10 P-38s shot down twenty transports—Junkers Ju 52s and Savoia-Marchetti SM.82s. That afternoon, P-38s escorting B-25s on an antishipping sweep claimed another 25 aircraft, including 21 transports, most of them carrying fuel. Then on April 18, the famous Palm Sunday massacre occurred. Three squadrons of P-40s from the 57th Fighter Group and one from the 324th Group, Ninth Air Force, with British Spitfires flying top cover, intercepted a huge formation of more than 100 Ju 52s, escorted by Bf 109s, Bf 110s, and Macchi-Castoldi MC.202s near Cap Bon. Seventy-eight Axis aircraft were shot down, 51 of them transports, while the Allies lost 7. On April 22, a formation of 21 fuel-carrying Me 323s were caught over the Gulf of Tunis by Allied fighters and completely destroyed, the gigantic aircraft blowing up in spectacular fashion. In seventeen days, total Axis transport losses on the Tunisian front reached a total of 435. Coming as it did after the disaster in Stalingrad, the Luftwaffe's transport strength in aircraft and crews was destroyed.

The Tunisian fighting ended on May 13, 1943, in an Axis defeat as great as that at Stalingrad, with 250,000 prisoners, 150,000 of them German, being taken. From this point on, Allied airpower would reign supreme, meeting only token Luftwaffe resistance through the invasions of Sicily, Italy, and southern France. The German infantryman, conceded even by his enemies to be the best in the world, soon learned to fight hard defensive battles without air cover, enduring even massive assaults like that on Monte Cassino in Italy.

In Italy, the Allied air forces would establish bases that permitted the bombing of Austrian, southern German, and Balkan targets.

With the Luftwaffe virtually absent, tactical air forces were free to launch Operation Strangle, a far-ranging attack on railroad lines, highways, and bridges over which supplies flowed. The bridges were a particularly important target, for they took less bomb tonnage to destroy than a railroad yard—and took much longer to repair. Operation Strangle was intended to cut off the German armies and starve them into submission; it didn't achieve that, for the Germans were able to smuggle a subsistence level of food and ammunition at night by truck, ship, and even horse-drawn wagon. But it did destroy the confidence of the German forces, giving them an overwhelming sense of helplessness in the face of relentless air attack.

The fighting in the Mediterranean theater had seen the introduction of several important new American aircraft to combat. The Lockheed P-38 proved to be highly versatile, being used for long-range escort, reconnaissance, and ground attack. Although the Lightning was never to be the success in the European theater that it was in the Pacific, it was a valuable commodity in the desert. The Bell P-39 was useful in a ground-attack role but had to be escorted because it could not hold its own against enemy fighters. Among bombers, the North American B-25 demonstrated again that it was a workhorse, while the Martin B-26 Marauder overcame its original notoriety as a crew killer to become one of the most highly regarded bombers of the war. Later in Sicily and Italy, the Republic P-47 Thunderbolt and the North American P-51 began their distinguished records. The effectiveness of the new Allied generation of fighter-bombers was enhanced by the advent of new communication systems that linked what would later become known as FACs, forward air controllers, with the aircraft. Experienced observers, first on the ground, and later flying in "Grasshoppers," small aircraft like the Piper Cub or the Auster, began picking up targets and actively marking them with smoke from rockets.

Thus the campaign in the Mediterranean theater that had been so bitterly opposed by the generals as a diversion actually proved to be the best possible school for war. The United States Army Air Forces learned the very demanding science of air-ground cooperation at relatively low cost, and would apply it well in the invasion of Europe. The lessons learned were synthesized and incorporated into a new Field Manual, 100-20, published on July 21, 1943, which would govern the great air armies that would demolish Hitler's Festunga Europa (Fortress Europe). Field Manual 100-20 stated that "land power and air power are coequal and interdependent forces; neither is an auxiliary of the other." This was the lesson the Germans never learned. The manual further emphasized that "the gaining of air superiority is the first requirement for the success of any major land operation." The same could have been said about any sea operation as well. Finally, it dictated that "control of available air power must be centralized and command must be exercised through the air force commander if this inherent flexibility and ability to deliver a decisive blow are to be fully exploited." The Germans believed this, the Russians had learned it the hard way, but the Allied air forces would exploit it to a degree never before achieved.

6

GERMANY'S THIRD
AND LAST CHANCE

Until 1942, the war had been an almost uninterrupted series of disasters for the Allies, endless retreats, defeats, evacuations, sinkings, and surprises in both the European and the Asian theaters of war. As depressed as the Allied leaders were, they knew full well that harder times were still to come. And yet, incredibly, the Germans had already twice *lost* chances for victory. The first time was in their failure to gain the requisite air superiority over England to permit an invasion. The second was in front of Moscow, where only a madman's will prevented a worse debacle than Napoleon's.

Germany was given a third chance to win the war, and came very close to doing so in the campaign that worried Winston Churchill the most, and over which he could exert the least control: the Battle of the Atlantic.

THE CLOSE-RUN MARITIME WAR

The two essential qualities of combat—endless periods of boredom suddenly punctuated by life-threatening terror—were magnified a thousandfold in the war at sea. U-boats would cruise the wild dark surface of the seas at night, or loiter for days in the chill depths waiting for word of a convoy. Patrol planes would drone on for endless hours above a monotonous, glassy-surfaced sea, peering into nothingness to try to pick up the white spray from a periscope. When battle came, it was sudden, sharp, and terror-filled, the aircraft trying to straddle the submarine with depth charges, the U-boat attempting to dive to safety or fighting back with a withering barrage of antiaircraft fire; the sailors fearful of drowning in their sardine can, the airmen dreading a long, violent plunge into a cold and hostile sea. Then, if the moment passed with good fortune, it was back to hours of uncomfortable boredom.

As ennui and fear melded in the maritime war, a mind-boggling set of numbers was generated. The U-boats carried out more than 3,000 patrols and sank 2,840 merchant ships with a total of 14,333,082 gross register tons. In the Battle of the Atlantic, more than one-third of the British merchant fleet was sunk and 30,248 merchant seaman drowned. It was as costly for the Germans; of their fleet of 1,126 U-boats, 784 were sunk. Out of the 40,900 men who served on board the U-boats, 27,491 were killed and more than 5,000 captured. The survivors became a tightly knit group after the war, and deservedly so.

THE SMALL BEGINNINGS

The man who, to his surprise, would become the last Führer of the Third Reich, Grand Admiral Karl Dönitz, had made himself unpopular in the prewar German navy by lobbying against the construction of capital ships like the *Bismarck* and the *Tirpitz*, contending that Germany could never build a surface navy to contest the dominance of the Anglo-Saxon powers. Less flamboyant than General Billy Mitchell, more personable than the Royal Air Force leader of Bomber Command, Air Marshal Arthur Harris, Dönitz nonetheless maintained that he knew the secret to winning the war against Great Britain: the creation of a fleet of three hundred operational, seagoing submarines. With three hundred submarines, he promised to strangle the British empire, starving England into submission.

But "big-gun" advocates ruled the German Navy as they did the British, and despite the tremendous achievements of the primitive U-boat fleet in the First World War, when England had come perilously close to defeat at sea, they assumed that submarines had been made obsolete by the development of the acoustical detection system known as "asdic." (The name derived from Anti-Submarine Detection Investigation Committee, and was one of the rare instances of a committee producing a functional product.) Familiar to all fans of submarine movies, asdic (later known as sonar) consisted of a noise emitter and a receiver; the pinging noise would echo off a submarine, permitting computations of distance of 1,500 yards and of direction. It also had a capacity for passive listening via hydrophones, a technique with a greater range than the active "pinging." In effect, it was an acoustic version of radar.

Dönitz combined the talents of "Bomber" Harris and Air Marshal Hugh Dowding to prove the experts wrong. Like Harris, he contended that his weapon, the submarine, could win the war by itself, and as a hands-on leader like Dowding, Dönitz developed a system of control and new tactics. The small, feisty admiral, like his patron Hitler a lover of German shepherds, was the beneficiary of the greatest German intelligence coup of the war. His B-Dienst (Beobachter Dienst, Naval Radio Intelligence Service) could read English naval codes, especially those of the merchant marine, for the most crucial period of the Battle of the Atlantic, and he used this information to track the progress of convoys from their painful assembly in port to the unloading of those ships that survived. Using an elaborate radio network and the Enigma code machines, Dönitz personally controlled the movements of his fleet, and, as soon as he knew a convoy's location, would assign one or two submarines to shadow it and maintain contact.

Dönitz would next direct his other U-boats to an ambush site. In place of the single lone-wolf raider of World War I, waiting passively for a target to happen by, Dönitz created the aggressive wolf pack, with as many as a dozen submarines stalking convoys and attacking in concert. He revolutionized tactics by insisting that they attack at night on the surface, effectively negating the dreaded asdic. His methods almost brought England to her knees, yet were ironically also part of his undoing, for the British developed high-frequency direction-finding equipments (H/F D/F, inevitably called "Huffduff"), which would deduce the bearing of submarines from their radio transmissions and locate them by triangulation.

Dönitz maintained close personal contact with each member of his fleet, attending the departure and arrival of every U-boat, awarding decorations himself, and going beyond that to speak to the crewmen in terms with which they could identify. Unlike his counterparts Dowding and Harris, Dönitz had charisma.

It is important to remember that he achieved his near-victory with a fleet one-fifth the size he considered the minimum necessary. Dönitz began the war with 59 submarines instead of 300, and of these, only 36 were oceangoing types—the rest were referred to as "Baltic Ducks." His ships at sea ranged from a low of 6 in late 1941 to a high of just under 100 in 1943. Yet even with these inferior forces, Dönitz almost reached his goal of sinking 800,000 tons of shipping per month, more than the Allies could build, and sufficient to strangle England. *If* he had had his 300 U-boats in September 1939, he would unquestionably have won the Battle of the Atlantic and, almost certainly, the war.

CONDORS AND U-BOATS

In some respects, the Battle of the Atlantic started dead even. The Germans had forgotten how important the submarine was, while the British had forgotten how deadly it was. As a result, the Germans started with too few submarines, while the British began with too few destroyers and an inadequate convoy system. Neither side had what it would soon find it needed most, a long-range aircraft for bombing and reconnaissance, nor did either side understand the implications of radar for the maritime war.

Aircraft were more valuable when they assisted centrally controlled submarine attacks with aerial reconnaissance than they were when making attacks themselves. As a long-range aircraft, the Germans had to rely on the Focke-Wulf Fw 200 Condor, another in the long series of Luftwaffe improvisations. An extremely advanced twenty-six-passenger airliner intended for use by Deutsche Lufthansa at the time of its debut in 1937, the prototype Condor had made headlines with a nonstop flight from Berlin to New York in June 1938. (Not quite seven years later, on April 14, 1945, Deutsche Lufthansa would make its last scheduled flight in a Condor, from Barcelona to Berlin.)

The Condor was hastily modified for combat use despite the fact that its structure was far too light for military work. A patchwork armament was fitted, with four MG 15 machine guns and a 20-mm cannon placed in the nose. Bombs were mounted in external racks under the nacelles and wings.

Deliveries were slow and the rigors of combat were hard on the fragile Condors, which sometimes broke in half behind the wing upon landing. Serviceability was low, with less than ten being available at any one time. The Condors were especially vulnerable to antiaircraft fire, for all of their fuel lines were routed on the underside of the aircraft.

Despite these shortcomings, natural enough in an airplane designed for commercial use, the Condor proved to be a lethal partner of the submarine and was an effective weapon. Condors sank eighty-five vessels totaling 363,000 tons between August 1940 and April 1941, while supplying the U-boat fleet with accurate information on convoys. Winston Churchill properly cited the Fw 200 as "the scourge of the Atlantic" in his *Second World War*.

If Germany's leaders had had the vision to provide all the resources necessary—resources that were well within their means—the Luftwaffe might have scored a tremendous victory in the Battle of the Atlantic, and England might have been starved into submission. During the earliest period of the struggle, when the greatest rewards could have been reaped at the least cost, Germany chose instead to send its bombers against English cities, in the vain hope that intimidation would force a quick end to the war. If only 50 percent of the effort devoted to the Battle of Britain and the subsequent Blitz had instead been given to the Battle of the Atlantic, the Germans might well have won the war against Britain before the invasion of Russia. Instead, the slow growth of German aviation and submarine forces was more than matched by a steady increase in antiaircraft armament on British merchant shipping, as well as more effective convoy protection.

ALLIED AIRPOWER VERSUS THE U-BOAT

In 1917, German submarines had nudged the goal Dönitz set for them one war later, sinking almost 7 million tons of shipping, and in April 1917, the month the United States entered the war, they destroyed more than 830,000 tons. England had reacted with a convoy system, and sought to bottle up the U-boat fleet in its Baltic ports by building up a formidable antisubmarine-warfare force in 1918.

By 1940, however, the U-boats were not confined to the North Sea, and England, for much the same reasons as Germany, lacked patrol planes with sufficient range to cover the enormous distances over open ocean. Instead, in the fight against submarines, it relied for a long period on the Short Sunderland flying boat. Though slow, the Sunderland was an attractive four-engine flying boat, possessing excellent flying characteristics. The Sunderland was dubbed the "Fliegende Stachelschwein" (Flying Porcupine) by the Germans because of its heavy armament—later models had as many as eighteen machine guns. It had an endurance of thirteen and a half hours, which meant it could lumber out to sea for 600 miles, cruise for two hours, and then return. But there were far too few Sunderlands when they were needed, and a 600-mile range was not enough—a very long-range bomber was needed, and none were available at the beginning of the battle.

COASTAL COMMAND

From its formation in 1936 until the darkest days of 1942, British Coastal Command had received short shrift in equipment, aircraft, and personnel. Fighter Command had rightly received first priority. That Bomber Command received second priority was as clear a mistake as the German decision to raid English cities rather than concentrate on the merchant marine, and for the same reason. Aircraft employed by Coastal Command could have had an effect on the war; aircraft employed by Bomber Command were, until 1942, almost useless to the war effort for a variety of reasons that will be discussed later. The full extent of this misuse of resources is typified in the ineffectual attacks made by Bomber Command on the German capital ships *Scharnhorst* and *Gneisenau* in port at Brest, France. In just under sixty days, almost 1,200 sorties were flown, dropping more than 800 tons of bombs—and registering only four direct hits. The *Gneisenau* was later put out of action for eight months by a torpedo from a sacrificial Coastal Command Beaufort, but Bomber Command did little more than pockmark the docks.

The inadequacy of Coastal Command can be appreciated by understanding the mismatch of its mission, its enormous geographic area, and the numbers and types of available aircraft. The Coastal

Command mission included not only the suppression of U-boats, but also the following:

- Cooperation with Bomber Command in the air offensive
- Coastal defense
- Air-sea rescue (shamefully neglected at first)
- Long-range night-fighter attack
- Antishipping strikes

In conducting these missions, Coastal Command, like the other commands, had to take a hand in aircraft development, weapon design, and, most important, in fostering electronic warfare.

All of these tasks have to be placed into the context of the hemispheric-scale geography involved, for the Battle of the Atlantic covered a great deal more territory than the *Queen Mary*'s 3,100-mile route from New York to Liverpool. The four defining points of the battle area were Murmansk in the northeast, Cape Town in the southeast, Rio de Janeiro in the southwest, and New Brunswick in the northwest. The maritime war even extended into the Mediterranean and the Indian Ocean. Where there were raw materials, there were ports; where there were ports, there often were U-boats.

Coastal Command, then under the leadership of Air Marshal Sir Frederick Bowhill, was pitifully weak at the start of the war, with but three squadrons of Sunderlands, just working up. (A total of 749 of the big flying boats were built by the end of the war.) Coastal Command's primary "strength" was ten squadrons of Avro Ansons, useless for anything but fair-weather coastal surveillance.

Help came in the form of the twin-engine Lockheed Hudson, which Sir Arthur Harris had championed as a member of the British Purchasing Commission in 1938, and which, among many other achievements, would score two memorable firsts. A No. 226 Squadron Hudson tallied the RAF's first aerial victory, shooting down a Dornier Do 18 flying boat on October 8, 1939. And on August 27, 1941, a Hudson flown by Squadron Leader J.H. Thompson captured the *U-570*, the first German submarine to surrender to air attack.

In the curious way of war, the Hudson never received the popular acclaim it deserved. An all-metal monoplane, it was the descendant of the type that Amelia Earhart flew on her ill-fated world flight, and similar to the Super Electra flown by Howard Hughes in his successful 1938 attempt. Lockheed turned out Hudsons in large numbers—2,941 before war's end—and the aircraft led to two equally good successors, the Ventura and the Harpoon. The Hudson laid the foundation for Lockheed's later successes, from the P-38 right down to today's F-22.

Less experienced pilots found the Hudson intimidating, for it was not without its limitations. With a greater wing loading, it was demanding to fly, especially out of short fields. The Hudson's range of 1,960 miles meant that it could be on station for two hours up to a distance of 500 miles from its home base—better than the Anson by far, but still not the answer to the submarine menace.

Coastal Command also acquired Consolidated PBY Catalina flying boats, direct descendants of Consolidated President Reuben Fleet's original Commodores, and they proved to be very successful, able to patrol at a range two hundred miles greater than the Sunderland, and possessing remarkable observation capability, thanks to extensive glazing. The latter contributed to the historic sighting of the German battleship *Bismarck*.

Even with the Catalinas, there were still extensive gaps in coverage, especially south of Greenland, and that's where the submarines gathered. Shipping losses continued at a high rate, and would do so until Allied airpower caught up. Yet by June 1941, when Bowhill turned command over to Air Marshal Sir Philip Joubert, Coastal Command had built up to forty squadrons. Joubert would preside over the worst period of the Battle of the Atlantic, when it seemed that the Germans had victory in their grasp, but he would also oversee the introduction of the weapons that would ultimately decide the battle. Having done the spadework for victory, Joubert then turned over the reins of Coastal Command, now with sixty squadrons and 850 aircraft, to Air Marshal Sir John Slessor. Bowhill also provided his successors with a first-rate scientific advisor, Professor P. M. S. Blackett. Blackett would lead the work of an Operational Research Unit that omnivorously gathered information from all sources to fight the U-boat war.

It's an interesting anomaly that the Germans, so rightly world-renowned for the quality of their scientists, never matched the British in what would later be called the "Wizard War." It was not a question of talent but of systems. The English pattern of academic freedom was better suited to the demands of war than the stern dictates of Nazi Germany. The cost was slight—most of the great contributors served at relatively low ranks and worked long hours in poor conditions. Yet time after time they were able to counter German advances, as with the Enigma machine or the various aids to bombing, or come up with war winners of their own, as with the many variations of radar.

THE DEADLY CYCLE

In today's environmentally conscious world, a sinking oil tanker receives immediate world attention, dominating headlines and the television news. In horrid contrast, sinkings were so frequent during the peak years of the Battle of the Atlantic that anything less than a liner like the *Athenia* rated little more than a paragraph on an inside page. After Pearl Harbor, tankers were sunk off the American coast with such frequency and ease that it was called "the Happy Time" by German submariners.

The sheer quantity of the U-boat successes is still difficult to comprehend. In 1941, at a loss of only 38 U-boats, the Germans sank 445 ships, totaling 2,171,890 GRT (gross register tons). In 1942, at a cost of 82 submarines, this jumped to 1,094 ships, totaling 5,819,025 GRT, with twin peaks reached in June with 131 ships of 616,904 GRT and in November with 118 ships of 743,321 GRT. Although he had not yet reached the full capability he sought, Dönitz had already achieved his principal aim: to sink Allied ships faster than they could be built. The grand admiral knew that if he could sustain that fatal arithmetic, England would have to surrender, perhaps in 1943, for with the introduction of *Milchkuh* (milk-cow) submarines able to refuel the operational boats at sea, U-boats could operate all over the world. Dönitz had succeeded in driving down imports from 61 million tons in 1940 to 33 million tons in 1942. A similar drop in 1943, at a time when the American buildup and its concomitant demand for supplies would begin to be felt, would alter the course of the war.

Submarine successes continued to build through March 1943, with 105 ships of 590,234 GRT sunk in that month. At that point Dönitz felt that his submarines had an incontestable advantage, and that despite his lack of resources he had achieved a war-winning position. In stark contrast, by that same spring, the Germans faced defeat in both Russia and Africa, and the full weight of the U.S. war potential was beginning to be felt. The maritime war was the only one Germany was winning—and it was obvious now that it was the only one it could win.

Just as Dönitz's euphoria soared with his sinkings, almost four years of continuous effort by the Allies suddenly paid off, and the U-boat fleet was first made vulnerable and then obsolete. After March, merchant-ship sinkings rapidly declined while U-boat sinkings skyrocketed, with an unprecedented forty-two lost in May 1943. Allied intelligence experts listened with satisfaction as call after call went out to U-boats that would never report in again.

At first, Dönitz could not understand what was happening and sent blistering messages to his submarine captains, virtually accusing them of cowardice in the face of the enemy. But as the figures came in, Dönitz admitted defeat. Where formerly 100,000 tons of shipping were sunk per U-boat loss, the ratio had declined to a mere 10,000 tons—an intolerable level that caused him to move his U-boats to areas where the air surveillance was not so complete. Unfortunately for his strategy, these were also areas where there were few ships to sink. By 1943, Germany had lost its third chance to win the war because Dönitz had lost the Battle of the Atlantic to Allied airpower and technology. In the bloody process, he had also lost his two sons, Peter and Klaus, both submariners, both drowned.

THE ELEMENTS OF VICTORY

At the Casablanca Conference, along with the more sensational notice that the Allies would accept only unconditional surrender, Churchill and Roosevelt also agreed that the defeat of the U-boat should have first priority on resources. The announcement coincided with the increasing availability of weapons that cumulatively would win the Battle of the Atlantic. These had been generated successively over time, and each one somewhat reflects the contemporary measure of desperation.

One of the first and most radical of these was the CAM ship (Catapult-Aircraft-Merchantman), in which a solid-rocket booster catapulted a Sea Hurricane like a Space Shuttle from the bow of a merchant vessel to drive off a marauding Focke-Wulf Condor. After the attack, the Hurricane pilot would ditch in front of the convoy, hoping to survive long enough in the frigid ocean to be picked up. It was not called a suicide mission, but it was close enough. Thirty-five vessels were so modified, and the first success came on August 3, 1941, when Lieutenant R. W. H. Everett was launched from HMS *Maupin*, and destroyed a Focke-Wulf Condor. By 1942, five more Condors had fallen to the Sea Hurricanes.

The MAC ships came in October 1941. These were merchantmen "scalped" to permit a tiny flight deck. Too small to have elevators and below-deck storage space, the MAC ships were just large enough to land upon, and so were vastly appreciated by the pilots.

The most important aircraft to be introduced was the Consolidated Liberator, the B-24 bomber, which had been built to complement the Boeing B-17. It would at last permit the closing of the gaps in surveillance allowed by smaller planes.

The B-24 was a remarkable aircraft; its design was not begun until 1939, but it was in service by 1941, and it was produced in greater quantity than any other American warplane, 18,432 being built. As a VLR (very long range) patrol plane, it could carry as many as twenty-four depth charges, which enabled it to persist in an attack long after a Hudson or a Sunderland would have exhausted its munitions.

Between Coastal Command and the air forces of the United States and Canada, the gaps in coverage in the North Atlantic, especially the vital one south of Greenland, had been closed by early 1943. It had not been an easy process, for the anglophobic Admiral Ernest J. King, the Commander in Chief of the U.S. Navy, cooperated only grudgingly, pursuing his own politics of seeking an independent long-range naval bombing arm, and stockpiling equipment for the Pacific war. Eventually, the teeming production lines were able to overcome even interservice rivalries, and there began to be enough airplanes to go around. But it had been very close; some British historians felt that the difference between victory and defeat in the early spring of 1943 was two squadrons of VLR aircraft—B-24s. By great good fortune, the Allies managed to have the essential two squadrons on hand.

Aircraft alone, however, were only part of the answer. Keeping the enemy below was not enough—the U-boats had to be found and sunk, and this required advanced technology.

THE OCEAN'S WIZARD WAR

Radar had its genesis in 1886 in Germany as a device to detect ships, when Christian Hülsmeyer deflected radio waves off large vessels in an attempt to develop a proximity warning device that would signal an impending collision in bad weather. There were parallel developments in other countries, including the United States, but the greatest strides were made in England. There, priority had been given to the Chain Home defense system, which was key in the Battle of Britain, but both airborne interception (AI) and air-to-surface-vessel (ASV) radar were also under development, all using the same basic equipment, modified for specialized needs. The ASV Mark 1 was installed in twelve Coastal Command Lockheed Hudsons by January 1940, but demonstrated only potential, not genuine, war-fighting capability. It would be many long, hard months before a reliable system was available. The ASV Mark I radar used a wave length of 1.5 meters. The British took an immense gamble and committed to the production of 4,000 of the follow-on ASV Mark II sets, without any certainty at all that they would be more successful than the very marginal Mark I. They embarked upon a technology that the Germans had proved to their own satisfaction would not work—very short, 10-centimeter wavelength (technically, 9.7 cm). After persuasion by Henry Tizard, scientific advisor to the Chief of the Air Staff, scientists at Birmingham University had abandoned work on nuclear energy to concentrate on microwave radar. By 1940, they had developed the magnetron, a cavity resonator that could handle all the power necessary for high-frequency transmissions. The magnetron was the key to more powerful ground stations, as well as smaller units to be carried in aircraft.

German Metox radar detectors had worked against the ASV Mark I, but could not detect 10-cm wavelength radar emissions, and German scientists had not considered the development of such short-wavelength radars feasible. Consequently, the Germans concluded that the British ability to track submarines stemmed from their detecting frequencies emitted by the submarines, and concentrated their development efforts on reducing radiation and on warning devices. It was not until early in 1943 when a British bomber was shot down over Rotterdam that the secret of the anti-submarine warfare campaign's success was revealed. The bomber carried one of the H2S airborne radars used for bombing, and it was a 10-cm wavelength type. The news was devastating to the German scientists, who could not believe that the British were so far advanced beyond their own efforts, and who knew that even duplicating the British technology would be almost beyond their means. They did hastily create the Naxos radar detector for the 10-cm wavelength radar, but in the ever-escalating electronics war, the Naxos in turn became an emitter that the British tracked.

One of the first uses of the ASV Mark II was in an intermediate approach. Squadron Leader H. de V. Leigh invented the "Leigh light," a twenty-four-inch naval searchlight installed in place of a Wellington's belly turret. In its first combat test on January 1941, the Wellington, equipped with the ASV Mark II radar, detected a submarine on the surface. At the last moment, the Leigh light was switched on, illuminating the submarine for a direct hit with a depth charge. Leigh, a pilot from the First World War currently acting as a personnel officer, had gone to great personal and career risk to thrust his device on his service; many submarines were sunk as a result.

The traditional U-boat tactic had been to crash-dive—twenty-five seconds was all that was required from the first warning horn till the U-boat was submerged, able to change course and depth without detection. The Leigh light robbed the submarines of that precious twenty-five seconds, and Dönitz's first reaction was typical—he insisted that the U-boats be given additional antiaircraft armament so that they could stay surfaced and fight back against their attackers. Modifications were made to existing boats as they returned and were added to new ones in production . These ranged from the addition of machine guns fore and aft to the installation of quadruple 2-cm guns or even 3.7-cm antiaircraft guns. The antiaircraft fire could be deadly, but a submarine rolling in the sea was both a poor gun platform and an easy target to attack. The "gunboats" were not a real match against an aircraft, and became almost helpless when two or more planes joined in an attack.

By April 1943, the new Commander of Coastal Command, Air Marshal Slessor, mounted a continuous surveillance of the Bay of Biscay. Slessor's aggressive tactics temporarily resulted in a high loss rate for the Germans, but the Germans revised their tactics to travel in packs and to spend as much time as possible submerged, which detracted from the duration of their patrol.

The combination of VLR aircraft and effective airborne radar won the Battle of the Atlantic. Germany's engineering genius would create new weapons like the schnorchel, and the later-model true submarines, the Models XXI and XXIII. The schnorchel was an extended ventilating tube that permitted operation of the diesel engines under water—albeit to the extreme discomfort of the crew, while Models XXI and XIII had entirely new shapes and power systems. The schnorchel boats didn't come into general use until after D-Day. Almost a hundred of the Models XXI and XXIII were completed by the end of the war, but they saw little use.

Both Germany and England had made mistakes in strategy prior to the war, the former not building enough submarines to be decisive, the latter not creating an adequate defense. In the hard contest after September 1939, England used its scientific skill and the assistance of United States reconnaissance aircraft to prevail. Germany, as in every other theater, and in every arm, could not match Allied resources on the sea or in the air.

THE LUFTWAFFE'S ANTISHIPPING WAR

Germany, however, was not completely dependent on the U-boats to disrupt Allied shipping. The Luftwaffe also conducted antishipping offensive operations, which ranged over vast areas, from France to far out over the Atlantic in great operational arcs emanating from Germany and Norway. In the Mediterranean, operations were undertaken from Italy, Sicily, Sardinia, Greece, and Crete. The Luftwaffe operated in conjunction with U-boats and attacked the convoys that supplied England, Russia, and the North African theater.

As happened so often, the Germans neglected a target of opportunity that would have paid a very high return for a relatively low investment. With almost every advantage in terms of geography, having bases ranging from Kirkenes in northern Norway to Bordeaux in France, and with a fleet of predatory submarines waiting for reconnaissance signals, the Luftwaffe devoted only meager resources to the Battle of the Atlantic, compared to the massive Allied effort.

The German effort, like that of its enemies, was harmed by interservice rivalry, for Göring resented diverting any of his Luftwaffe assets to help the German Navy. But while assisting submarines was not attractive to the Luftwaffe, attacking shipping was, and in 1939, two Luftwaffe bomber units, Kampfgeschwadern 26 and 30, operating the Heinkel He 111 and the Junkers Ju 88, respectively, were selected to undertake that mission. From this small beginning eventually grew the famous Fliegerkorps X, which shuttled from Norway to Sicily to attack Allied convoys. Colonel Martin Harlinghausen was named Commissioner for Torpedoes, and was at last able to use the knowledge he had begun to gather on maritime tactics during the Spanish Civil War. He targeted the convoys picking their way around the Arctic Circle to Murmansk. The Luftwaffe soon developed a deadly proficiency in low-level attacks on shipping with its Heinkel He 111s, He 115s, and Junkers Ju 88s, using both bombs and torpedoes. By the time the RAF's local air superiority had made attacks on shipping around England too hazardous, a new target became available in the north.

Winston Churchill had reacted instantly to the German attack on the Soviet Union, offering aid all out of proportion to his resources to a country he once considered a mortal enemy. Much to the distress of the British Admiralty, he promised to have convoys laden with all the materials of war arriving every ten days. The Admiralty had neither the merchant ships nor the naval vessels to fulfill his promise, and England did not yet have the material means to fill the convoys, but they began anyway on August 21, 1941, only sixty days after the invasion. Initially, they did not sail so often or so heavily laden as Churchill had promised, but ultimately more than eight hundred ships made the Arctic run. (The majority of Lend-Lease goods to the Soviet Union were sent through Iran.)

The Arctic route was dangerous, passing west of Iceland, through the Denmark Strait, then skirting as far north of Norway as the ice would allow before turning south to Archangel or Murmansk. For more than 1,500 miles, they sailed through seas hazardous enough in peacetime, and now freighted with the menace of U-boats, surface raiders, and aircraft. Almost the entire route to the destination Russian ports was within the range of the Luftwaffe units stationed in Norway, and during the summer, the long daylight hours gave the Germans plenty of time to find, fix, and attack. The hazard was reflected in the statistics—of Atlantic convoys, some .7 percent of the cargo was sunk; of the Arctic convoys, 7.5 percent was lost—more than 100 ships sunk, almost 3,000 sailors dead.

The most notorious German success came with convoy PQ 17, composed of thirty-five merchantmen and one tanker, with the usual escort vessels. Under Harlinghausen's tutelage, the Luftwaffe had developed potent tactics for antishipping attacks. Both the Heinkel He 111 and the Junkers Ju 88 had proved to be excellent torpedo planes, and experience had shown that a combined attack of high-level bombing, glide bombing, and torpedoes split the convoy's defenses and lowered the risk to the attackers. The torpedo planes used the "Golden Comb" attack, coming in low in line-abreast formation, with the convoy's ships silhouetted against the skyline, and fanning out their torpedoes to get the maximum number of hits.

The attack on PQ 17 began on July 4, 1942. Four ships were sunk, and the British Admiralty was spooked by the report that the German superbattleship *Tirpitz* had put to sea. Orders were given for the convoy to scatter, which allowed the Luftwaffe to pick off single ships one by one. The Germans claimed that the entire convoy was sunk, but a British account showed that 23 out of 34 had been lost, still a grievous figure.

In November 1942, the Allied invasion of North Africa had offered the Luftwaffe the most lucrative target ever presented. There were already almost 1,000 aircraft in Sicily and Sardinia (400 Luftwaffe, 515 Italian), and these were reinforced by another 500, including heavy-bomber units from the Russian front and antishipping units from Norway. It was another splendid demonstration of Luftwaffe mobility, with one unit relocating to the new theater in less than forty-eight hours. In the Mediterranean, antishipping strikes continued, but the operational emphasis had shifted to attacks on Allied ports. The Luftwaffe achieved some successes, but, as was coming to be the case in all theaters, the German Air Force was now overextended and unable to cope with the growing numbers of Allied aircraft. In overall terms, the Luftwaffe failed in its antishipping efforts because it lacked a long-term policy, and because the crews trained in the specialized techniques were often lost when called to perform routine bombing duties over England, in the Mediterranean, or in Russia.

Another effective antishipping strike was made on September 9, 1943, and in a way it symbolized all that was right, and all that was wrong, with the German war effort.

The Italian battleships *Roma* and *Italia* were sailing from Spezia to surrender to the Allies. Dornier Do 217K-2s of III/KG 100, operating from the south of France, were sent to attack it. The lead Dornier was flown by Major Hajo Herrmann, the wildest tactician in the Luftwaffe, who had as his bombardier Lieutenant Heinrich Schmetz, a specialist in the use of the new Fritz-X guided missile. The Fritz-X, a "smart bomb" before the term was coined, was based on a standard SD-1400 armor-piercing bomb, but equipped with four wings in an X array and a complex tail unit, which contained the receiver portion of the radio control unit. The Fritz-X was dropped from about 18,000 feet; the bombardier guided it with a small joystick, using a flare at the rear of the missile to assist in sighting. Schmetz put his Fritz-X right down the *Roma*'s funnel, and became the first, and probably the only man, ever to sink a battleship with a missile. The *Italia* was damaged by an attack from another bomber. It was a stunning technical accomplishment, one that the Allies would not have been able to duplicate.

Yet the sinking of the *Roma* provides insight into the extreme contrast between England and Germany. In England, scientists worked hand in hand with the military and received support from Churchill. In Germany, Hitler's penchant for interference was so great that the military did everything to avoid it. Hitler was told that the *Roma* had been sunk by conventional bombs, because it was feared that if he learned of the Fritz-X's success he would deem it another miracle weapon and give it priority over fighter production.

CONCLUSION

Early successes and a natural hubris kept German leaders from realizing that the maritime war was the one arena where time, strategy, geography, and the balance of forces combined in their favor. Preoccupied with the land battles, confident it had as large an air force as it needed, equipped with the right types of planes, Germany treated the air component of the maritime war as less important than bombing civilian targets or cooperating with the panzer forces. If someone at the highest level—Hitler with a flash of intuition perhaps, or Göring with rare insight—had insisted that first priority be given to cooperation with submarine forces, the war might have ended favorably for the Axis in 1941.

Allied leaders were no more farseeing, but they were more sensitive to their problem than the Germans were to their opportunity. As a result of an intense effort, the Allies were able to alter the odds so completely in their favor that the Luftwaffe was forced to withdraw from the maritime war. It was a pattern that the Allies would repeat in the Pacific war, albeit with far more difficulty.

7

THE BIGGEST
BATTLEGROUND

From the broiling sands of Africa to the frigid steppes of Russia, nowhere was the air war more closely tied to surface conditions than in the South Pacific. Savagely fought land and sea battles both determined air superiority and were determined by it. In part, this was because the ratio of ocean to land was great and the distances over which battles were fought were enormous. But the distinguishing characteristic lay in the strategic and tactical approaches of the combatant forces.

In the beginning, neither Japan nor the United States had sufficient aircraft, and grandiose strategic aims were undertaken with token tactical forces. Even though the air forces available to fight were often absurdly small, both sides obtained results out of all proportion to their strength.

The destruction of U.S. battleships at Pearl Harbor forced the abandonment of Plan Orange and all other preconceived U.S. notions of conducting a war with Japan: the Carrier Task Force came into being by default. The United States was determined to strike at Japan, and the untried aircraft carrier was the only tool available. The importance of the innovation has overshadowed how small the forces involved were, particularly when compared to the simultaneous buildup of massive forces in England.

Large American carriers such as the *Yorktown* or the *Enterprise* could carry 80 aircraft deep within enemy waters; there they could fence with their Japanese counterparts, such as the *Shokaku* and the *Zuikaka*, each capable of embarking 72 planes. While carrier task forces could do effective work, pecking at the periphery of an enemy's defenses as the U.S. Navy had pounded Japanese outposts in the Marshalls and elsewhere, all naval authorities were sobered by the fate of the *Prince of Wales* and the *Repulse*. Consequently, the use of carriers within the range of long-distance land-based aircraft was considered too dangerous. Carriers were at their best— that is their most destructive—when engaged in battle with each other.

Unlike the U.S. Navy, the Japanese had built up a land-based naval air force equipped with a relatively large number of excellent aircraft suitable for operating over long distances. These included the familiar G4M Betty and the A6M Zero, the latter of which in 1941 had a range that was not achieved by the Mustang until 1944. The Zero's long range and otherwise excellent performance were obtained only by sacrificing structural strength and combat necessities including armor and self-sealing tanks.

Yet Japanese strategy in 1942 was not concerned with defensive capabilities. It was posited on obtaining great results from small numbers of aircraft that could fly long distances, inflict crucial damage, and return. That strategy succeeded until Midway; it would fail at Guadalcanal, where the initial arrival of a handful of fighters and dive-bombers enabled the United States not only to endure but to prevail.

BICKERING INTO BATTLE

The battle at Guadalcanal began on an even basis, with the Japanese Air Force initially having the edge in numbers and quality, despite their bomber bases being six hundred miles away. As we will see later, during the first weeks of the campaign, it was a war in microcosm, with small numbers of Japanese attackers being met by equally small numbers of American defenders. After an agonizing ninety days, when the battle could have been won or lost on the turn of a ship or the flight of an aircraft, the situation changed dramatically as American numbers steadily built and Japanese strength declined.

Guadalcanal had never figured in either Japanese or American preliminary planning. That there was a battle there at all, much less one fought so tenaciously, if often erratically, by both sides, was because of incidents and personalities totally unrelated to the island. The fight began there accidentally and then took on a life of its own, one that clearly presaged how the war must ultimately end. Japan's misadventure at Guadalcanal, like the unexpected German diversion in the Balkans in the spring of 1941, shows how strategy can become subordinate to unexpected events. Guadalcanal also showed that air, sea, and land power were no longer just complementary, but inextricably intertwined.

Far more than the war in Europe, the Pacific war was characterized by sharply divided opinions on how it was to be conducted and by even greater rivalries among its fighting forces.

The multiple Allied divisions and rivalries had begun long before Midway, and they existed at the very top, between Roosevelt and Churchill. The argument was not Europe versus the Pacific but rather where in Europe the Germans should be engaged. Roosevelt was normally quick to succumb to Churchill's combination of charm, persistence, and experience, but his own inclination, steeled by the strong belief of the majority of his military staff, was to meet the pledge to Russia of a second front by an invasion of France followed by a thrust to the German heartland. Churchill and his commanders feared involving England in a land war against the Germans, preferring other options that ranged from Norway to North Africa to Italy. The British wanted to fight anywhere on the periphery that would weaken Germany, not kill too many British soldiers, and perhaps fulfill their pledge to Josef Stalin.

Yet there were rifts even within the fabric of Roosevelt's staff. Steely-eyed Admiral Ernest Joseph King was Commander in Chief of the U.S. Navy and Chief of Naval Operations. King, who described himself as the son-of-a-bitch they sent for when the going got tough, didn't like the English, and wanted to throw the Japanese out of Alaska and then out of the Pacific. On the latter point, but few others, he was backed by General Douglas MacArthur, who had survived the bankruptcy of his plans for the defense of the Philippines to become a hero of folkloric proportions. King and MacArthur, opposed by General George Marshall, General Henry H. "Hap" Arnold, and many others, were overruled. Europe was to come first, even if the invasion of France had to be delayed while it was being forced upon the English. The majority of Allied men and matériel were to be devoted to the defeat of Hitler, and a much smaller amount to the containment of the Japanese with what was termed an "offensive-defensive." The allocations indicated just how serious Roosevelt and Churchill were about the primacy of the European war but didn't reckon with service politics.

King and MacArthur had their orders, but they also knew how to play the system, and they would play it well in the months to come in every way except orchestration of a sound chain of command. Neither man could be forced to serve under the other, so neither could be given command of the entire Pacific theater. A July 2, 1942, directive made MacArthur Commander in Chief of the Southwest Pacific, while King's designated representative, Admiral Chester Nimitz, would command the rest of the Pacific. Beneath this awkward organizational split, ill defined not only geographically but in terms of forces, there were many additional confusing divisions concerning the control of amphibious operations, airpower, and supplies.

The same directive ordered that the two commanders be assigned three tasks. Task I, code-named Operation Watchtower, was assigned to Admiral Nimitz, who, by August 1, 1942, was to capture the Santa Cruz Islands in preparation for an attack on Tulagi in the Solomons. Task II was a simultaneous operation by General MacArthur to drive the Japanese out of New Guinea. MacArthur would then undertake Task III, invading New Britain and seizing the main Japanese base at Rabaul. With war's typical irony, these plans would be upset by disagreements within the Japanese hierarchy.

JAPANESE DISSENSION

At the same time that the Allied leaders squabbled about priorities between and among theaters, the Japanese armed forces were split along traditional army-navy lines, each service wanting a different strategy and neither willing to cooperate with the other at command levels. The degree of dissension can be judged by the fact that the admirals refused to let the generals know just how extensive the defeat at Midway had been, while the generals did not advise the admirals that an airfield was being built on Guadalcanal. The same inability to coordinate existed all down the chain of command, except at the very lowest operational levels, where Japanese naval captains would gallantly beach their ships upon an island shore just to ferry another few hundred troops to battle, and Japanese Army units would die to the last man to defend a naval outpost.

Despite having conquered all the territory that the proponents of the Greater East Asia Co-Prosperity Sphere had always lusted for, Japan soon found that its conquests were not unalloyed blessings. Where before the war the Island Empire had been able to import millions of tons of iron ore and thousands of barrels of petroleum from the very areas it now owned by conquest, an acute and growing shortage of shipping steadily shrunk these imports to negligible levels. Both the army and the navy agreed that the conquered territory should be maintained at all costs, and the shipping constraints relieved by creating an impervious defensive barrier, but they disagreed on how to do it. The army, still forced to maintain fifteen divisions on the border of the Soviet Union and another twenty-six in China, wanted to bring all of New Guinea under its control so that Australia would be threatened. The navy emphasized the defense of the Solomon and Bismarck islands, to be better able to defend the naval base at Truk. In this, as with the decision to attack Pearl Harbor, the army prevailed.

The problems deriving from the divisions in the Allied command structure were solved in part by two things. The first was the squabbling within the ranks of Japanese military leaders, and the second was the geography of the area where the war was to be fought.

A determined Japanese attempt to take Port Moresby by an overland drive across the Owen Stanley Mountains preempted MacArthur's Task II. The discovery by FRUPAC, the Fleet Radio Unit Pacific, commanded by Commander Joseph J. Rochefort, that the Japanese were building an airfield on Guadalcanal similarly forced Admiral Nimitz's hand with Task I.

THE GEOGRAPHY OF THE PACIFIC WAR

Millions of years ago, continental drift separated the land masses, and, augmented by a fiery chain of volcanoes, left a spiny ridge of islands stretching in parallel lines running southeast from Malaya to the Fijis. On maps, the numerous islands seem strung together like stepping-stones, separated by only a short journey across a sparkling sea, but the hard fighting showed instead that the islands stretched out over enormous distances of water. It was this unusual geography of attenuated island chains that dictated Allied strategy, for Japan's opening thrust had reached all the way to the Solomon Islands, where thousands of harbors served as havens for small ships, barges, flying boats, and submarines.

The distances between island bases was great, more than a thousand miles from Japanese-occupied New Guinea to Guadalcanal, and 650 miles from MacArthur's New Guinea outpost, Port Moresby, to Bougainville. From the main Japanese naval bases at Rabaul, New Britain, and Kavieng, New Ireland, it was 600 and 840 air miles, respectively, to Guadalcanal. Japan, after all its railing about Western colonial oppression, had adopted colonial military tactics, establishing strongpoints all along the chain, and in doing so, spread its army, navy, and land-based naval air forces to the point of indefensibility.

South of this canopy of islands lay Australia, vulnerable even after the Battle of Midway, and dependent upon supply lines that ran 7,500 great circle miles to the United States. General MacArthur's headquarters were in Australia, and he was determined to return to the Philippines by driving the Japanese out of New Guinea and then New Britain. Nimitz wanted to take the Central Pacific route, through Micronesia, capturing the Gilberts, the Marshalls, and the Carolines. Ultimately, the route would reach to the Marianas, from where it could bring the war to the home islands of Japan. The two offensives would support each other, keeping the Japanese from concentrating against just one, and the carrier forces could be rapidly switched as required.

The geography had another curious effect, unanticipated by either side. Although the vast ocean spaces permitted the deployment of virtually unlimited naval resources, the land masses were such that only relatively small numbers of men could be engaged in combat, a factor that limited Japanese thinking to an almost fatal degree. While only small armies could take part in the land battles—fewer than 40,000 soldiers on each side at Guadalcanal, far fewer than that at Tarawa or Iwo Jima—even those armies had to be supported by sea. And control of the sea was rapidly passing to the Allied side.

GUADALCANAL CALENDAR

The battle for Guadalcanal was long and complex, comprising six major and many minor sea engagements and continual engagements of the land forces, punctuated by several major land campaigns, all under the umbrella of daily air battles from land and sea bases. In addition, it was perhaps the only campaign in history in which the mastery of the sea switched every twelve hours like the changing of the guard, the Americans dominating by day, the Japanese by night. The very narrow margin of victory at Guadalcanal, combined with the wide variety of engagements, makes it an excellent case study for the entire Pacific campaign. Later the marked difference in strength between the Allies and the Japanese made the outcome of battles certain, no matter how desperately the defenders fought. For these reasons, the battle for Guadalcanal will be covered in greater depth than other Pacific campaigns.

The many battles at and around Guadalcanal also offer snapshots of rampant heroism. When the respective air forces first engaged, the Japanese held several advantages, including more and better aircraft. They had the advantage of the initiative and were able to strike the U.S. base at Henderson Field at will, for their own bases were beyond the range of Marine forces. They also had the advantage of experience; most of the Japanese pilots engaged in the early battles at Guadalcanal had at least eight hundred hours of flying time and had been in combat often. Their American opponents had less than half that amount, and most had never been in combat. Over time, these green American forces, fighting under appalling conditions, would break the back of the Japanese air forces, bleeding them of their most experienced pilots and ultimately driving them from the skies over Guadalcanal.

It is convenient for clarity to divide the ebb and flow of battle into monthly segments.

August 1942
Guadalcanal, considered uninhabitable by the white plantation owners of the area, was about a hundred miles long, and, at its widest point, thirty miles across. Owned by the British for more than a hundred years, it had been seized by the Japanese on May 5, 1942. On August 7, the Allies totally surprised the Japanese by bringing a seventy-six-ship invading force to take Tulagi, Tanam-

bogo, Gavutu, and Guadalcanal islands with overwhelming force. Nimitz had dispatched three of the navy's four remaining aircraft carriers—the *Saratoga*, the *Enterprise*, and the *Wasp*—to provide air cover for landing the men of the 1st Marine Division, Major General Alexander "Archie" Vandegrift commanding. The carriers were commanded by Rear Admiral Frank Jack Fletcher.

A bewildered Japanese radioman on Tulagi sent out this plaintive radio message—"LARGE FORCE OF SHIPS UNKNOWN NUMBER OR TYPES ENTERING SOUND WHAT CAN THEY BE?"—before being obliterated by shellfire from American ships. On Guadalcanal, about 600 Japanese soldiers and 1,500 construction workers fled into the jungle, leaving behind them bowls of warm rice. On Tulagi, 1,500 Japanese soldiers fought to the last man.

Yet Guadalcanal was not secure, and possession of the airfield would hang in the balance for months. The first Marines established a perimeter around the airfield and then began the process of searching out the remaining Japanese. Their efforts would be frustrated by continual Japanese reinforcements being sent to an island slowly transforming itself into a meat grinder for men, planes, and ships.

Even though surprised by the invasion, the Japanese Naval Air Force reacted swiftly. Rear Admiral Yamada Sadayoshi, commanding the 25th Air Flotilla, launched the first of many Japanese attacks from Rabaul—27 Bettys and 18 Zeros. An additional 9 Aichi D3A1s were sent on a one-way mission, the Vals not having the range for a round trip. This attack was typical of the Japanese air war modus operandi—a relatively small number of aircraft, flown by highly skilled crews, sent to make a precision strike against what they hoped was an ill-prepared enemy defense.

But things were changing. The defense was relatively well prepared, thanks to the still-primitive radar sets, but more especially to the efforts of one of the most unusual intelligence-gathering groups in history, the Coastwatchers. The Australian Navy had had the foresight to recruit planters, natives, retired servicemen, and others to hide out on the small islands in the chain and broadcast Japanese naval and air activity as they observed it. The network operated as Chennault's had in China, and, as there, the Coastwatchers were few in number, highly intelligent, and subject to certain death if captured.

On August 7, the Coastwatchers warned Admiral Fletcher of the

inbound bombing raid, and his tough Grumman F4F Wildcats re-
pulsed the onslaught in a dogfight that signaled just how ferocious
the air war over Guadalcanal was going to be. The Japanese lost 2
Zeros, 6 Vals, and 5 Bettys, 13 out of 54 aircraft, a 22 percent loss
rate. The Americans lost a grievous 20 percent—1 SBD and 8 Wildcats out of the 44 aircraft to engage from the *Saratoga* and the *Enterprise.* Thirty aircraft from the *Wasp* attacked the seaplane base
at Tulagi, destroying 19 floatplanes and 2 four-engine Kawanishi
H6K flying boats. It might be said that the battle for Guadalcanal
had been almost won, for these and the next day's losses diminished the Japanese Naval Air Force's appetite for battle and gave the
Americans time to dig in.

One of the Japanese victims was the most famous of their aces,
Flight Officer Sakai Saburo. Sakai, who already had 59 victories,
quickly dispatched a Wildcat and an SBD and then dove on what he
thought was another formation of 8 F4Fs. A hail of machine-gun
bullets from their rear cockpits told him, too late, that they were instead SBDs. His canopy blown off, blinded in one eye, and terribly
wounded, Sakai nonetheless managed to fly his Zero on an epic
four-hour-and-forty-seven-minute flight back to Rabaul. Probably
no other plane nor any other pilot could have pulled it off—low on
fuel, without navigation aids, periodically unconscious, Sakai
showed the true samurai spirit, as he did later, when after a long
convalescence and despite the loss of an eye, he returned to fly,
fight, and raise his victory toll to 64.

Sakai's achievement was all the more heroic in view of the basic
philosophic flaws of the Japanese Air Force. In his 1957 autobiography, *Samurai,* Sakai tells of the harsh discipline he encountered in
training, but it was not until much later that he revealed his resentment of the way the Japanese Naval Air Force discriminated
against noncommissioned officers. Even as a leading ace, Sakai
could be, and was, treated as a servant by a newly commissioned
officer who had never flown a combat mission. This caste system
extended to quarters, food, recreation and even the in-flight
"kokko-bento" box lunches necessary for the Zero's seven-hour
missions. Sakai's resentment is clearly not a personal one; instead
he feels that such unfair treatment vitiated the strength of the service for which he and so many others sacrificed themselves.

A second attack the following day was also beaten off, with 18
Japanese aircraft shot down, but the threat of land-based air su-

premacy gave Admiral Fletcher a crisis of nerves and he pulled his Carrier Task Force out, leaving the Marines without air cover. More than one historian has termed Fletcher's withdrawal "desertion," but Fletcher was aware that his were the only carriers available, and to lose them either to land-based aircraft or the hard-fighting Japanese surface fleet would have been catastrophic.

Fletcher's apprehensions about the threat from the surface fleet were validated on August 9, when Admiral Mikawa Gunichi administered the worst surface naval defeat to the United States since the War of 1812, sending a force led by five heavy cruisers into Savo Bay. Using the brilliant Japanese night-fighting techniques that were to prevail for the next year, Mikawa's ships sank four Allied cruisers and two destroyers. Unaccountably, he did not press on to destroy what should have been his main target, the vulnerable transports still unloading troops and supplies. It was the first of many major Japanese mistakes, some of which bordered on a miraculous snatching of defeat from the jaws of victory, and it stemmed from the apparently universal concern of navy commanders to avoid losing ships no matter what the prize.

A priceless, if uneasy, eleven-day period followed, during which the Marines used the primitive Japanese construction equipment to turn a tamped coral Japanese strip into Henderson Field. The code name for Guadalcanal was "Cactus," and on August 20, the first aircraft of what came to be known as the Cactus Air Force arrived—19 Grumman F4F Wildcat Fighters of VMF-223, led by Major John Smith, and 12 Douglas SBD dive-bombers of VSMB-232, led by Lieutenant Colonel Richard Mangrum. Two days later, Captain Dale D. Brannon brought in elements of the first Army Air Forces unit, the 67th Fighter Squadron. They had only five clapped-out Bell P-400s, export models of the P-39 Airacobra. The P-400 was a very modern-looking aircraft with a tricycle landing gear, a 37-mm cannon mounted in the nose, and the engine mounted behind the pilot. Unable to handle the Zero in air-to-air combat, it excelled in bombing and strafing duties. This small force would be bled down almost to extinction; the pilots flew continuously, and it was soon evident that thirty days was about the maximum time that could be endured given the stress of combat and the unhealthy living conditions.

The growing proficiency and confidence of American pilots was shown by a contest between VMF-223's commander, Smith, and Captain Marion Carl to become the top ace over Guadalcanal. Carl had scored 1 victory at Midway, and quickly scored 4 more at Guadalcanal to become the Marines' first ace. The two men ran neck and neck for weeks, when, tied with 12 each, Carl was shot down. Aided by friendly natives, he managed to get back to the base after five days in the jungle. When he arrived, he found out that by then Smith had 16 victories. Carl jokingly asked that Smith be grounded for five days to give him a chance to catch up, knowing that conditions were far too tough to give anyone a rest. Carl scored 15½ victories on Guadalcanal and another 3 before the war ended, then went on to become a distinguished test pilot, fight in Vietnam, and retire as a major general. Smith ultimately wound up with 19 victories and the Medal of Honor, the latter given to him as much for his brilliant leadership of VFM-223 as for his kills. Smith's squadron would fight with unremitting intensity against the Japanese, and he and his pilots would down 110 enemy aircraft in the fifty-four days before they were at last relieved on October 12.

Even though the Japanese Navy and its air force had reacted quickly to the American invasion, the Japanese Army moved slowly, completely misinterpreting Fletcher's departure. They considered the incident merely a raid by 2,000 troops, who were now abandoned following the disastrous naval battle at Savo Bay, and presumably disorganized and demoralized. The Japanese sent a 1,000-man invasion force led by the arrogant Colonel Ichiki Kiyano, to be landed by what soon became known as the "Tokyo Express." Ichiki proudly radioed notice of his success even as he marched to a defeat as complete as Custer's. Trapped by the 1st Marine Regiment, all of his force was slaughtered and Ichiki committed hari-kari. In the scheme of later battles, the toll was not great—almost 900 Japanese troops lost at the cost of 35 Marines dead—but it was terribly significant, for it was the first clear-cut victory by American troops over the Japanese Army, and dispelled the idea that the Japanese were invincible jungle fighters.

Ichiki's defeat was a more powerful portent than anyone could realize. The Japanese Army would consistently underestimate both the numbers and the fighting power of the Americans, even after suffering several drubbings at their hands. Further, they would ignore Guadalcanal's geography and terrain in their planning. Using ancient maps, the commanding generals repeatedly devised complex maneuvers depending upon widely separated bodies of troops to make simultaneous attacks on the American positions. These called for split-second coordination with naval and air forces, even though Japanese communication systems were totally inadequate and there were shortages of such basic items as watches. Even after experiencing the concentrated firepower of American machine guns and artillery, the attacking forces remained equipped with the light weapons they had used on the red sorghum plains of China.

Belatedly, Admiral Yamamoto was beginning to understand that it would take a full-blown combined operation to retrieve Guadalcanal, and, while mobilizing his Combined Fleet and the Eleventh Air Fleet, ordered Admiral Tanaka Raizo to ferry in troops to the island on his destroyers—the Tokyo Express. The Japanese Navy would display exceptional bravery and skill over the next six months, regularly sending ships down "the Slot," the narrow reach of water that split the Solomon Islands and terminated in "Ironbottom Sound," a forty-five-by-twenty-five-mile body of water so filled with sunken ships that the compass needles of vessels passing over them spun like tops.

Tanaka demonstrated how a single leader can make a difference. His cruisers and destroyers would load up with men and supplies and leave Buin, on Bougainville, in the early afternoon, steaming at 30 knots to arrive off Guadalcanal around midnight, only ten miles from Henderson Field. There Tanaka's ships would throw the supply drums and the troops overboard to be recovered by small boats, lay down fire on Henderson Field and other targets, and speed away. Land-based airpower ruled the seas around Guadalcanal during the day, forcing the Japanese to this piecemeal reinforcement that spelled their ultimate destruction. In his new operation, code named KA, Yamamoto once again showed his penchant for the complex approach, dividing his force into many small commands despite the known problems with communications and intelligence. The fleet, under Admiral Nagumo, consisted of the large carriers Shokaku and Zuikaku, the light carrier Ryujo, 3 battleships, 9 cruisers, 13 destroyers, and no less than 36 submarines—all to cover a troop reinforcement. A fleet carrier force, commanded by Vice Admiral Kondo Nobukate, and consisting of the veteran large carriers Shokaku and Zuikaku, 2 battleships, and 2 cruisers, sailed to the waters northeast of the Solomons. A smaller force under Admiral Hara Chuichi was intended to seduce Fletcher into an attack, which would be followed by a riposte from the Shokaku and the Zuikaku. Hara's force included transports and was escorted by the heavy cruiser Tone—whose seaplane had missed the American carriers at Midway—and the light carrier *Ryujo*.

Hara's detachment was caught east of Bougainville Island by a Navy Catalina patrol plane, and Fletcher took the bait, sending 30 Dauntlesses and 8 Avengers against *Ryujo*. The small carrier was masterfully conned, running in tight circles to avoid damage from the dive-bombers, but was caught by torpedoes from the Avengers boring in from both sides simultaneously. Gutted by flames, the *Ryujo* drifted for seven hours before sinking.

Nagumo ordered the counterstroke from the *Shokaku* and the *Zuikaku*, sending two waves totaling about 60 aircraft into the towering cumulus clouds covering the American fleet—and into the guns of the 50 Grumman F4Fs Fletcher had on Combat Air Patrol.

The resulting battle was inconclusive. Twenty-four aircraft of the attacking force broke through, scoring hits on the *Enterprise*, while Fletcher's forces failed to find the Japanese carriers but sunk a seaplane carrier, the *Chitose*. On balance, it was a U.S. victory by a slender margin in terms of ships, serving notice to the Japanese that reinforcing Guadalcanal was going to be bitterly contested no matter how powerful the naval escorts.

September 1942
The battle for Guadalcanal moved from crisis to crisis like a soap opera. The veteran carrier *Saratoga* was torpedoed by the submarine *I-26* on August 31, and Guadalcanal's air cover was left to the slender forces on Henderson Field and the limited capability of a patched-up *Enterprise*. Henderson Field was now a 3,800-foot strip, 1,000 feet of which were covered by the pierced steel planking known as Marston mat. The runway ran roughly northeast to southwest in the middle of a plain of razor-sharp kunai grass; one pilot saltily described it as the only place in the world where you could be up to your ass in mud while having dust blown in your face. The 1st Marine Division was dug in around the field perimeter, and from the field's center it was only two and a half miles to the enemy in any direction.

The pilots fought and slept in the clothes they'd flown in with, and lived with the rest of the troops on a diet of dehydrated potatoes, canned hash, and captured Japanese rice. Spam was a treat; there was no liquor and only Japanese cigarettes. Everyone lived in tents in the coconut groves, most without floors, many without beds, and all equally disturbed by the nightly visitations of "Washing Machine Charlie," the small single-engine float biplanes that the Japanese used in harassment tactics. ("Louie the Louse" was a larger, twin engine aircraft that came over less regularly.) These didn't offer the danger comparable to the naval bombardments, but they prevented sleep for the exhausted Americans.

Yet the pilots flew mission after mission, landing to rearm, refuel, and take off again; the mechanics worked night and day to patch up the aircraft. Everyone was beset by malaria and dysentery, and almost everyone was young—the enlisted men averaging about nineteen years in age, the pilots, twenty-one. For most, it was their first experience in the service, in the South Pacific, and in combat. They fought well and too many died—the attrition rate for the Marine squadrons at Henderson was 57 percent for the first twenty-five days of combat. These were the Americans that the ruling military clique in Japan had considered to be too soft to fight.

The nights were endless, with shellfire from artillery and ships, bombs from Bettys, and annoyance from Louie the Louse. The days were long. American offensive flights began soon after dawn, with the Marine SBDs and the army Bell P-400s bombing and strafing. Daily combat action began for the bulk of the fighters about 1130, and lasted until almost dark. The Japanese bombers' arrival would be heralded by reports from the Coastwatchers, then verified by the radars, which could pick up incoming Bettys about 125 miles out. This gave the Grummans ample time to get to altitude, climbing in two-plane sections grouped into four-plane divisions. They would cruise about 5,000 feet above the passé V-formation of Bettys, then fly on the opposite course until they could do either a direct overhead pass or a high side attack, in either case avoiding defensive fire from the Bettys' 20-mm tail cannon. If the Bettys were escorted by Zeros—or Zekes, as they were code-named in July 1942—the Marine pilots would dive through the formation shooting, then head either for cloud cover or back to Henderson. If, as often happened, there were no Zeros, the Grummans would attack until fuel or ammunition was exhausted, trying to flame the Bettys' vulnerable wing-root fuel tanks.

The almost awesome respect in which the Mitsubishi A6M Zero had been held since Pearl Harbor slowly began to fade. After a month of close encounters, it was apparent that while one F4F could not dogfight with a Zero successfully, two F4Fs, working together using the famous Thach weave, could handle four or five Zeros. (Named after Lieutenant Commander John S. "Jimmy" Thach, a seven-victory ace, the maneuver called for a pair of Wildcats to fly in a widespread formation. When a Zero attacked, the two Wildcats banked toward each other; if the Zero followed his target, it led him inevitably into the guns of the other Wildcat.)

The Zeros were lightly built, their fuselages skinned with almost paper-thin duralumin, their wings covered with a gauge only slightly heavier. The pilot's seat was not armored, nor were the three fuel tanks self-sealing. Consequently, the Zero could absorb only a few seconds' burst from the F4F's six .50-inch machine guns without exploding, while the tanklike Grummans could take an endless hammering from the Zero's armament (two small 7.7-mm machine guns and two slow-firing 20-mm cannon) and keep on flying. And though the A6M was slightly faster in level flight, it could not follow the Wildcat in a turning dive. At speeds above 360 miles per hour, the Zero's ailerons stiffened to the point of immovability. A diving Grumman at speed could escape by making a sharp turn that the normally more maneuverable Zero could not follow. The Zeros were further hampered by the weight of the fuel they carried for the long round trip; unlike the practice in all other air forces, they did not usually jettison their belly tanks when engaging in combat.

The Japanese had thrown two air flotillas into battle—the 25th and 26th, of the Eleventh Air Fleet. Commanded by the one-armed Vice Admiral Tsukahara Nishizo, the units were under strength, with only 36 Bettys, 46 Zeros (of which only 30 had the range to reach Guadalcanal), 6 Val dive-bombers, and 10 Kawanishi H6K flying boats. The Kawanishis, code-named Mavis, were elegant four-engine aircraft not unlike the American Sikorsky S-42, and were used both as patrol plane and bomber.

Yet Tsukahara's strength was greater than the Americans', whose force had declined to a low of only 11 flyable F4Fs on September 11. Reinforcements came shortly thereafter but the numbers remained small for a crucial campaign.

The Japanese Army and Navy remained at odds. Although Yamamoto had committed most of the Combined Fleet to retrieve the situation on Guadalcanal, the army had not yet divined that there were now 17,000 Americans ashore, and sent a force of 5,000 men under Major General Kawaguchi Kiyotake to retake the island. Kawaguchi, like Yamamoto, was partial to elaborate plans. He divided his small force into three elements and proceeded with a frontal attack that became known as the "Battle of Bloody Ridge," from the blood of six hundred Japanese soldiers drenching the high ground at the jungle's edge. Forty Marines died defending the position. Three of the USAAF's much-maligned Bell P-400s did a magnificent job of strafing the enemy, earning praise from the Marines, no easy task.

The worst was not over for Kawaguchi, who had been so confident of success that he had left his food supplies behind, certain that he would feast on the Marine bounty at Henderson Field. The week-long starvation trek back through the jungle cost him more than half his force.

Japanese submarines avenged this defeat on September 15, the *I-16* sinking the *Wasp*, and the *I-19* holing the battleship *North Carolina* and the destroyer *O'Brien*, which later sank. This left the Americans more vulnerable than they had been since Pearl Harbor, for there was only one carrier in the area, the *Hornet*, from which Doolittle's raid had been launched so few months—and such a long time—before.

In compensation, aircraft from the wounded *Saratoga* and elsewhere had been ferried to Henderson Field, where Brigadier General Roy Geiger, a squadron commander in World War I in France, a veteran of the invasion of Nicaragua in 1933, and a prototypical Marine, was now commanding the Cactus Air Force. Geiger was fifty-seven years old, but soon demonstrated that he was a hands-on commander by having a 1,000-pound bomb loaded on an SBD and dropping it on an enemy troop concentration.

September ended as it had begun, with the outcome of the battle balanced on the razor edge of a minimum of airpower, and airpower hinging in turn on the strength of the Marine perimeter. The Japanese continued to reinforce the island via the Tokyo Express, but bigger things were planned.

October 1942
The Japanese High Command now decided that Guadalcanal must be taken at whatever cost and, most significantly, that Henderson Field had to be captured and the defending air forces destroyed. The army began to strip units from the forces fighting MacArthur's troops in New Guinea. As was apparently their custom, they even set the date for the American surrender ceremony—October 21, 1942. (They might not have continued to underestimate American fighting power if they had known of the saga of VMF-224's Lieu-

tenant Richard R. Amerine, who had bailed out of a Wildcat thirty miles behind Japanese lines. It took him six days to get back to base; in the process he had to kill four Japanese soldiers in hand-to-hand combat.) General Hyakutake Harukichi planned to use two infantry divisions, heavily supplied with artillery and tanks, to defeat the 7,500 Americans he estimated to be on the island. It is difficult to imagine now that Japanese intelligence could have been so faulty as to miss by 12,000 the actual number of troops opposing them.

Rabaul had been reinforced to have 180 aircraft, and new bases were built at Buin in southern Bougainville and at Buka in the northern Solomons. These reduced the flying time to Guadalcanal, giving the 11th Air Flotilla much more time over target. Yamamoto dedicated the Combined Fleet to escorting Hyakutake's forces, and for the first time assigned battleships to an artillery support role. His combined fleet sailed from Truk with 5 carriers, 5 battleships, 14 cruisers, 44 destroyers, and a host of auxiliaries.

On Guadalcanal, General Geiger's Cactus Air Force received desperately needed reinforcements on October 5, when 20 new F4F-4s of VMF-121 were flown off the escort carrier *Copahee*; two days later, the USAAF 339th Fighter Squadron arrived with 11 Bell P-39 Airacobras. The executive officer of VMF-121 was twenty-seven-year-old Captain Joe Foss, who would begin his phenomenal scoring streak on October 13; by October 25, he would raise his total to 16. Foss ultimately scored 26 victories, tying Captain Eddie Rickenbacker's World War I record. He would receive the Medal of Honor and then go on to a distinguished political career as governor of South Dakota.

On October 13, the Japanese unleashed two air attacks, the first by 27 Bettys and 18 Zekes, the second by 18 Bettys and 18 Zekes. These put the runway at Henderson Field out of action, destroyed several aircraft on the ground, and set fire to 5,000 gallons of precious gasoline. At the same time, Hyakutake's 150-mm cannons began dropping shells on the runway. The rate of fire was so slow the Marines thought only one weapon was involved; they quickly dubbed it "Pistol Pete."

All this was but a prelude. At 0138, Louie the Louse arrived, dropping a red flare over the west end of the runway, a white one in the center and a green one on the east end. It was a signal to the battleships *Haruna* and *Kongo* in Ironbottom Sound. For the next hour, their 14-inch guns pumped 918 shells into Henderson in rippling cascades of explosions that would have warmed the hearts of big-gun admirals from Nelson to Yamamoto. The 293 high-explosive shells did most of the damage with their concussions; the remaining armor-piercing shells tore big holes into whatever they hit, but lacked blast effect. The shelling was devastating, for it would have taken 900 Bettys, thirty-seven times the number in the typical raid, to deliver an equivalent amount of ordnance, and the guns were far more accurate than the bombers could ever have been.

All gasoline supplies were destroyed. The barrage knocked out all the Avengers, 32 out of 39 SBDS, and left only 6 P-400s. Fortunately, only 12 of the 41 F4Fs were blown up, primarily because they were located on a tiny auxiliary airstrip, Fighter One, that had been hacked out of the coconut grove.

The runway had been heavily hit; repair facilities were destroyed, the radio put out of action, and even the pagodalike control tower toppled. The next night, two cruisers, the *Chokai* and the *Kinugasa*, hit Henderson again with 752 eight-inch shells. These did not have the destructive power of the fourteen-inch monsters but were sufficient to destroy almost everything missed the night before.

The suppression was almost complete. Any American pilot able to taxi around the shell holes to take off could see as soon as he was airborne the Japanese transports unloading troops and supplies at Tassafaronga. Less than a dozen miles from Henderson Field, the transports disgorged enough troops to allow General Hyakutake to build his forces to 20,000, including a company of tanks and lots of heavy artillery.

The Japanese had achieved their primary objective, rendering Henderson Field impotent. General Hyakutake then proceeded to throw his advantage away by making a series of ill-coordinated frontal attacks on Marine positions, now supplemented by the army's 164th Infantry Division. The Japanese light-division tactics that had worked well in China and elsewhere melted away in the face of the American machine-gun, mortar, and semiautomatic-rifle fire. Banzai charges were terrifying to experience, but they could not overcome the firepower, and Hyakutake had to repeat his predecessor Kawaguchi's humiliating retreat, taking his beaten, starving troops back through the jungle to the bases where they started, and postponing the surrender ceremony once again.

Beaten but unbowed, Hyakutake next set the stage for a demonstration that Billy Mitchell would have relished. He called for

12,000 more men to reinforce the 15,000 he had remaining. They would be brought to Guadalcanal the following month in a great transport armada—and American airpower would be waiting.

THE BATTLE OF SANTA CRUZ

The balance of effort now shifted back to the carriers. Admiral Nagumo, with the *Shokaku*, the *Zuikaku*, the *Zuiho*, and the *Junyo*, sailed to sink the *Hornet*, which they believed to be the only U.S. carrier remaining in the area. Unknown to Nagumo, the *Hornet* had been rejoined by the *Enterprise*, and reinforced as well by the new battleship *South Dakota*, which bristled with twenty of the latest quadruple-mounted 40-mm Bofors antiaircraft guns, true plane killers.

The American carriers, under Admiral Thomas "Fighting Tom" Kincaid, drew first blood on October 26, when he threw 16 SBDs from the *Enterprise* against the *Zuiho*. Two scouting SBDs, one flown by Lieutenant Stockton Birney Strong, and the other by Ensign Charles B. Irvine, sighted the light carrier and dove on it at 0840. A 500-pound bomb blew a huge hole in the *Zuiho*'s flight deck, rendering it unable to recover aircraft, but, undaunted, still able to launch 9 Zeros for the next strike.

Nagumo's strike of 67 aircraft was commanded by Lieutenant Commander Seki Mamoru, the best dive-bomber pilot in the Pacific, leading a formation of 22 Vals and 18 Kate torpedo planes, escorted by 27 Zeros. It was a formidable force, made much more so by the expertise of its crews, most of them veterans of Pearl Harbor and Midway.

The American fleet was about to have a bad day, in large part due to inexpert work by the air controllers aboard the *Enterprise* and the *Hornet*. The first mistake was positioning the Combat Air Patrol of Wildcats too low to intercept the incoming Vals. The second, and even worse error, was a breakdown in radio communications; the controllers gave the pilots bearings to their targets relative to the direction of the target from the ship—worse than useless information.

The *Enterprise* was spared for the moment by taking advantage of a providential rain squall. The Japanese launched a well-coordinated attack on the *Hornet*, the Vals peeling off in precise seven-second intervals as the Kates sped in from all quarters. The first two dive-bombers missed the *Hornet*, but the third—Seki's aircraft—was hit by flak and plunged into the flight deck, Seki's bombs setting off fires in the hangar. Three more bombs and two torpedoes set the *Hornet* afire. Destroyers were dispatched to take her under tow while the fires were fought.

Even as the *Hornet* burned, her aircraft were savaging the *Shokaku*. Lieutenant James E. "Moe" Vose took 11 SBDs directly down on Nagumo's flagship, planting four 1,000-pound bombs in her flight deck. Fortunately for Nagumo, all aircraft had been launched, and the *Shokaku* didn't suffer the secondary explosions that had ravaged the *Hornet*. Unable to recover her aircraft, the *Shokaku* left to be repaired, out of the war for nine months.

A second strike of 78 planes—12 Kates, 38 Vals, and 28 Zeros—next attacked the *Enterprise* and the *South Dakota*. After taking severe losses, the planes broke through the Combat Air Patrol and the antiaircraft fire to hit the *"Big E"* three times and put a bomb into the *South Dakota*'s number-one turret. The antiaircraft cruiser *San Juan* was also hit. In the fight, Lieutenant Stanley W. "Swede" Vejtasa of VF-10, the Grim Reapers, lived up to the squadron name by becoming an instant ace. Vejtasa shot down 2 dive-bombers and 5 torpedo planes, including the Kate flown by the Japanese strike leader, the famous Lieutenant Commander Murata Shigeharu.

Vejtasa couldn't stop all the Kates, however, and it remained for the *Enterprise*'s skipper, Captain Osborne B. Hardison, to skillfully steer clear of repeated torpedo attacks. Just as 4 of the Kates had been shot down and the rest driven off, their torpedoes expended, 18 Vals dropped out of the sky on the *Enterprise* and the *South Dakota*. Eight were shot down, including the one flown by the flight leader, Lieutenant Yamaguchi Maseo, but single hits were scored on the *Enterprise*, the *South Dakota*, and the *San Juan*.

Damage-control parties on the *Enterprise* showed the skill gained by experience, and despite heavy submarine attacks, which sank a destroyer and damaged a cruiser, the carrier was able to begin recovering aircraft just after noon. The air was filled with returning planes from both the *Hornet* and the *Enterprise*, and suddenly the entire focus of the battle shifted to a single man, Lieutenant Robin M. Lindsey, who was the landing-signal officer. With incredible skill, Lindsey managed to land 95 aircraft on the *Enterprise* before a lack of deck area forced him to halt operations. He had been ordered to stop long before, but aware of his skill and of the need, he disobeyed and continued to bring planes in. As it was, 54 planes had to ditch in the ocean.

The fires on the *Hornet* had been almost contained, and she was under tow when another attack from the *Zuikaku*'s Kates forced her to be abandoned again around 1400. American destroyers put sixteen torpedoes into her, but she drifted on, a burning commentary on the quality of American torpedoes at the time. She was sunk eight hours later by four Japanese torpedoes. There were many who thought—and some still do—that the *Hornet*'s abandonment was shameful, and that her ultimate destruction as a practice target for the Japanese was unworthy of all the achievements in her short, intense life.

The Battle of Santa Cruz was a tactical victory for the Japanese, having sunk the *Hornet* while suffering damage to only two of their carriers. The United States had entered the war with seven carriers. Four had since been sunk by the Japanese, and only one remained in the Pacific, the damaged *Enterprise*.

The United States had also lost 74 planes and 316 officers and men in the engagement. Nagumo had lost 100 planes, further draining his rapidly diminishing pool of experienced pilots.

The cold statistics do not tell the full story, however, for the U.S. fleet was growing stronger every day and was able to replace ships, planes, and pilots on a prodigious scale. In contrast, the Combined Fleet was severely weakened, without immediate prospect of replenishment, and the pride of the Imperial Japanese Navy, its fighter and bomber crews, was being consumed in a fatal war of attrition. The damage to the two large carriers was severe; they would not return to battle for nineteen fateful months, and then in a virtual kamikaze role.

With both navies' carrier task forces weakened to the danger point, the principal air combat shifted back to land-based forces. Henderson Field, after reaching another low point on October 26, when the Cactus Air Force was reduced to 30 fighters, was being steadily reinforced. By the end of October, it became possible for the first time to rotate pilots out for rest. Far too many, however, had already flown their last missions, consumed in the sky over Guadalcanal. Of the eleven Medals of Honor won by Marine pilots during World War II, five were won on Guadalcanal.

NOVEMBER 1942

The recidivistic Japanese High Command set about mounting another mid-month major air, land, and sea attack on Guadalcanal. The Western image of the highly disciplined Japanese was faulty. The Japanese tolerated insubordination from junior officers—*gekokujo*, as it was called—to a degree unheard of in Allied armies. In effect, junior officers objected to decisions of senior officers, particularly if they were not radical enough, and frequently made the decisions themselves, putting forth staff papers and orders to be signed that the senior officers didn't dare refuse, for fear of being considered either cowardly or lacking in patriotism. Colonel Tsuji Masanobu was one of the most insanely nationalistic practitioners of *gekokujo*, and he has been called the Rasputin of the Japanese military. It was Tsuji whose arguments drove the Imperial Japanese Army into a piecemeal commitment of its forces in Guadalcanal, where they were serially ground down by the hard-pressed American defenders.

Bowing to Tsuji's clamor, the Japanese next added the army's 38th Division strength to the troops already ashore, supported once again by the firepower of the Combined Fleet. The first weeks in November passed in the usual fashion, with the Tokyo Express spiriting in small quantities of troops and supplies at night, while powerful elements of the Combined Fleet circled like Sumo wrestlers at a distance.

THE BATTLE OF GUADALCANAL

Guadalcanal's ultimate fate was decided in the series of land, sea, and air battles that began on November 12, 1942. In numbers of ships, the odds were very uneven. To oppose a reported Japanese force of 2 carriers, 4 battleships, 5 heavy cruisers, and 30 destroyers, Admiral Halsey could muster only 5 cruisers and 12 destroyers. Just as work had been rushed on the *Yorktown* before the Battle of Midway, repairs were accelerated on the *Enterprise*, and it sortied from Noumea, New Caledonia, on November 11, accompanied by 3 cruisers and 6 destroyers. The *Enterprise*'s forward elevator had been damaged, and it was left as it was—mechanics were afraid that if they lowered it, it would not go back up, and thus make the flight deck useless.

On November 12, two Japanese battleships, the *Hiei* and the *Kirishima*, surprised a small American fleet of 2 heavy cruisers, 2 light cruisers, and 4 destroyers. The Japanese immediately sank a light cruiser and 2 destroyers, but the American ships attacked with such fury that the Japanese admiral commanding, Abe Hiroaki, decided to retire only twenty-four minutes after the battle had started. The next morning, the submarine *I-26* sent a torpedo into the cruiser *Juneau*, sinking it with 700 casualties, among them the five Sullivan brothers.

Once again the Japanese had won a tactical victory while losing their strategic goal, the suppression of Henderson Field. Nor was the battle quite over. At first light, the *Hiei*, Abe's flagship, had been spotted trying to crawl painfully away to safety. Admiral Kinkaid, still 280 miles away on the *Enterprise*, had had the foresight to dispatch eight torpedo-armed Grumman Avengers to Henderson Field. Led by Lieutenant Al Coffin, they arrived around 1100 and began an immediate attack on the *Hiei*. Splitting his formation into two units of four, Coffin used "anvil tactics" to attack from both sides, dropping the torpedoes from a thousand-yard range at 170 knots airspeed, then banking away for the deck. Three hits were claimed, and the *Hiei* lay dead in the water, rudderless, an inert target for a daylong series of bombing and torpedo attacks. By nightfall, fires raged uncontrolled throughout the ship, where almost 500 members of the crew had already perished. Abe eventually scuttled his ship to avoid its capture. It was the first Japanese battleship to be sunk by airpower; it would not be the last.

The two adversaries continued to exchange blows as, bloody but unbowed, the Japanese sent in heavy cruisers to bombard Henderson Field while Admiral Tanaka drew close with his fleet of eleven transports escorted by a dozen destroyers. The 8-inch guns of the cruisers could not do the job the battleships' 14-inchers might have, and only a handful of aircraft were destroyed. The next morning, torpedo planes from Henderson Field caught the cruisers on their way home and put two torpedoes into the *Kinugasa*, which was sunk by planes from the *Enterprise* a few hours later.

Tanaka's force sailed on down the Slot. The usual lack of communications caused Tanaka to assume that the cruiser attack had in fact knocked out airpower on Henderson Field. Shortly after noon, however, the Cactus Air Force, reinforced by the *Enterprise*'s air group, arrived on the scene in force, and began systematically to slaughter Tanaka's ships. Seven transports were sunk and four were forced to beach themselves at the Tassafaronga beachhead. The next day, Avengers from Henderson Field shuttle-bombed them with antipersonnel bombs dubbed "Molotov breadbaskets," killing the troops as they struggled down the rope ladders and burning the supplies within the ships. Of the 10,000 Japanese soldiers in the transport, only 4,000 made it to what they now called "the Island of Death." (The Japanese Army was to refer to many islands by the same term.) Many of the remaining 6,000 were rescued by destroyers, but many others drowned. Yamamoto's mammoth effort had landed only a trivial amount of supplies: 260 cases of ammunition and 1,500 bags of rice.

There was one last bitter flurry of activity when the Japanese sent their bombardment force, including the *Kirishima*, to attack Henderson Field again. This time they were intercepted by two battleships, the *Washington* and the *South Dakota*. In the last battleship-versus-battleship action of the war—and almost certainly in history—the Americans sank the *Kirishima* and a destroyer, at the cost of three of their own destroyers sunk.

Admiral Halsey later correctly assessed the situation when he noted that until November 15, 1942, the enemy advanced at its will; from then on, it retreated at the Allies'.

Tanaka continued to slip in reinforcements with his destroyers and, with a brilliant torpedo attack, administered a stinging defeat to a U.S. cruiser force in the Battle of Tassafaronga at the end of November. It was one of the last Japanese victories at Guadalcanal.

DECEMBER TO FEBRUARY

General Tojo Hideki, the Prime Minister, ordered the evacuation of Guadalcanal on January 4, 1943. It was a wise decision, for American strength was growing rapidly. After four months of the most bitter fighting in history, the battered 1st Marine Division was relieved, and the U.S. Army assumed the predominant ground-fighting role. In early December, Henderson Field had almost 200 aircraft, including 71 Wildcats and 17 of the new Lockheed P-38s, the beautiful twin-engine fighter that was so well suited to the Pacific theater. In the next few weeks, dozens of squadrons flew into Henderson, which was being rapidly improved. The Japanese Naval Air Force, while not reinforced on a similar scale, was still capable of minor offensive activity, and on January 31, 9 Bettys sank the heavy cruiser *Chicago* with torpedoes.

One of the anomalies of the war was that Japan was so far ahead of the United States in the design of its torpedoes and its bombs. The Japanese Type 93 torpedo, nicknamed "Long Lance" because of its 40,000-yard range, was superior to those of every other nation. Powered by liquid oxygen, the Long Lance had over twice the range of comparable American and British torpedoes and was equipped with a far more reliable fighting system. In a similar way, it was not until late 1943 that the United States was able to obtain bombs with explosive power equal to those used by the Japanese.

Tanaka's destroyers continued to come down the Slot, but, unknown to the Americans, their task was now evacuation rather than resupply. Certainly not a victory, it was perhaps a moderate deliverance, for the destroyers were able to evacuate more than 11,000 Japanese troops from the island without the Americans being aware of it. In the months to come, Japanese troops would be left to die on island after island of what had been intended as an "impermeable barrier" to American attack. By February 9, Lieutenant General Alexander M. Patch, the army commander, was able to wire Halsey that "TOKYO EXPRESS NO LONGER HAS TERMINUS ON GUADALCANAL."

The cost to both sides had been terrible. Each had lost 24 combatant vessels, including 2 Japanese battleships and 2 American carriers, but not including transports, patrol boats, and similar auxiliaries. The Japanese lost 14,800 killed or missing, 9,000 dead from disease, and 1,000 captured, most of the latter either wounded or too ill to commit suicide. The Americans lost 1,600 killed. Estimates of plane losses are more difficult to assess, but the combined total of Japanese land- and carrier-based aircraft lost may have been as high as 900 aircraft. Because Japanese bombers had relatively large crews—the Betty required seven men—also lost were more than 2,400 irreplaceable pilots, navigators, radiomen, and gunners. The Cactus Air Force lost 101 planes, and the U.S. carriers a similar number.

GUADALCANAL: CAUSE AND EFFECT

Guadalcanal demonstrated that air, sea, and land power were no longer just complementary, but inextricably intertwined. It was also an incontrovertible signal to the Japanese leaders that the

United States was not going to seek a negotiated peace; instead, it was going to bring the full weight of its enormous resources to bear.

There would be many bitter battles after Guadalcanal, but none where the issue was in doubt. For the next two years, Japan would suffer one disaster after another, an attenuated humiliation that was without parallel in history, and for the citizens of a nation that had prided itself on never losing a war, a period of almost ingenuous incredulity. The American strength grew so quickly and so formidably that it was able to impose its will wherever it chose, and further, was able to do so at minimum human cost to itself. As in Europe, the United States elected to fight the war on its own terms, substituting firepower for manpower on a scale undreamed of, to minimize casualties.

There would still be grievous losses, for as part of his Field Service Code, the Japanese soldier had sworn not to be taken alive. To use a term from a later era, the soldiers were continuously brainwashed to believe that death in battle would ensure their being eternally honored. This was a curious extension of the traditional samurai concept of death rather than surrender; in feudal Japan, it was honorable for the defeated leader of a band of warriors to take his life, but this did not extend to his followers, who were presumably too low-caste (or perhaps too sensible) for the honor. But both officers and men of the Japanese armed forces took it seriously, and later in the war, as on Saipan, they would include indigenous populations in the final sacrifice.

THE LONG, HARD ROAD TO TOKYO BAY

The future of the air campaign had been written in the skies over the eastern Solomons. The United States would enlarge the dimensions of its air superiority at an increasing tempo until it achieved air supremacy, demonstrated over the burning cities of Japan and given the ultimate confirmation in the 492 aircraft flyover on September 2, 1945, as the surrender was being signed on the USS *Missouri*.

In many respects, after Guadalcanal it was a totally new war. Over the next three years, America would vastly expand the land-based Army Air Forces, field fleets of new aircraft carriers, and produce hundreds of thousands of aircraft, the majority of them new types not seen before in battle. In response, the Japanese would launch some new carriers as well, and introduce some new combat planes, but in pathetically smaller numbers. For the most part, the Japanese Army and Navy would fight the remainder of the war with updated versions of the Zeros, Oscars, Bettys, and Kates with which it started, and suffer terribly without the veteran pilots upon which its strategy had depended.

While the Battle of Guadalcanal had not of itself settled the question of air supremacy in the Pacific, the great production and training capability of the United States had. As the war moved relentlessly closer to the home islands, the Japanese attempted to overcome their inadequacies in planning and matériel with what became known to the West as kamikaze tactics. Frightening to experience and deadly when successful, they were really only signals of Japan's desperation and not a substitute for effective armed forces.

In the grand move to establish a defensive bastion encircling half the Pacific, the Imperial High Command never for a moment imagined that the Americans would gain such sea and air superiority that they could choose to bypass the Japanese island garrisons, leaving them to wither on the vine. Yet by the fall of 1943, less than two years after Pearl Harbor, the United States began island-hopping. Although the ultimate object was always the invasion of Japan, it transpired that securing island air bases for the United States Army Air Forces would prove to be enough. But island-hopping was a year away; in the meantime, Tasks II and III had to be addressed.

TASK II AND BEYOND—THE GREEN HELL OF NEW GUINEA

Just as Admiral Nimitz had been preempted by the Japanese Army's construction of an airfield on Guadalcanal, so was General MacArthur caught out by the Japanese push to take Port Moresby and the rest of New Guinea, beginning July 22, 1942.

The Japanese Army, convinced that it could not depend upon naval support, decided to conquer the Papuan Peninsula and Port Moresby by the most difficult possible route—across the Owen Stanley Mountains, which combined extremely difficult terrain with an almost impenetrable jungle. General Hyakutake Harukichi, who would later be defeated on Guadalcanal, directed that the crack South Sea Detachment, 16,000 of the best Japanese troops, be landed at Buna. From there, with 1,000 native bearers, they were to push across the Kokoda Trail, which ran a hundred crooked miles to Port Moresby. Led by Major General Horii Tomi-taro, the Japanese brushed back the weak Australian defending forces and for weeks made good progress, primarily because their sea-lanes were secure. Lack of food, medical supplies, and the dif-ficult terrain wore them down, however, and as they progressed along the tortuous Kokoda Trail, it became a cemetery for them. Australian resistance, backed by an increasingly powerful ground-attack air force, bled them down. With many already ill from de-liberately tainted food the Australians had allowed them to capture, the retreating Japanese soldiers ate insects, leaves, bark, earth, and ultimately, their dead comrades, as cannibalism was forced upon them. Falling by the wayside meant death, and the trail was thickly marked with the skeletons of Japanese soldiers. Before the campaign was over, thousands would die, many more of star-vation and disease than from bullets.

The collapse of the Japanese system was simultaneous with the growth of American airpower, now gathering strength and experi-ence from every campaign. Even before the jungle joined in Japan's long and bitter defeat, the air war's new dimension was heralded by the arrival of a great leader. Lieutenant General George Churchill Kenney, United States Army Air Forces, was assigned to replace Lieutenant General George H. Brett, whom General MacArthur blamed for the USAAF's alleged lack of discipline and fighting spirit. (Curiously, however, MacArthur's headquarters praised the airmen's role in fighting as infantry on Bataan after their planes had been destroyed.)

Kenney, short, affable, and determined, was a perfect choice. He had shot down two planes during World War I and had served in at-taché jobs in Europe, which allowed him to make many recom-mendations for improvements to U.S. aircraft prior to its entry into World War II. Selected by General Marshall to take over the Allied Air Forces in the southwest Pacific, Kenney's energy, practical bent, and leadership would in short order revolutionize army airpower. A gifted leader who went right to the troops to find out what the difficulties really were, he was not only able to stand up to MacArthur, but also to inspire confidence in him. Perhaps more important, given the fate of many others, Kenney had the tough-talking ability to intimidate Brigadier General Richard Sutherland, who reveled in playing a Martin Bormann role as MacArthur's Chief of Staff.

Upon arrival, Kenney found a solid basis for MacArthur's complaints, for his new command was disorganized to the point of fragmentation. Australian, New Zealand, and American crew members were assigned to fly together on a random basis, and attacks were carried out almost informally, without the usual precise orders prescribed by USAAF procedures. The result was that only a few aircraft at a time went on raids, and then only in loose formation. Further, Kenney discovered that his crews mistakenly thought that a single machine-gun bullet in a bomb would result in instant detonation; as a result, they had immediately jettisoned their bombs upon the approach of an enemy fighter. In short, they were as ineffective as the "boulevard shock troops" MacArthur had complained about.

With the foresight of a good commander, Kenney had sent some able leaders on ahead of him. Brigadier General Kenneth M. Walker was an experienced bomber commander who had been one of the small group who created the Air War Plan by which the USAAF was fighting the war. (Walker would lose his life on January 5, 1943, leading an attack on Rabaul.) Brigadier General Ennis C. Whitehead was a veteran fighter commander who eventually became Kenney's deputy commander for the Fifth Air Force, which was formed on September 2, 1942. Both men would serve Kenney well.

Kenney's charter had been to organize existing forces into a competent defense of Australia and to organize a new air force, the Fifth, to undertake offensive operations. In new-broom tradition, Kenney ruthlessly shook up his command, sending home people he considered too tired or insufficiently aggressive and replacing them with younger men who wanted to fight. He knew how to delegate; if an officer showed initiative, Kenney gave him the go-ahead, and backed him up even if mistakes were made. One of his great protégés was the famous "Pappy" Gunn. Major Paul I. Gunn had come to the Philippines with his wife and four children in 1939. During the Japanese invasion, he turned the small Beechcraft D-18s of the Philippine Air Lines into a vital component of MacArthur's defenses, operating his planes in secret out of Grace Park Cemetery near Manila. He flew the little Beechcraft through the heart of Japanese defenses, delivering personnel and parts, and occasionally acting as navigation ship for overwater flights by fighters.

Gunn's unorthodox field modifications became legendary. The first was performed in New Guinea on the Douglas A-20 Havoc. The Havoc was a handsome twin-engine light bomber, armed with four forward-firing .30-inch machine guns, but too short-ranged to be useful in New Guinea. Using an intuitive approach that defied conventional engineering inhibitions, Gunn added four .50-inch guns to the nose and installed two huge fuel tanks in the bomb bay. The A-20 was converted on the spot to a fearsome long-range weapon, one that helped the Fifth Air Force secure an early and undisputed mastery of the air over the Papuan Peninsula.

A longtime specialist in attack aviation, Kenney fostered the concept of skip bombing, which was to be so destructive to the Japanese merchant marine, as well as the use of "parafrag" bombs, parachute-retarded antipersonnel fragmentation bombs that permitted low-level drops.

Kenney was infuriated by the low in-commission rate of his most potent weapon, the Boeing B-17; more than half were out for lack of engines or tail wheels alone. He ordered an immediate stand-down on all bomber flying and instituted a crash maintenance program so that sufficient B-17s would be able to make an attack on the Japanese air base at Vunakanau on August 7, 1942, coincident with the landings on Guadalcanal. An initial force of 20 B-17s was intended to fly from Australia, refuel at Port Moresby, then bomb its target near Rabaul. Only 16 got off, and of these only 13 made it to the target area, where one was shot down. The Japanese had 150 aircraft lined up wing-to-wing, and intercepted radio reports indicated that many had been destroyed on the ground. But even more important than the harm done to the Japanese was the good done to American morale. Kenney had proved that they were capable of striking out, reversing a process of defeat that had begun on December 7, 1941.

The air superiority Kenney gradually obtained over New Guinea was initially a tenuous one, for the Japanese, preoccupied as they were by Guadalcanal, still had more than 100 aircraft available at Rabaul. Yet they rarely intruded over New Guinea, where Kenney was able to begin an aerial resupply service that materially affected the outcome of the land campaign.

As Australian and American troops drove the beleaguered Japanese forces back, Kenney's Douglas C-47s, the redoubtable Gooney Birds, ferried in tons of supplies to forward detachments. Kenney's transports also flew the sick and wounded out. The army's 32nd Division had more than 10,000 casualties during the campaign; of these only 700 died, thanks in large part to their quick evacuation by the Fifth Air Force.

Organized Japanese resistance ended on the Papuan Peninsula on January 22, 1943, a land victory made possible by the Fifth Air Force's dominance. Many lessons were learned, the most important of which was that Japanese soldiers would continue to fight, even in circumstances where there was no possible hope for their survival, much less their victory. In the bunkers at Buna, where one of the last battles of the Papuan campaign was fought, the starving soldiers fought on, even as they, too, were forced into cannibalism.

A SAMURAI'S APPOINTMENT IN SAMARRA

Allied code breakers learned that Admiral Yamamoto Isoruku was planning an inspection trip that would take him to the Kahili area in the southern part of Bougainville. Yamamoto was famous for his precise adherence to schedules, and the code breakers were able to determine his exact itinerary. The timetable called for him to arrive in a bomber at Ballale, an island off the southern tip of Bougainville, at 0945 (American time) on April 18, 1943—Easter Sunday and the first anniversary of Doolittle's raid on Tokyo.

Upon learning from Admiral Marc A. Mitscher, Air Commander in the Solomons (COMAIRSOL), that the Army Air Forces P-38s on Guadalcanal had the range to make the interception, Admiral Nimitz gave the authorization for the assassination. Even after his recent defeats at Midway and Guadalcanal Yamamoto was highly regarded by his American opponents and revered in the Japanese Navy, where he was considered, despite his taste for high living and his recent setbacks, to be almost as precious as the Emperor.

Major John W. Mitchell, commander of the 339th Fighter Squadron, was given responsibility to execute the attack. Eighteen P-38 pilots were chosen, eight each from the 12th and 339th squadrons and two from the 70th. It was decided that there would be an attack section—the killers—who would destroy Yamamoto's airplane, while the remaining fourteen would fight off the fighter escort. Six Zeros were known to be accompanying Yamamoto's flight of two Bettys, and the Japanese were expected to put up a large welcoming escort force from their bases in Bougainville.

The navigation challenge alone was formidable; Mitchell's plan called for a 435-mile flight at wave-top level, entirely over the open ocean and out of sight of any land-based observers. Done entirely by dead reckoning—i.e., flying compass headings and computing distance based on airspeed and predicted winds—Mitchell determined that the route would bring them to a point thirty-five miles off the coast of Kahili at 0935.

The odds against the interception were high. P-38 compasses at that stage of the war were notoriously unreliable (Major Mitchell had insisted on having a navy compass installed overnight in his P-38), there were no radio navigation devices, and the curling sea would give no directions. There was also the probability that they would be discovered en route by a Japanese vessel or patrol plane. Finally, although Yamamoto was rigidly punctual, his airplanes were as subject to mechanical malfunction as anyone else's, and he might not arrive on time; if so, the P-38s couldn't wait. It would have to be a split-second ambush, or just a wasted effort.

The Lockheed P-38 was an extraordinary airplane, the first twin-engine single-seat fighter ever put into mass production. The twin-engine safety and long range of the P-38 made it perfect for the Pacific. Two of America's most famous war aces, both winners of the Medal of Honor, flew P-38s. Major Richard Bong finished the war with 40 victories, while his nearest rival, Major Thomas B. McGuire, was shot down just after scoring his 38th kill.

Mitchell buckled down to work out the problem, saying later that he regarded the job as just another mission. From Yamamoto's itinerary, he deduced that the admiral's plane would be flying at 180 mph, which indicated that it was probably a Betty bomber. Working backward from the announced arrival time at Ballale, and figuring a gas-conserving 197-mph ground speed for his P-38s, Mitchell devised a five-leg, two-hour-and-forty-two minute flight low over the ocean, estimating Yamamoto's interception at a point thirty miles from Ballale.

Except for the fact that two Lightnings had aborted, the interception took place precisely as planned, to the utter surprise of the Japanese pilots in the two Bettys and six Zero escort planes. The American pilots were disappointed that the larger escort hadn't materialized, for it meant fewer victories to share. Ironically, sharing the victories would eventually become a fifty-year dispute.

The Lightnings were still at wave-top height when they caught sight of the Japanese formation, exactly on time and on course, at about 4,500 feet altitude and descending. One aircraft of the "killer flight" couldn't jettison its tanks and pulled out, with his wingman covering him. The two remaining aircraft, flown by Captain Thomas G. Lanphier and Lieutenant Rex Barber, headed for the eight-aircraft Japanese formation, while the protection flight climbed to altitude.

What happened in the ensuing moments is shrouded in mystery except for the most important facts: both Bettys were shot down, and Yamamoto was killed by gunfire before he crashed in the jungle. In the wild melee of the attack, the American pilots claimed three Bettys and three Zeros. Postwar records show that of Yamamoto's eight-plane formation, only the two Bettys were shot down. It is possible that Zeros were scrambled from Kahili, and were the victims claimed, but no investigation has confirmed this. One P-38 was lost.

Lanphier put in the earliest and most vocal claims for having downed the Betty carrying Yamamoto; Barber believed the victory was his. It is at least possible that both men had fired on the aircraft, and that it was a shared triumph. Over time, the weight of the evidence has tended increasingly to support Barber's claim.

There is no little irony in that Yamamoto's death may well have saved him tremendous loss of face when the full implications of the battles of Midway and Guadalcanal were evaluated. Instead, his ashes were returned, in two boxes, to Japan for a state funeral. One box was then interred in the Tama Cemetery, next to the grave of Admiral Togo, victor of Tsushima. The other box was buried in a Zen temple, the Chokoji in Nagaoka. Even in death, Yamamoto split his forces.

THE COST OF
INCOMPETENCE

THE AMERICAN ADVANCE TOWARD RABAUL

For as long as they could, the Axis powers routinely moved large units of their air forces from hot spot to hot spot, depending upon the inherent flexibility of airpower to optimize the limited number of aircraft they possessed. By 1942, the United States could afford a totally different approach, which was well organized by 1943 and operating at maximum capacity by 1944. Like the Pacific war strategy, it followed two lines. The first was the great expansion of its naval task forces. In the first six months of 1943, 9 new aircraft carriers joined the Pacific Fleet. Included were the CVs, large 27,100-ton Essex-class carriers with a complement of 85 aircraft, and the smaller CVLs, 11,000-ton *Independence*-class carriers with 40 aircraft. By January 1944, a single unit, Task Force 58, had 6 fleet carriers and 6 light carriers assigned, with far more aerial strength than the entire U.S. Navy had possessed in 1941. (By the end of the war, more than 130 U.S. carriers were in service.) The Navy's growing power would be applied to Admiral Nimitz's strategy of leapfrogging island by island toward Rabaul, the key Japanese outpost in New Britain, and then Japan.

The USAAF adopted a second approach, creating whole new air

forces in each theater, as required. These were often small units at first, consisting of a single group of bombers or fighters, with the rest of the organization on paper only. But the massive U.S. training schemes soon generated all the necessary personnel, and then supplied them with massive amounts of superb equipment, backed up by an efficient logistics system. Although supply and communication lines were thousands of miles long, both naval and air forces were able to swamp enemy opposition.

BATTLE OF THE BISMARCK SEA

The Bismarck Sea lies between the Admiralty Islands to the north and New Britain and New Guinea to the south. The sea-lanes plowed by Japanese ships were patrolled regularly to the range limits of General Kenney's B-24s and B-17s—dangerous, dreary work. Every flight was a hazard, with the fuselages filled with gasoline fumes from the overladen tanks and the weight of bombs and fuel making for long takeoffs over the short coral runways. The patrol sweeps lasted as long as twelve hours over the trackless waters; if the bombers were damaged by enemy fighters or antiaircraft fire, getting back to base was problematic. (One of the best accounts of this sort of lonely heavy-bomber war is John Boeman's *Morotai*. By the end of 1944, the USAAF would operate more than 6,000 Liberators in the Pacific.)

On December 30, 1942, a Lockheed F-4 Lightning reconnaissance plane brought back photos that showed the heaviest concentration of shipping ever seen at Rabaul—21 warships and 70 merchants (marus)—with a combined total of 300,000 tons. These became prize targets for the next ninety days as the Fifth Air Force mounted attacks on Rabaul and on the convoys sent to reinforce garrisons at Lae and Salamaua on Huon Gulf, New Guinea. The latter were General MacArthur's next objectives.

The Japanese responded with increasingly heavier fighter escorts for their convoys, playing directly into Kenney's hands, for his goal was to destroy the enemy's airpower in the air and on the ground. On January 6, 1943, in what was to become a typical mission, Fifth Air Force planes hit a convoy hard, sinking only 2 transports but shooting down more than 70 escorting fighters. Ten USAAF aircraft were lost.

The Japanese found themselves unable to disengage from the war of attrition thrust on them by their far-flung positions and American strategy. As Japanese aerial strength declined, General Kenney's forces built up. By March 1943, he had a striking force of 114 bombers and 154 fighters, including those of the Royal Australian Air Force. It was an extremely mixed bag, including 60 Curtiss P-40s, 35 Lockheed P-38s, 28 North American B-25s, 28 Boeing B-17s, 9 Consolidated B-24s, 21 Douglas A-20s (including 6 RAAF Bostons), 13 Beaufighters, and 13 Beauforts. Such disparity of types made maintenance, scheduling, and even formation flying difficult, but the situation was so vastly improved that no one noticed, much less protested.

The most promising of aircraft were the new B-25C1s of the 90th Squadron of the 3rd Bombardment Group. Under the direction of "Pappy" Gunn, the Mitchells had been specially modified for strafing with eight fixed forward-firing .50-inch machine guns and an upper turret armed with two more of the same type. With eight or ten machine guns firing forward, the B-25C1s could suppress most shore or shipboard antiaircraft fire. The B-25s would sweep in at masthead height to sling a 500-pound bomb equipped with a five-second delay fuse inside a thin-walled enemy merchant ship, blowing its bottom out. Dozens of Japanese garrisons were condemned to slow starvation as Japan's merchant fleet was eradicated by aerial attack, and by mines and submarines.

Ignoring the defeat at Guadalcanal and the continual losses at sea, Japan remained determined to reinforce New Guinea, and in early March sent the 51st Infantry Division down the Bismarck Sea in a convoy of eight destroyers and seven merchant ships. The weather was bad, and the Japanese hoped to make the five-day journey hidden from Kenney's forces.

Despite the wide variety in aircraft types, with all their differences in performance, Kenney's forces began a coordinated action on March 2 that sank all of the transports and four of the destroyers in what General MacArthur later described as "the decisive aerial engagement" in the Pacific theater of war. Kenney had established more than air supremacy—he had created an aerial blockade, one that doomed Japanese troops on New Guinea to fitful resupply by submarines or small barges operating at night.

The Fifth Air Force continued to hammer at Japanese targets, including shipping, ports, and bases, in a unique gestation process that saw the birth of a modern combat air force. On his arrival, Kenney had found a broken and dispirited air force, the shattered remnants of the defeat in the Philippines and the flight to Australia. Kenney honed his weapon in combat, continually raising performance standards even as new personnel and new equipment were brought on board and new units were formed. It was like a baseball farm club transforming itself into a World Series winner in the course of the spring season.

Kenney's air force kept busy even though other U.S. efforts were at a virtual standstill because of the increasingly violent argument between MacArthur and Nimitz over which should be the main axis of attack on Japan and who should control the majority of the forces. The two men neither liked nor respected each other. Their argument confirmed the American Joint Chiefs' agreement to limit the Pacific offensive in favor of Europe. The bickering between MacArthur and Nimitz led to a cutback on the objective to capture Rabaul and advance beyond the Solomons in 1943. Oddly enough, the dispute resulted in a well-designed strategy that saw the Allied forces pin down and chew up the Japanese troops along both lines of advance.

ISLAND-HOPPING

The bitter losses at Guadalcanal and in New Guinea made it obvious that island-hopping tactics should be adopted to isolate islands harboring Japanese aviation installations or large troop concentrations. The islands would be neutralized by bombing, then bypassed and left to starve. Frontal assaults were to be avoided wherever possible, while the Japanese Navy and merchant marine were to be systematically hunted down and destroyed, so that they would have to abandon the Bismarck-Solomons line of resistance.

Not all barriers could be bypassed, and the road to Bougainville led through New Georgia, another rugged, mountainous, jungle-infested island where the ground fighting turned out to be far more difficult than anticipated. The initial planning called for a 15,000-man invasion force to wipe out the 9,000 Japanese estimated to be on the island. Before it was over, 50,000 men were required because of fanatic Japanese resistance, typified by the action at Munda Point. There the enemy had built an intricate fortress of coral dugouts strengthened with log and well camouflaged. The island's strongpoints were mutually supporting and were manned by troops who would die rather than surrender the airfield that was the goal of the American forces. The strongpoints had to be taken one by one, using flamethrowers, tanks, and hand grenades. The attempt began on July 2, and the airfield was not secured until August 5, when the Japanese survivors escaped to join 10,000 others on Kolombangara Island to the north—where they would be bypassed and left to starve.

Within a week, Marine fighters were flying out of the strip, augmenting Marine and army airpower operating from airfields on Guadalcanal and the Russell Islands to fend off persistent Japanese attacks. The Cactus Air Force had come a long way.

The Japanese had slugged it out toe-to-toe against a stronger opponent until they fell from the weight of the blows—and from the superior strategy. Close air support was difficult in a jungle that was far worse even than that of Guadalcanal, but the Americans strafed everything that moved on the water, from canoes to barges to the rare destroyer. Barges, often the metal-hulled, diesel-powered craft manufactured by Diahatsu, were the most lucrative target, for they carried up to 120 men or 15 tons of cargo. At their 8-knot top speed, they were sitting ducks to the American fighters and bombers swarming over the area.

To the southwest, General MacArthur used his newfound airpower capability in his movements up the New Guinea coastline. A landing would be made, a perimeter established, and an airfield built. C-47s would fly in the necessary fuel and supplies, and within days, the P-38s and the new Republic P-47 Thunderbolts would be operating to cover the next landing. Yet Allied forces were still subject to threats from Japanese aircraft at Rabaul and bases near Wewak.

Kenney decided to deal with the two threats consecutively, hitting Wewak first. On August 17, 1943, 41 B-24s and 12 B-17s smashed airfields at But, Borum, Dagua, and Wewak with 200 tons of bombs. These were followed two hours later by 33 B-25s, escorted by no less than 82 Lightnings. At Borum, the B-25s decimated more than 100 Japanese airplanes warming up for takeoff, 50 fighters and at least 60 bombers. At Wewak, 30 fighters were slaughtered on the ground by 12 B-25s. The Japanese later referred to the "Black Day of August 17," when more than 150 aircraft and their irreplaceable air and ground crews had been destroyed.

THE LEAP TO BOUGAINVILLE

As the lynchpin of a defensive system that was being systematically dismantled, Rabaul became the graveyard of the Japanese Naval Air Force. As Japanese Army pilots were drawn off to other battlefields, they were replaced from the rapidly diminishing pool of experienced naval aviators, despite the vehement protests of the carrier admirals.

The succession of victories following Guadalcanal had given the American forces a surge of confidence, and in preparation for the invasion of Bougainville, General Kenney undertook to "kill" Rabaul with a series of air raids. On October 12, 1943, in the biggest raid yet seen in the Pacific theater, he sent every plane he had in commission in a devastating attack on the already beleaguered port. The 349-plane force included 87 Liberators, 113 of the heavily armed B-25 low-level attack planes, 125 P-38s, and 12 Australian Beaufighters. The attack opened with Kenney's trademark low-level sweeps on the Japanese airfields. B-25s of the 3rd Bombardment Group worked over Rapopo, flying in shallow V-formations 12 to 15 planes wide and separated by about a mile. The B-25s began firing their eight nose-mounted machine guns at long range, softening up the antiaircraft batteries, then dropped 23-pound parafrag bombs on aircraft and personnel with devastating effect.

Two B-25 squadrons of the 38th Group and four more from the 345th Group smashed Vunakanau with the same technique. The attacks, which destroyed or damaged 151 planes and set off explosions in the fuel and ammunition dumps, were over in minutes. Replacement of fuel and ammunition was even more of a problem than airplanes, which could be flown in. To get fuel and ammunition to the island, ships had to break Kenney's blockade.

Seven squadrons of B-24s, from the 43rd and 90th groups, each Liberator carrying six 1,000-pound bombs, had a field day over Simpson Harbor, sinking 3 large merchant ships and more than 100 smaller vessels. Of the 35 enemy fighters that climbed up to oppose the attack, Kenney later claimed 26 victories for his P-38s. American losses were light; antiaircraft fire had shot down 2 B-24s, 1 B-25, and 1 Beaufighter.

The vise slowly closed on Bougainville. By October 15, Major General Nathan Twining, who had replaced Admiral Mitscher as Air Commander in the Solomons, possessed a striking force of 223 aircraft, including Marine and navy SBDs, Lockheed Venturas (a Hudson development), and TBFs.

There were 264 fighters, among them the tried-and-true Grumman F4Fs, Bell P-39s, and Curtiss P-40s. In addition, however, Twining had 163 of the new Vought F4U Corsairs, 48 new Grumman F6F Hellcats, and 22 P-38s. These were the backbreaking difference, for all of the newer aircraft had superb performance, dramatically outclassing anything the Japanese had to offer in speed, range, armor, armament, and even, for the Hellcat at least, maneuverability.

The gull-wing Corsair, known to the Japanese as the "Whistling Death" was in production longer than any other U.S. fighter, from 1940 to 1952, during which time 12,571 were built. Powered by a huge Pratt & Whitney R-2800 engine that generated 2,100 horsepower for takeoff, the Corsair was extraordinarily rugged and versatile, able to lift huge ordnance loads and deliver them with precision. With a top speed of 446 mph and a range of 1,005 miles, the Corsair provided the Marines with a weapon that made the beloved Wildcat seem like a toy. It achieved an eleven-to-one kill ratio against Japanese fighters, and in postwar interrogations, some Japanese officers rated it as the best fighter they had faced.

The Corsair's chief rival, the Grumman F6F Hellcat, was designed specifically to counter the Zero, and it did just that. By the end of the war, the Hellcat had racked up over 5,000 victories, against about 250 losses. Like the Corsair, the production versions were powered by the Pratt & Whitney R-2800 engine, giving the Hellcat a maximum speed of 376 mph. It was extremely maneuverable and extraordinarily rugged, able to take on the best Japanese aircraft and pilots in one-on-one combat. In just three years, Grumman built more than 12,600 of the F6Fs, improving them continually.

The American portfolio was expanded with new equipment as well as new aircraft. The 5th Bombardment Group began flying SB-24s, Liberators equipped with radar sets that permitted the bombing of ships through an overcast. Given the early development stage of the equipment, results from radar bombing were surprisingly good, for the enemy ships were usually unaware they were being stalked and did not take the wild evasive tactics customary when being attacked under visual flight conditions. Other new equipment ranged from engines with increased horsepower, better armament, improved radios, and much better lifesaving equipment to an increasing number of creature comforts. As soon as bases were stabilized, shipping space was somehow found for ice-making machines, fans, washing machines, and other items that had been undreamed of in the early days on Guadalcanal. It was part of an American pattern of making life comfortable that could never be eradicated, even under wartime conditions. The Japanese soldier, who felt fortunate if he had rice to cook, looked on captured American K rations with awe. Even though the Japanese would ordinarily have considered the contents unpalatable, the K rations seemed to be unimaginably rich, including, besides canned food, such incredible luxuries as toilet tissue, soap, and even candy.

Some of the most poignant comments on the relative luxury of American supply practice were heard after the war from those few hardy Japanese holdouts who had refused to surrender. Starving and clothed in rags, they had hidden in jungle dens near the bases, amazed at the profusion of electric lights, food supplies, and, *mirabile dictu*, entertainment in the form of films, radios, and even touring USO groups. Over time, the Americans became aware of these holdouts and joked about their being seen in pay lines or at the mess halls. Some hardy souls held out for decades, sad patriots who still believed the imperial dream, even as their brothers made fortunes in a revived Japan.

In contrast to the wealth of American supplies, the Japanese situation became ever more rigorous. They were flying for the most part only updated versions of the Reisen, as they called the Zero, and even had to regress in the matter of bombers, pressing some of the earlier Mitsubishi G3M Nells into action to supplement the fast-diminishing supply of Bettys. Because they totally lacked the "instant airfield" capability being demonstrated in ever-more dramatic fashion by the U.S. Navy construction battalions—the famous "Seabees"—they placed more reliance on floatplane fighters, specifically the Nakajima A6M2-N, essentially a Zero with a center pontoon and wingtip floats. It is a tribute to the basic Zero design that the A6M2-N was fast and maneuverable for a floatplane, but it was no match for Allied fighters. All the Japanese aircraft received marginal improvements over time. By the Battle of the Philippines, in October 1944, for example, the A6M5b version of the Zero had armor glass and its fuel tanks had automatic fire extinguishers.

One new Japanese fighter debuted in New Guinea, the Kawasaki Ki-61 Hien (Swallow), code-named "Tony" by the Allies because they assumed it had derived from an Italian design. It was the only Japanese fighter to use a liquid-cooled engine, the 1,100-horsepower Kawasaki Ha-40. Germany had sold Japan engineering plans and sample copies of the Daimler-Benz DB 601A, which powered the Messerschmitt fighters, and Kawasaki hastened to copy it.

The Tony had built-in armor protection, self-sealing fuel tanks, and as many as four 12.7-mm machine guns as armament, and was well liked by the Japanese pilots as soon as they got used to its high wing loading. The aircraft was effective in New Guinea, although it was difficult to maintain. Raw materials and skilled labor were already scarce in Japan, and quality-control problems plagued the Ha-40 engine, which was unreliable, rarely able to deliver the rated performance. The Tony was kept in production until January 1945, by which time a total of 2,654 had been built.

BOUGAINVILLE INVASION

The Bougainville invasion, commanded by Admiral Halsey, began on November 1, 1943, and provoked a sharp reaction from the Japanese, who reinforced their air strength at Rabaul with almost 300 Japanese naval aircraft, drawing forces from several carriers, along with land-based fighters. These were gathered at the four operational fields around Rabaul, raising the Japanese strength to almost 550 aircraft. Of these, 390 were fighters, supplemented by an additional 36 floatplane fighters at seaplane anchorages. The resupply effort at Rabaul would come to typify the fate of the Japanese air forces in the future. There would be a stand-down to gather strength, a quick mustering to oppose the Americans, and then massive defeat in battle, followed by another stand-down. It was a policy of desperation, one that consumed the very substance of the two Japanese air forces.

Japan still felt strong at sea, and in a replay of tactics that had worked well at Guadalcanal, the High Command sent a powerful group of cruisers and destroyers to counterattack the American landings at Cape Torokina, Empress Augusta Bay. There, adverse terrain had hampered movement inland, offering the cruisers' heavy guns a chance to destroy the American invasion. Instead, the

Japanese were beaten in a brilliant night action by Rear Admiral A. S. "Tip" Merrill's outnumbered and outgunned fleet, which used radar-ranging to sink one cruiser and a destroyer and send the rest in retreat. It was yet another case where a Japanese admiral, faced with a golden opportunity to make a decisive difference in a battle, fled to save his ships.

Perhaps embarrassed by the defeat, the Japanese deployed six additional heavy cruisers of the Combined Fleet to Rabaul to crush Merrill's forces. Halsey responded by calling on his carriers and Kenney's bombers to attack the Japanese fleet in the harbor at Rabaul November 5 and 11. Aircraft from the carriers *Saratoga, Princeton, Essex, Bunker Hill,* and *Independence* destroyed the aerial opposition and mauled the enemy fleet so badly that heavy cruisers were never again sent to the area. The Japanese, badly shaken by the loss of so many experienced aircrews, withdrew their ships and remaining aircraft more than 600 miles north to Truk.

Not every new American aircraft was an immediate success. The SB2C-1 Helldiver, the last in a long series of dive-bombers from the venerable Curtiss firm, earned the nickname "the Beast" because it was difficult to handle and had so many mechanical malfunctions. Nonetheless, it made a splash in its November 11, 1943, combat debut at Simpson Harbor, when Lieutenant Commander James Vose, C.O. of VB 17, dive-bombed a Japanese destroyer that was apparently being loaded with torpedoes. The resultant explosion damaged a nearby cruiser and sent visible shock waves echoing across the harbor.

For a long time, however, the Helldiver was not popular with its crews, many of whom preferred the old Douglas Dauntless. The later-model SB2C-4 was fast at 295 mph, and could carry a 2,000-pound bomb load, but it took months in action for the aircraft to prove itself, and it never gained the degree of acceptance accorded so willingly to the Dauntless or the Avenger.

THE FIGHTING GRINDS DOWN

On Bougainville, the ground battle followed the Guadalcanal scenario, with the 27,000 American troops forming a perimeter around the beachhead within which airfields were soon built. General Hyakutake had more than 40,000 soldiers and 20,000 sailors under his command, but they were miles from the invasion site, and he experienced extraordinary difficulty in bringing his troops to battle via the jungle trails, often resorting to barging them at night down the coastline. In the end, an uneasy stalemate grew as the Japanese remained concentrated in the area in the south around Buin, where they spent much of their time growing food to survive. The battle continued well into 1945, with some Japanese troops, sick and malnourished, holding out until the end of the war. In the meantime, Allied airfields on the island were operating at full capacity.

In the course of a six-month period, from October 1943 through March 1944, the Bismarck Archipelago had been isolated, thanks to the effective cooperation of air, land, and sea forces. The Japanese Air Force at Rabaul was destroyed, the ships in the harbor were sunk, and ground installations obliterated. As the American island-hopping tactics evolved, it became evident that Rabaul would not have to be invaded. Instead, it was isolated, its 100,000-man garrison left in idleness. The bombing of its airfields and installations eventually became routine training missions. One of the curious facts about the Japanese Army in Rabaul was its increasingly top-heavy administrative nature. Fighting units being sent to Guadalcanal, New Guinea, and elsewhere all passed through Rabaul. The Allied dominance of the sea forced the Japanese to transfer the fighting elements in small packets to the most critical point. In the process, the administrative elements were left behind to a relatively pleasant life in Rabaul, for it was also a major supply depot, and there was plenty of food and even minor luxuries. In typical army fashion, the fighting troops were transported to battle areas to be killed or starved, while the "barracks-square warriors" were left behind in relative comfort. In one postwar memoir, a retired officer looked back fondly on Rabaul, regretting only that when he was promoted to lieutenant general there was no transportation available to take him to a post suitable for his rank.

OPERATION GALVANIC

During almost the same period of MacArthur's slow but steady triumphs, Admiral Nimitz's forces executed Operation Galvanic, which saw some of the most one-sided aerial fighting of the war coincident with the bloodiest hand-to-hand combat on the ground.

The operation began with a week of bombing strikes by the Seventh Air Force's Liberators to soften up Makin and Tarawa. They hit the islands daily from November 13 to 20, 1943, and then continued on in support of the actual landings.

The Navy's Fifth Fleet, consisting of more than 200 ships, and spearheaded by the new *Lexington* and the new *Yorktown*, sailed with impunity, for the main Japanese fleet had been paralyzed by the air attacks at Rabaul. Japanese carriers were inactive because of the shortage of trained naval aviators.

Despite absolute U.S. air dominance, the Japanese resisted stoutly on Tarawa, and the navy learned a great deal about amphibious operations. After four days of fighting, at the cost of 1,000 dead, Tarawa was taken.

By January 1944, the Fast Carrier Force of the Pacific Fleet had reached an undreamed-of level of strength, with four *Essex*-class carriers, six light carriers of the *Independence* class, and the old tried-and-true *Enterprise* and *Saratoga*. In addition, there were enough new battleships, cruisers, and destroyers to provide an effective antiaircraft screen, and to take on the Japanese Combined Fleet in case it managed to sortie out for a confrontation.

As his strength built, Rear Admiral Marc Mitscher became confident enough to go in harm's way, confronting Japanese island-based aircraft. And just as the Japanese had run riot in the early months of 1942, so did the Americans decide to maintain 1943's momentum in the early months of 1944, striking Kwajalein, the world's largest coral atoll, with one of the most complicated amphibious operations in history. Once again, aside from an occasional bombing raid, there was no Japanese aerial resistance. The measure of American superiority can be inferred from the battle statistics. Of 41,000 American troops, 372 were killed. Of 8,675 Japanese defenders, 7,870 died.

The incredibly swift manner in which the Americans had gobbled up the Gilberts and the Marshalls unnerved the Japanese, leaving them no time to prepare their next line of defense in the Marianas adequately. Nonetheless, wherever the Japanese soldier was well dug in, he fought a tough defensive battle, never expecting to do more than die in the attempt, and following instructions to regard his bunker as his grave. It was a sad and heartless mission, for the defense of the islands came to be regarded in Japan as buying time to delay the invasion of the mainland.

In effect, the Japanese High Command had exchanged one illusion for another. At the beginning of the war, they had hoped that a series of sharp defeats would bring a cowed America and Great Britain to the surrender table. They now hoped to secure a negotiated peace by making too costly the prospect of an invasion in which everyone—man, woman, and child—would resist, even if they had only bamboo sticks as weapons. Such wishful thinking was possible only because the High Command managed to believe its own propaganda, never admitting to the real disparity in losses, nor acknowledging that a banzai charge against murderous heavy-weapons fire achieved nothing.

Yet Japanese strategy had been forcibly altered. The threat from American air bases in China had caused Japan to embark on a large and successful land operation in China and to continue the battle in Burma. Seventeen divisions were spread across the island outposts from islands near the coast of Australia in an arc that reached westward to the Marianas and then all the way to Japan itself. The duty of protecting those possessions fell upon the Combined Fleet, which was now firmly on the defensive, and, its carrier strength vitiated, could operate only under the protection of land-based aircraft.

WINDUP IN NEW GUINEA

General MacArthur had continued his series of leapfrog movements along the northwest coast of New Guinea, as a preliminary to his return to the Philippines. The Fifth Air Force cleared the way for him. Between March 11 and 16, 1944, Kenney's bombers dropped 1,600 tons of bombs and fired a million rounds of ammunition on the Japanese strips at But, Dagua, Wewak, and Borum, devastating the runways and leaving the bulk of the Japanese Air Force derelict wrecks. More than 100 planes were destroyed on the ground, and 68 fighters were shot down in air-to-air combat.

Showing surprising resilience, by late March the Japanese had scraped together 351 aircraft, stationing them at three air bases near the port of Hollandia. Antiaircraft defenses were known to be heavy, and a new strategy was followed. On March 30, 92 Liberators, escorted by 59 P-38s, made the first strike against dispersed aircraft, plastering the airfields with 1,286 of the 120-pound frag cluster bombs and 4,612 of the 20-pound fragmentation bombs. The Japanese antiaircraft fire was far lighter than expected and the fighter reaction apparently confused, with only about 60 Oscars and Tonys appearing, and these not making determined attacks. (The Oscar was the army's counterpart to the Zero and was often confused with it. Officially the Nakajima Ki-43 Hayabusa [Peregrine Falcon], the Oscar was, like the Zero, very maneuverable, but lightly built and lacking armor and self-sealing fuel tanks.)

The attack was repeated the following day with similar results. Reconnaissance showed that 209 aircraft had been destroyed, and the Japanese were observed flying many of their remaining aircraft out of the area, ceding air superiority once again. A three-wave attack on April 3 destroyed Hollandia as an air base. Sixty-three B-24s dropped 1,000-pound demolition bombs and were followed this time by 96 Douglas A-20s at treetop height, dropping 100-pound parademolition bombs to blow up aircraft, fuel and munition dumps, and housing areas. The third wave consisted of 76 of the now-notorious B-25s, dropping bombs and strafing everything still standing. All the Japanese aircraft and the entire fuel supply had been destroyed and 2,000 ground crewmen had been killed. Counting those destroyed in air-to-air combat, the strikes on Hollandia had cost Japan more than 450 aircraft.

Japanese air opposition in New Guinea was now negligible, and it was apparent the caliber of the average Japanese pilot had declined markedly. The Japanese persisted with their night-bombing attacks, which, while occasionally effective, lacked their former impact. Japanese resistance on New Guinea continued through August, with sporadic fighting even longer, but MacArthur was at last poised for a return to the Philippines.

OPERATION FORAGER

The early defeats and later hard-won victories had taught the United States a great deal, and one of the lessons most adhered to was "no inadequate measures." The armada being dispatched against the Marianas consisted of Admiral Raymond Spruance's Fifth Fleet, with 7 battleships, 21 cruisers, and 69 destroyers. It was complemented by Admiral Mitscher's four carrier groups, with 15 aircraft carriers and 956 aircraft. The commander of amphibious operations for Operation Forager, as the campaign to take the Marianas was called, Vice Admiral R. Kelly Turner, had no peer in the world for his knowledge, experience, and dedication. Turner's forces were formidable, with three Marine divisions for the assault and two army divisions in reserve. A tough disciplinarian but open to new ideas, Turner enjoyed the prospect of plucking at Japan's very vitals by reaching out more than 1,000 miles to bypass Truk and the Carolines and take the Marianas.

The islands there—Guam, Saipan, and Tinian—respectively manned with 18,000, 32,000, and 9,000 troops, controlled the sealanes of the Central Pacific; holding them would sever Japan's jugular vein. In addition, the Boeing B-29 would have bases within range of the Japanese mainland.

Curiously, the American move fit perfectly with its opponent's plans, and corresponded somewhat to the prewar Japanese plan of luring the American fleet deep into Japanese waters for the decisive engagement. Admiral Toyoda Soemu had adopted his predecessor Yamamoto's "A-Go" plan to engage the American navy in a final, decisive battle by sandwiching it between carrier forces and landbased aircraft operating from the islands. Despite open criticism, Toyoda remained at his post in Tokyo, giving command of the fleet to Vice Admiral Ozawa Jisaburo.

Only six months earlier, Ozawa's fleet would have been considered overpowering, with 5 fleet carriers, 4 light carriers, 5 battleships, 11 heavy cruisers, 2 light cruisers, 28 destroyers, and 14 other vessels. The battleships included the two largest and most powerful ever built, the *Musashi* and the *Yamato*. These 74,000-ton giants each carried nine 18-inch guns, the most powerful battleship armament in history. In theory the perfect instrument for crossing the American T (that is, crossing the enemy line at a right angle), they were one war out of date.

On his carriers, Ozawa had 222 fighters, all Zeros, 113 divebombers, and 95 torpedo bombers. There were also 43 floatplanes for reconnaissance. Two modern types of aircraft were on strength, the Yokosuka D4Y Suisei (Comet), code-named Judy, and the Nakajima B6N Tenzan (Heavenly Mountain), code-named Jill. The Judy was small for a dive-bomber, with about the same dimensions as a Zero, and had a superb performance, with a 343-mph top speed and a range of 850 miles. Incredibly, given the experience of the war, it lacked armor protection for the crew, or self-sealing fuel tanks. The Jill was essentially a more powerful Kate, faster and longer-ranged, but prone to engine trouble and difficult to handle on a carrier.

The latter was no small consideration, for Ozawa's flight crews were no longer the peerless professionals of Pearl Harbor and Midway. Instead, they were ill trained, just able to operate off a carrier and totally inexperienced in combat.

After so many defeats, Japan was thirsting for a victory, and Ozawa counted on two tactical advantages to provide it. The first was the use of the 100 aircraft based in the Marianas that figured so prominently in Operation A-Go planning. The second was the greater range of his aircraft, which could reach out to search for 560 miles, and to bomb for 300. American search planes would be at their limits at 350 miles, and the bombers could not safely go beyond 200 miles to attack. If he could catch the Americans napping, Ozawa hoped to give Spruance's carriers a one-two punch with his land- and carrier-based aircraft.

Misfortune stalked the Japanese, and half of their plan was rendered inoperative by Mitscher's Task Force 58, which included 470 Grumman F6F-3 Hellcats, 199 Grumman Avengers, 57 of the veteran Douglas SBDs, 165 Curtiss SB2C Helldivers, and even three Vought F4U-2 night fighters. At 1300 hours on June 11, Mitscher sent 211 Grumman Hellcats, given navigational assistance by eight Avengers, to hit airfields at Guam, Saipan, Tinian, and a smaller island, Pagan. Eighty-one aircraft were shot down and another 29 destroyed on the ground, while 21 Hellcats were lost. The carnage was but a prelude to what became known as the "Great Marianas Turkey Shoot" a few days later.

On June 15, Rear Admiral J. J. "Jocko" Clark, with four carriers (*Hornet, Yorktown, Belleau Wood*, and *Bataan*) of Task Groups 58.1 and 58.4, struck Iwo Jima and Chichi Jima, where the Japanese mustered aircraft to stage to the Marianas. Clark launched 44 Hellcats, 16 Avengers, and 16 Helldivers from a position 135 miles south of Iwo Jima. Thirty-eight Zeros intercepted the Americans, who promptly shot down 28 of of them and proceeded to strafe the airfields, fuel dumps, and small vessels. A 1,900-ton transport, the *Tatsutakawa Maru* was sunk off Chichi Jima, and American destroyers rescued 118 of its crew.

THE BATTLE OF THE PHILIPPINE SEA

Saipan had been invaded on June 15 after an unprecedented bombardment by the American fleet; before the day was out, 20,000 Marines were on shore, complete with their artillery. They brushed off a 1,000-man banzai charge the next day, and, in a pattern that would be repeated, the Japanese retreated to their prepared fortifications, awaiting rescue by Ozawa's fleet. Spruance issued orders calling for the complete destruction of that fleet, specifying to Mitscher that the enemy carriers should be knocked out first, followed by an attack on the capital ships.

Ozawa had received similar instructions from his own boss, Admiral Toyoda, who asked for a victory as significant as that of Tsushima almost forty years earlier. Ozawa placed an advance unit of three light carriers and their supporting vessels to act as a decoy, reserving the rest of his force, 100 miles to the rear, to make the decisive attack. It was not bad strategy for his carriers, but it was pointless for his battleships, which had to close to within twenty miles at the least to be more than floating antiaircraft batteries—and targets.

The fighting opened with the destruction of 30 fighters and 5 bombers sent to Guam from Truk to support Ozawa. Then, at 0830, the Japanese began the greatest carrier battle in history, launching their first strike of 8 Jills, 43 Zero fighter-bombers carrying a single 251-kilogram bomb, and 14 Zero fighters.

More than 200 Grumman Hellcats from the *Essex*, the *Cowpens*, the *Bunker Hill*, and the *Princeton* scrambled and were amazed to see the incoming force suddenly begin turning in a wide circle while its individual elements were given on-the-job combat training on how to make the attack. Each minute of delay was precious to the Americans, whose one goal was to halt the Japanese before they broke through to the carriers. The Hellcats fell on the aging Zeros and shot them out of the sky, with pilots claiming 3 or 4 victories in a single dogfight. After almost thirty minutes of one-sided combat, a few Japanese aircraft broke through to attack the fleet, where they encountered a withering hail of antiaircraft fire that claimed 17 more victims. One bomb hit was scored on the battleship *South Dakota*, but at a cost of 40 to 60 of the 65 attackers.

The second attack was launched by Ozawa's main fleet, 100 miles behind the vanguard, and included 53 of the Judys, 27 Jills,

At one point, Spaatz was concerned that Doolittle was afraid to take risks; by March 1945, when this photo of a bomber crew briefing them was taken, those fears were allayed. (*Air Force Association Photo*)

The man who had built the Eighth Air Force, Lieutenant General Ira Eaker, had been named Commanding General of the Mediterranean Air Forces, to his severe displeasure. Typically, he immediately set about to do a first-rate job there, and did. Here he decorates an Italian fighter pilot fighting for the Allied cause. (*Air Force Association Photo*)

General Hap Arnold, smiling (albeit not as broadly as usual), and Brigadier General Claire Chennault, dour and taciturn. The aircraft are the famous sharkmouthed P-40s of the China Air Task Force, which later became the Fourteenth Air Force. (*Air Force Association Photo*)

Many former members of the Flying Tigers served with the 23rd Fighter Group. From left to right: Major John R. Alison, Major David "Tex" Hill, Captain Albert Baumler, and Lieutenant Mack Mitchell. Baumler had fought in Spain. (*Air Force Association Photo*)

Despite failing health, Hap Arnold drove himself hard, making inspection trips worldwide. Here he talks to one of the most effective and popular generals in the USAAF, George Kenney, who saw his Far East Air Force grow from a ragtag collection into a massive force. (*Air Force Association Photo*)

The theme "Remember Pearl Harbor" was not just a cinematic device; there was a genuine desire to inflict punishment on the Japanese who had done this to Wheeler Field. (*Air Force Association Photo*)

By 1944, the U.S. Army Air Forces were able to respond with force in the Pacific war. Here B-24, B-25, and A-20 bombers attacked airports in the Philippines, destroying 104 aircraft in the air and 252 on the ground. This is Clark Field; note the parachute-retarded bombs descending in the center of photo. (*Air Force Association Photo*)

One new American weapon was an improvisation by the legendary "Pappy" Gunn, the installation of a 75-mm cannon in a North American B-25. (*Air Force Association Photo*)

The cannon-armed B-25s could be devastating; this sinking Japanese frigate is still under attack. (*Air Force Association Photo*)

During the Battle of the Bismarck Sea, in a single attack on a 22-ship Japanese convoy, bombers destroyed 90,000 tons of shipping. (*Air Force Association Photo*)

Circling frantically, a *Yamato*-class battleship tries to escape an air attack. Ultimately, both the *Yamato* and its sister ship the *Musashi*, the largest battleships ever built, succumbed to air attack. (*Air Force Association Photo*)

Allied command of the sea forced the Germans to desperate aerial resupply measures in the Mediterranean theater. Here a formation of Junkers Ju 52s scuttle across the Sicilian Straits, under attack by Lockheed P-38s and North American B-25s. (*Air Force Association Photo*)

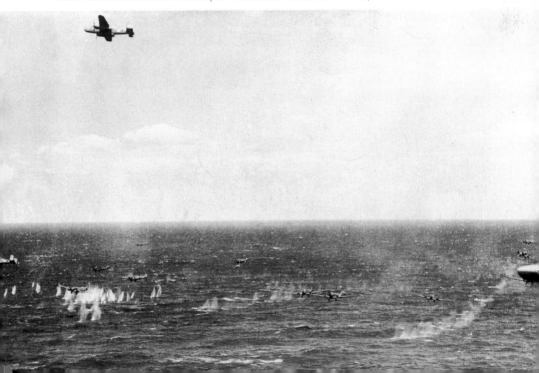

The air war did not go easily in Europe. The strain of combat is shown on the face of Lieutenant Allen F. Bunte, of the 4th Fighter Group. He was later shot down and made a prisoner of war. (*Warren Bodie Photo*)

Captain Walker "Bud" Mahurin scored $20^3/4$ victories in World War II and was shot down in both the European and Pacific theaters. In the Korean War, he accounted for $3^1/2$ MiG-15s before being shot down and made a prisoner of war. His record of having scored victories in all theaters and having been shot down in all theaters must be unique. (*Warren Bodie Photo*)

Captain John Godfrey, who with Captain Don Gentile made up one of the most formidable killer teams in Army Air Force history. Godfrey's aircraft, *Reggie's Reply*, is named for his brother, who died when his ship was sunk in the North Atlantic. (*Warren Bodie Photo*)

American aircraft were rugged, and none more so than the Republic P-47 Thunderbolt. This is Major Harry McAfee's *Jug* on Saipan, 1945. (*Warren Bodie Photo*)

Some airplanes performed vital services without ever getting headlines. Called "grasshoppers" for their ability to leap in and out of small fields, predecessors of this Piper L-4J were used for thousands of tasks. (*Warren Bodie Photo*)

Another workhorse, one that General Eisenhower considered to be one of the most significant workers of the war, was the Douglas C-47, shown here towing Waco CG-4 gliders filled with airborne infantry men on D-Day. (*Air Force Association Photo*)

Flying the gliders was hazardous, and many ended like this one, crashed in an enemy field in Holland in September 1944, during the ill-fated Arnhem operation. (*Air Force Association Photo*)

Helicopters became available toward the very end of the war. This is the Sikorsky R-4 Hoverfly, very possibly the prototype. (*Warren Bodie Photo*)

American aircraft lent themselves to continual improvement, reaching such extraordinary lengths as this Lockheed P-38M-6-LO Night Lightning. Seventy-five P-38Ls were modified to this two-seat configuration. The ASH (AN/APS-4 radar) was carried for interception. (*Air Force Association Photo*)

Germany was so ravaged by the round-the-clock bombing that it put its factories underground. Here a V-1 assembly line has been abandoned in the ghastly tunnel factory at Nordhausen, dug and manned by malnourished slave laborers. (*Air Force Association Photo*)

In pointed contrast to the Nazi slave laborers were these "Rosie the Riveter" prototypes, who were starting a revolution not only in wartime production but also in the women's movement. Curiously, Germany failed to mobilize the women in its work force until it was far too late. (*Author's Photo*)

American factories, untouched by war, put forth aircraft at the rate of 100,000 per year in 1944. More than 18,000 Consolidated B-24 bombers were built. (*Courtesy Eric Hehs, Lockheed*)

Two of the top American aces flew Lockheed Lightnings: Major Richard I. Bong and Captain Thomas McGuire. Bong is shown here with Colonel David W. Hutchinson and Bong's old friend, General George Kenney. Bong had 40 victories to lead all American pilots in the war; he was killed after the war in the crash of a P-80 fighter. (*Air Force Association Photo*)

Lockheed P-38s were complex aircraft but were produced in great numbers. (*Warren Bodie Photo*)

Two GIs inspect the ravaged hulk of the most advanced production aircraft of the war, the Messerschmitt Me 262 jet fighter. (*Warren Bodie Photo*)

The Boeing B-29 was to bombers what the Messerschmitt Me 262 was to fighters: simply the best. It was an expensive gamble on the part of both Boeing and the USAAF, but it paid off. (*Author's Photo*)

Despite, or perhaps because of, great expectations, the B-29 campaign against Japan was initially a failure; the damage inflicted was in no way proportionate to the cost of the program, including building the bases. Then Major General Curtis E. LeMay arrived, fresh from triumphs in Europe, to turn things around. He's seen here with General Lauris Norstad (left) and Brigadier General Thomas Power, right. All three did well in their postwar careers. (*Air Force Association Photo*)

LeMay introduced new techniques that turned the B-29 into an instant success; flying low, at night, carrying primarily incendiary bombs, the B-29s burned Japan from end to end. The Asukasa residential area of Tokyo contained many small industries. Yet even as Tokyo burned, an elemental new force was brewing. (*Air Force Association Photo*)

In perhaps the most incongruous codename of the war, this 120-inch-long, 28-inch-wide bomb was called "Little Boy." It was the first nuclear weapon, detonated over Hiroshima on August 6, 1945. It weighed 9,000 pounds and had a yield equivalent to 20,000 tons of high explosives. (*Air Force Association Photo*)

The bomb was dropped by the B-29 *Enola Gay*, named for its pilot's mother. The air and ground crews of the *Enola Gay* are gathered here; the aircraft commander, Lieutenant Colonel Paul W. Tibbets, is shown in cap and flying suit in front of the propeller blade. At this time, few people, from President Truman down, had any real inkling of the implications of Hiroshima. (*Air Force Association Photo*)

Hiroshima after the attack. (*Air Force Association Photo*)

The Japanese were instructed to paint aircraft carrying members of their peace commission white with green crosses. It was an unprecedented loss of face for the proud Japanese airmen. This is a Mitsubishi Betty, similar to the aircraft in which Admiral Yamamoto Isoroku was killed. (*Warren Bodie Photo*)

Two of the great aerial tacticians of the war, the U.S. Navy's first ace, Lieutenant Commander Edward "Butch" O'Hare (left), and Commander John S. "Jimmy" Thach, creator of the effective counter to the Japanese Zero, the Thach weave. Thach is congratulating O'Hare for downing five Japanese planes attempting to attack the USS *Lexington*. O'Hare was awarded the Medal of Honor but later lost his life in action. (*Robert Lawson Photo*)

This scene from the Luzon campaign in the Philippines would have been repeated dozens of times over had there been an invasion of Japan. Here Lockheed P-38s napalm Japanese infantry emplacements. (*Air Force Association Photo*)

A Japanese Zero kamikaze plane, its tail shorn off and wing ablaze, drops toward a deck filled with Wildcats on board the USS *Petrof Bay*, on October 26, 1944, off the Philippines. (*Robert Lawson Photo*)

Commander Douglas McCampbell, the leading Navy ace at war's end with 34 victories, and a recipient of the Medal of Honor, smiles broadly from the cockpit of his Grumman F6F-5 Hellcat *Minsi III* on board the USS *Essex*, on October 29, 1944. (*Robert Lawson Photo*)

Designed specifically to meet the Zero threat, the Grumman F6F Hellcat did that and more. It was faster and stronger than the Zero, and almost as maneuverable. In one of the great engineering triumphs of the war, the Hellcat moved from drawing board to combat in twenty-five months. The Hellcats achieved almost 75 percent of the Navy's aerial victories, shooting down more that 5,000 enemy aircraft. (*Warren Bodie Photo*)

Flight-deck crewmen aboard a Pacific Fleet escort carrier disengage a Grumman TBF Avenger from the arresting gear following a landing. It was in an Avenger that Ensign George Bush attacked the enemy before he was shot down and rescued by a submarine. (*Robert Lawson Photo*)

The Vought F4U was in production longer than any other U.S. fighter of World War II, and achieved an 11–1 victory ratio. Its excellent overall performance makes it a contender for "best fighter of World War II," and it did outstanding work in Korea and Indochina as well. (*Warren Bodie Photo*)

and 48 Zeros. As brave and inexperienced as the first wave, these were slaughtered by Hellcats and antiaircraft fire; 41 Judys, 23 Jills, and 32 Zeros, were shot down. The Japanese High Command was making the same mistake that Hitler was making in Europe, confusing units filled with new and ill-trained personnel with the old-line organizations of the past. The numbers looked the same on a morning report; it was very different in the field.

Ozawa was already defeated, and two of his carriers, the 33,000-ton flagship *Taiho* and the veteran *Shokaku* were torpedoed by the U.S. submarines *Albacore* and *Cavella*, respectively. The *Shokaku* blew up and sank at 1500 hours, while the *Taiho*, the newest and biggest Japanese carrier, suffered the same fate about twenty minutes later. Had the two ships been manned by the experienced seamen of two years before, both would almost certainly have been saved, for the explosions were caused by fuel vapors being allowed to fill the fire-ravaged hulls.

Before these disasters, the Japanese had launched two more raids with similarly disastrous results. By day's end, the Americans had claimed a total of 413 victories, somewhat more than the actual Japanese losses of 315, but close enough given the confusion of battle. Two important Japanese carriers had been sunk. It was the greatest single day's victory in the Pacific war, and more was yet to come.

Very late the following afternoon, the main Japanese fleet was finally located, and Spruance ordered an attack. The light carrier *Hiyo* was sunk by two Avenger torpedo hits, while the *Zuikaku*, veteran of so many battles, survived again, taking a direct hit and several near-misses. Two light carriers, the *Junyo* and the *Chiyoda*, were damaged by bombs. The Japanese lost at least 65 Zeros, as well as the other aircraft on the *Hiyo*.

The American planes were now faced with a 335-mile night flight over the trackless ocean, flying back low on fuel and in radio silence to a blacked-out fleet. Jocko Clark ordered the *Hornet* to turn on a vertical searchlight beam, notifying Mitscher of his action. Mitscher made a courageous decision to order every vessel to turn on its lights. Even though the returning planes landed on the first available aircraft carrier (some even tried to land on other types of ships) it was impossible to recover them all. Out of 104 aircraft lost, 80 losses were due to fuel exhaustion or landing accidents. Thirty-six crewmen had died in the attack on the Japanese fleet, and a further 13 were drowned in emergency landings.

Spruance was subsequently criticized by some for allowing the Japanese fleet to escape. Although still formidable on paper, Ozawa's force was a hollow shell, with only some 35 aircraft remaining. Four hundred planes had been shot down or lost on the three sunken carriers. An entire second generation of naval aviators was killed, as well as several of the leading Japanese aces and many of the few remaining experienced formation leaders.

On the American side, a few flyers scored multiple victories. The man who would become the leading U.S. Navy ace, Commander David McCampbell, claimed 7 victories and one probable on June 19; he ended the war with a total of 38. The leading U.S. Navy ace at the time of the Turkey Shoot was Lieutenant Commander Alex Vraicu, who claimed 6 Judys and raised his score to 19.

The battle for Saipan ended July 9, after the man who had begun his nation's war so brilliantly at Pearl Harbor, Admiral Nagumo, and the island's commanding general committed suicide. U.S. casualties were high, with 3,426 killed or missing in action, but the Japanese lost most of their 32,000-man garrison. The U.S. forces were stunned when hundreds of Japanese civilians leaped to their deaths from the cliffs of northern Saipan, even though interpreters had broadcast that there was nothing to fear from surrender.

Saipan had seen some new additions to island warfare, including the continuous orbiting of fighters and bombers to respond immediately to calls for ground support. The USAAF Seventh Air Force lent its weight to the attack, beginning June 22, when Captain Harry E. McAfee made an unaccustomed takeoff from the "jeep" carrier *Natoma Bay*, to lead the P-47s of the 19th Fighter Squadron to the just-opened Isley Field landing strip. The 73rd Fighter Squadron from the *Manila Bay* joined them the next day on Saipan. The Thunderbolts became famous for conducting air support so close that their ejected cartridges sometimes landed behind American lines.

Guam and Tinian were liberated by August 12, 1944. It had been a long and bloody campaign, during which more than 600 Japanese aircraft were destroyed at a cost of 65 U.S. Navy planes. The almost ten-to-one victory ratio showed how markedly superior U.S. aircraft, pilots, and tactics had become. What it did not reflect was the intensity with which the carrier crews fought, nor how fatigued they were becoming. Yet in ninety days their task would grow to a level never seen before. In that brief period, they would launch almost 20,000 sorties and lose almost 300 aircraft.

In the meantime, work began immediately on Saipan to create runways for Boeing B-29s. When the island's loss was finally admitted in Tokyo on August 18, it was accompanied by notice of the resignation of Premier Tojo Hideki. If Emperor Hirohito had decided to intervene at this point, rather than waiting until thirteen months later, he would have saved many cities and many lives.

LEYTE GULF AND THE LOGICAL SOLUTION

Despite their profound weariness, the Americans had become professional warriors, rich in their weapons and increasingly proficient in execution of their strategy. Japan strained every fiber to do as much as it could, but increasingly it found itself relying only on the spirit of *gyokusai*, a mystic euphemism. Its meaning, a "crushing of jewels," implied that the proud Japanese people would prefer death to defeat or surrender. The Japanese public responded through the entire war to poignant haikus left behind by fallen warriors, or to last radio calls of "SAKURA" (cherry blossoms) from units about to be overrun. Individual soldiers who didn't subscribe to the concept of *gyokusai* were swept along because they assumed their comrades believed in it. Continual defeats and starvation diets took their toll, however, and in the final years of the war, surrenders became slightly more common. About 1,800 prisoners were taken in the Marianas, about 50 percent of them Koreans.

The character of the South Pacific air campaign had assumed its final form, with two important exceptions. The first of these, to be covered in the concluding chapter, was the final phase of the aerial bombardment of Japan by B-29s and carrier-based forces. The second was the introduction of suicide attacks by what the Japanese called Shimpu Tokubetsu Kogekitai, the Divine Wind Special Attack Corps. The Japanese abbreviated this to Tokko, but the name later became immortalized in the United States as the Kamikaze Corps.

The indoctrination of the Japanese people, especially the servicemen, in the idea of *gyokusai* combined with the irresistible force of the American onslaught to create a climate in which a suicide attack became perfectly logical. It was already apparent to any

Japanese pilot that he could not live through combat, given the overwhelming force of the American opposition. Even if a Japanese plane eluded the prowling Combat Air Patrols, the withering anti-aircraft fire of the fleet had now been enhanced by the introduction of the proximity fuse, which detonated if it passed near the target. It was but a small step to decide that a suicide flight would make the inevitable sacrifice vastly more useful to Japan by taking out a valuable ship—an aircraft carrier if possible, if not, then a battleship. The equation of one life for one aircraft carrier was heroic and appealing, yet filled with unconscious irony, contrasting strongly with the American spirit demonstrated in the Marianas when an entire fleet was put at risk by illuminating at night to save the lives of aircrew members.

Not unexpectedly, the most vociferous advocates of Tokko-tai were those who did not have to make the final sacrifice. Although the Tokko-tai was portrayed to the Japanese people as a totally voluntary effort by patriots who became war gods, and thus by definition were the perfect example, the program became increasingly a psychological con game. Many of the early kamikaze pilots (and their spiritual brethren who manned the kaiten suicide submarines) were volunteers who understood what they were doing and felt they were fulfilling the Bushido tradition. Many others were simply tricked into volunteering and then kept in the corps by a combination of peer and family pressures and direct military orders. Peer pressure was so great that a kamikaze or kaiten volunteer who returned from a mission, unable to make his attack for whatever reason, might be beaten insensible by his comrades.

From an economic point of view, Tokko-tai was the only alternative to passive acceptance of total destruction or surrender. There was no prospect of creating conventional weapons that would stop the Americans, and the kamikaze weapons could be made very inexpensively. A wide array of special suicide weapons evolved, ranging from the exotic to the merely sad. On the one hand, the latest aircraft were packed with explosives, to be used in a single diving attack. On the other, there was the pathetic concept of arming individuals with mines placed on a bamboo spear—to be used against landing craft by scuba-diving warriors. Between these extremes there were midget submarines, human torpedoes, explosive-laden powerboats, and a variety of other makeshift devices.

From a hard-eyed military point of view, the most practical approach was to convert the thousands of aircraft on hand into "body-hitting" planes, for pilot training could be streamlined to accommodate the simplicity of a one-way, no-return mission. Although the idea of suicide attack had many sources, it is most often attributed to a Captain Jyo Eiichiro, who advocated the idea of "human aerial bullets" as early as mid-1943. Ultimately, however, the driving force behind the Kamikaze Corps was the roughneck Admiral Onishi Takijiro, a hard-drinking, inveterate gambler who in his younger days had been admonished both for pulling geishas behind him in a rickshaw and for slapping them around. Among his other exploits, Onishi had fought against the Germans in 1914 at Tsingtao, and then helped found the Nakajima aircraft company in 1916. He was a rabid airpower advocate who roundly condemned the battleship admirals. The degree of his ability can be assessed by the fact that he was not sacked early on, as many a junior officer was. Instead, he was ultimately handled in the time-honored military way, being assigned in the fall of 1944 to an important position far from Tokyo's political center.

Onishi was given command of the 1st Air Fleet, which was to have a key role in the defense of the Philippines, Operation SHO-1 (Victory-1). Although the Japanese Army was strong in the Philippines, and led by the redoubtable "Tiger of Malaya," General Yamashita Tomoyuki, everything was staked on a climactic sea battle. Characteristically, there was no command link between the Japanese Army and Navy in the Philippines. Everything had to go to the Imperial General Headquarters in Tokyo.

Japanese plans called for airpower on Formosa and the Philippines to be switched as required by events. When it was apparent that General MacArthur's invasion force was en route, Admiral Toyoda Soemu initiated the SHO-1 plan. A Northern Force under Admiral Ozawa was to decoy Halsey's carriers north, out of the battle area, while two heavy surface forces, the Center and the Southern, came together to destroy the amphibious ships and transports in Leyte Gulf. The plan was notable for its complexity, requirement for rigid timing and good communications, continued reliance on the efficacy of battleships—and a minimum of carrier airpower. Ozawa had two hybrid battleship-carriers and four aircraft carriers—but only about 100 aircraft. The fuel shortage gripping Japan had prevented adequate training and the pilots were so inexperienced that Ozawa ordered them not to attempt to land

back on the carriers after they were launched but to return to land
bases in the Philippines. It was indeed a very long way from Pearl
Harbor to the battle of Leyte Gulf.

Aircraft on Formosa had been earmarked to reinforce Onishi's
1st Air Fleet; they were instead destroyed in a slashing carrier attack by Task Force 38, beginning October 12, 1944. In three days,
four carrier groups flew 2,498 sorties, supplemented by a 109-plane
B-29 bombing raid by XX Bomber Command. Admiral Fukudome
Shigeru, commander of the Imperial Navy's 6th Air Fleet, later reported that more than 500 of his planes had been shot down like
"so many eggs thrown against the stone wall of indomitable enemy
formations."

Despite Fukudome's gloomy but realistic assessment, there transpired one of the most absurd propaganda fiascoes in history.
Tokyo Rose and the Japanese radio trumpeted that Halsey's entire
fleet had been wiped out and nineteen aircraft carriers had been
sunk. The emperor announced a national holiday in honor of the
event, the first in more than two years. The paroxysm of self-
congratulation showed how desperate the Japanese were for good
news.

Before he left Japan, Onishi had been given the recommenda-
tions of two veteran combat leaders, Captain Okamura Motoharu
and the famous Pearl Harbor leader, Commander Genda Minoru.
These two men, who had done so much to further Japan's cause,
suggested that the only remaining chance Japan had was full utilization of the suicide attack. Onishi's instinctive reaction to what
seemed to be an utterly wasteful measure was negative. This attitude may in part have stemmed from the fact that a trickle of much-
improved fighters was now reaching the front, of which two are
worthy of note.

The Nakajima Ki-84 Hayate (Gale), code-named Frank, was
nominally the equivalent of any American fighter, but was unable
to demonstrate its full potential for a variety of reasons. Fast, at
392 mph, and rugged, the Frank was equipped with armor and self-
sealing fuel tanks and well armed with two 12.7-mm machine guns
and two 20-mm cannons. The pilots liked it, for it didn't sacrifice
much of the Zero's maneuverability but it had more speed and armor. Deliveries were slow, however, and the decline in manufacturing quality control resulted in numerous mechanical malfunctions,
including hydraulic leaks and landing-gear struts that tended to

collapse under side loads. Its 1,800-horsepower Nakajima radial engine often ran rough, due to a loss of fuel pressure, and this problem was never corrected.

The second aircraft, the Kawanishi N1K1-J Shiden (Violet Lightning), code-named George, had an unusual genesis, deriving from a floatplane fighter designed to replace the Zero. Intended to meet and defeat the U.S. Hellcats and Corsairs, the George was almost as maneuverable as the Zero, and about 30 mph faster. An improved version, the Shiden-kai, was brought into production in 1944 and, in the hands of a qualified pilot, was equal to any fighter in the theater. But, like the Frank, the George suffered quality-control problems, particularly with its Nakajima Homare radial engine.

Both the Frank and the George arrived in small numbers, and both were difficult for the Japanese to support logistically. The hopes Onishi had for a powerful conventional force evaporated, and he realized that with less than 100 aircraft available to him, and the biggest naval battle in history looming on the horizon, the Tokko-tai was the only alternative. Once committed to the concept, he pushed it with all his energy and drive. On October 20, 1944, orders were cut authorizing the commander of the 201st Air Group to form a special attack group, a "body-hitting" unit of 26 fighters, 13 of which were intended to crash into enemy ships. Twenty-four volunteers under the leadership of Lieutenant Seki Yukio were selected for the honor. It was the small beginning of what became an almost unsolvable problem for the U.S. Navy.

THE DEATH OF THE JAPANESE NAVY AND

THE DEBUT OF THE KAMIKAZE CORPS

General MacArthur's promised return to the Philippines began to be fulfilled on October 17, with the first landings on A-Day, October 20. American troops met little opposition as they moved inland and began improving the airfields at Dulag and Tacloban.

In the meantime, uncoiling like some giant sea serpent, Operation SHO-1 lumbered along, its 64 Japanese ships about to be pitted against 216 American and two Royal Australian Navy vessels. The first of four separate naval actions began with the Battle of the

Sibuyan Sea, between the islands of Mindoro and Luzon, on October 23. There the Japanese Center Force under Vice Admiral Kurita Takeo lost two cruisers to submarine action.

On October 24, the enemy scored their first success east of Luzon when a Judy dive-bomber slipped through the Hellcats to put two bombs directly into the light carrier *Princeton*'s torpedo storage area. The tremendous explosion eventually sank the *Princeton* and badly damaged the cruiser *Birmingham*, which was alongside.

The Americans responded with a furious attack by 259 aircraft, vindicating Billy Mitchell with nineteen torpedo and seventeen bomb hits on the superbattleship *Musashi*, which rolled over and sank. Her sister ship the *Yamato* and the smaller battleship *Nagato* were also slightly damaged. With these and two others, Kurita continued on toward his rendezvous off Leyte, as SHO-1 had prescribed.

While smoke still hung over the *Musashi*'s grave, another portion of the complex Japanese plan was working. Admiral Ozawa's decoy force of carriers lured Admiral Halsey into a stern chase 190 miles west of Luzon. The deception would endanger the U.S. landing forces and cause Halsey considerable embarrassment.

On the night of October 24, the Japanese Navy got its longed-for surface fleet encounter in Surigao Strait, where Rear Admiral Jesse B. Oldendorf so skillfully deployed his PT boats and destroyers and his line of battle that he demolished the van of the Southern Force, led by Admiral Nishimura Shogi.

The following day, October 25, Kurita's fleet of four battleships, six heavy cruisers, and eleven destroyers burst upon the Leyte Gulf transports in an almost perfect execution of his portion of the SHO-1 plan, resulting in the battle off Samar Island. With Halsey's fleet far to the north pursuing Ozawa's Potemkin carriers, nothing but three destroyers, four destroyer escorts, and six small escort carriers, CVEs, stood between the Japanese and the invasion force. (The CVEs were jokingly referred to as "Combustible, Vulnerable, and Expendable" by their crews, who knew that their thin sides would not withstand fire from shells or torpedoes.)

Kurita totally miscalculated American strength, assuming that he had surprised Mitscher's Task Force 38. His mistake was parlayed into an American victory in one of the most brilliant feats of arms of the war, when Rear Admiral Clifton A. F. "Ziggy" Sprague reacted by ordering an attack. His tiny, tinny destroyers and destroyer escorts raced in to savage the Japanese with torpedoes and small-gun fire, while the carriers launched their torpedo-armed Grumman Avengers and then began evasive maneuvers. Sprague was assisted by aircraft from two other similar groups of CVEs, so that Kurita had to contend with 253 fighters and 143 torpedo planes.

In his confusion, Kurita gave the order "General attack,"—i.e. every ship for itself—which diluted his advantage in firepower as each Japanese ship chose different targets. The American crews responded heroically, flying sortie after sortie, sinking the heavy cruisers *Chokai, Suzuya,* and *Chikuma* with torpedoes. When the Grummans ran out of torpedoes, they were rearmed with depth charges and antipersonnel bombs; when these ran out, they made dry runs, drawing fire and forcing the Japanese vessels to alter course. Then suddenly, incredibly, Kurita folded, ordering his Center Force to retire.

It was a monumental American victory, the stuff of which John Wayne movies were once made. Samuel Eliot Morison recounts two conversations, possibly apocryphal, of seamen in the battle. In one, a chief gunner sings out to hold fire for just a little longer so the destroyers could "suck the battleships into 40-mm range"; in another, a signal man on an escort carrier sees the massive Japanese fleet leaving and yells, "Goddammit, boys, they're getting away."

But it was a victory won at great cost, and there was more to come in the form of the first attacks by the Kamikaze Corps. The initial sorties had not been successful, but on October 25, Lieutenant Seki, a gentle and reflective man by all accounts, led four Zeros laden with 251-kilogram bombs through the escort carriers' defensive screen. One Zero crashed into the side of the *Santee,* while others caused the *Petrof Bay* and the *Sangamon* minor damage. A few minutes later, a single Zero crashed into the center of the *Suwanee*'s wooden flight deck, causing heavy casualties.

A second wave of five Zeros now broke through Wildcat fighters flown off the escort carriers. Four Zeros caused only minor damage before being destroyed, but the fifth sent its bomb crashing through the flight deck of the *St. Lo,* setting off fires and explosions that ultimately sank the ship. While the *St. Lo* struggled in its death throes, another attack, this time by the fast Judy dive-bombers, severely damaged the *Kalinin Bay.*

Not one of the six carriers had gone unscathed. It was an inauspicious beginning for a drama that would rise to greater heights before the battle for the Philippines was over, and then go on to a zenith in the battles to come off Okinawa.

HALSEY'S REVENGE

Meanwhile, to the north, achingly aware of the danger to which he had exposed Sprague's little fleet, Halsey began the Battle of Cape Engaño on October 25. The Northern Force had consisted of four carriers, with a total of 116 aircraft on board, and the two hybrid battleship-carrier combinations, without any planes. These were accompanied by three light cruisers, nine destroyers, and the associated tankers and auxiliaries.

Halsey threw Marc Mitscher's three carrier groups against Admiral Ozawa's decoy force, using Helldivers, Hellcats, and Avengers to savage the Japanese. The first wave sank the converted seaplane carrier *Chitose* and a destroyer. The old warrior *Zuikaku*, wounded in so many battles since Pearl Harbor, was torpedoed and badly damaged. The second wave damaged the carrier *Chiyoda* so badly that it was later sunk by gunfire, carrying the indomitable Captain Jyo to his death. The third wave was devastating, finishing off the *Zuikaku* and damaging the *Zuiho*. Wave four sank the *Zuiho* and damaged other ships, including the hybrid *Ise,* which was proving to be a formidable antiaircraft vessel. Ozawa's Bushido pride must have been devastated as he made his getaway, with four carriers gone in a single battle and absolutely nothing to show for it.

The Battle of Leyte Gulf was finished, and with it, for all practical purposes, the Japanese Navy. But the United States had been presented with a new, and apparently unsolvable problem, the determined kamikaze attack. In actions off the Philippines, Japanese Army and Navy aircraft would harass the American fleet. Heartened by their victories, and learning from their defeats, the Japanese carefully husbanded their kamikaze assets, trying to concentrate on important targets—aircraft carriers preferably, battleships or cruisers when possible, but not sparing destroyers, tankers, or transports.

In response, new defensive tactics were developed. Destroyers were placed as picket ships as far as sixty miles away from the carriers, in the direction of the expected attack, to provide early warning. The Combat Air Patrols were divided up into HiCAP, flying at up to 25,000 feet, MedCAP, flying at 10,000 feet, and JackCAP, flying as low as 3,000 feet. Far-ranging fighter sweeps, nicknamed the "Big Blue Blanket" for the color of the aircraft, were sent deep into the Philippines to catch the kamikazes forming up.

Although the attacks could not be stopped, an inherent weakness emerged in the Japanese attacks: even when they struck a ship squarely, the aircraft often did little damage. Of all the hundreds of attacks made in the Philippine Islands after the *St. Lo* went down, only two ships were sunk and two damaged beyond repair. Many others were damaged, and there were 2,000 casualties, including more than 700 killed. The Japanese, who lost more than 500 aircraft in the attacks, never grasped the hard physical fact that most of their planes, even at the end of their fatal plunge, didn't have the mass required to cause fatal damage. A bomb dropped by a speeding dive-bomber reaches its terminal velocity, multiplying its mass upon impact. The kamikaze aircraft, even those that dove into their targets, were unable to reach the speed required to do ship-sinking damage. The resultant fires and explosions caused casualties, but the increasingly expert U.S. Navy damage-control teams saved the ships. Training and equipment had been vastly improved. Among the many new fire-fighting systems was the "fog nozzle" technique, which delivered massive amounts of atomized water in a dense spray that was far more effective than using regular pumps and hoses.

The Japanese used experience gained in the Philippines and in battling the Fast Carrier Forces to improve their kamikaze tactics. Although there were more airplanes of advanced type on hand than at any time before, pilots were few and poorly trained, often entering combat with as little as a hundred hours of flying time. A veteran pilot would go out as an advance scout to be sure of the target location. Then escort fighters would precede the kamikaze planes. Given the numerical and qualitative superiority of the American air defenses, the escort fighters functioned more as diversionary bait than as an effective defense. They would attempt to engage the American fighters to allow the kamikaze aircraft to slip through.

Another tactic was reserved for more experienced pilots. Small groups of Japanese aircraft would attempt to conceal themselves from radar by making their attack at the same time American for-

mations were returning to land. Using clouds or night as concealment, individual Japanese planes could often sneak in for a quick
attack. The Americans soon understood the tactic, however, and
alerted the defensive fighter CAP to search for intruders in what became known as "delousing tactics."

A new weapon appeared, one that seemingly offered promise but
in fact reflected Japan's desperate situation and its naive hopes for a
miracle weapon. Like many of its German counterparts, it substituted human sacrifice for technology. In the Yokosuka MXY7 Okha
(Cherry Blossom), the Japanese created a true "smart bomb," a
rocket-powered attack plane with a human being as its computer
system, designed to be flown against battleships and carriers. Made
mostly of wood, its spartan cockpit equipped with a minimum number of instruments, the tiny seventeen-foot-wingspan aircraft carried a 2,646-pound warhead. After release from its mother plane,
the Okha pilot fired three tail-mounted solid-propellant rockets.
Level speed could reach 403 mph, while the terminal diving speed
was 576 mph, giving it the penetrating power that conventional
kamikazes lacked.

The Okha was reserved for the Thunder God Corps, and its pilots were called Thunder Gods. The title was not a mere public relations gimmick. Upon death in battle, the pilot was deified in
ceremonies at the Yasukuni Shrine on the top of Kudan Hill in
Tokyo, there to continue the spiritual fight for his country.

Despite its technical innovation, the Okha had a range of only
twenty miles, and had to be carried into battle strapped beneath the
slow and vulnerable Mitsubishi G4M2e Bettys. This awkward
combination of design achievement and severe operational handicap would characterize most of the new weapons.

In the Okha's combat debut in the Philippines on March 21,
1945, sixteen of the little planes, their noses bright with cherry blossoms painted against blue backgrounds, were loaded into the Bettys and sent on an almost impossible mission to attack U.S. carriers
more than three hundred miles off the coast. Sixty miles out from
the carriers, an avalanche of Hellcats fell on the formation. The
Bettys immediately jettisoned their Thunder God-laden Okhas for
a terrifying, utterly wasteful death glide into the faceless sea, far
short of their intended targets. One can only imagine the frustrated
rage of the helpless Thunder God pilots who had dedicated themselves to their country and were now discarded as so much excess

baggage. Their release did not save the Bettys, which were all shot down within ten minutes.

THE GROUND WAR

General MacArthur had returned to the Philippines to conduct a methodical ground war against the numerically strong Japanese, who had 350,000 troops spread out over the islands. General Yamashita made the best possible use of the rugged terrain but was unable to resist the relentless onslaught of American air and ground forces. Japanese land-based airpower was wiped out early on, and Marine Corsairs and USAAF Thunderbolts, operating almost without air opposition for most of the time, brought close air support to new heights of proficiency. The Fifth Air Force's P-47s and P-38s worked over the Japanese positions systematically, with lavish use of napalm to ease the way for the ground forces. In one attack against Japanese positions near the Ipo Dam on Luzon, 144 P-38s, 48 P-47s, and 64 P-51s dropped 200,000 gallons of napalm in a three-day period. Japanese morale crumbled, and the American Sixth Army was able to move in three days ahead of schedule.

In his defense of the islands, Yamashita lost 262,000 killed and 15,000 captured in combat; the remainder were pinned in small enclaves on the eastern coast of Luzon when the war ended on August 15, 1945. There were 23,000 American troops killed, the ten-to-one ratio being a tribute to MacArthur's genuine concern about saving lives and to the profligate use of American airpower.

CHANGE OF STRATEGY

By the fall of 1944, the Pacific theater was receiving enough men and matériel to wage war on an unprecedented scale, and the island-hopping strategy was working perfectly. On October 3, 1944, the Joint Chiefs of Staff ordered the B-29 bombings to be stepped up, using Saipan and bases to be acquired on Iwo Jima and Okinawa, both of which would prove to be formidable fortresses, defended to the death by well dug in soldiers.

Iwo Jima was located in the Bonin Islands; only four and a half miles long and two and a half miles wide, it was vital both as an intermediate base where B-29s could make emergency landings and as a fighter base for the long-range escort P-51 Mustangs that were now becoming available in the theater. In preparation for the February 19, 1945, invasion, carrier planes from Task Force 38 struck mainland Japan, hitting airfields and factories around Tokyo and effectively reducing any air support the Japanese might have been able to provide.

Once again the Japanese soldiers fought valorously without air-power, for Iwo's defenses were virtually impervious to bombing and to the heaviest preinvasion naval gunfire in World War II. It remained for the Marine soldiers to contest each pillbox and each cave until the final surrender on March 24.

In the Iwo Jima bloodbath, 6,766 Marines and sailors were killed or missing in action, while almost 23,000 were wounded. The Japanese casualties exceeded 21,000, all killed in battle or sealed within their caves. Ultimately, 2,500 prisoners were taken, mostly wounded, and little pockets of resistance persisted for weeks.

As will be discussed in the final chapter, the American air campaign was scoring its most decisive victory of the war even as the Japanese resisted on Iwo Jima. On the night of March 9–10, B-29s firebombed Tokyo, killing 83,793.

OKINAWA: THE *YAMATO'S* LAST HURRAH

The Ryukyus, only 400 miles from the Japanese homeland, had been an independent kingdom until 1879, when Japan took it over; as in Korea, the indigenous population was not assimilated. The largest island, Okinawa, was 57 miles long and 12 miles wide at its broadest point. It was strategically located, only 350 air miles from the Japanese mainland, and directly athwart communication and supply lines to Formosa and mainland China. The United States wanted Okinawa as a springboard for the invasion of Japan, for it offered plenty of room for airfields and enough harbors to accommodate the Pacific fleet. Ominously, Okinawa was as eminently suitable as Iwo Jima had been for a prolonged defense by its 100,000-man garrison, and the ground battle became the most costly in the Pacific theater. But, it was the Kikusui (Floating Chrysanthemum) air campaign that broke new ground.

The ground war began on Easter Sunday, April 1, 1945, with the invasion going smoothly, the first 60,000 men of the 175,000-man force landing with training-film precision. By afternoon, two airfields were secured. It was a deceptive beginning. The fighting was now far different from those early days on Guadalcanal, when the Japanese contested daily for Henderson Field and were resupplied at night by the Tokyo Express. Instead, the Japanese gave up the airfields, resigned themselves to live on the supplies at hand and retreated to the south, allowing the invaders to overrun three-fourths of the island.

The retreat reduced the Japanese exposure to naval bombardment while pinning down the huge American fleet of 318 combat vessels and 1,390 auxiliaries and transports for air attack. Okinawa was within the range of almost eighty airfields, from which the Imperial General Headquarters planned to launch kamikaze attacks on an unprecedented scale.

The kamikazes had shown their teeth again in attacks on the American carriers striking Japan in March, hitting the *Franklin*, the *Yorktown*, and the *Wasp*. A conventional bombing attack cost the *Franklin* more than 1,100 casualties, 830 of them killed, before it was towed away by the cruiser *Pittsburgh*. Brilliant damage control and a stouthearted crew saved the vessel, which subsequently steamed 12,000 miles to its home berth in New York to be repaired.

Apparently out of equal measures of desperation and frustration, the once-proud Imperial Navy ordered a sacrificial run by the huge battleship *Yamato* and an escort of the light cruiser *Yahagi* and eight destroyers, but no air cover. The vessels were provisioned with food for five days, and only enough fuel for a one-way trip. The *Yamato* was given an impossible assignment. After destroying the two carrier task forces, it was to eliminate the invasion fleet in concert with a huge kamikaze air attack, then beach itself and use its huge 18-inch guns as artillery while its crew joined the fighting on land.

On April 7, 1945, a vigilant Grumman Hellcat from the *Essex* passed the *Yamato*'s location back 240 miles to Admiral Mitscher's Fast Carrier Force.

Mitscher's fourteen carriers sped to the attack, launching at 1000 on receipt of the *Yamato*'s location from Catalina and Mariner patrol planes. A second wave was launched forty-five minutes later, so that Mitscher had 386 dive-bombers, torpedo planes, and fighters streaming in to settle the aircraft-battleship controversy forever.

When the first American planes burst through the heavy rain

clouds in the area, the *Yamato* and its attendant vessels began a radio-jamming operation that effectively blanked out all American communications, inhibiting a coordinated attack. The aircraft split up into small packets, with Helldivers, Avengers, and Hellcats attacking from different angles and different heights, confusing the poorly trained Japanese antiaircraft gunners.

The first wave damaged the *Yamato*'s steering with one torpedo and several bombs. Within ten minutes, the light cruiser and a destroyer had been knocked out. The swarming American aircraft hit the *Yamato* with many bombs and at least seven torpedoes; it assumed a thirty-five-degree list to port, then slowly rotated to ninety degrees as water poured in. Within two hours of the first attack, the *Yamato* was sunk, carrying with her 2,488 officers and men in a last hurrah for the super battleship. The light cruiser *Yahagi*, as tough as the *Yamato*, didn't sink until hit by seven torpedoes and twelve bombs. Another 1,167 men drowned on the *Yahigi* and the four destroyers that were also sunk. The Americans lost 10 aircraft and 12 crew members.

On land, the fighting was the most intense so far experienced in the Pacific war. When, after eleven weeks of bitter fighting, the island was finally secured June 22, 1945 (there was no formal surrender), more than 135,000 Japanese soldiers had been killed, 20 percent of them entombed forever in caves. While a great fleet fired its guns and hordes of aircraft dropped bombs, it remained for the infantry grunts to poke flamethrowers into each cave or pillbox to winkle the defenders out. The ruthless conduct of the battle by the Japanese overlords caused 75,000 Okinawan civilian deaths. The Americans' land battle casualties were 7,374 dead and 31,807 wounded. Both sides lost their commanders. The American Army commander, General Simon Bolivar Buckner, was killed June 18 by flying coral churned up by an artillery shell. Five days later, the Japanese Army commander, Lieutenant General Ushijima Mitsuru, committed seppuku, ritual suicide, with his dagger and was beheaded by his dutiful aides, the macabre scene occurring within fifty yards of American positions.

The fanatical resistance of the Japanese and the high American losses on Okinawa showed how high a price would have to be paid to invade Japan. A simple extrapolation of numbers indicated that the Americans would suffer hundreds of thousands, if not millions, of casualties; Japanese casualties would be many times higher.

FLOATING CHRYSANTHEMUMS AND FALLING CHERRY BLOSSOMS

In the air war, the Japanese had raised the ante at Okinawa with Operation Ten-go, which called for a series of Kikusui attacks, these to be interlaced with individual suicide sorties. The Americans countered with radar picket screens of destroyers and other small craft placed as far as ninety-five miles and as close as forty miles from the island. Fighter-director teams were placed at each location, to bring the Combat Air Patrols to the most crucial point in the shortest possible time. Task Force 58 was positioned to the north, and carried out strikes against airfields on Kyushu, while Task Force 57 of the Royal Navy's Pacific Fleet, including the carriers *Indefatigabile, Illustrious, Indomitable*, and *Victorious*, operated to the south, warding off attacks from Formosa. (The British carriers' armored steel decks proved invulnerable to the kamikazes.)

Duty on the picket ships was dangerous; more than twenty ships were sunk and hundreds of sailors killed. A series of small-scale Kamikaze attacks had begun the week of March 26, a little less than a week before the invasion. The first full-scale Kikusui took place on April 6, when more than 700 aircraft were launched, of which 355 were suicide planes. The Americans were ready, and 250 enemy aircraft were shot down even before they reached the radar picket screen. The attackers lost another 55 inbound to Okinawa and 171 while making the attack. In just a few minutes, 476 chrysanthemums floated no more.

But 180 of the suicide planes got through to deliver their attacks, sinking the destroyer *Emmons*, two ammunition-laden merchant ships, and an LST (landing ship tank), and scoring hits on the British carrier *Illustrious* and six destroyers. In this first attack, the Americans lost 466 killed and 568 wounded, many by fire, and morale was sharply shaken by the inhuman way the Japanese planes bored in, even after they were hit and burning.

Kikusui 2, while strong, was not as forceful as its predecessor. One hundred and eighty-five suicide planes, 45 Jill torpedo bombers, 30 Val dive-bombers, 9 Bettys with Okhas attached, and 150 fighters hit on the afternoon of April 8.

The inexperience—or the wisdom—of the Japanese flyers showed in their target selection. Most attacked the radar picket stations in the north, where a Zero fighter-bomber and an Okha hit and sank the destroyer *Mannert L. Abele*.

The intensity of the kamikaze attacks dwindled as the Japanese ran out of planes and pilots. In the ten Kikusui assaults, there were almost 2,000 kamikaze attacks amid the 6,300 sorties by fighters and bombers of the army and navy air forces. The attackers sank 21 ships, damaged 43 others so badly that they were scrapped, and forced another 23 out of action for more than a month. The United States Navy's personnel losses exceeded those it had incurred in all wars prior to World War II—4,907 officers and men killed and 4,824 wounded. Most of these were due to the kamikaze attacks.

ACES HIGH

The mass attacks gave the pilots flying on Combat Air Patrols a chance to run up their victory totals. It was not always an uneven contest, for there were still some old hands flying, veterans of thousands of hours of combat since the early days in China, and they now flew far better aircraft than the Zeros. The situation was reminiscent of the Luftwaffe's last days, in which most of the pilots were inexperienced, but a few were old stagers, masters of the game.

American combat experience, now widespread through the fleet, greatly reinforced the excellence of American equipment. A typical example was Commander Eugene A. Valencia, who was not only a 23-victory ace, but also a master teacher and tactician. Valencia and his three wingmen flew what he called "mowing machine" tactics, which allowed one Hellcat to remain continuously on the attack while being covered by the other three. Flying with the *Yorktown*'s VF-9, "Valencia's Flying Circus" included Lieutenants Clinton O. Smith, Harris E. Mitchell, and James French. On April 17, the four-man unit dove from out of the sun to attack the rear of a 38-plane Japanese formation inbound on a raid. When the first two Japanese fighters blew up, the bombers jettisoned their bombs and tried to escape. The mowing-machine tactics scythed the scattered aircraft down; when low fuel forced them to break off combat, the team claimed 14 victories, 9 probables, and 6 damaged. In their tour of duty, the four men scored over 50 victories, 16 of them going to Valencia.

THE KAMIKAZE COVER-UP

Official U.S. government pronouncements minimized the effect of the kamikaze attacks in what in later years would have been called a cover-up. The truth was that the kamikaze attacks hurt the navy, and if Japan had been able to sustain them at the level of Kikusui 1, the casualty figures for the war would have been vastly increased.

During the entire kamikaze campaign, special attention had been given to carriers. Three escort carriers (the *St. Lo*, the *Ommaney Bay*, and the *Bismarck Sea*) were sunk and another 25 carriers (including 13 heavy carriers) were damaged. More than 3,250 officers and men were killed.

A kamikaze attack was terrifying, for it seemed to each sailor on each ship that the suicide plane was heading directly at him. Only in the last few moments of the attack could it be determined what the target was, and whether it would be hit.

More important, the attacks certainly raised important questions about what might happen during an invasion of Japan, when the ranges would be shorter and where the numbers of airfields from which attacks could be made were so much greater. It was known from intelligence sources that Japan was producing aircraft at the rate of 28,000 per year, which could provide a potential kamikaze force ten times greater than that at Okinawa.

With the fall of Okinawa and the occupation of the Philippines, the strategic hopes of both Admiral Nimitz and General MacArthur were now fulfilled. The way had been prepared for a final aerial assault on Japan, after which the hard task of the invasion would at last be possible.

THE OVERLOOKED CAMPAIGNS

The American advance through the South Pacific, with its brilliant carrier battles and hard-fought island campaigns, has overshadowed the long and hard wars fought in other parts of the Pacific theater, with the possible exception of the contributions of the American Volunteer Group, the Flying Tigers.

The reasons for this are many. Important political, economic, and geographic considerations caused the China-Burma-India theater to be regarded as a distinct and almost separate theater of war against Japan, subordinate to both Europe and the South Pacific. The American public, and indeed, top American officials, had great sympathy for the Chinese people, but were doubtful of the integrity of the Chiang Kai-shek government and its ability to resist. The British were immensely concerned about the implications of the Japanese victories for their colonial empire; Burma had fallen quickly to the Japanese, and was now a wedge between India and China. In India, the independence movement was gathering momentum, and Subhas Chandra Bose had raised three Indian divisions from prisoners to fight on the side of the Japanese.

The problems in command were almost insuperable, due to the mix of national loyalties and difficult personalities. The result was an anarchic chain of command that hampered operations at every level. As an example, as late as August 19, 1943, when Major General George Stratemeyer assumed command of the Army Air Force Units, India-Burma Sector, China-Burma-India Theater, he found seven chiefs giving him orders, ranging from the President of the United States to Generalissimo Chiang Kai-shek to the acerbic Lieutenant General Joseph "Vinegar Joe" Stilwell. The principal task of Stratemeyer's Tenth Air Force was the protection of the aircraft flying supplies from India to China. The supplies were flown by both the India Air Task Force and the China National Aviation Corporation, the latter initially doing a much more efficient job. Later the task was given to the Air Transport Command.

The flow of supplies began slowly; there were insufficient airfields and too few aircraft. Living conditions were deplorable, with inadequate food, irregular pay, poor medical support, and frequently even a stoppage of mail. Many of the pilots were inadequately trained, some never having had twin-engine experience before their arrival in the theater.

Flying the Hump between India and China was a dangerous business; the route between Dinjan and Kunming, splashed with the wreckage of more than 450 aircraft, was called "the Aluminum Trail." Flying conditions were abominable. The aircraft would take off in the dense, moist heat of the Brahmaputra valley, 90 feet above sea level, then climb to meet turbulence and heavy icing over mountain ranges of 14,000 to 16,000 feet. There were few radio aids and no emergency landing fields. Not until late in the war was there even the semblance of an effective search-and-rescue operation for the aircraft that did go down.

The C-47s had difficulty reaching the necessary altitudes, and the Curtiss C-46s brought in to supplement them proved initially to be maintenance nightmares, prone to blowing up in flight. An added hazard was attacks by Japanese fighters, particularly during the winters of 1942–43 and 1943–44.

Yet in time, the wealth of American production reached even the remote areas of the China-Burma-India theater and was reflected in the steady growth in tonnage. In July 1942, 85 tons were lifted; in July 1943, 2,916 tons; in July 1944, 18,975 tons; and in July 1945, 71,402 tons. It was a tremendous effort that saw proficiency go up and accident rates go down even as the tonnage climbed.

The official history of the Army Air Forces in World War II raises an intriguing question about the Hump operation, asking, "What good end was served by the emergency delivery of 650,000 tons of this and that into China?" It answers its own question somewhat ambiguously with a statement that little went to aid the Chinese people or the Chinese armies, but that it did sustain Chennault's men, who in turn prevented the collapse of Chiang Kai-shek's regime. Then it suggests that the greatest value was that the Hump operation was the proving ground for mass strategic airlift like that carried out later for Berlin.

Veterans of the Tenth and Fourteenth Air Forces would disagree with this official view. The Hump operation enabled the building of airfields from which the B-29s operated, but more important, it provided the wherewithal for attacking Japanese shipping off the southern coast of China and in Indochina. The Tenth Air Force was important in the campaigns in Burma, despite its relatively small numbers. The essence of the Tenth Air Force was improvisation; 1,000-pound bombs were fitted to P-40s for dive-bombing bridges; B-25s were sent out for night attacks on harbors; millions of pounds of supplies were dropped by B-24s, and other millions of pounds of freight were evacuated from Burma to India.

The Fourteenth Air Force was an outgrowth of the China Air Task Force, and really represented the desire of Generalissimo Chiang Kai-shek to have an independent air force under General Chennault. Despite the opposition of General H. H. Arnold and General George Marshall, President Roosevelt authorized the establishment of the Fourteenth Air Force on March 10, 1943. It never became a large force, beginning with about 350 aircraft and ending the war with close to 800.

The Fourteenth Air Force began operations with a shortage of both fuel and aircraft. Those aircraft on hand were in desperate need of overhaul. As a result, operations got off to a slow start. In time, however, all of the difficulties were overcome, and with the arrival of the 308th Bombardment Group's B-24s, activity began to accelerate. The Fourteenth destroyed coastal shipping, ferried supplies, did close-support work, and always rose to meet intruding Japanese bombers. Ironically, it achieved its greatest successes in 1944, when the Japanese swarmed forward in a 1,500-mile advance, conquering much of southeast China (including many of the Fourteenth's bases) but dissipating their resources for the defense of the Southwest Pacific.

ALASKAN INTERLUDE

The Japanese seizure of American territory in the Aleutians had been a grievous blow to U.S. national prestige, and it was decided to recover the islands of Kiska and Attu in early 1943. There the Eleventh Air Force fought under the worst weather conditions in the world, with high winds, low ceilings, epidemic icing, and runways choked with snow, mud, ice, or flowing water. When the Eleventh was attacking Kiska, during the period from June to October 1942, it destroyed 32 aircraft in the air, and a further 13 on the water. In the process, it lost 9 aircraft to combat—and 63 to adverse weather conditions.

Eleven thousand American troops invaded Attu on May 4, 1943, bypassing the larger garrison at Kiska. The fighting was exceptionally fierce as the Japanese, well dug in, resisted to the last man. In twenty-six days of bitter fighting, the Japanese were wiped out, with only 28 prisoners taken from a force of 2,500. There were 1,000 Americans killed in the action. When Kiska was invaded later in the year, it was discovered that the Japanese had quietly evacuated their troops. That withdrawal eliminated the Eleventh Air Force's reason for being, and it spent the rest of the war posing a threat to the garrisons in northern Japan.

CONCLUSION

The Pacific war was long and hard, and fought with a fury not found in Europe, even in cauldrons like Stalingrad. The air war became increasingly one-sided as months passed, but the Japanese never lost their offensive spirit, or their willingness to die. The Americans learned quickly in combat, and created the training and logistics base to teach the growing band of newcomers the hard facts of combat. By the summer of 1945, the bombing campaign in Japan was under way and, for the first time, the idea of an invasion began to be questioned. By the end of the summer, that question was answered.

A cumulative series of errors by the Imperial Japanese High Command had placed the empire in a fatal position long before the Battle of Midway. Not realizing how detrimental it would ultimately be to the conduct of the war, the Japanese military had conditioned the public to think that any criticism of the military government was a criticism of the Emperor, and thus impermissible. Without the counterweight of informed public opinion, and with any military dissent labeled as treason, the High Command fashioned an artificial climate in which realistic assessments even from top leaders like Yamamoto were disregarded.

Strict security kept the Japanese public ignorant of military reverses for as long as possible, the closely controlled media continuing to whip up patriotic fervor with blatant lies about Allied losses. This security also deceived the Allies, who were unaware until after the war as to just how badly beaten the Japanese actually were. Early in the war, the Japanese military police, the Kempe-tai, instituted strict measures on all aspects of Japanese life, extending it beyond even Gestapo standards to include thought control, so that anyone could be denounced for even a suspicion of having a defeatist thought. These measures stemmed from the very top, for it was not a coincidence that the man guiding Japan's destiny, Prime Minister Tojo, had been Commander in Chief of the Kempe-tai in China.

The hubris of the Japanese military fostered blunders of omission and commission in military affairs, diplomacy, and relations with conquered territories so egregious that they make those of Adolf Hitler, Joachim von Ribbentrop, and Alfred Rosenberg look trivial in comparison. In the first place, they began a war with the West at a time when the war in China had already drained Japanese matériel and manpower sources. Despite overwhelming evidence on Wake Island, Corregidor, and elsewhere to the contrary, Japanese at all levels had a profound naïveté, rooted in provincial chauvinism, that maintained their belief that the United States was morally weak and would sue for peace after the initial defeat. The same naïveté led them to grossly overestimate the time it would take the United States to recover from the first strike. The Japanese thought it would take two years; it took just over six months.

At the same time, the hostility and suspicion between the army and the navy in Japan was so intense that military operations were sabotaged from the beginning to the end of the war and beyond. Further, Japan suffered an economic planning fiasco, failing utterly to expand its industry to meet the requirements of a world war. Like Germany, it did not begin to reach its industrial potential until 1943, when it was far too late. Making a bad situation worse, Japan failed to exploit the resources of the areas it conquered, primarily because of the brutally repressive policies it used even as it spoke of the "Co-Prosperity Sphere." As a nation in the embrace of racism, the Japanese refused to "stoop" to eliciting cooperation from the countries it had conquered. Postwar Japanese accounts reveal the ruthless cruelty of the occupation troops, for whom the phrase "sharpen their sword" was a euphemism for random decapitation of prisoners.

The military-planning failure, however, exceeded even the economic fiasco. Japan switched its emphasis from battleships to aircraft carriers but was utterly unable to provide the planes and pilots for them. Neither the army nor the navy expanded pilot training to the degree that it easily might have, even though all of Manchuria was available as a protected training ground. The army continued to depend upon its light-infantry division concept and did not develop the types of tanks, antitank weapons, armored personnel carriers, and related equipment that had been proved in Europe, and which the Americans would use with such effect against it. And even when the light-infantry divisions could put up a long defensive fight—without hope of winning, but still able to inflict casualties—the army often sacrificed them in futile banzai charges. Far worse, the army was incapable of creating a suitable logistics and supply base, so that its troops fought with inadequate clothing, medicine, fuel, and food. The soldiers and sailors were told to fight until they died, simply to keep the war away from the homeland for a little longer.

After the war, the Allies conducted war-crimes trials for some of the Japanese military. There should have been another, conducted by the Japanese soldiers and sailors themselves, indicting their leaders for an abysmal failure to provide the basic food, water, and medicine essential to survival. That the Japanese officer corps was brave, from Tojo down to the ensigns and second lieutenants, is undeniable, yet the calloused, criminal incompetence of the staff officers is without parallel in military history.

Finally, the vaunted Japanese intelligence system failed miserably, unable to pierce the Allied cryptographic systems and remaining unaware that Japanese codes were being read on an almost real-time basis.

Japanese soldiers, sailors, and airmen fought with courage and dignity; they deserved better of their leaders.

9

ROUND-THE-CLOCK BOMBING

THE EUROPEAN BOMBING OFFENSIVES

The Allied bombing campaign began in 1939 as an ineffectual pecking around the perimeter of enemy defenses. It grew slowly for the first three years, then accelerated in late 1944 and early 1945 to reach a degree of frightfulness that the world had never dared to contemplate. The worst visions of Douhet, Mitchell, Trenchard, or even that most malevolent of men, Adolf Hitler, had never encompassed the extent of death and destruction visited by aerial bombing upon Europe, and most particularly upon Germany.

Early concepts of the "knock-out blows" were rendered puny by 1944. In the conventional prewar wisdom, 40 or 50 tons of bombs were considered enough to destroy London or Paris and cause a rioting populace to force chastened governments to sue for peace. By the end of World War II, the combined efforts of the Royal Air Force Bomber Command and the United States Strategic Air Forces had rained down 2,790,000 tons of bombs upon Axis targets in Europe and the occupied territories. Of this amount, 85 percent were dropped after June 1, 1944, and 72 percent after December 31, 1944. The massive escalation was possible only by 1944, when the Allied air forces and logistics systems had reached the size necessary to fight a genuine air war.

In the process, German air defenses grew as well, proving for the greater part of the war to be equal, and sometimes superior, to both of the opposing air forces. Hard-pressed on all fronts, the Germans elected to expand their defenses gradually, at a rate just sufficient to blunt the current level of enemy effort. Over time, the German day- and night-fighter forces grew from just a few airplanes to hundreds; in the same period, the Allied forces grew from a similar few to thousands of aircraft. It was a losing strategy for the Germans, who might have won both the night and the day air battles permanently if they had trebled their early efforts.

At the end of the bombing, Germany was prostrate, its land overrun by foreign armies. It had suffered 6 million war dead, including 510,000 casualties of the bombing, and the entire country was in ruins—transportation, utilities, industry, and, not least, political system, for the Nazi government simply evaporated overnight. Until May 7, 1945, there was still a functioning Nazi system. On May 8, it vanished with a whistle in the dark as everyone changed from brown uniform to drab civilian clothes. Fortunately for the hardworking, long-suffering German populace, the peasants continued to farm, the fishermen continued to fish, and the anonymous apolitical civil service continued to function so that a minimum level of subsistence could be maintained. The bitter German joke "Enjoy the war, the peace will be terrible" was not quite true—after the Nazis, the war, and especially the bombing, bare existence seemed quite tolerable.

There were a thousand aspects to the long and bitter air war, but four cities and one aircraft came to symbolize the heart of the campaign. The cities were Hamburg, where the first man-made firestorm occurred; Schweinfurt, where the Germans asserted daytime air superiority; Berlin, where the Bomber Command lost a costly battle; and Dresden, which became the symbol of the depths of the campaign when it was destroyed in an anticlimactic bombing horror in February 1945.

The one aircraft was the North American P-51 Mustang, the long-range fighter that reversed the losses at Schweinfurt and over Berlin, and made it possible for the Allies to secure air superiority, allowing the bombing campaign to reach its final intensity.

PERSONALITY PROBLEMS

Even more than in other combat arenas, personalities played a tremendous role in the bombing campaign on both the Allied and the Axis sides. From heads of state to the military commanders and right down to the individual crews, the course of the bombing campaign turned upon individuals. Perhaps because of the awful nature of bombing, with its endless destruction and harm inflicted upon the innocent, the commanders of both Allied and German units were under tremendous scrutiny. No matter how remarkable their achievements, most of the top military commanders on both sides received far more criticism than praise for their efforts. Churchill first backed his bomber commander, Air Chief Marshal Sir Arthur Harris, then sidled away from him in the controversy over Dresden. Lieutenant General Ira Eaker built the American Eighth Air Force into a formidable force despite every obstacle; just when it was reaching maturity, it was jerked from him like a toy from a child. The German generals faced similar rebuffs; after creating an efficient night-fighting force from virtually nothing, Generalleutnant Joseph Kammhuber was banished. His daytime opposite number, Generalleutnant Adolf Galland, did equally well and was given even more humiliating treatment.

And all the time, on both sides, the bureaucratic barracudas circled—men who wanted top posts and didn't care who or what they sacrificed to get them, totally indifferent to the fact that their politics were awash in the blood of the aircrews. In one of many coincidences of the war, the three major western opponents endured strikingly similar losses among their aircrews, the Germans losing 80,588, the British 79,281, and the Americans 79,625 lives. Losses among staff members were considerably lower.

The bombing ended with the war, but the multifaceted arguments about both the morality and the efficacy of the bombing campaign did not. These are so complex and involve so many issues that they must be discussed before the campaigns themselves are dealt with.

THE ISSUE OF MORALITY

The question of morality is difficult to resolve except with a simple syllogism: War is immoral. Bombing is part of war. Therefore, bombing is immoral. All other means of killing incident to war are implicitly immoral as well, from the bayonet thrust to premeditated horrors like the Allied blockade of Germany during and *after* World War I, which starved 750,000 to death.

Yet the morality of bombing must be considered within the context of World War II politics, where, as a famous historian has noted, the greatest immorality would have been to allow Hitler to win and to establish the perverted Nazi rule over much of the world. Further, some argue that there are degrees of morality, and that area bombing is more immoral than the precision bombing techniques advocated by the United States.

This, however, is essentially a nonargument, for the implacable factors of weather, wind, size of the bombing formation, inexperience, mechanical flaws, and German resistance tended to make *most* bombing area bombing, whether it was intended to be so or not. Precision bombing—the precise surgical strike that attempts to place all the bombs only on hard military targets—was the goal of the United States Strategic Air Forces, and was, indeed, often the goal of Bomber Command. But it was a goal usually impossible to attain. The question that daily faced Allied leaders was not "Do we bomb precisely?" but "Do we bomb at all?"

PRECISION BOMBING VERSUS AREA BOMBING

The U.S. Army Air Corps intended that a modern bomber would be able to fight its way through any enemy fighter formations without incurring excessive losses, and, equipped with the secret Norden bombsight, do precision bombing, the proverbial "dropping bombs in a pickle barrel." Fighter escort was deemed "highly desirable" but it was considered impossible to build a fighter that had the speed and maneuverability of opposing interceptors, yet could still carry the necessary fuel to get to the target and back.

The British belief in precision daylight bombing was shattered by a high attrition rate; later they learned that they did not possess the equipment or the skill to do precision night bombing either. By that time, however, the events of war and the momentum built up for Bomber Command dictated that the bombing had to go on in the only way it could: night area bombing. The die was cast.

When the Americans arrived in Europe, the British tried to dissuade them from the idea of daylight precision bombing, but both American doctrine and equipment were dedicated to the task and could not readily be converted to night work.

To the dismay of the Americans, the abominable weather over the Continent meant that precision daylight bombing was impossible. The Eighth Air Force was forced to rely on the technical equipment that had been developed for blind bombing. The result was that, contrary to popular belief, the American effort was also largely an area-bombing campaign.

Precision bombing was in fact difficult even on a clear day, with no fighter opposition, when the bombs were dropped from a formation of large aircraft. If it were possible to fly wingtip to wingtip (which no one would do with an overladen bomber in turbulent air), the combat-box formation would be more than 1,800 feet wide. All the airplanes dropped their bombs when the leader dropped, creating a swath of bombs 1,800 feet wide, each one subject to the vagaries of wind at various altitudes. And even with the excellent Norden bombsight, the precise moment of the drop depended upon the skill of the bombardier-pilot combination. With the formation covering approximately 300 feet per second, a decision to drop that was even four seconds off would mean that the bombs would be dropped 1,200 feet short of the intended aiming point or 1,200 feet over. The most well-intended bombing meant a shower of bombs from a moving mass that could not be less than 1,800 feet wide, and could easily be 1,200 to 5,600 feet or more off target. Precision in the sense of hitting *only* the *exact* targets aimed at was impossible.

Even with this caveat, the leaders of both the RAF and the USSTAF would have preferred to do 100 percent precision daylight bombing for a wide variety of reasons. It would have meant easier navigation, better target identification, more harm to the enemy war potential, and less likelihood of the need for a return trip. They were inhibited from doing so by the size of the formations, the nature of the bombing problem, the weather, and not least, the Germans, who used fighters, antiaircraft fire, decoy fires, electronic counterwarfare, smoke screens, and other devices to combat the attack. So instead of bombing as they wished, the Allies bombed as they could, and for the most part this meant area bombing.

THE EFFICACY OF BOMBING

Opinions on the effectiveness of bombing varied wildly before the war. Most leaders thought that bombing of civilian targets would be an effective war-winning strategy. Yet no one had any idea of the immense effort that a successful bombing campaign would require, nor of the tremendous resilience and strength possessed by a modern industrial country such as England or Germany. Both sides also completely underestimated the apparently inexhaustible ability of civilians to endure the ravages of bombing.

When the war ended with Germany in ruins, with city after city mere gutted shells, the streets filled with rubble, the utilities destroyed, it seemed that bombing had, after all, been effective. It had taken a long, hard fight to beat the Germans on the ground with the assistance of bombing, and the question "What would it have been without it?" had to be asked. The answers seem obvious. In the first place, there would have been no invasion without the air superiority obtained through the bombing campaign. Had there been no invasion, then there were only two probable outcomes for the ground war. Russia might have made a separate peace, leaving Germany still master of the Continent. Alternatively, Russia might have crushed Germany in the field and then continued its victorious land assault across Europe to the English Channel.

After the war, captured Germans didn't seem to doubt the efficiency of the bombing or the disastrous effect that it had upon their war effort. Albert Speer called it the unrecognized second front, as it diverted 2 million men, 30 percent of the gun output, 20 percent of the heavy ammunition, 50 percent of electronic equipment, and 33 percent of optical equipment to antiaircraft units. Perhaps most important, 75 percent of the vital dual-purpose 88-mm guns were diverted to antiaircraft duty from their primary task of killing tanks on the Eastern Front. Hermann Göring attributed the loss of the war to the American long-range escort fighter achieving air superiority. Field Marshal von Rundstedt stated unequivocally that airpower had made the difference. Most other German leaders, military and civilian, agreed that airpower had won the war for the Allies.

The bulk of the arguments about the efficacy of the bombing campaign would have been avoided if the correct assumptions on the scale of the effort required had been made in 1938, rather than in 1942, and the necessary size of forces recognized. Then, by 1943, the bombing forces could have reached the size and efficiency they achieved in late 1944. In that case, bombing would have won the war in Germany just as it did later in Japan. It would also have precluded the need for an invasion, provided western Allies had been willing to accept Russian occupation of the European Continent, which they had not.

SHIFTING POLITICS AND THE RUSSIAN FACTOR

Both the English night and the American day bombing campaigns were subjected to political influence that directed their execution. On July 8, 1940, just as the Battle of Britain was building, Winston Churchill wrote to Lord Beaverbrook at the Ministry of Aircraft Production that he could see only one sure path to winning the war "and that is an absolutely devastating, exterminating attack upon the Nazi homeland. We must be able to overwhelm him by this means, without which I do not see a way through."

When the Germans invaded the Soviet Union on June 22, 1941, Churchill promised Stalin that he would visit a "terrible winter of bombing" upon Germany. The night bombing offensive was accelerated, as it was the only thing Churchill could—or wanted to—offer Russia in the form of a second front.

A curious circular process then began by which the air effort was enormously increased in intensity, but was restrained from ending the war. Airpower was at first correctly seen as the only way of harming Hitler, and then as the only way to keep the Soviet Union from collapsing. Two political elements intervened to prevent airpower from defeating Germany by itself. As the bombing offensive built in intensity, the United States eclipsed Great Britain in strength and began to dictate the course of the war. The American leadership was as dedicated to the concept of an invasion of the Continent as the British leadership was to its avoidance. The second political element was the growing realization that an invasion was necessary to contain the Russians in Eastern Europe, an often-overlooked influence on the bombing campaign. An invasion required air superiority. The only way to get air supremacy was to defeat the German Air Force in the air and on the ground. And the only way to do that was by bombing critical targets, for the Luftwaffe declined to engage the enemy over a target it did not feel was critical.

THE EARLY BRITISH CAMPAIGNS

The British learned the hazards of daylight bombing in one mission. On December 18, 24 Vickers Wellington twin-engine bombers, the best the RAF possessed, made an armed reconnaissance of the Schillig Roads waterway and Wilhelmshaven.

German fighters shot down 10 Wellingtons into the sea, most in flames, for the fuel tanks were vulnerable. Two more ditched en route, and 3 crashed on landing. The first lesson had been learned: unescorted aircraft could not bomb in daylight from medium altitudes and live.

British training and doctrine were destroyed at a stroke. Very little effort had been devoted to night navigation or bombing and few crews were capable of finding the Ruhr in the dark, much less a city and still less a particular factory in that city.

Yet the war had to be fought, leaflets had to be dropped, and the enemy had to be hurt. The British turned to night raids, and, according to the crew reports, did amazingly well. Reports were made of great fires caused by the raids, and wishful thinking translated tons of bombs dropped into acres of destroyed factories and great percentage losses in German output.

The crews were brave and believed their reports. RAF leaders based further actions on the reports. Churchill directed his war economy to the service of a massive bombing campaign, which was the only thing going well for the British, who had thrice been driven from the Continent in ghastly evacuations (Dunkirk, Greece, and Crete) and were under attack from all quarters. In the fall of 1940, two staff changes occurred that would have subsequent effect upon the execution of the bombing campaign. Air Chief Marshal Sir Charles Portal left Bomber Command to become Chief of the Air Staff, succeeding Sir Cyril Newall. At Bomber Command, Portal's place was taken by Air Marshal R. E. C. Peirse.

Portal is universally described as the perfect choice, a man of immense intellect, formidable education, polite address, and determination, able to work as well with Churchill as with his aircrews. Portal was perhaps the best example, next to General Eisenhower, of the importance of an appealing personality, for despite some egregious errors, he survived the war beloved by almost all. Once one of the most vociferous advocates of area bombing, Portal created a plan for "Target Force E." Four thousand bombers in 250 squadrons were to win the war by killing 1 million Germans, injuring another 900,000, and making 25 million homeless by totally destroying forty-three major German cities. Yet in the end, when area bombing began to be criticized even in England, Portal distanced himself from Dresden, area bombing, and the Bomber Command. Portal also turned his back on the commanders who had won battles for him, first Dowding and later Harris, and he resolutely quashed the idea of the feasibility of the long-range escort fighter. Despite these flaws, his other qualities sustained both his position and the admiration of his colleagues.

Peirse was a less fortunate choice to handle the difficult task with which Bomber Command was tasked, not having the means to accomplish what he was directed to do, nor the acumen to detect how far short he was falling. Peirse's career would be plagued with difficulties and eventually go up in smoke in a bizarre 1943 incident. While serving as Allied Commander in Chief, South-East Asia Command, Peirse was smitten by the lovebug and eloped with another man's wife. It was not a good career move; the lady was the wife of General Sir Claude Auchinleck, then Commander in Chief, India, and this diminished Peirse's promotion prospects.

It must be noted here that Peirse, Portal, Churchill, and the entire bombing campaign were undone by a universal malady of aircrews, the natural desire to believe in the successful execution of a mission, and the reporting of that success in an exaggerated fashion. Aircrew optimism was pandemic; it was reflected in the reported accuracy in bombing, in the numbers of aircraft shot down, in the effect upon enemy actions. All air forces of all countries acted in the same way. As a result, air force reports were discounted and rediscounted to the point that the real efficiency of the bombing was never appreciated.

BUTT BUTTS IN

Churchill's Scientific Advisor, Professor Sir Frederick Lindemann, Lord Cherwell, was a nonconformist, a man of unusual accomplishments and greater ego, a peculiar combination of broad insight and tunnel vision. Lindemann was cursed by the not-invented-here syndrome, and resolutely supported the development of infrared detection of aircraft, as opposed to radar, and was for a long time the advocate of ineffective parachute-cable mines as an antiaircraft weapon.

Following a hunch, in early August 1941, Lindemann asked D. M. B. Butt of the War Cabinet Secretariat to make a statistical analysis of the results of the British bombing of Germany, using photographs taken during night operations of the previous two months, encompassing a hundred raids on twenty-eight targets.

Butt's report was shattering. It revealed that on average, only one in three aircraft *of those attacking* got within five miles of the target. Over France, it was somewhat easier, three in four did; over the Ruhr, only one in ten made it to within five miles.

Butt reported that the bombing was severely affected by both ambient light and weather. On a moonlit night, the overall average was two in five reaching within five miles; on a moonless night, the average degraded to one in fifteen, the same ratio that obtained in thick haze. These numbers applied only to the planes successfully attacking; if the entire number of sorties was included in the figures, they were diminished further by one-third.

Reactions to the Butt report were predictable. The RAF, particularly Bomber Command, refused to believe it, not even when its results were confirmed by day reconnaissance photos. Yet the facts were indisputable. The RAF did not possess the means to navigate to the target area, or the means to drop bombs accurately when—or if—it found the target.

The conclusions of the Butt report were reinforced by serious reverses in battle. On the night of November 7, 1941, 400 aircraft were dispatched to attack targets from the Ruhr to Oslo, reaching as far east as Berlin itself. The entire attack was a disaster; 37 aircraft were lost, for a 9.25 percent loss rate. The worst showing came at Berlin, where only 73 aircraft of the 169 dispatched attacked, and of these, 21 were lost—more than 28 percent. Few bombs hit Berlin; there were only 41 casualties, including 9 dead. The other components of the raid did almost as poorly. Tragically, most of the losses resulted from fuel exhaustion—the planes simply glided down to crash or ditch, and were never heard from again.

Peirse blamed the weather and inexperienced crews, so totally reprehensible an admission after two years of warfare that he had to go. He was succeeded on February 22, 1942, by a man who came to personify area bombing, Air Chief Marshal Sir Arthur Travers Harris.

Portal and Harris were old friends, and Churchill soon took a liking to the new man. Harris was big, gruff, and outgoing—with superiors at any rate—and he had the fighting instinct that Churchill always admired.

Harris found Bomber Command in sad shape, with only 378 serviceable aircraft and crews. Of these, only 69 were heavy bombers, while 50 were the blighted Blenheim light bombers. British heavy-bomber production had so far failed miserably, as the new models were having development problems.

To the new commander, the bomber campaign meant one thing only: the defeat of Germany by aerial bombing. He threw himself wholeheartedly into this effort, protesting vigorously when his assets were withdrawn for use in the Middle East or in the Battle of the Atlantic. In the process, he adamantly opposed "panacea targets" like the enemy oil, ball-bearing, or transportation industries, maintaining that there was no way to defeat the Germans but to bomb them to oblivion.

Only three days after Harris's appointment, the first official parliamentary doubt was raised over the effectiveness of Bomber Command. A firm pacifist, Sir Stafford Cripps, noted that the United States and the Soviet Union were now in the war and asked whether "the building up of this bomber force is the best use we can make of our resources."

It was the start of an antibombing, anti-Harris campaign that would grow over time, flaring into its maximum intensity after the bombing of Dresden. In the meantime, however, Harris went about his business, striking both the Germans and his critics with Operation Millennium, the thousand-bomber raid on Cologne. His ability to conduct Millennium must be considered first in the light of his maturing equipment and the German defense systems.

BRITISH AIRCRAFT AND EQUIPMENT

The three principal Royal Air Force medium bombers were workmanlike examples of the first generation of modern, all-metal enclosed-cockpit bombers, and what they lacked in sophistication they made up for in good old-fashioned aerodynamic virtues.

The Vickers Wellington made its first flight on June 15, 1936, and continued to be built until October 1945, by which time 11,461 had been produced. It was the principal RAF bomber until the advent of the four-engine heavies. With a 235-mph top speed, a 180-mph cruise speed, and a range of 2,200 miles with a 4,500-pound bomb load, the Wellington was a remarkable aircraft for its time, but far from adequate for Harris's needs.

The Wellington was supplemented by two smaller aircraft, the Handley Page Hampden, nicknamed the "Frying Pan" because of its unusual tail-boom arrangement, and the Armstrong Whitworth Whitley. All three aircraft had individual idiosyncracies, but one thing that they had disastrously in common was vulnerability to the foul weather and icing encountered for so much of the year over Europe.

The Whitley, affectionately called the "Flying Barn Door" because of its slab-sided disregard for streamlining, first flew on March 17, 1936. In an effort to reduce ground run on takeoff and landing (sophisticated high-lift flaps were not yet available), the wing was given an exceptionally large 8.5-degree angle of incidence (the angle of the wing relative to the fuselage). As a result, the Whitley flew with a peculiar nose-down flight attitude that imparted the distinct impression to an observer that the wings and fuselage were traveling along diverging paths. But handsome is as handsome does, and the Whitley was beloved by its crews. It was the first British aircraft to drop bombs on German soil and was not removed from night bombing operations until the spring of 1942, when its work continued in leaflet-dropping and maritime reconnaissance roles.

THE HEAVY BOMBERS

In October 1938, in sharp contrast to German planners, the British Air Ministry began development of Program L, which called for the delivery of 3,500 heavy bombers by April 1942. A unique feature of the plan was the concept of "quantity groups," which divided production among several manufacturers and created a dispersal system under which large components were built in as many as twenty different factories, while smaller components were the product of a widespread subcontracting network. The system anticipated the methods to which bombing would drive the Germans a little later in the war.

Program L called for 1,500 Short Stirlings, 500 Handley Page Halifaxes, and 1,500 Avro Manchesters. The Stirling suffered an extreme operational handicap due to a shortsighted official specification, which was that the aircraft's wingspan had to be less than the hundred-foot width of the standard door opening of RAF hangars! As a result, the Stirling's designers had to use a wing of low aspect ratio (the relationship of span to width) and high induced drag. This, coupled with the slab-sided fuselage, gave the Stirling a clumsy appearance. Clumsy it was not—the Stirling was highly maneuverable, but it had a limited ceiling that made its operations increasingly hazardous as antiaircraft fire improved. On some missions to Italy, heavily laden Stirlings had to fly *through* the Alps, rather than over them. Despite, or perhaps because of, these difficulties, *A Thousand Shall Fall* one of the most gripping accounts of the air war, was written by a Stirling pilot, Murray Peden.

The Stirling first flew on May 14, 1939, and entered combat on February 10, 1941, with an attack on Rotterdam. The Stirling was used in bombing raids until September 8, 1944; as it was supplanted by the more capable Lancasters, it was relegated to the usual obsolete bomber tasks of mine laying, radio countermeasures, airdrops to French resistance groups, and glider-tug work.

The second bomber of Program L, the Handley Page Halifax, would come to constitute 40 percent of Bomber Command's strength at the height of the bomber offensive. Handley Page had originally planned to use two Rolls-Royce Vulture engines, but decided in 1937 to change to four Rolls-Royce Merlins. It was a happy decision, and the first flight on October 25, 1939, led to the eventual production of another 6,176 aircraft. The "Hallie" had a top speed of 282 mph, a range of 1,030 miles with a 13,000-pound bomb load, and a maximum gross weight of 65,000 pounds.

Program L's third heavy bomber, the Avro Manchester, was unsuccessful because of the failure of its two Rolls-Royce Vulture engines, which did not deliver the designed power and were completely unreliable. Avro saved the day, however, by redesigning the Manchester with four of the proven Rolls-Royce Merlins, thereby creating the best British bomber of the war. Unlike most of its contemporaries, the Lancaster was a handsome aircraft with a 287-mph top speed and a service ceiling of 24,500 feet. Its bomb capacity was its major capability. The Lancaster could carry a normal load of 14,000 pounds of bombs (compared to a B-17's 4,000 pounds), and a relatively simple modification enabled it to carry the 22,000-pound "Grand Slam," the heaviest bomb of the war.

Rushed into production even before its January 9, 1941, first flight, the Lancaster gave Harris the airplane he needed for Bomber Command, and he bought the plane in quantity—ultimately, 7,374 Lancasters were built. Yet as capable as the Lancaster was in terms of speed, range, altitude, and bomb load, its utility would have been minimal if the necessary navigation and bombing equipment had not been created to ensure that its huge bomb load found the proper targets.

THE BOFFIN'S WAR

During the war, English scientists proved more adept than their German counterparts at devising each round of an escalating system of measure and countermeasures. The test of their success was not so much in original thinking, for the German scientists often met or exceeded their efforts in this regard, but rather in the design and application of their ideas.

In England, a central organization, the Telecommunications Research Establishment (TRE), had been set up in Dorset to bring the various radio direction-finding systems under one control. TRE prospered under the leadership of Dr. Bernard Lovell and Dr. Alan Hodgkin, both of whom were subsequently knighted for their work. From the TRE laboratories would come a series of developments to assist in navigation and bombing, including Gee, Oboe, and H2S.

Gee (for the Grid map used with the system) had originally been developed as an aid to instrument landings, but its war potential was recognized by an expert engineer, Professor R. J. Dippy. Gee permitted a navigator to determine his position easily and accurately, without making any transmissions from the aircraft that might reveal its position. The Gee system consisted of three ground transmitters, located at a considerable distance from each other, and each transmitting pulse signals simultaneously.

Gee was a tremendous improvement over conventional navigation techniques, but the curvature of the earth limited its range to about 350 miles, and the Germans would soon learn to jam it, just as the British had interfered with the similar German Knickebein system.

Oboe was a ground-to-air-to-ground blind-bombing system in which two ground stations (called "Cat" and "Mouse") calculated the range and track of the aircraft, guiding the pilot by notes resembling that of the musical instrument that gave it its name. Introduced on December 20, 1942, by de Havilland Mosquitoes of No. 109 Squadron, it was successfully used for the first time on February 16, 1943. Oboe was used primarily for single aircraft acting as target markers for the mission and, like Gee, was limited in range by the curvature of the earth. A later development, G-H, reversed the Oboe process, the aircraft measuring the distance from two RDF stations in England, tracking itself over the target by measurement from one and determining the time for bomb release from the other. Its great advantage was that as many as eighty aircraft could use the system simultaneously.

Oboe was quickly followed into action by development of the airborne intercept radar. Called H2S (for Home Sweet Home), it was a radar scanner carried within the aircraft that gave a rough picture of the terrain below as the variations in terrain painted an image on the cathode ray tube. When the variations were quite distinct, as in the case of a shoreline, the picture was easy to interpret. Learning to use H2S took practice, and some navigators became far more skilled than others in interpreting subtle variations of the images. The demanding skills of the discipline required a special sort of personality, and so radar observers acquired an identifiable air, the 1940s equivalent of today's computer hacker, and they could be picked out by other aircrew members at a glance.

Electronic equipment transformed the air war by giving Bomber Command's four-engine heavies an accuracy never before possible, reducing the range of error from five miles to perhaps 1,000 feet. The developments did not yield precision bombing as interpreted by the USAAF, yet they did permit useful bombing at night and in bad weather, and the American air force would come to rely upon them.

The bombing and navigation aids were enhanced by the development of new tactics and more effective electronic counterwarfare measures and target-marking indicators, all of which will be discussed below.

THE GERMAN DEFENSE SYSTEMS

After the war, Field Marshal Erhard Milch was asked what he regretted most, and his reply was "the 140,000 unbuilt fighter planes." Milch's number was probably high, but it is representative of the unrealized production of German aircraft because of administrative inefficiencies, lack of leadership, and, ultimately, the Allied bombing campaign.

The slack effort stemmed from many sources. In the prewar period, German leaders lacked the vision to fight a global war, just as their Allied counterparts did. The crucial difference came after the war started, when the Allies began an all-out campaign to win the war at all costs, while the Germans persisted with a business-as-usual attitude. Göring's assertion that guns came before butter was only partially correct, for the Nazi leaders, particularly Hitler, were concerned with public opinion. As a result, German consumer industries employed 6 million workers well into the fourth year of the war, and for most of the war the German civilian populace ate better than their English counterparts. In April 1942, more than 90 percent of German industry was still on a single shift and was closed one or one and a half days on the weekend. In 1943, German households still employed 1.4 million domestic workers, supplemented by 600,000 young girls imported from the Ukraine.

The successful repulse of the RAF attack on Wilhelmshaven added to the Luftwaffe's confidence level. As a result, just sufficient emphasis was placed on both day and night air defenses to maintain a rough parity with the Allied forces, when, with only slightly more effort, a decisive superiority could have been achieved. As the war spun out, the defense efforts were on two occasions adequate to win air superiority—against the Americans in the fall of 1943, and against the British in the awful winter of 1943–44. But air superiority has to be won every day, and the Germans became unable to match the rising Allied ante.

EARLY DAY DEFENSE EFFORTS

In many respects, the Germans had adopted a prudent and economic mode of defense for the period 1940–43, given their far-flung commitments. After the Battle of Britain, the RAF continued to build its fighter defenses and found itself in the embarrassing position of having a large and powerful force not being actively employed. Air Chief Marshal Sir Sholto Douglas had replaced Dowding and wanted to earn new laurels with offensive fighter sweeps across the channel. His ideas were embraced by Air Marshal Sir Trafford Leigh-Mallory, the "big wing" advocate who now commanded No. 11 Group. Missions were undertaken in the true Trenchard spirit to force the German Air Force to fight—in "Rhubarbs," sweeps by fighters only, and "Circuses," combined bomber and fighter missions.

Rhubarbs and Circuses were melded into what the British called a "nonstop offensive" during the summer of 1941. In six months, a total of 190 bomber and 2,700 fighter sorties were made. The advantages held by the RAF in the Battle of Britain now accrued to the Germans, who could elect to fight or not as they chose. The German radio intelligence services and radars gave ample warning of incoming RAF flights, so that they could be met by an appropriate force. If a German pilot bailed out, he was returned to his squadron by the quickest route; when an RAF pilot bailed out, it meant a prison camp. Perhaps more important, the Messerschmitt Bf 109F-1 and F-2 fighters were fully equivalent to the intruding Spitfires, while the new Focke-Wulf Fw 190s were clearly superior. The only Luftwaffe fighter to use a radial engine, the Fw 190 was about 30 mph faster than the Spitfire V at all altitudes up to 25,000 feet and had the fastest rate of roll of all fighters in World War II.

The British attacks were mere pinpricks that the Germans could choose to ignore if they wished. For the most part of this early period, only two German *Jagdgeschwadern*, 26 and 2, were deployed in the west, while the RAF maintained seventy-five day-fighter squadrons in England at a time when they were badly needed in the Middle East and in Southeast Asia. The Luftwaffe pilots grew experienced with the good hunting while their veteran RAF counterparts were sent to other theaters, leaving less-experienced pilots for the contest. (This was the beginning of a process that, by the end of the war, found the Luftwaffe manned by a few of the very best combat pilots the world had ever seen, supplemented by a large number of ill-trained novices who rarely survived their first five missions.)

The British plan failed miserably, for the Luftwaffe achieved an approximate four-to-one victory ratio over the RAF through 1943. The adverse numbers would probably have impelled the British to stop the attacks if it had not been for the need to do something to assist the hard-pressed Russians. Thus Sholto Douglas and Leigh-Mallory were hoisted on their own petard, forced to continue a campaign with an unfavorable attrition ratio that they would gladly have halted.

Both sides were unaware that the scale of combat was small compared to what would happen only a year later, and the main result of the RAF offensive was the gradual improvement in German defenses by the spring of 1942. Freya early warning radars were in place all along the coast, supplemented by an increasingly expert radio intercept service. Another chain of Freya stations was located well inland, as far as fifty miles from the coast. However, despite the improvements in equipment and training, the Germans did not add substantially to their day-fighter forces until 1943, and in fact periodically drew down on them to reinforce other theaters. In January 1943, fewer than 100 day fighters were available in Western Europe. By the end of 1943, the pressure of the American Eighth Air Force forced an increase to 342 single-engine and 139 twin-engine fighters.

NIGHT DEFENSE

Night flying was hardly an innovation. The first night flight had been a balloon ascent in London in 1836. Aircraft began flying at night as early as 1909 at College Park, Maryland, when Wilbur Wright and his student, Lieutenant Frederic E. Humphreys, flew in the bright moonlight. Both the Allied and the Central Powers had engaged in extensive night flying during World War I, conducting bombing, clandestine operations, and night fighting. Yet the science had since been thoroughly neglected in Germany, one reason being that Germany relied almost entirely upon flak for air defense at night. The German searchlights, target predictors, and guns were excellent for their time, and the flak units were considered to be an elite, receiving some of the best personnel joining the Luftwaffe. Like the French, the Germans believed that flak could put up an almost impenetrable shield against intruding aircraft. Unlike the French, the Germans backed up their belief by investing heavily in the necessary weaponry. It was in fact a heady rush of euphoria after a tour of the German antiaircraft defenses that inspired Hermann Göring to comment publicly that he could be called "Meier" (an antisemitic slur) if any foreign aircraft ever penetrated to the Ruhr. The remark would live to haunt him.

British incursions soon made it apparent that night fighters were necessary, and in June 1940, one of the elite *Zerstörergeschwadern*, ZG 1, was sent with its Messerschmitt Bf 110s to Düsseldorf airfield to train and create new tactics for night fighting. Designated the Nacht und Versuchs Staffel (Night and Experimental Squadron), it was commanded by Major Wolfgang Falck. Falck, known as the "Happy Falcon" as much because of his smiling, hook-nosed visage as for his name, had gained national fame leading the relentless December 1939 attack on the Wellingtons. Falck was soon appointed Wing Commander of *Nachtjagdgeschwadern*. It was an excellent choice, for Falck first proved that the Bf 110, with modifications, could be used at night, and also developed the first night-intruder tactics, sending Dornier Do 217s over England to ambush British bombers returning after a mission.

As Falck's unit grew, Göring realized that he had to incorporate the flak, searchlights, and night fighters in a single command, and in July 1940 called on Oberst Joseph Kammhuber to command the newly established 1st Night Fighter Division, in Brussels. A small man, Kammhuber had plenty of drive and set up a defense system that became known to the Allies (but not the Germans) as the "Kammhuber Line." Although he and Falck quickly developed a mutual personal antipathy, they managed to work together nonetheless.

Kammhuber's defenses originally were relatively short and narrow, but were extended over time. They at first depended upon a fifteen-mile-deep strip of searchlights, which would work in cooperation with flak guns and night fighters. After October 1940, the early German Würzburg A parabolic reflector radar units became available, permitting the night fighters to operate ahead of the search light zone.

Observing the general path of RAF bombers to the Ruhr enabled Kammhuber to set up three night-fighter zones contained in an area 54 miles in length and 12 miles in depth. Each had two Würzburg A radars and a searchlight battalion. The night fighters were linked through one Würzburg to a ground control, while the searchlights were linked through the other Würzburg. In the area plotting room, three night fighters (one in each zone) could be controlled and vectored to the incoming bombers, which were illuminated by the searchlights. The whole procedure was called *Helle Nachtjagd*, illuminated night fighting. It was an excellent concept, making maximum use of the capabilities of existing equipment to match Bomber Command's potential.

Kammhuber knew instinctively that "illuminating" the target by a radar network was far more effective than using searchlights, for it was more accurate and not inhibited by clouds. Incoming formations were first detected by the Freya radar, which could scan for about 100 miles in all directions. The tracking task was then turned over to the new narrow-beam Würzburg Riese (Giant Würzburg), which could scan over a radius of 36 miles. One Giant Würzburg followed the bomber coming in, while another controlled the night fighter, which was maintained on station, at altitude, orbiting a radio beacon located central to its "box," the area in which it operated. The aircraft courses were plotted in the control room, and vectors were given to position the fighter where its own radar could take over the interception. This became famous as the *Himmelbett* (four-poster bed) system.

Eventually, a series of boxes was created that stretched from Norway to southeast of Paris. The Kammhuber Line proved to be an effective defense against the RAF bomber tactics of the time, which consisted of flying single aircraft, well separated in time and distance. However, a subtle but important difference in the two enemies' methods was slowly emerging. The British were experimentative, investing more time, money, effort, and brainpower in new offensive systems. The Germans were reactive, failing to devote comparable resources to either anticipating or solving the defensive problems the British were about to force upon them.

The effectiveness of the early German defenses was further enhanced by the development of airborne radar, for which Kammhuber had announced a requirement in June 1940. By July 1941, Telefunken had produced an effective airborne intercept radar called Lichtenstein. The early sets were heavy, not too reliable, and encumbered with a radar antenna system (known as Hirschgeweih, or Stag's Antlers) whose drag cut about 25 mph off the interceptor's speed. This made many of the pilots reluctant to use radar, for the differential between the speed at altitude of the night fighters and that of the bombers was already relatively slight.

By early 1943, the Luftwaffe was able to field five *Geschwader* of twin-engine aircraft. The Messerschmitt Bf 110, which had failed so miserably in its vaunted Zerstörer role, now came into its own as a night fighter. Many variants were produced, over time, but the most numerous were the Bf 110G-4s, which had two 1,475-horse-power Daimler-Benz engines, four MG 17 machine guns and two 20-millimeter cannon. Some later versions were modified to have the schräge Musik (Jazz Music) installation, in which two 20-millimeter cannon were placed behind the cockpit and arranged to fire upward at an angle of 70 to 80 degrees. As most British bombers lacked belly turrets, the schräge Musik provided a means to approach the target closely to deliver a devastating attack. Like their British night-fighter counterparts, the German crews soon gathered a proficiency in reading the blurred signals on the radarscopes and became progressively more effective. In addition to the Lichtenstein SN2 radars, the Bf 110s picked up the pace of the electronic countermeasure war with two new devices. The first was the FUG 27 Flensburg, which homed in on the tail-mounted "Monica" radar that RAF bombers used to detect night fighters. The second was the FUG 350 Naxos, which homed in on the airborne H2S radar.

The Bf 110s bore the brunt of night fighting through 1943, along with the Junkers Ju 88 and Dornier Do 217s, and by the summer of 1943, the system had acquired a deadly expertise. The night fighters were complemented by the flak (mostly 88-mm, but also including 105-mm and 128-mm guns) and the radar-controlled searchlights, whose brilliant grip was feared by all the bomber crews because it was almost incapacitating—and because it pointed them out so clearly as a target.

The old saying that "no good deed goes unpunished" had particular application to Generalmajor Kammhuber, who not only created the night-fighter force but provided for its ability to adapt to Allied advances. Kammhuber was sacked on June 24, 1943, because he told Hitler that since the Americans were producing aircraft at the rate of 5,000 per month, he would need eighteen night-fighter groups instead of six and that the German ground- and air-based radar systems would have to be vastly improved. Hitler told him that the American production figures were ridiculous and that the current night-fighter operations were satisfactory. Kammhuber was replaced by the erstwhile chief of the Luftwaffe Command Intelligence Staff, the inept Major General Josef "Beppo" Schmid. Kammhuber was posted to Norway, where he survived to return to duty and became chief of staff of the postwar Luftwaffe.

FIRST INNINGS FOR THE AMERICAN EIGHTH AIR FORCE

The Eighth Air Force was originally conceived as a mobile tactical air force for use in one of Churchill's pet ideas, Gymnast, a projected invasion of northwest Africa. When Gymnast faded away, Major General Carl Spaatz advocated sending the Eighth Air Force to the United Kingdom, where Brigadier General Ira C. Eaker and his small staff were already in place.

Eaker masterminded the transition of the Eighth Air Force from its original role to that of strategic bombardment of Germany. In the process, he became Harris's intimate friend, a confidant and advisor to Churchill, and the architect of the greatest air force in history. In doing so, he suffered endless torment from the normal exigencies of war, continuous harassment from his friend and mentor, General Hap Arnold, and ultimately, the greatest disappointment of his life.

The Eighth Air Force, originally commanded by Spaatz, consisted essentially of VIII Bomber Command, to be headed by Eaker, and VIII Fighter Command, to be commanded by a World War I ace, Brigadier General Frank O'Donnell "Monk" Hunter, along with the associated support and administrative units. It grew from six men and no airplanes in February 1942 to 400,000 officers and men and 8,000 aircraft by June 1944. It occupied some 250,000 acres of British soil in 43 airfields and 40 other major installations. The growth was possible only through the generosity and courtesy of the Royal Air Force, which put everything from quarters to secretaries to laborers at Eaker's disposal.

Even as it began its buildup, the Eighth Air Force took on an additional role as the rapidly expanding United States Army Air Forces' milk cow, used to succor new initiatives as they arose. After Churchill had persuaded Roosevelt on the idea of Operation Torch, the invasion of North Africa, the creation of the Twelfth Air Force became an immediate, crippling drain on the Eighth Air Force's resources and was in fact a pattern for the future.

Despite the diversion of its assets, expectations remained high for the Eighth Air Force. No one, from General Marshall on down, had any idea of the enormous lag time involved in the creation of the airfields, logistics chains, and training, and this led to extreme dissatisfaction and fretting that was passed on to Eaker. Although much could be done concurrently, many things had to be done consecutively, and these delayed the Eighth's operational capability.

For example, airplanes could be produced at the same time crews were being trained, so that new crews could pick up new airplanes and fly to England rather expeditiously. But to create an airfield, you had to secure the land, hire the labor force, do the necessary land preparation (drainage was a vital problem in England), construct the buildings and the runways, put in the utilities and housing, and so on. Most of these things necessarily happened in succession, so that only a limited time compression was possible. In addition, aircraft arriving from the United States were far from combat-ready, and many took weeks in modification and repair shops before making their way to an operational airfield.

The rapport General Eaker enjoyed with his RAF counterparts made things happen more quickly than otherwise could have been expected, but it was never fast enough to suit Arnold. Eaker served as a shock absorber, taking the bad news from the top and not passing it along to those who served under him. It was a role he performed well, but it exacted a toll on his physical resources. Eaker excelled in community and public relations, and he endeared himself to all in a now-famous arrival speech in which he said only, "We won't do much talking until we've done more fighting. After we've gone, we hope you'll be glad we came."

The Eighth's first mission was flown on July 4, 1942, when six crews were selected to join six RAF crews in a daylight raid on four enemy airfields in Holland, using American-built Douglas Bostons, the RAF version of the A-20.

The raid was a tactical failure, redeemed by an episode of extraordinary heroism. Two planes flown by Eighth Air Force crews were shot down and a third was heavily damaged. But the day was saved and the future forecast by Captain Charles C. Kegelman, who attacked the De Kooy airfield. On his run-in, Kegelman's right propeller was shot away by flak that bounced his plane into and off the ground. Kegelman kept it flying, first turning to blast a flak tower into silence, then crossing the Channel on one engine. He was awarded the Distinguished Service Cross, and deserved more, for he foreshadowed the bravery, ability, and perseverance that would characterize Eighth Air Force crews.

On August 17, the Eighth Air Force flew its first heavy-bomber mission, with twelve B-17s attacking the marshaling yard at Rouen. RAF Spitfire squadrons escorted the formation, and there were no losses. General Eaker rode in the *Yankee Doodle*, the lead bomber of the second flight of six, and reported that the bombing was highly accurate. Flak and fighter opposition was light, the only injury coming from a pigeon shattering the nose of one aircraft, injuring the bombardier and navigator slightly.

The Eighth began a slow buildup, limited both by the arrival of aircraft and their reassignment to other theaters. Eaker tried to get the maximum effect from them, sending all that he had available whenever weather made daylight precision bombing possible, and bombing targets in the occupied territories for the most part. The missions were escorted by fighters, mostly Spitfires at first, and then, as they arrived, Lockheed P-38s. The following spring, they were augmented by the Republic P-47s, which had to overcome initial engine and radio problems.

The first VIII Bomber Command raid on Germany took place on January 27, 1943; its target was Wilhelmshaven. Bombing was not particularly effective, but neither were the German fighters or flak. Twenty-two fighters were claimed shot down, while the Germans actually lost 7. Ninety-one bombers were dispatched, and 55 made effective runs on the targets; 1 B-17 and 2 B-24s were lost.

This minor effort was the start of a campaign that would bring Germany to its knees. For the next thirty months, the Eighth fought the best the Germans had to offer in the way of fighters and flak; for most of that time, it suffered an almost constant barrage of criticism that not enough was being done, that aircraft were not being used effectively, that crews were not working hard enough, and, at one point, that too many crews were landing in Switzerland or Sweden. The men at the top, particularly Arnold, Marshall, and Roosevelt, failed to see that the Eighth's expansion had been inhibited by their own changes in strategy. Further, they were unaware of the massive difficulties getting crews trained to a satisfactory level for combat in bombing, formation flying, and gunnery. Maintenance and personnel difficulties had to be overcome; at one point, 49 percent of Eaker's planes were grounded because of a shortage of spare parts, tools, and aircrews. The incidence of damage in bombing missions was far higher than anyone had predicted, with the rate running at 42.1 percent in December 1943.

Then there was the weather, always the weather, an impossible problem that sometimes allowed only five bombing days a month. Commanders were always concerned that they might launch a mission on the basis of reports of good weather over Germany, only to have the aircraft return to find England completely covered with clouds and fog. Weather became an increasingly important factor as the numbers of aircraft grew; by 1944, as many as 2,000 aircraft would be taking off to climb through the clouds over England, with only the most primitive procedures to avoid collisions—of which there were many. Once assembled on top, there remained the mission itself, the return, and the descent through the clouds back to land.

The February 16, 1943, raid on St. Nazaire (known to the crews as "Flak City") showed early on just how difficult a task daylight precision bombing was. Of the 65 bombers attacking the submarine pens there, 6 were shot down and 2 more were lost in a collision. This represented a terrifying 12.3 percent loss rate, one that would mean the loss of the total force in just over eight missions.

THE ODDS AGAINST LIFE

The loss rate was a fundamental problem tormenting the minds of combat leaders and crews alike, especially because the critics at the top seemed to have no inkling of the deadly mathematics of the missions. The theoretical tour of duty was twenty-five missions—seemingly reasonable until one computed that a 4 percent loss rate would ensure that no one, statistically, would live to complete his tour. Even if the loss rate dropped to 2 percent, crews had only a fifty-fifty chance of surviving. But the hard truth was that by early 1943 the Eighth Air Force was averaging an 8 percent loss rate, which meant that, on average, no one could expect to complete his thirteenth mission.

The situation demanded new leaders and new tactics, and both emerged. One of the greatest fighting commanders in airpower history, Colonel Curtis E. LeMay, was the Commander of the 305th Bombardment Group. Only thirty-five years old, LeMay was a brilliant leader whose laconic manner and ability to make hard decisions earned him the nickname "Iron Ass" early in his career, a title that he successfully defended until his retirement as Chief of Staff of the U.S. Air Force in 1965.

LeMay insisted on intense training, which he personally supervised, flying in the top turret of a B-17 to call out instructions to his aircraft commanders. He adopted a realistic attitude toward the feared German flak, calculating that on the bomb run, German guns would have to fire 372 shells to down a bomber. (His calculations were conservative; on the average, nearly 5,000 antiaircraft shells were expended for each bomber shot down.) Working with Brigadier General Laurence S. Kuter, who commanded the 1st Bomb Wing, LeMay developed the combat-box and combat-wing formations, which were intended both to intensify defensive firepower and improve bombing accuracy.

Each combat box had eighteen to twenty-one bombers in a group, and three groups formed a combat wing. The lead group flew slightly ahead of the other two, one of which flew 1,000 feet higher and echeloned to one side, while the other flew 1,000 feet lower and echeloned to the opposite side. With fifty-four bombers in a formation, an attacking German fighter would be covered by up to 540 .50-inch machine guns.

The granite-faced, stubble-jawed LeMay was quick to adopt other ideas as well. He evaluated the results of the attacks and selected the best bombardiers and navigators to fly with highly trained crews and lead the missions. In the past, each aircraft had bombed separately, and the results varied as widely as the skills of the individual crews. Now all the aircraft in the formation dropped when the lead crew did, ensuring a far-higher average accuracy. LeMay's insistence that the last minutes of the bomb run be flown straight and level to permit the bombardier a chance to stabilize his sights, kill the wind drift, and improve his accuracy undoubtedly caused some losses, for it gave the German antiaircraft gunners a better, more predictable target. The result was that bombing targets were hit far more frequently than in the past, with greater accuracy.

On March 18, 1943, the 305th Bomb Group placed 76 percent of its bombs within 1,000 feet of the mean point of impact on the Vulcan submarine yards at Vegesack, Germany. A total of 73 B-17s and B-24s had bombed the small target, which measured only 2,500 by 1,000 feet, and was no more than a collection of sheds and shops along the Weser River near Bremen. On this one mission, the Eighth had combined the combat box, dropping when the lead crew dropped, and the steady bomb run with an innovation, the automatic flight-control equipment (AFCE). With the AFCE, the bombardier could send signals to the autopilot so that he, rather than the pilot, was flying the airplane on the last portion of the bomb run, reducing communication error and increasing accuracy.

The success at Vegesack validated precision bombing, lessening the pressure to convert to night bombing. Congratulations poured into the Eighth Air Force from every important critic, including Churchill, Portal, Harris, and Arnold. Yet the triumph was a mere palliative; in the next nine months, the Eighth would grow slowly and suffer terrible losses, and the concept of precision daylight bombing would again be closely questioned. The Luftwaffe was learning, too, and as its strength and skills grew, the Eighth Air Force would be defeated in the skies over Germany.

THE THOUSAND-BOMBER RAID

Ten months before Vegesack, "Bomber" Harris had achieved his first great victory for Bomber Command in Operation Millennium, the thousand-aircraft area-bombing raid against Cologne. In planning the attack, Harris had in mind impressing his critics in England as much as his enemies in Germany; he knew that the public was thirsting for a victory, and that a massive attack on a famous German city would be widely applauded, quieting parliamentary opposition.

Harris had already achieved considerable success in the March 28–29 raid on the ancient, vulnerable city of Lübeck, and the April assault on Rostock. The reaction of the top Nazis to these raids was revealing. The first reports of heavy damage were immediately discounted as enemy propaganda and provoked a flood of recriminations. Next, intense concern would be expressed about the loss of historic buildings or art objects. Finally, there would be a call for retribution in the form of attacks against English cultural centers.

After the two raids on these venerable cities, Goebbels, in a curious reversal of psychological warfare technique, had handbills printed with pictures showing the damage done by the British to Rostock and Lübeck, and ordered them dropped over the English cultural centers slated for attack in what were termed the Baedeker raids, after the popular guidebook. Goebbels reported in his diary that Hitler viewed the English as belonging to "a class of human beings with whom you can talk only after you have first knocked out their teeth." The Führer was to find to his dismay that it was the British who were about to administer the dental work, steadily increasing the fury of their assaults even as the weight of the German attack steadily diminished.

Goebbels managed to capitalize on the German bomb damage by ensuring that the majority of relief efforts were conducted by party organizations, so that victims of the raids saw the Nazi party apparatus in a positive role. The early efforts were comprehensive. Relief supplies streamed into bombed cities from other areas and special teams of carpenters and glaziers set about repairing the houses. Immediately after the raid, canteens were set up and extra rations, often including liquor, were issued. Compensation payments were made promptly for damage incurred in the raid. Later on, as more and more cities were bombed, the relief efforts were still appreciated even when they were limited to providing soup kitchens and carving a path through the rubble. The gauleiters, normally despised for the luxurious way they lived, exerted themselves on the people's behalf and worked especially hard to get the defense industries running again. In most circumstances, the Nazi system of duplicative party organizations for normal governmental functions was costly and ineffective, yet it was to prove itself invaluable in its response to Allied bombing.

OPERATION MILLENNIUM—RESULTS VERSUS EFFECT

The RAF effort had slowly built to the point that it was able to get 250 to 300 aircraft into the air for a maximum effort. During sustained operations, as a result of both ordinary maintenance requirements and combat damage, the number declined quickly. In his desire to smite the enemy and secure friends in the press and Parliament, Harris wanted to send 1,000 aircraft in a single strike against a single city. By desperate efforts, straining all of Bomber Command's resources, he mustered 1,043 aircraft. The bulk of the force was composed of 598 Wellingtons, but he also had 292 of the new four-engine types—131 Halifaxes, 73 Lancasters, and 88 Stirlings. Thirty-five percent of the aircraft were manned by instructors and students from the operational training units. This was an especially risky business, for if the training crews were destroyed, the bomber offensive would be set back for a year until they were reconstituted.

On the night of May 30–31, 1942, the weather was good from takeoff to landing, and the chosen target, Cologne, was bathed in bright moonlight. Harris used saturation tactics, compressing the bulk of the force so that within ninety minutes, 898 aircraft dropped more than 1,500 tons of bombs on the ancient city, starting enormous fires that continued to rage the following day. More than 600 acres of the city were destroyed. Harris had achieved both his short- and long-term political aims. The immediate effect was to silence his opponents in Parliament, whom he considered far more dangerous to his mission than the Germans. The long-run effect was that England's resources were tipped irrevocably to Harris's mission, so much so that eventually more than one-third of Great Britain's manufacturing effort went to support the bomber offensive. By the time serious doubts rose again about the efficacy—and the morality—of area bombing, it was too late. England had committed not only vast aircraft-building resources to the campaign, but all the ancillary resources as well—the manufacture of bombs, test and maintenance equipment, airfield construction, training, and all the myriad other requirements of a massive bomber force. After Cologne, there was no turning back; the British Empire was committed to Harris's strategy.

In sharp contrast to the energy being expended by British leadership, the German reaction to the raid on Cologne was both typical and ineffective. Göring adamantly refused to believe the telephone reports of Cologne's gauleiter, Josef Grohé, for if correct, the reports meant not only total failure of his flak and fighters; they proved that the RAF had reached a level of strength unattainable by the Luftwaffe. Göring insisted to Hitler that the attack had been made by about 70 planes, and of these, more than 40 had been shot down. Göring's rose-colored glasses momentarily turned Cologne into a great victory for the Luftwaffe, but Hitler talked directly to the gauleiter and soon knew the truth. (Grohé was an unpleasant fellow; late in the war, he exhorted the citizens of Cologne to resist the advancing Americans to the death, while he himself fled to safety.) Göring had already started to fall from grace; Cologne was grease on the slide.

Properly so, for the devastation was tremendous. Police reports indicated that more than 18,000 buildings had been destroyed, and another 39,000 damaged. Only about 500 people were killed, but 60,000 were "dehoused" in the cold English phrase of the time. Intensive photo reconnaissance was conducted to see what could be learned, and the analysis would have great effect upon future raids. The photos showed that each ton of high explosive destroyed, on the average, approximately one and three-quarters acres of built-up property, while each ton of incendiary bombs destroyed three and one-quarter acres. In the past, Harris had been a great believer in the efficacy of high-explosive bombs; now he knew that he had to arrive at an optimum mixture with incendiaries.

Bomber Command made two other 1,000-plane raids in the next month, hitting Essen on June 1–2 with 956 aircraft and Bremen on June 25–26 with 1,056. It was an immense effort that could not be sustained; the training crews had to go back to school, the mechanics had to have time to repair the airplanes, and the crews had to have rest. For Bomber Command, the five raids actually masked the underlying problem of aerial bombing, for the Allied leaders continued to confuse the *results* of a raid with its *effectiveness*. In all these raids, and in many to come, the *result* was the destruction of large areas of the city and the obvious damage inflicted upon factories. Inferences made from the statistical analysis of these results would begin to verge on lunacy. One early 1944 report estimated that each ton of bombs dropped resulted in a loss of 22,500 man-hours, a totally unrealistic number in view of the fact that German production was increasing at a rate never before achieved.

The early bombing, all the way through the middle of 1943, had, in fact, little *effect* upon production and less upon morale. In the five cities struck in the first half of 1942––Lübeck, Rostock, Cologne, Essen, and Bremen—production of war materials was resumed almost immediately and within a few days was back to normal. There were many instances in which a surge of patriotic resentment would drive production levels *above* the projected levels.

The difficulty was that while interpreters could study the daytime reconnaissance photos and determine exactly how many square feet of factory area had been destroyed, how many aircraft had been blown up, and how many houses had been burned, they could not determine how quickly repairs would be made, how much harder people would work, what substitute space and tools would be used, or how little production was affected.

First British, and later U.S., planning was based on the optimistic analysis of results, and the damage to German morale, production, and general capability was vastly overestimated. This in turn led to a failure to make repeat raids. Albert Speer would comment later on his surprise that hard-hit targets were usually left alone to recover, while the bombers turned their attention elsewhere.

The German night-fighting force was learning as rapidly as its day-fighter counterpart, and, as it gained in strength and experience, it would make the British raids more and more costly. Harris would continue his area-bombing campaign confident that he was on the correct path to winning the war without an invasion, and always protesting when his bombers were diverted to other tasks. Yet even as he took satisfaction in the damage to German cities and began a fateful assault on Berlin, the German night-fighter force was preparing to win a victory in the spring of 1944.

THE COMBINED BOMBER OFFENSIVE

All through 1943, despite the constant drawdowns for other needs, the Eighth Air Force continued to grow, its strength reflected in the numbers of aircraft and the importance of the targets as the following table of selected raids shows:

DATE	TARGET	AIRCRAFT DISPATCHED	AIRCRAFT ON TARGET	AIRCRAFT LOST	PERCENT LOST
Feb. 26	Wilhelmshaven	93	65	7	7.6
Mar. 18	Vegesack	103	97	2	2.0
Apr. 17	Bremen	115	107	16	13.9
May 21	Wilhelmshaven	161	123	5	3.0
June 11	Wilhelmshaven	227	182	26	11.5
July 26	Hannover/Hamburg	284	199	24	8.5
Aug. 12	Bochum/Bonn	330	243	25	7.6

The table does not reflect the many raids where the aircraft on target were a very small percentage of those dispatched, primarily due to adverse weather. It does reflect the growing cost of operations, as the Eighth plunged forward into Germany without an adequate long-range fighter escort. The efforts in July sent a clear signal—128 four-engine bombers shot down, 1,280 crewmen removed from the war, at a cost of 40 German fighters. German fighters and antiaircraft took their toll on every mission; in addition to combat losses, from 25 to 50 percent of all aircraft returning from a deep penetration of Germany suffered battle damage. The burden on repair establishments, replacement aircraft, and spare-parts supply became intolerable.

THE RAF AGAINST THE RUHR

While the Eighth Air Force battled the German day fighters, Bomber Command was fighting a similar battle at night. It would attack the Ruhr for ten long months in 1943, with the most intense period stretching from March through June, when twenty-six heavy attacks were made, including the famous if less-than-decisive "Dam Buster" attacks on May 16–17. As Germany's industrial heartland, the Ruhr was hotly defended by flak and night fighters. Two-thirds of all high-grade steel, 75 percent of the coal and coke, and 60 percent of all iron and steel poured from the Ruhr, yet it was a miserable target, its factories blending together like modern suburbs, making target identification almost impossible. The Germans, already faced with bad news in Russia and Africa, responded to the attack by bringing so many new flak emplacements that the Ruhr soon contained 40 percent of all the Reich's antiaircraft guns. More night fighters were deployed, and it became evident to Bomber Command, as it was to the Eighth Air Force, that the German fighter force had to be destroyed if bombing operations were to continue.

Although General Eaker's concept of the combined bomber offensive had been smiled upon at Casablanca, there was no official directive for such operations until June 1943. Previously, the practical concerns of the Bomber Command and the Eighth Air Force had prevented extensive cooperation. The first important instance of combined operations would occur during the bombing of Hamburg, an epochal battle that forced Germany's unbelieving leaders to realize the true magnitude of the aerial threat. But before that, a number of important decisions were made at the Trident Conference held in Washington in May 1943. Operation Overlord, the invasion of France, was now set for May 1, 1944. This gave Harris and Eaker twelve months to accomplish the objectives of Operation Pointblank, the combined bomber offensive. By the time of the Trident Conference, it was increasingly clear that the first task was still the destruction of the Luftwaffe and the establishment of complete air superiority. However, the only way air superiority could be achieved was by forcing the German Air Force to fight, and this in turn was possible only by the sustained bombing of vital targets. It meant that the Eighth Air Force and Bomber Command had to throw themselves upon the German sword to blunt it—a bloody and costly process that twice would lose air superiority rather than win it. The battle would have remained lost if a new factor had not intervened, one that leaders on both sides had insisted was impossible to achieve—the long-range fighter. It came in the form of the North American P-51 Mustang, with Rolls-Royce Merlin engines, and it revolutionized the air war over Europe.

OPERATION POINTBLANK

By the late spring of 1943, the Luftwaffe was increasing its strength, improving its tactics, and introducing important innovations into the battle, including effective head-on attacks that were later offset by adding more forward-firing machine guns to the bombers. In January 1943, the Luftwaffe had 1,045 fighters for the defense of the Reich (635 single- and 410 twin-engine), compared to only 445 on the Russian front (395 single- and 50 twin-engine.) One year later, the total had grown to 1,650 fighters in the west (870 single- and 780 twin-engine), while the strength on the Russian front had declined by 20 to 425 fighters, of which only 345 were single-engine. In the simplest terms, defending Germany against the bombers cost her air superiority in Russia. In addition, the concentration of production on fighters meant the virtual elimination of the Luftwaffe's bombing force.

Management of the air battle was shifted by the creation of new defensive zones and of many simple auxiliary fields, each one amply stocked with fuel and ammunition so that more than one sortie could be made per mission. The Luftwaffe made its night fighters do double duty, calling them in to undertake standoff attacks against the formations once the fighter escorts had departed.

Armament was beefed up by a variety of means. The Weapons Proving Ground at Tarnewitz had adapted an infantry rocket-mortar shell to be air-launched from tubes suspended under the wings of both single- and twin-engine fighters. The mortars could be fired from a distance of more than half a mile and were relatively accurate, having a plus or minus flight deviation of only 130 feet horizontally and 23 vertically at that range. Called Pulk Zerstörers (*Pulk* meaning "herd," Luftwaffe slang for the American combat box), the single-engine fighters were equipped with one launcher under each wing, while the twin-engine fighters had two. So equipped, they would linger outside the range of the American bombers' guns and lob rockets into the formation. It was a terrifying sight, for the USAAF crews could watch the smoke trail from the launch of the big 250-pound mortar shells from invulnerable aircraft sitting out of range. A hit from the 21-pound warhead was fatal and usually broke up the tight formation, allowing single-engine fighters to close with the survivors.

German fighter aircraft were also modified with heavier armament, including the installation of two 30-mm Mk 108 cannon in underwing gondolas on some of the Bf 109Gs and Fw 190A-8s, increasing their firepower but severely limiting maneuverability. Another tactic, initially used with success but later found to be impractical, was the airdrop of the 550-pound SC 250 bomb on enemy formations.

All of these innovations had made the suppression of the German Air Force urgent, and on June 10, 1943, the Pointblank directive was issued. It called for a combined offensive by Bomber Command and the Eighth Air Force against seventy-six targets in six target systems, recognizing fully that this wholesale attack was fully dependent upon destroying German fighter strength either before or during the attack. The Luftwaffe was to be destroyed in the air, on the ground, and in the factories.

The Eighth Air Force was given the assignment of destroying the German airframe, aero-engine, aircraft component, and ball-bearing industries, while Bomber Command was ordered to effect the "general disorganization" of German industry. The Allied fighter forces were tasked to engage enemy aircraft in the air or on the ground and to keep bomber losses at a minimum.

Even though the means at his disposal were limited, Eaker began a faithful execution of the directive he had authored. Sir Arthur Harris continued on his own way, convinced that his prescription for area bombing was still what the patient called for, and that a salutary dose of medicine could be dispensed at Hamburg.

OPERATION GOMORRAH—THE BOMBING OF HAMBURG

The decision to destroy Hamburg, the second-largest city in Germany, home to a major submarine base, an oil refinery, and more than three thousand other factories, was made when Arthur Harris had been in command just over a year. In that year, his force had matured, now being largely equipped with four-engine bombers, with only a few units still using Wellingtons. The new bombing aids had been augmented by new tactics.

Harris reluctantly agreed to the formation of what he called "Pathfinder Force," to be headed by Air Commodore (later Air Vice Marshal) D. C. T. Bennett. Bennett, an unsmiling hard-charger, promptly selected the best crews from across Bomber Command to create what became No. 8 Pathfinder Group. (Harris, after opposing the concept of a target-finding group, was human enough to insist on both selecting their name and seeing to it that they had a distinctive badge to wear.)

But an idea is not a proven tactic, and the Pathfinders had to undergo their own training period to achieve the desired results. Tactics evolved over time; initially, two aircraft would use Gee to lay down parallel lines of flares on either side of the target. Then other aircraft, called "illuminators" would drop groups of red flares outlining the target area. Finally, "marker" aircraft would drop incendiaries to start fires on the target area. It was a demanding task, and absolutely horrifying to the potential victims below, who knew all too well what the "Christmas trees" meant.

There were many problems, the most crucial of which was that when the Pathfinders missed the target, *everyone* missed the target. There was a tendency for each succeeding wave of bombers to drop early and avoid the flak—as a result, the center of the bombing would creep backward, sometimes completely out of the target area. The Germans set decoy fires and attempted to duplicate the colors and the disposition of the illuminating flares. However, the Pathfinders gained efficiency with experience, improving both their techniques and their pyrotechnics. A later further sophistication was first called a "master of ceremonies," and then a "master bomber," who was always an experienced leader, acting as on-scene commander. Typically, the master bomber would be first over the target, and then stay, orbiting the target area, vulnerable to flak and fighters for an extended period, to direct operations. If the line of falling bombs began to creep back, the master bomber would instruct the next wave to drop farther in; if decoy fires were spotted, he would call them out. It was a hair-raising job, but records of the master bomber's comments are characterized by a cool sportsmanship and often good humor, interlaced with savage criticisms of bombers apparently not coming up to the mark.

JULY 24 TO AUGUST 3, 1943

The British and the Americans had been bombing Germany for three years and for six months, respectively, when their efforts converged over Hamburg. For the RAF, it would be their 138th visit to the city; for the USAAF, the first. Hamburg had suffered but had grown strong; besides the night fighters, it was defended by 278 flak guns and 24 searchlight batteries.

Harris planned to drop 10,000 tons of bombs on Hamburg over a period of several days; on the first night, an especially heavy proportion of incendiary bombs was intended to saturate the enemy fire-fighting capability to take full advantage of the interesting new weapon up his sleeve: Window.

Window was the simplest of all electronic countermeasures and would today be called "chaff." Originally, it consisted of sheets of metal coated paper, about 14 by 21 inches; later it was found that a bundle of 2,000 foil strips, each about 1/16th of an inch wide and 11 inches long, not unlike the tinsel used to decorate Christmas trees, was the electrical equivalent of a bomber to German radar screens. The strips were cut to half the wavelength of the German radar they were being used against, and operated as antennas, resonating with the radar signals with which they were illuminated. When dropped, the bundles of Window opened, and millions of strips spread out, confusing enemy radar scopes with thousands of targets and completely blinding them to the real targets, the bombers.

On the night of July 24, 1943, Harris launched 791 bombers against Hamburg. The Stirlings, sent first because they climbed so slowly, were just creeping toward altitude when the now-expert German defensive apparatus sprang into action, unlimbering the Himmelbett system that had served it so well—until this fateful night. Just as the British had to revise their entire offensive philosophy after their disastrous daylight raid on Wilhelmshaven, so now would the Luftwaffe have to completely revise its carefully crafted methods of defense.

The first Window was dropped by Pathfinder aircraft as they approached within the estimated forty-five-mile range of the Würzburg radar. The bundle of chaff thrown overboard exploded into more than 2,000 twirling strips of tinfoil, each echoing the same bright blur that an aircraft did on German radar screens. As each bomber came into range of the radars, it began dropping Window, one bundle every minute for the entire trip into the target and back out until once again beyond radar range. Each bundle took about fifteen minutes to flutter to the ground, filling the screens with more than ten targets for each bomber. It became impossible for the radar operators to distinguish real from false targets, and no meaningful directions could be provided the German night fighters. As the number of bundles increased, both the Würzburg radar system and the Lichtenstein airborne radars were inundated with false targets. (The Freya radars were not affected.) The new electronic countermeasure was in fact ill named. Instead of Window, it should have been called Curtain, for it rang down a curtain of brightly glowing phosphor dots on the radars of the Himmelbett system.

On board a night fighter, the radar observer would acquire a target, close on it, then find that it was moving so slowly that it was impossible to track—a bit of drifting tinsel in the sky rather than a lumbering Stirling or a swift Lancaster. British intelligence operators, monitoring the German frequencies, sensed tension rising to panic in the voices of the controllers and the crews.

Window had a devastating effect, totally disrupting the Himmelbett system with reports like that from a Würzburg radar on the island of Heligoland that indicated 11,000 bombers were attacking. The 740 aircraft that arrived at Hamburg attacked almost at their leisure, some swinging around to make second bombing runs, as 2,396 tons of bombs, 980 of them incendiary, rained down. Yet in another testimony to the hardy German civilians, the severely wounded city rallied under the leadership of Gauleiter Karl Kaufmann and Bürgermeister Carl Krogmann, both convinced Nazis, and both excellent men in emergencies.

The Eighth Air Force hit Hamburg during the next two days. On July 25, 100 B-17s from the 1st Bomb Wing dropped 196 tons of bombs; the next day, another 54 aircraft from the 1st dropped an additional 134 tons. The weight of effort was small compared to the RAF's attack, but the precision strikes were directed against important aero-engine factories and the U-boat yards, and they maintained the pressure on the German air-raid-protection system and the citizens' nerves.

The British returned on the night of the twenty-sixth with only six Mosquitoes, enough to set off the alarms and deny sleep to the already battle-fatigued crews fighting the fires. July 27–28 was quite different, for Bomber Command put 729 aircraft across Hamburg in forty-five minutes, dropping a higher percentage of incendiary bombs, 1,200 tons in all. The previous raids had seriously weakened the German air-raid-protection services, and many fires were still smoldering. The heavier proportion of incendiaries combined with the weather and fate were to create a new phenomenon: the man-made firestorm. Even before the last aircraft had departed, the multiple fires in Hamburg had become a single holocaust, with temperatures reaching 1,000°C, creating an enormous tornado of fire that uprooted huge trees, set asphalt streets afire, and sucked human beings huddling in their homes into the heart of the storm. Bomb shelters were turned into crematoriums, where the victims were first asphyxiated by carbon monoxide and then burned to ashes by the ovenlike intensity of the heat. As many as 50,000 died; the exact number will never be known because there were no accurate records of the thousands of displaced persons, foreign workers, and slave laborers whose anonymous lives were communally consumed by the flames.

It was by far the worst bombing disaster of the war to date, and Germany was shaken by a wave of horror. Most of the Nazi leaders realized that the bombing offensive had reached a new level of terror. Albert Speer estimated that similar attacks on six more major German cities would bring the war to a halt. But the only man who could have changed things, Adolf Hitler, was not moved by his people's suffering. Just as he had not been cold when he forced his troops to hold in the snows before Moscow, he was now not burned as were the victims in Hamburg. Safe in his headquarters, he was confident that the German people would continue the war no matter what they had suffered. He dismissed Speer's protests, telling his Armament Minister that he would straighten out the production problems again, and that people could survive even if they had only a hole in the ground to live in, with a board to put over the top to keep out the rain. Hitler, in effect, condemned his entire population to the same troglodyte life he had lived at the front in the First World War.

From a purely pragmatic point of view, the Führer was correct. Speer did straighten out production problems, the people did return to work, and their morale did not break even when Bomber Command struck again on July 29–30. The heavy raid caused severe damage to previously undamaged areas of the city because the fire-fighting systems had completely broken down. But there was no firestorm and "only" 800 people were killed. The fourth raid, on August 2–3, was ineffective due to extremely bad weather en route.

In four raids on Hamburg, Bomber Command launched 2,592 sorties and dropped 8,344 tons of bombs. So jaded had commanders become that losses were considered to be low—only 87 aircraft, merely 870 crewmen lost, a livable 2.8 percent loss rate, well worth the killing of approximately 50,000 people, most of whom died in the firestorm. Nine hundred thousand people were homeless, thousands of buildings were destroyed, and there was a general dislocation of utilities, transportation, and ordinary commerce. Yet the people rallied quickly; after the war, it was estimated that the raids had cost Germany less than two months' production effort from its Hamburg factories.

And just as the people recovered, so did the Luftwaffe.

10

AIR SUPERIORITY LOST, THEN WON

Immediately after the raid on Hamburg, neither Harris nor his opponent Kammhuber could have guessed that even though the efficient Himmelbett radar system was rendered ineffective by Window, the aluminum strips that mimicked airplanes, a new and ultimately more effective system of night fighting would almost immediately evolve.

The code name "Wildsau" (Wild Sow) was derived from a slang term for a reckless, unpredictable person, something like "a loose cannon" in English. The great advocate of Wildsau tactics was Major Hajo Herrmann, himself a loose cannon by any standards of military discipline, who regarded the Himmelbett system as too limiting. He preached that standard single-seat day fighters could be flown at night against the bomber formations. A bomber pilot by trade, Herrmann borrowed Bf 109s and Fw 190s to try out his theory, wading into the British bomber stream and ignoring the German flak. Herrmann determined that the bombers were vulnerable if the searchlights caught them for as little as thirty seconds.

It was a risky business, for nighttime takeoffs and landings were difficult in these fighters, and the exploding flak did not distinguish between enemy bomber and friendly fighter. Herrmann had eighty-five-gallon external tanks installed on his fighters so that they could stay airborne for two hours and move from city to city as the attack progressed. Success with the single-engine fighters encouraged similar tactics by the twin-engine Junkers Ju 88s and Bf 110s. These combined with the radar-equipped night fighters to present the British with a new defensive problem that would ultimately defeat them in the Battle of Berlin.

THE FIGHT FOR AIR SUPERIORITY

The Eighth Air Force remained determined to push its bomber offensive into Germany, despite being able to put only 250 to 300 bombers in the air on a mission. A pattern evolved in which the Eighth would mount a series of stinging attacks, recoil from the losses, then stand down to recuperate before attacking again. The lingering, almost wistful, belief that heavily armed "self-defended" bombers could penetrate Germany without a fighter escort persisted primarily because there *was* no long-range fighter to escort the bombers. The Spitfires and the Republic P-47s were useful only for sweeps over France, although the Thunderbolt's radius of action got a boost to 400 miles in July when useful droppable fuel tanks became available. The Lockheed Lightning, which became available later in the year, could ultimately reach out to a distance of 600 miles when equipped with two 165-gallon drop tanks, but the Lightning was never highly regarded as an air-superiority fighter in European skies.

Sophisticated tactics were developed to extend the range of the escort fighters as much as possible, including phasing arrival of the various sections of the escort, but these were matched by the ever-observant Luftwaffe, which timed its attacks to coincide with the escort's departure. A massive engineering effort was made to increase the internal-fuel-tank capacity of the fighters, even though the increased weight had adverse affect upon climbing and handling characteristics. External tanks grew in size from 75 to 108 to 150 gallons, and instead of carrying one on the center line, engineers put two under the wings. These, too, adversely affected performance, but the loss was acceptable.

As his assets grew, General Eaker was under increasing pressure to obtain results. General Arnold sent message after message criticizing the level of effort by the Eighth, demanding to know why more was not being done and making invidious comparisons with the performance of other units. Bowing to the inevitable, Eaker was forced to replace two old friends, Brigadier General Newton Longfellow, Commander of VIII Bomber Command, and Brigadier General Frank Hunter, Commander of VIII Fighter Command. The dashing, mustachioed Hunter had insisted on sending his aircraft on fighter sweeps, but didn't draw the correct conclusion from the fact that they made few contacts and scored even fewer victories. The Germans quite properly declined to squander their resources in pointless dogfights, and simply refused to come up and fight. Much to Hunter's chagrin, he was replaced by the aggressive Brigadier General William Kepner.

Brigadier General Frank Armstrong, Jr., the brilliant bomber leader who had quietly obtained permission to fly in a Lancaster on the Hamburg raid, took over VIII Bomber Command. The two new men would make a difference in the air war, but Eaker's days as commander of the Eighth were already numbered, and, by coincidence, a plausible reason for his removal was established later in the year.

By the fall of 1943, when the Eighth Air Force was locked in a desperate struggle with the Luftwaffe, Allied troops fresh from victories in North Africa and Sicily had moved well up the Italian peninsula toward Rome. General Hap Arnold decided to split the Twelfth Air Force into two parts. Twelfth Bomber Command became the Fifteenth Air Force (Strategic), a heavy-bomber unit. Twelfth Fighter Command became the Twelfth Air Force (Tactical). The reasoning was sound; England was overcrowded and would have difficulty supporting more aircraft. The bases in Italy would have better weather. Major General James Doolittle was given command of the Fifteenth, effective November 1, 1943.

JULY 24 THROUGH AUGUST 17: THE GRISTMILL OF SCHWEINFURT

On July 24, 1943, the Eighth Air Force began what became known as "Blitz Week," with strikes that ranged from the longest raid to date, a 1,900-mile round-trip attack on targets in Norway, to attacks on Kiel, Hannover, Hamburg, Kassel, and Warnemünde. Eaker had begun the week with 330 aircraft and crews on strength who made 1,720 sorties. Of these, 1,080 hit the target and 88 were lost, 8.5 percent of the attacking force. With many other aircraft too damaged to fly, VIII Bomber Command was whittled down to less than 200 heavy bombers, an ominous prelude to the first raid on Schweinfurt.

The out-of-theater demands on the Eighth Air Force continued, highlighted on August 1 by the contribution of two bomb groups to take part along with the Ninth Air Force in the low-level raid on Ploesti, Rumania, which provided Germany with 66 percent of its crude oil. The raid was marred by lack of secrecy and inaccurate navigation, and of 177 planes attacking, 54 were lost. Though the damage was severe, it was easily repaired, and the follow-up attacks were too long in coming, a persistent flaw in Allied bombing operations.

On August 17, the anniversary of the first Eighth Air Force raid on Rouen, a double strike was made on the ball-bearing factories at Schweinfurt and the Messerschmitt factory at Regensburg. General LeMay, wearing his new single star, led the 4th Bombardment Wing against Regensburg with 146 aircraft, while the veteran 1st Bombardment Wing, commanded by Brigadier General Robert B. Williams, attacked Schweinfurt with 230 aircraft.

Almost nothing went well. The original plan called for the 4th Bombardment Wing to receive the brunt of the Luftwaffe's attack, so the 1st, departing England ten minutes after the 4th, would be able to hit Schweinfurt while the enemy fighters were refueling and rearming. Weather intervened and plans were changed in order to give the Allied escorts (eighteen squadrons of Thunderbolts and sixteen squadrons of RAF Spitfires) time to return from their first escort mission, rearm, refuel, and then accompany the 1st. Consequently, Williams's force got under way three and a half hours after LeMay's wing had departed. This gave the Luftwaffe plenty of time to regroup.

Both units ran into continuous, well-disciplined German fighter opposition. The Luftwaffe was up and ready, attacking in groups initially, then coming back in for individual attacks. Strung out in a fifteen-mile-long column, the 4th received only one of two P-47 groups as escort, and the Germans began their attacks over Belgium, concentrating on the rear units, especially the 100th Bomb Group, the notorious "Bloody One Hundredth." LeMay was in the lead plane, a B-17F of the 96th Bomb Group, and hit the target along with 126 other aircraft. It was precision bombing of the first order, with 300 tons of bombs devastating the Messerschmitt works, disrupting its production of Bf 109s for five months. Unknown at the time, but perhaps even more important, the production fuselage jigs for the Messerschmitt Me 262 jet fighter were destroyed.

As planned, LeMay led his force on over the Alps to land at Telergma, in North Africa. The raid had cost 24 aircraft, almost 19 percent of the attacking force.

The Luftwaffe had hit the lst Bombardment Wing as it appeared over Antwerp, and continued the assault for the entire mission. Despite heavy losses to the lead squadrons, the 1st put 183 bombers over Schweinfurt; opposition was heavy all the way in and all the way out, and 36 aircraft were lost, a 19.7 percent rate.

Bombing results were fair—80 hits were recorded on the two main ball-bearing plants and production was reduced from 140 tons in July to 50 tons in September. These losses were offset by purchases from Sweden and the substitution of other types of bearings in less critical applications. Speer, apprehensive about follow-up raids, began a dispersal program for the industry.

Schweinfurt was a significant victory for the Luftwaffe. In addition to the 60 U.S. aircraft shot down during the mission, another 30 aircraft had to be left in North Africa because of battle damage, while a further 28 of those that got back to England were heavily battered. The German Air Force had shown that it was still a dangerous opponent, able to use its resources to the best possible advantage and to press attacks home bravely. Curiously, the German High Command did not see it this way, however, and Hitler upbraided the Luftwaffe Chief of Staff Generaloberst Hans Jeschonnek unmercifully. That night, the RAF made a devastating attack on Peenemünde, where the secret development of the V-1, V-2, and other wonder-weapon projects took place.

Göring was infuriated by the Peenemünde raid because a diversionary ruse by 8 Mosquitoes had tricked the Nazi air-defense system into ordering 200 fighters to Berlin, where they were fired on by their own flak. He blasted Jeschonnek, holding him personally responsible. The double disgrace was too much for Jeschonnek, who, despite (or because of) a meteoric career, was totally out of his depth as Chief of Staff, as indicated by the two quotes he is best remembered for. One was to the effect that he would not know what to do with a production rate of more than 360 fighters per month. The other, equally notorious, was his joyful comment on the invasion of Russia: "At last, a proper war." The war was no longer proper, and Jeschonnek shot himself, leaving a baleful note saying,

"I cannot work with Göring anymore. Long live the Führer."

(The Luftwaffe suffered from a too-rapid turnover in chiefs of staff, having eight in its short twelve-year existence. Three chiefs of staff followed Jeschonnek; the first, Generaloberst Günther Korten, tried to rectify Jeschonnek's errors by concentrating on building up the fighter force and revitalizing the Luftwaffe's strategic bombing capability. Korten died as a result of injuries suffered during the July 20, 1944, assassination attempt on Hitler. Korten's successor, General der Flieger Werner Kreipe, was too independent for Hitler, who soon fired him. The last Chief of Staff, Generalleutnant Karl Koller, an excellent officer, although disliked by Göring, could do little more than preside over the Luftwaffe's funeral.)

The losses at Schweinfurt and Regensburg caused the Eighth Air Force to refrain from attacking targets in Germany until September 6, when 312 heavy bombers hit Stuttgart and some targets of opportunity; this time 45 (14.4 percent) were lost. Despite all his difficulties, Eaker was still pugnacious, continuously pushing the Eighth toward a turning point in the bombing war, seeking air superiority through the attrition of the Luftwaffe, even as the Luftwaffe was achieving just the opposite.

The denouement came during the second week of October 1943. From October 8 through 10, 1,074 bombers were dispatched against targets in Germany: Bremen, Vegesack, Marienberg, Anklam, and Münster. At Marienberg, precision bombing came into its own—every bomb landed in the target area, and none in the town. In the series of attacks, 855 bombed successfully, and 88, just over 10 percent were lost. Then, on October 14, the Eighth Air Force went back to Schweinfurt, again with fighter escorts for only part of the trip.

A total of 291 B-17s were sent against Schweinfurt, with P-47 escorts taking them to Aachen, Germany, 240 miles from England. When the P-47 escort turned back, the Luftwaffe led off with the first of 500 sorties, attacking the bomber stream all the way to the target and back to the coast.

The official U.S. Army Air Force history relates that the German Air Force "turned in a performance unprecedented in its magnitude, in the cleverness with which it was planned, and in the severity with which it was executed." The Luftwaffe expertly coordinated rocket attacks by rocket-mortar-armed Messerschmitt Bf 110s with air-to-air bombing and massed attacks by cannon-armed fighters to savage the Eighth's formations. A total of 60 aircraft were shot down out of the 229 attacking, an un-bearable 26.5 percent. Another 17 B-17s were scrapped upon their return to England, and 121 more were damaged. The Eighth Air Force could not continue to sustain such losses; no air force could. The Luftwaffe had achieved day air superiority.

THE CRISIS IN AIRPOWER

The Allied commanders were stunned by the defeat, which seemed to vitiate the very concept of Operation Pointblank. Instead of the Luftwaffe being worn into the ground, it was growing stronger by day and by night. The reasons were not obvious then; they became so upon analysis after the war. The Allies had grossly underesti-mated German aircraft production capacity, while grossly overesti-mating the claims of the number of German aircraft destroyed in battle. In the second battle of Schweinfurt, for example, 288 Ger-man planes were claimed shot down, while actual German losses on all fronts from all causes for the day were only 38. But the Eighth Air Force persisted, against the strongest possible evidence, in believing that bombers could make unescorted long-range penetrations.

The second raid on Schweinfurt disabused the Eighth Air Force of that belief. Air superiority had to be won back from the Ger-mans, but it could only be done with the help of a long-range escort fighter.

Bad weather and the need to recoup its forces kept the Eighth Air Force from making deep penetrations into Germany for the re-mainder of the year, and depending primarily upon radar bombing to reduce the limitations imposed by weather. The Fifteenth Air Force, attacking Austria and southern Germany from Italy, forced the Luftwaffe to regroup, but there were no attacks comparable in weight to the October 14 Schweinfurt raid.

The import of the Eighth Air Force defeat went far beyond the question of the efficacy of airpower. The invasion of Europe de-pended upon securing air superiority from the Luftwaffe, which was increasing rather than decreasing in strength. The combined efforts of Erhard Milch and Albert Speer were contributing to a production miracle that would produce 44,000 airplanes in 1944. The improved versions of the Fw 190 and Bf 109 were considered to be equal to the best American fighters and had proved them-selves deadly against the bombers. Even the quality of German fighter pilots seemed to be improving, thanks to new training methods introduced at the unit level. All of this had its effect upon American leadership.

On December 23, Lieutenant General Eaker was relieved as the commanding general of the Eighth Air Force; Lieutenant General Carl Spaatz was named commander of the new United States Strategic Air Forces (USSTAF). It was an ugly situation. Eaker fought hard not to be removed, appealing for support to his new friends in the RAF and to his old friends, Arnold and Spaatz, for mercy. The matter was cloaked in congratulations, for Eaker was given a more prestigious position as commander of the Mediterranean Allied Air Forces. Eaker did not buy the rationale, having himself booted more than one subordinate upstairs. Operation Overlord, the invasion of Europe, was coming up, and the Mediterranean would be a subsidiary theater. It was especially galling to him to be relieved just when, at long last, his resources were beginning to increase. He felt that after all he had done to build up the Eighth Air Force, despite the constant diversions to Operation Torch, the South Pacific, preinvasion bombing, and attacks on V-weapon installations, he deserved more consideration. In the end, he took the bitter pill like a good soldier, and went on to do an equally good job in the Mediterranean, where he in fact did have command of considerable forces, including the U.S. Twelfth and Fifteenth Air Forces, the French Air Force, and the RAF's Balkan Air Force, Desert Air Force, and Coastal Command.

THE BATTLE OF BERLIN

One of the great difficulties confounding advocates of airpower was that no matter how great their enthusiasm, nor how deep their understanding, none was able to grasp either the scope or the complexity of World War II in the air. Thus, in the early months of 1944, two titanic battles raged, one of which would end in a resounding defeat of Bomber Command, while the other would result in the virtual annihilation of the Luftwaffe. The first battle was Sir Arthur Harris's obsessive campaign to obliterate Berlin. The second battle was the renaissance of the Eighth Air Force's bombing command and the subsequent establishment of air superiority by the USAAF when it obtained a long-range escort fighter. The Luftwaffe was ground to a husk between the two.

Churchill had long called for air strikes against Berlin, which slowly came to symbolize victory in the air war. Sir Arthur Harris and Carl "Tooey" Spaatz both sincerely believed that if Berlin were destroyed as Hamburg had been, it would not be necessary to invade the Continent.

When it began its preliminary offensive against Berlin in late August 1943, Bomber Command strength was approximately twice that of the Eighth Air Force, with 700 four-engine aircraft available. More important, a tidal wave of strength was flowing, for the entire foundations of an air force—training, logistics, intelligence, industrial base, everything—were solidly in place, generating more crews, more aircraft, and more ordnance every week. In addition, Bomber Command had a string of remarkable successes, including the Dam Buster raid, Hamburg, and Peenemünde, which prepared it fully for a championship bout against the Luftwaffe for Berlin. Tactics had been remarkably improved—the bomber stream was now shrunk from an endless 300-mile smorgasboard of targets for the Luftwaffe to a dense wedge, 3 miles across and only 70 miles long, able to cross a city in twenty-two minutes. Electronic countermeasures were much more sophisticated, as illustrated by the new Serrate device used to pick up the emissions from an enemy night fighter's radar. Dedicated RAF bombers, sometimes in modified Boeing B-17s, now carried radio operators fluent not only in German but in Luftwaffe argot, so they could give spurious instructions to enemy night fighters. Diversionary tactics had become extraordinarily sophisticated, and the ubiquitous Mosquitoes faked raids when they were not serving as marauding intruders patrolling the bomber stream and enemy air fields in search of German night fighters.

A less optimistic man than Sir Arthur Harris might have seen some difficulties in the results of the first heavy raids on Berlin in the late summer of 1943. In three separate night attacks, 1,719 sorties were flown against Berlin, during which 123 aircraft were lost and a further 114 damaged. The Luftwaffe had recovered its night-fighting prowess after the debacle at Hamburg, supplementing Herrmann's Wildsau tactics with Zahme Sau (Tame Sow) methods that inserted twin-engine night fighters into the bomber stream to acquire targets on their own radar sets. The ground-based Observer Corps became much more important, and was provided with modern radar equipment to assist with a revised plotting and control system. Luftwaffe crews gained confidence as new models of tried-and-true aircraft were joined by a few new types. From July 1943 to July 1944, the night-fighter force grew from 550 to 775 aircraft, with the improved Junkers Ju 88G-1 and G-6 variants coming in increasing numbers. These had more powerful 1,700-horsepower engines and improved armament, including six 20-mm cannon, two in an upward firing schräge Musik installation, and four firing forward.

The best German night fighter of the war, the Heinkel He 219 Uhu (Owl), made its debut on the night of June 11–12, 1943, when Major Werner Streib took a preproduction model into combat and destroyed five Lancasters in thirty minutes. The Uhu was the only German aircraft capable of combating the Mosquito. It combined superb handling characteristics, high speed, excellent radar, and heavy firepower from six 20-mm cannon, making it the ideal night fighter, and it was the first operational aircraft to have an ejection seat, which several German pilots used to save their lives. The Uhu fell prey to the almost customary German bureaucratic squabbling, and the program was repeatedly canceled and reinstated. In the end, only 268 Uhus were built, but those that reached squadron service wreaked havoc on the bomber streams.

The heavy losses in the August raid had not deterred Sir Arthur Harris, and he wrote on November 3 to Winston Churchill: "We can wreck Berlin from end to end if the USAAF will come in on it. It will cost between 400–500 aircraft. It will cost Germany the war." This was written at a time when the Eighth Air Force was still in a state of shock from Schweinfurt, as Harris must have known. Yet later, years after the battle, he said that he would never have begun the campaign on Berlin if he had known that the Americans were not going to take part.

Bomber Command began its formal Battle of Berlin on the night of November 18–19, 1943, and waged it until March 1944. Concealed beneath the flak and falling bombers was an internecine battle between Sir Arthur Harris and the Air Staff. Harris paid no more than lip service to the Pointblank directive, while continuing to devote the main weight of his effort to the destruction of German cities. His boss, Portal, wanted to fire him, but didn't dare since Harris had the implicit support of Winston Churchill, who had relished the destruction of Hamburg and wanted nothing more than to visit the same upon Berlin.

Harris won out and mounted an all-out assault against Berlin. In the next four months, Bomber Command would fly 20,224 sorties;

of these, 9,111 were against Berlin. Almost 2,700 planes were shot down or heavily damaged; 1,047 were lost over Germany.

It was a more difficult campaign than the raids on Hamburg. Metropolitan Berlin's 833-square-mile area was almost thirty times larger than Hamburg's, and was both well out of range of Oboe or Gee and a far more difficult target to acquire on the H2S radar system. The weather over northern Germany was miserable for the entire winter, and the bombers (mostly Lancasters, with some Halifaxes, as the Stirlings had to be withdrawn because of their high loss rate) fought high winds, heavy icing, and the constant concern over night fighters. The latter were especially worrisome, for they could appear anywhere in the 1,150-mile round trip from landfall to landing.

It might be well to consider for a moment the psychological differences between the two battles for the crew members in Bomber Command and those in the Eighth Air Force. Each was a special kind of hell.

The Eighth flew in strong formations in daylight and had to maintain straight-and-level flight on the bomb run into the teeth of the flak. Plumes of smoke from flak and burning aircraft hung in the sky for minutes and there was nothing more agonizing than to see a Fortress rear upward and then lurch into an endless spin to the ground, with everyone watching to see how many—if any— parachutes appeared. The British flew alone at night, each crew an entity to itself, the camaraderie of the formation absent but with the importance of the crew relationship intensified. The RAF was aware of losses as the pitch-black night was illuminated by bursting flak and exploding aircraft, but the impact was less sustained, and there grew up a system of denial. A belief persisted that the Germans were firing "scarecrow" shells that *looked* like exploding bombers. They were not—what looked like exploding bombers were in fact exploding bombers.

There were equal, if different, senses of vulnerability. The American formations could see the Luftwaffe form up, then turn in, guns winking. They could see debris being blown off their comrades' aircraft and even bodies plummeting through the air. In contrast, the RAF bombers could only watch for the German night fighters, trying to pick up a flash of exhaust that would give them away. And while the German fighters made fierce headlong attacks during the day, the German night fighters were stalkers who would edge toward their quarry, foot by foot, totally invisible, until they fired at point-blank range. The night fighter's capability had been improved by ad hoc methods, including the development of the surprisingly fruitful "running commentary" method of guiding fighters to a target. A system of radio and visual beacons was used to muster the defending fighters in adequate strength, and a continuous radio commentary on the speed, altitude, and direction of the bombers was used to get the night fighters into the bomber stream.

Both the bomber and the night-fighter missions were hazardous. Each required a special kind of courage. For the Americans, early in the war, 25 missions were considered to be sufficient for a tour of duty; later, when the situation demanded it, this was raised to 30 and then 35, but by then the chances of survival had greatly improved. The British found that the maximum return could be obtained from the investment in crew training with an initial tour of 30 missions, followed by a tour of duty in a training capacity, with another tour of 20 missions to follow.

It was different with the Luftwaffe. There were no tours of duty. Crew members flew until they were killed or the war was over, whichever came first.

Despite its losses, Bomber Command's strength grew throughout the bleak winter. All of the great preparatory effort to mass-manufacture Lancasters was now bearing fruit, and aircrews were pouring from the hundreds of training schools scattered around the world. By March 1944, Harris had an average strength of about 1,050 heavy bombers, compared to the 59 that he had begun with a little over two years before. But Bomber Command's losses were high. The Air Staff was staggered when 72 aircraft were lost over Berlin on March 24, and then that catastrophe was exceeded only a week later in a raid on Nuremberg. On the night of March 30–31, 1944, a force of 976 heavy bombers and 15 Mosquitoes was launched in perfect weather on a route notable for its lack of subtlety. Ninety-six aircraft were shot down and 960 crew members were lost in a raid that resulted in 138 German civilian deaths. The numbers were not adding up.

It was an impossible situation—even for a man of Harris's indomitability. It was fortunate for him and for the bomber crews that fate was intervening on two fronts. Politically, the requirements for Operation Overlord forced Harris to place Bomber Command at the disposal of General Eisenhower, ending the awful attrition of the Battle of Berlin. More important, while Bomber

Command had been bleeding itself white in the night skies over Germany, the USAAF had done what many considered to be impossible. It had fielded increasing quantities of a long-range escort fighter, the North American P-51 Mustang, had wrested air superiority from the Germans, and had created an entirely new climate for the air war.

OPERATION BIG WEEK AND AIR SUPERIORITY AT LAST

One of the curious anomalies of World War II aviation is that the most versatile German bomber, the Junkers Ju 88, was designed in large part by two Americans, W. H. Evers and Alfred Gassner. Both men returned to America, Gassner to work with the famous designer Virginius Clark on the Duramold process that was used in the construction of Howard Hughes's famous flying boat. To even things up, the most important American fighter, the Mustang, was designed by the German-born Edgar Schmued. In a further coincidence, Schmued had also worked for Virginius Clark, at the General Aviation Corporation, the company that became North American Aviation.

The Anglo-French Purchasing Commission had invited North American Aviation, in Downey, California, to become a second source to build Curtiss P-40 fighters. Edgar Schmued believed that he could design a more modern aircraft that could be put into production as quickly as the P-40 could. He sold the idea to his boss, James Howard "Dutch" Kindleberger.

Within five weeks, Kindleberger had a contract for 320 aircraft, the North American NA-50A. The British demanded that the aircraft have the American Allison engine and eight machine guns, and cost no more than $40,000 each. It was to prove to be the best buy they ever made.

Schmued created a beautifully streamlined fighter with a laminar-flow wing and equipped with an innovative radiator system that minimized drag. The prototype was completed, initial design to roll-out, in just 102 days. The first flight took place on October 26, 1940, and it was soon evident that North American had produced the best American fighter to date. Perhaps operating under the "not invented here" principle, the U.S. Army Air Forces expressed no interest in buying the aircraft in quantity. Instead, it purchased two XP-51 aircraft for test purposes.

The Allison engine handicapped the Mustang's performance at high altitude, and when it entered RAF service in April 1942, it operated as a high-speed, low-altitude reconnaissance aircraft. The Mustang soon proved extremely popular with its pilots, being considered far smoother in all maneuvers than a Spitfire, high praise indeed. By October 1942, the Mustang had cast a very long shadow by becoming the first fighter aircraft based in the United Kingdom to penetrate the German border, on a photo mission to Dortmund.

An assistant air attaché at the American embassy in London, the famous polo-playing playboy Major Thomas Hitchcock, made a recommendation that the Mustang, the best airframe so far developed, be powered by the Rolls-Royce Merlin engine, the best engine so far developed. It was a marriage made in heaven, for the Merlin conferred upon the Mustang outstanding high-altitude performance. There were some problems on the honeymoon, however, for it developed that copper castings in the Rolls-Royce engine-cooling system and the aluminum radiator of the P-51 were incompatible, and corrosion promptly sealed up the radiators. The interim solution, provided to Schmued by the Bureau of Standards in Washington, was to coat the system internals with the lacquer used in beer cans, to isolate the liquid from the metal. It worked like a charm, and shows how insightful engineers can find ingenious solutions to seemingly intractable problems.

The Mustang's performance was now sensational. It was faster than both the Fw 190 and the Bf 109 at all heights, and outperformed both fighters in almost all characteristics. Yet the Mustang was still not a long-range escort fighter, however, for it lacked sufficient internal tankage. With drop-tanks, it had the range to go all the way to Berlin and return *only* if the fuel in the tanks was fully consumed. But drop-tanks had to be dropped in a dogfight, and the Germans became specialists at the feint attack that would cause the escort fighters to "pickle-off" their tanks, and with them their range capability.

The P-51B, with its internal 184 gallons and 150 gallons in drop-tanks, had an endurance of four and three-quarters hours, insufficient for the Berlin mission. There was virtually no vacant space in the airframe, but Schmued and his engineers crammed an 85-gallon tank immediately behind the armor plate behind the pilot, a roughly 650-pound weight addition that moved the center of gravity to the rear and adversely affected stability. Pilots were instructed to use extreme care until at least thirty gallons had been burned off from the new tank, moving the center of gravity in the correct direction. But with the new tank behind the seat, the Mustang had an endurance of seven and a half hours—enough for the round trip to Berlin.

The first P-51Bs arrived in England on September 17, 1943. It took time to get them assembled and checked out, and the first sortie was flown by the 354th Fighter Group on November 11. The first long-distance escort to Germany was flown on December 13, on a raid on Kiel, a round-trip distance of 980 miles escorting 710 bombers, the largest force dispatched to that date. The Mustang had arrived.

ARGUMENT

By the fall of 1943, German factories were again producing more fighters every month than the Luftwaffe was losing. The Luftwaffe's loss rate had been reduced because the USAAF made the same mistake that Göring had in the Battle of Britain—having its escort fighters fly in relatively close formation with the bombers.

General Doolittle took over the Eighth Air Force on January 6, 1944; shortly afterward, he directed VIII Fighter Command's Major General Bill Kepner to "release" his fighters. Doolittle later related that when he arrived in Kepner's office, he saw a sign reading, THE FIRST DUTY OF THE EIGHTH AIR FORCE FIGHTERS IS TO BRING THE BOMBERS BACK ALIVE.

Doolittle directed that it be changed to read, THE FIRST DUTY OF THE EIGHTH AIR FORCE FIGHTERS IS TO DESTROY GERMAN FIGHTERS.

It was a welcome change of direction for Kepner and his command. The newfound freedom was applied only gradually, with first just one squadron from each group being free to attack and follow any Luftwaffe fighters. This produced such quick results that soon two-thirds of an escorting group and then whole groups were released to freelance. It was soon found that sweeps out as much as fifty miles from the main bomber stream could catch the Luftwaffe units at their most vulnerable time, as they were forming up for an attack. The hunters suddenly became the hunted, with Allied radio experts monitoring German radio communications to learn the locations of mustering enemy units and then vectoring the Eighth Air Force fighters in to attack. One of the immediate and most important benefits of the new tactic was the virtual elimination of the slower, twin-engine German fighters used to lob rockets into the formation with such deadly effect. In the past, they had been able to loiter just out of range; now they were dead meat.

In essence, the bombers had now become bait for the long-range escort's trap. Doolittle's decision to free the fighters was consistent with Operation Argument, a subset of Pointblank, formulated under Brigadier General Orvil A. Anderson's guidance. Argument called for the elimination of the Luftwaffe by continuous attrition and by attacks on fighter, synthetic rubber, and ball-bearing production. Bad weather had prevented Eaker from initiating Argument, and it fell to Doolittle to execute the plan, but not before he himself was engaged in strictly one-way arguments with Spaatz, and, indirectly, Arnold.

Doolittle, who had become known in his racing and test-pilot days as "the master of the calculated risk," twice calculated that bad weather made the odds against a successful bombing mission too heavy, and he recalled the bombers. Everyone in England dreaded the very real prospect of a bombing mission being launched, and then the weather shutting down the bases so that the entire force would be lost.

After the second recall, Spaatz gave Doolittle a severe dressing down, cutting him to the quick with the remark, "I wonder if you've got the guts to lead a big air force. If you haven't, I'll get someone who has." It was the first, and very probably the last, time anyone had ever questioned Doolittle's guts, especially after February 20, 1944, the start of "Big Week."

BIG WEEK

Increasing demands were placed upon the Eighth Air Force, including the diversion of almost half of its missions in Crossbow operations against the V-1 launch sites. Continuing bad weather—many said it was the worst winter in Europe's history—limited operations.

On February 19, 1944, the weather over Germany began to clear, and Operation Argument was put into play with an intensive series of attacks against German aircraft final-assembly plants, ball-bearing factories, and factories for the manufacture of subcomponents. Bomber Command joined the Eighth and Fifteenth Air Forces in this series of attacks. The weight of the Allied effort was demoralizing to the Germans, both military and civilian, who were kept up all night by the RAF and then had to witness the spectacle of a thousand U.S. aircraft on one mission, the contrails streaming behind proud combat boxes of bombers surrounded by fighters.

The Luftwaffe was up in strength with new tactics, attacking early in the penetration and engaging in a running battle for the whole mission. But the advent of the long-range fighters completely changed the rules of the game. The Mustangs reached out to strike the German fighters as their formations assembled, then dropped to the ground to strafe parked aircraft. The German pilots now faced attack at all times, from takeoff to landing. The Mustang revolutionized the air battle over the year; it was the realization of the impossible dream—a fighter with enough range to escort the bombers and enough speed and maneuverability to defeat the defending fighters.

When Big Week was completed on February 25, the Eighth and Fifteenth Air Forces had flown a combined total of 3,800 sorties and had dropped almost 10,000 tons of bombs, more than the Eighth had dropped in its first year of operations. A total of 226 heavy bombers were lost, for a loss rate of 6 percent. The fighters had flown 3,673 sorties and lost only 28 aircraft, less than 1 percent.

The German Air Force, which had gamely traded blow for blow for more than four years and had achieved day superiority over the Americans in the fall of 1943, was defeated, having lost 2,121 aircraft to all causes in February alone. March was to prove almost as disastrous, with 2,115 aircraft destroyed. Even the tremendous production effort being pushed by Milch and Speer could not redress losses of this magnitude, because of the staggering aircrew losses. After March, there was an obvious decline in the quality of Luftwaffe pilots. The combination of high attrition and insufficient fuel to provide adequate training had gutted the Luftwaffe's proficiency.

The Luftwaffe's night fighters would continue to fight and win the Battle of Berlin, but they were soon to be overwhelmed as well. In contrast, Allied strength grew every day, both in quantity and in quality.

From February on, the Luftwaffe declined to oppose the daylight bombing campaign on a full-scale basis, sometimes electing not to sortie at all, sometimes putting up a token resistance, and sometimes assembling in mass for a major attack.

The Eighth Air Force sensed the change and now used every possible device to force the Luftwaffe into combat. The long-range fighters were cut loose from escort duties and given the task of rooting out and destroying the Luftwaffe on the ground. Soon everything that moved in Germany became a target, from trains to trucks to couriers on bicycles.

The Luftwaffe would occasionally strike a sharp blow, as when on March 6, 1944, the Americans made their first raid on Berlin, 660 aircraft dropping 1,626 tons of bombs through the overcast. The largest force of enemy fighters since Big Week reacted, including a sizable portion of the night-fighter force, and they destroyed 69 American bombers.

By April, however, it was apparent that the objectives of Operations Pointblank and Argument had been achieved. The Allies had the requisite air superiority to permit an invasion by methods that no prophet of airpower had ever forecast. Air superiority had been won not by bombing the enemy's factories into oblivion; instead, it was won by the long-range fighter, using the bomber formations as bait to entice the Luftwaffe to fight.

FINALE IN EUROPE

The Allied Air Forces had attained air superiority over Germany despite diversions like Crossbow, the attack on German V-1 and V-2 launching sites, which would result in 25,150 bombing sorties dropping 36,200 tons of bombs and costing 154 aircraft. The Germans were forced to drop their plans for using steel and concrete launching pads (known as "No Balls" or "ski sites" from their shape) for the production-line delivery of V-1s against England and instead had to resort to improvised delivery techniques. The German V-1 onslaught was delayed by three to four months, and when it finally came on June 13, 1944, the invasion was already established.

The Allies' ability to turn to diversionary tasks like Crossbow was only possible because of the continuously growing strength of new air armadas, like that epitomized by the Ninth Air Force. The Ninth, which distinguished itself in the days leading up to the invasion and in the subsequent pursuit into Germany, had lived two separate lives as an air force. When it had finished its work in the North African campaign, a new Ninth Air Force was formally established in England on October 16, 1943, with an organization parallel to that of the Eighth Air Force. IX Bomber Command was equipped with medium bombers, initially Martin B-26 Marauders and Douglas A-20s. The second major component, IX Fighter Command, used P-38s, P-47s, and P-51s, while the third major element, IX Troop Carrier Command, had Douglas C-47s and Waco CG-4 gliders for troops and cargo. In addition, there were the usual support commands.

In the nineteen months after its formation in England, the Ninth flew 368,500 sorties during which it dropped 240,000 tons of bombs, fired almost 75 million rounds of ammunition, and destroyed 4,200 enemy aircraft. In the process, it lost 2,139 fighters and 805 bombers, troop carriers, and gliders. When fully mature, it possessed more strength than the entire Luftwaffe.

Yet the buildup in Allied airpower was still plagued by organizational difficulties. The problem was not at the very top, for as Supreme Allied Commander, General Dwight D. Eisenhower had selected Air Chief Marshal Arthur Tedder as his deputy. The two men worked so admirably together that eventually the division between USSTAF and RAF activities blurred into a single Allied activity. However, below their level there was considerable controversy over people, turf, and objectives, with understated, stiff-upper-lipped Great Britain having most of the personality problems. The mammoth egos of such prima donnas as Air Chief Marshal Sir Trafford Leigh-Mallory and Field Marshal Sir Bernard Montgomery clashed with the no-nonsense manner of Tedder and Air Marshal Sir Arthur Coningham, Commander of the Second Tactical Air Force. In many ways, the situation was a repeat of the North African campaign, where the lessons learned by the Desert Air Force were forgotten and had to be relearned. The upshot was the failure of the RAF and the army to cooperate during the most crucial months after the invasion.

Leigh-Mallory, who was notorious for being difficult to work with, was Air Commander in Chief of the Allied Expeditionary Air Force, which consisted of the RAF's Second Tactical Air Force and Fighter Command, and the U.S. Ninth Air Force. In addition, he demanded control of both Bomber Command and the Eighth Air Force, an idea vigorously opposed by both Sir Arthur Harris and General Carl Spaatz.

The turf question was soon submerged in an argument over objectives. Spaatz considered German oil production to be the most vulnerable target, and believed that he now had sufficient forces to destroy synthetic oil production in Germany and bring the country to its knees. Harris didn't believe that the oil industry was a better target than any other, but he certainly preferred it to the alternative that Leigh-Mallory endorsed: Professor Solly Zuckerman's insistence on concentrating on the German transportation system.

Zuckerman, the author of the plan to disrupt the Italian railway system, was asked in January 1944 to look over the air plan for the Overlord invasion. Zuckerman's extensive quantitative analysis proved to him—and ultimately to those who counted—that the proposed air plan was totally inadequate. He decreed that it had chosen the wrong targets, didn't take sufficiently into account the possibility of bad weather, and did not have adequate forces assigned. In essence, he agreed with Leigh-Mallory, suggesting that the weight of the Combined Bomber Offensive be transferred to the enemy transportation systems in France and Germany.

Zuckerman was a friend of Lord Cherwell, and both Tedder and Eisenhower were conscious of Cherwell's great influence on Churchill. They accepted Zuckerman's proposal that precision attacks made on seventy-five selected railway targets, the major maintenance and repair centers in northern France and Belgium, would make a crucial difference to the success of the invasion. Harris disagreed, saying that a diversion from the bombing of German cities to bombing the railway systems would release vast resources in the form of fighters, antiaircraft guns, and soldiers to defend against the invasion. Spaatz also demurred, stoutly maintaining his preference for an attack on the oil industry, asserting that this would certainly bring the Luftwaffe up to fight and be destroyed. He also argued that because there were so many fewer key synthetic oil installations, they could be obliterated with a weight of bombs that would not make a dent in the vast rail systems, which had tremendous slack capacity in terms of plundered railway equipment, alternate routes, and the ability to substitute military for civil traffic as necessary. And, although he never said so at the time, Spaatz also had in the back of his mind the desire to keep his forces independent so as to continue laying the basis for a separate air force after the war.

Both Harris and Spaatz expressed a possibly hypocritical concern that Zuckerman's plan might cause 100,000 French civilian casualties. Eisenhower contacted the French commander in the

United Kingdom at the time, General Pierre Koenig, who with a Gallic shrug said essentially *"C'est la guerre,"* indicating that the losses were a price the French were prepared to pay for their freedom. Mercifully, there were only about 12,000 casualties.

Zuckerman, an academic arguing against two of the most accomplished bomb commanders in history, prevailed, not least because he was focused on the same question as Tedder and Eisenhower. While Spaatz and Harris were still arguing for a strategy that *might* so damage Germany that the invasion could be a walk-on, Eisenhower was concerned with making sure that the invasion succeeded under any and all conditions. When, on April 14, 1944, the Combined Chiefs of Staff placed both Bomber Command and the Eighth Air Force directly under Eisenhower's control, he decided to proceed with what was now officially called the Transportation Plan but known privately as "Zuckerman's Folly" in bomber circles.

Bomber Command was given thirty-seven railway targets and the Eighth Air Force forty-two. Both units turned to it with a will, with Bomber Command surprising even Harris with its newfound ability to do precision bombing, demonstrated the previous month, on March 6–7, when 236 planes from Bomber Command devastated Trappes, the major railway center south of Paris, with 1,256 tons of bombs. This was the beginning of an offensive that would confound the enemy railway network with 22,000 British and American sorties and more than 66,000 tons of bombs dropped before D-Day. German rail movements were stopped in their tracks, and even the Germans' phenomenal ability to repair tracks and reroute trains could not mitigate the damage.

The improvement in Bomber Command's precision was a natural concomitant of more experienced crews and leaders, better training, and improved techniques, allowing it to do in 1944 what had been impossible before. The benefits from the air superiority gained in the early months of 1944 were never more evident than in the statistics on Bomber Command's losses. After recovering from the unsuccessful Battle of Berlin, Bomber Command losses had declined to 1.34 percent through the end of September 1944; by December 1944, the rate had gone down to .86 percent. From January to the end of the war, the rate did not exceed 1 percent. It is an undeniable, if unquantifiable, fact that it is easier to bomb precisely when you know you will probably not be shot out of the sky.

(It must be noted that although the percentage loss numbers

seem comparatively innocuous, they are disguised by the high sortie rate, a total of 245,728 from May 1944 through May 1945. During that period, 2,625 aircraft were lost, a terrible price to pay.)

D-DAY TO VE-DAY

The extent of the crushing Allied air superiority was demonstrated on D-Day and in the weeks to follow. Between June 6 and September 1, 1944, the Allied Air Forces flew almost 500,000 sorties, losing 4,100 aircraft in the process. The Luftwaffe was totally suppressed, confined to isolated attacks that had no measurable effect.

The Allied advance swept the German radar line back, so that by the end of August, Luftwaffe night fighters were deprived of their early-warning network, an almost insuperable handicap that was exacerbated by the increasing number of Allied night fighters intruding into their skies. Although it was feeling the fuel pinch by late summer, the Luftwaffe had more airplanes than ever before, and brave, if less-experienced crews, the pilots entering combat with little more than a hundred hours of flying time. But the Luftwaffe no longer possessed the necessary territory to employ night fighters effectively.

The attack on fuel supplies, in which Spaatz had persisted, took effect, and the Luftwaffe's day and night operations were both severely curtailed after July. So complete was Allied air superiority that the Germans didn't attempt to move anything on the roads or railroads by day unless it was an extreme emergency; all movement was at night and even then was at risk. The Allies were able to establish "caps" over enemy airfields, so that even a German cadet on a training flight was vulnerable.

The wounding of Field Marshal Erwin Rommel is a perfect example of Allied control, so complete that it could single out for attack even a single automobile on a back road. At about 1600 hours, July 17, 1944, Rommel was returning by car from a visit to SS-Oberstgruppenführer Josef "Sepp" Dietrich. Rommel had to get back to his headquarters because he'd received word of an Allied breakthrough on another part of the front. At about 1800 hours, Rommel's party saw eight fighter bombers attacking the main road to Vimoutiers in Normandy. They decided to proceed, confident that they hadn't been seen. A few moments later, their spotter warned that two aircraft were headed for them. Rommel's driver sped up to get to a wooded area, futilely trying to outspeed Spitfires. Two aircraft from 602 Squadron fired, wounding Rommel, causing the car to crash, and effectively removing one of Germany's greatest generals from the war. Credit was given to 602's Squadron Leader Chris Le Roux for the attack. With war's typical cruel irony, Le Roux, a 23½ victory ace, was himself lost on a routine flight to London later in the month.

The Allied air superiority permitted their own truck convoys to move in tightly packed nose-to-tail arrays, confident that any aircraft that appeared overhead was a friend, and Allied forward airfields were jammed with aircraft parked in the open, without concealment or revetments.

CARPET BOMBING

After less than successful attempts by the British, the first major use of carpet bombing by the Americans was Operation Cobra, which took place on July 24–25. The Americans committed all of the Eighth's heavy bombers and all of the Ninth's medium bombers and fighters. A compromise bombline was arrived at, 1,500 yards in front of American positions and marked by red and yellow panels.

More than 1,500 B-24s and B-17s joined 380 medium bombers to drop a total of 3,437 tons of bombs. This was supplemented by 559 fighter-bombers dropping another 212 tons, along with quantities of napalm. A few Luftwaffe fighters appeared, made ineffectual passes, and departed; antiaircraft fire downed 5 heavy bombers and 1 medium bomber. Because the bombers dropped parallel to the front line, instead of in a line perpendicular to it, a total of 102 Americans were lost to "friendly fire," including Lieutenant General Lesley J. McNair, the highest-ranking U.S. officer killed in the war.

Despite the fact that they were well dug in, with deep foxholes and communication trenches, the German troops were stunned. Morale was shattered because communications had been broken off with the rear, breeding a feeling of isolation that lead to the surrender of many small groups. Morale was also affected by the efficiency of the bombers, making their bomb runs as if they were on parade. Field Marshal Günther von Kluge reported that it didn't make any difference whether the troops being bombed were good or bad—the effect was the same, total paralysis. Major General Fritz Bayerlein, veteran of North Africa's defeats and a tough customer not given to exaggeration, called the battlefield a *Mondlandschaft*—a lunar landscape. And after the war, the laconic Field Marshal von Rundstedt attributed the American success to the air bombardment, combined with the follow-on initiative of American armor.

There was more air domination to come. Major General Elwood Quesada, who had been a fellow crew member with Ira Eaker and Tooey Spaatz on the *Question Mark*'s endurance flight in 1929, and was now commander of IX Tactical Air Command, suggested that an "air support party" (ASP) be placed in each tank column, with direct VHF radio communication with USAAF planes. Soon afterward, every tank column was covered at all times by a four-ship flight of fighter-bombers as advanced reconnaissance. The universal air umbrella that Winston Churchill in 1942 had said was impossible to achieve was now permanently in place.

During the first weeks of August, General George Patton's Third Army broke out, calling upon XIX Tactical Air Command to cover its southern flank at a time when German air opposition, for the first time, was mounting. The Luftwaffe had raised its sortie rate to 400 per day, and in quick hit-and-run raids had damaged armored columns, ammunition dumps, and even Patton's headquarters.

The Luftwaffe buildup was a part of Hitler's last desperate attempt to throw the Allies out of France with a counterattack by the German Fifth Panzer Army and the Seventh Army. Although the battle lasted for a week, the issue was decided in the first twenty-four hours when the German forces were halted by fierce American resistance and the combined assault of hundreds of American and British fighter-bombers whose rockets destroyed German tank and vehicle concentrations.

The German attack collapsed into a mass retreat into the gap between Allied forces at Falaise. The Luftwaffe attempted to cover the retreat but was hammered by aggressive American tactics such as the action on August 16, when eight P-51s of the 354th Fighter-Bomber Group saw no less than 70 Focke-Wulf Fw 190 fighter-bombers en route to an attack on American armor. The Mustangs attacked immediately, shot down two for a loss of two of their own, but dispersed the formation, forcing most of the Fw 190s to jettison their bombs.

THE MASSACRE AT FALAISE

Hitler's counterattack had left German forces almost encircled in the Falaise-Argentan pocket. The densely packed targets, a disorganized mass of tanks, vehicles, artillery, and troops, was matched overhead by a concentration of Allied airpower so thick that formations had to wait in line for their turn to dive in and attack. It became standard technique to seal off a column by destroying the first and last vehicles, then making continual rocket and cannon attacks against stationary targets. Occasionally, a tank or an armored car would turn and attempt to escape cross-country, setting off an aerial fox hunt, the individual Typhoon or Thunderbolt pilot happy to have the challenge of a moving target.

As the torture in the Falaise Gap ground down, the Germans finally abandoned their equipment and fled on foot through the narrowing gap. Allied aircraft were everywhere, ferreting out targets as small as couriers on bicycles and called in to destroy each vestige of enemy resistance. It reached the point that German infantrymen complained petulantly that their opposite numbers were unwilling to fight until they'd received overwhelming fighter-bomber support. They were right; the Allies had the power and they flaunted it.

THE OIL RUNS OUT

In the meantime, the strategic bombing, day and night, went on, now at last with particular emphasis on the oil industry. On September 14, 1944, Bomber Command received a new set of priorities that listed the petroleum industry as number one, with special emphasis on gasoline. Second priority was accorded to German rail and transportation systems, tank production, and truck production. Tooey Spaatz, who had been demanding the oil industry as a target since March, reiterated his belief that German oil reserves were already so low that the effect of bombing the synthetic oil plants would be felt immediately. The Ploesti oil fields had been destroyed, and by September were occupied. German production was down to less than 300,000 tons of oil from all sources, only 23 percent of what it had been only six months before.

Yet the Germans had become expert in the reconstitution of the synthetic oil plants and refineries, eliminating all frills and safety procedures in the interest of turning out product. More than 350,000 workers were dedicated to the task of repairing and dispersing the industry.

The USSTAF and Bomber Command at last combined their offensives, the Eighth and Fifteenth Air Forces hitting synthetic oil plants while Bomber Command hammered targets in the Ruhr, where benzol was derived as a by-product of the coke ovens. In the process, an argument that had by now become academic was settled: precision bombing using the Norden bombsight could do more damage with 250 tons of bombs than could an attack using radar with 1,000 tons.

The oil offensive reached a peak in November, with the three air forces dropping a total of 37,096 bombs. Incredibly, despite the damage, German oil production had risen 8 percent, to 31 percent of that of the previous spring. It took several missions spread out over two or three weeks to destroy a complex, and the Germans could have it back in operation in a little over a month. By December, the focus of the bombing effort forcibily shifted from the synthetic oil industry to stopping the German offensive in the Ardennes. Fittingly, however, that very offensive was doomed by a shortage of gasoline. It had been possible to launch what was known as the von Rundstedt offensive, but what was really Hitler's last play in the west, only by saving every possible drop of fuel for a period of months. Even so, when the offensive was launched, there was fuel available only for five days of heavy operations, and German plans depended upon a quick capture of American stocks, which did not materialize. Spaatz's oil campaign had paid a totally unexpected dividend. By the end of the war, the 220,000 tons of bombs rained down on the German oil industry had reduced its output to 5 percent of the previous year's production, resulting in bizarre anomalies like the latest thing in aviation, jet fighters, being towed to their takeoff positions by teams of horses to save on the fuel required for taxiing.

RAILS AND JABOS

Even as all Germany was going up in flames, the German motor-vehicle industry reached new peaks of production, with the tank industry reaching toward a production rate of 30,000 units per year. As a second-priority target, factories and repair depots all over the country were hit. Yet these were tougher targets even than the oil industry, for no matter how extensive the damage to the plant, the machine tools were invulnerable to almost anything but a direct hit or a massive fire.

But, like the aircraft industry, the armored-vehicle industry was dispersed, and another path to halting production was to destroy the rail and canal networks that linked dispersed subcontractors to the main assembly plans.

The strategic bombers took on the rail centers, while the tactical fighter-bombers—known to the Germans as *Jabos,* from *Jagdbomber*—cut the railway lines and attacked individual trains, canal traffic, and motor transport.

The roving bands of fighter-bombers ranged farther into Germany, destroying the transport infrastructure upon which the system of widely dispersed manufacturing depended. In the end, the destruction of railroads, trucks, and barges contributed as much to the breakdown of German production as did bombs on factories. Yet incredibly, amid the endless rain of bombs and bad news in 1944, German production rose, and with it, German inventiveness.

THE PARADOX OF THE LUFTWAFFE—RISING NUMBERS,
DWINDLING POWER

The Luftwaffe's fighter arm had seen a vast increase in the numbers of aircraft available to it, as a result of the remarkable achievements of the Jägerstab, a typical wartime special production operation set up under Albert Speer's Ministry for Armaments and War Production and led by Karl Otto Saur. Incredibly, in a nation fighting for its very life, the move was as much a bureaucratic power grab by Speer as anything, for it resulted in the removal of Field Marshal Erhard Milch, who always accused Speer's ministry of refusing him the materials, transport, and even rations that would have helped him expand production further. Now under Speer's aegis, although Saur was the de facto manager, monthly fighter production shot upward, reaching 3,000 in September. In 1943, Germany produced 24,807 aircraft and in 1944, 44,000, almost five times the 1939 figure. (As a comparison, in 1944, the United States produced 96,318 aircraft, Great Britain 26,461, the Soviet Union 40,300, and Japan 28,180.)

For the most part, German production consisted primarily of improved models of aircraft types with which it had begun the war. A few new models had been introduced, the most important of which was the Focke-Wulf Fw 190, for which design work had begun in 1938.

There was a strange dichotomy within the German aviation industry, which on the one hand was able to produce aircraft like the Messerschmitt Bf 109 and Junkers Ju 88, which were extremely versatile, susceptible to modification, and produced in large numbers, and on the other, also put forward a long series of abortive new designs that failed after costing millions of marks and man hours.

The development of new German types had to overcome a series of leadership problems. The first of these came after the victory in the west in 1940, when it seemed to Hitler that he had won the war, and Göring personally put a hold on all aircraft developments that would not come to fruition within one year. For a much longer period of time, however, sensible development was impaired by the inept leadership of Colonel General Ernst Udet, who was totally unqualified to lead the Technical Department of the State Ministry of Aviation.

But even as the Technical Department produced some terrible planes, it was capable of producing the most advanced aircraft of the war, including the world's first operational jet fighter, first rocket fighter, and first jet bomber, as well as an array of experimental aircraft that dumbfounded the world's aeronautical engineers when their existence became known after May 1945. In addition, Germany produced a formidable series of exotic weapons, including the V-1 and V-2.

Without question, the single most advanced aircraft the Germans put into the field was the Messerschmitt Me 262 jet fighter. With its twin jets, swept wings, heavy armament, and 540-mph top speed, the Me 262 was easily the best fighter of the war and a clear harbinger of the future, for it influenced the design of the postwar North American F-86, Boeing B-47 and, at least in plan form, the Boeing 737 airliner.

The Me 262, called officially either Schwalbe (Swallow) for the fighter version, or Sturmvogel (Stormbird) for the bomber version, but more often termed "Turbo" by the pilots, was arguably the most beautiful aircraft of the war. Its pilots liked it for more than aesthetic reasons; by the time it began to appear in service in late 1944, the Allies dominated the air, and the Messerschmitt Me 262 gave Luftwaffe pilots at least a slim chance for survival. It was, as one of the leading aces wrote, "an insurance policy."

Approximately 1,433 Me 262s were delivered to the Luftwaffe, and of these only about 300 got into operation, the rest being destroyed on the production lines or en route to the combat units. Adolf Hitler is often blamed for the delayed entry of the Me 262 into combat, because he had decreed that the aircraft be used as a *Schnellbomber* (fast bomber) rather than a fighter. In fact, the 262 was delayed because of the difficulty in producing a satisfactory number of the radical new jet engines. Even when the Junkers Jumo 004 jet engines finally began coming through the production pipeline, the supply was erratic, permitting delivery of 28 Me 262s in June, 59 in July, but only 20 in August.

There is no question, however, that if someone had been prescient enough when Me 262 development started in 1939 to have placed the utmost priority on the development of the jet engine, the 262 could have entered service in mid-1943. If it had, the air war over Europe would have been vastly different. The Allies would not have won air superiority, nor would they have invaded Europe in 1944. American and British jets would have arrived eventually to counter the 262, but the war might have extended into 1946. (With this scenario, the "what if" possibilities are endless, including a separate German-Soviet peace and/or the first atomic bomb being dropped on Berlin rather than Hiroshima.)

Another German engineering triumph was the Arado AR 234 Blitz, the first operational jet bomber and a superb reconnaissance plane. Almost as fast as the Me 262, but with a greater range, the single-seat, twin-jet Blitz was built in small numbers and used primarily for reconnaissance. An Arado Ar 234 was the last Luftwaffe aircraft to fly over England, making a final sortie in April 1945.

Other radical German aircraft included the Messerschmitt Me 163 Komet, a rocket-powered flying-wing interceptor. Dr. Alexander M. Lippisch's airframe and Professor Hellmuth Walter's rocket engine were combined in a tiny prototype which flew at 624 mph in 1941, a feat so fantastic that any self-respecting Allied spy would have refused to believe it. (In 1944, test pilot Rudy Opitz reportedly achived 702 mph in a more advanced version.)

The Me 163 design indicated the increasing willingness of the

Luftwaffe to barter risk to its pilots for increased performance. The Me 163's liquid rocket motor used two extremely volatile fuels, T-Stoff and C-Stoff, which were hazardous to handle and with any mishap, even a bounced landing, susceptible to explosion. The T-Stoff was so corrosive that in a crash it could literally dissolve a pilot's body. Three hundred Komets were built, but they achieved only nine kills in combat, including two probables.

There were many other advanced projects in the Luftwaffe arsenal but one aircraft, the Gotha Go 229, has special resonance for today, incorporating as it does many of the features found in more sophisticated form on the Northrop B-2 stealth bomber. The Go 229 was designed by brothers Reimar and Walter Horten, who independently followed a flying-wing development program similar to that pioneered by Jack Northrop in the United States. The Go 229 was the production designation of the Horten Ho IX flying-wing jet fighter. With a projected top speed of 640 mph and a service ceiling over 51,000 feet, the Go 229 would have been a formidable opponent, but its relationship to the B-2 rests on the fact that it was by chance also a stealth aircraft. Constructed primarily of wood and plywood, and coated with a material that made it resistant to radar pickup, the Go 229 had an extremely low radar signature.

The other longbows in the German wonder-weapon arsenal were the *Vergeltungwaffe* (Retaliation) weapons, the V-1 flying bomb and the V-2 missile. The V-1 (actually the Fieseler Fi 103) was a pilotless, pulse-jet-powered aircraft built of inexpensive materials and controlled by a gyroscopic control unit that kept it on a preset compass course while an aneroid barometer maintained it with certain altitude limits. A small propeller in the nose drove an airlog that measured the distance flown; at the desired point, the engine was shut off and the aircraft dove to the ground. (The airlog was a distance-measuring instrument not unlike that used by the Wright brothers on their 1903 Flyer.)

The V-1 had a maximum speed of about 400 mph, but many flew at lesser speeds and so were vulnerable both to RAF fighters and the special antiaircraft belts set up to combat them. The raucous sound of the V-1's pulse jet was especially terrifying because its sudden cutoff signaled an imminent explosion. Although employed too late to be more than a cause of anguish to the English populace, had the V-1 been introduced at the time and in the quantity planned, it might have had a tremendous effect on the war.

A total of about 6,725 V-1s crossed the coast of England; of these, 3,900 were destroyed by aircraft, antiaircraft guns, or balloons. The remaining 2,825 destroyed 23,000 houses and killed 5,500 civilians. The last one reached England on March 29, 1945.

The second wonder weapon, the V-2, was a rocket-powered ballistic missile that carried, like the V-1, a one-ton warhead. Known officially as the A4 rocket, the weapon weighed 28,380 pounds, reached a trajectory height of 60 miles, had a range of 189 and was immune to interception, approaching its target from beyond the atmosphere at supersonic speeds. Almost 6,000 V-2s were built, many by slave labor, and 1,054 fell in England while another 1,675 fell on the Continent, primarily on Antwerp, which received 1,265 hits.

Although terrifying, and presaging the future in a way that only a few understood, the V-2 was actually counterproductive for Germany, consuming engineering man hours, materials, and labor at a tremendous rate. The only way that the V-2 could have altered the war—and it would have done so decisively—was if Germany had been able to create a nuclear warhead for it. With the one-ton warhead of conventional explosives, Germany never could have manufactured enough of the necessary alcohol and liquid oxygen to fuel a fleet of V-2s to deliver explosives on England at a rate comparable to the bombs being dropped on Germany.

The German military had long been dazzled by the possibilities of rockets, and the impressive nature of the V-2 performance led them down a costly path. The whole project was actually a hobby-shop adventure of an enthusiastic group of scientists led by Wernher von Braun, who "aimed for the stars, but kept hitting London." The group used the V-2 development program primarily as a means to advance their interest in space travel, an interest realized after the war in both the United States and the Soviet Union.

THE LUFTWAFFE'S LAST THROWS OF THE DICE

Even though hammered down, the Luftwaffe maintained its recuperative powers to the very end. Aircraft were still flowing from the factories, and when fuel could be husbanded for them, the Luftwaffe could still put on brilliant performances, displaying the old initiative and skills. One of its more brilliant exploits occurred as a result of Operation Frantic, the USAAF's shuttle bombing of Germany on June 21–22, 1944. The Eighth Air Force participation in Frantic began well when 114 B-17s and 71 fighters bombed a synthetic oil plant south of Berlin, then went on to land at Poltava, Mirgorod, and Piryatin in Russia. Unknown to them, a Heinkel He 177 trailed the bombers to Poltava, and that night, General Rudolf Meister's Luftflotte 4 delivered a precisely executed attack on the parked aircraft. More than 110 tons of bombs fell, destroying 43 B-17s and damaging 26 more. Fifteen Mustangs and many Russian aircraft were destroyed, along with 450,000 gallons of gasoline.

There were no German losses in the brilliant attack, which gave a significant boost to Luftwaffe morale. The Americans were strongly suspicious of collusion on the part of the Russians, who had long resisted the concept of shuttle bombing and who failed to pick up the incoming German bombers on their early-warning systems. The Soviet authorities refused to let either their own or the American fighters take off to engage the intruders.

In December 1944, the Luftwaffe had planned a great aerial offensive in concert with the December drive in the Ardennes, but bad weather had intervened. Instead, all available fighter aircraft were prepared for a final, last-gasp effort on New Year's Day, in Operation Bodenplatte. With about 800 aircraft in the attacking force, the Luftwaffe achieved complete tactical surprise in an attack on sixteen Allied airfields in Holland and Belgium and one in France. A total of 134 Allied aircraft were destroyed and another 62 damaged, but the Germans lost 220 aircraft, many to their own flak, which was not accustomed to seeing German aircraft in the air. The Allies could replace their aircraft losses far more easily than the Germans could, and the Luftwaffe could ill afford its loss of pilots. It was the end of the road; for the next five months, Germany would throw its air force at the relentless armies advancing in the east, the west, and the south, with as little effect as throwing a cup of water on a forest fire. The war was lost, and the continuing bravery and élan of the Luftwaffe could do nothing to change things, not even when it was driven briefly to suicidal ramming tactics late in the war.

The final Luftwaffe statements were made by Jagdgeschwader 7, the world's first operational jet-fighter unit, and by Jagdverband 44, the elite "Squadron of Experts" flown by the most distinguished fighter pilots of the Luftwaffe, and commanded by Adolf Galland.

JG 7 was created in August 1944, and its first unit, Staffel 3, was built on the foundation of the 262 operational test unit, Kommando Nowotny. Galland, at that time still *General der Jagdflieger,* had long known that the war was lost, but this did not deter him from funneling men and equipment to the new unit. The brilliant leader, 170-victory ace, and future Chief of Staff of the postwar Luftwaffe, Oberst Johannes Steinhoff, was named the unit commander.

It was JG 7 that would conduct the first large-scale operations with the Me 262, employing it with deadly effect into the last months of the war. By March 1945, the collapse of the Luftwaffe had left the defense of Germany virtually in the hands of the sixty Messerschmitt 262s of JG 7, able to put up a maximum of thirty to fifty sorties on any given day. The strength of the Allied fighter escort had become so great that the jets were usually able to make only one pass at the bombers before being forced to break off the battle.

By this stage of the war, the range of talent among German jet pilots varied widely. Some were experts with thousands of hours of flying time, but perhaps as little as one-hour's training in the Me 262, while others were fresh from flying school with only a little over a hundred hours of flying time. A few—a precious few—were aces with lots of flying time and well experienced in the Me 262. When they made their attacks with the jet fighters' four 30-mm cannon and, for a brief period, the R4M rockets, they were dangerous opponents. But even aces could not make a decisive difference when a main Allied attack of as many as 1,300 bombers and 700 fighters was supplemented by scores of other attacks by smaller numbers of heavy and medium bombers and fighter-bombers. The Luftwaffe was physically overwhelmed—but not in spirit, especially in the most elite of all jet units, Jagdverband 44.

Galland's outspoken nature had caused him to fall into disfavor with both Hitler and Göring, and he was assigned to command a special Me 262 unit, which quickly gathered in the very best of the surviving Luftwaffe aces, including Colonel Günther Lützow (108 victories), Lieutenant Colonel Heinz Baer (220 victories), and Majors Gerhard Barkhorn (301 victories, and Germany's second-ranking ace), Walter Krupinski (197 victories), and Erich Hohagen (55 victories). JV 44 got into action quickly and scored some victories, but not even the Me 262 could redress the balance. Time had at last run out for the Luftwaffe.

WHY THE LUFTWAFFE LOST THE WAR

The Luftwaffe was defeated because it had not been conceived on a scale necessary for the gigantic combat Hitler had embroiled it in. While it had caught the design tide to have the best aircraft available when the war started, it missed the production tide by two vital years. When aircraft production at last rose toward its peak in 1944, it was too late.

The Luftwaffe was also ill served by its leadership. Reichsmarschall Hermann Göring had been of vital importance in establishing the Luftwaffe, but was derelict in his direction of it after 1939. Colonel General Ernst Udet was incapable of performing the duties assigned to him, and Göring was too uninvolved to remove him. Colonel General Hans Jeschonnek was simply too immature for his responsibilities. All three men were to commit suicide, Göring to evade the hangman's noose after Nuremberg, the other two as expiatory acts, although their deaths did nothing to mitigate the harm they had done the Luftwaffe.

With such leaders, not even the formidable talents of Field Marshal Erhard Milch, Lieutenant General Adolf Galland, or Field Marshal Wolfram von Richthofen could prevent the Luftwaffe's defeat. All the heroism of the many aces, all the selfless duty of the mechanics and the factory workers, and all the stoic heroism of the civilian populace were wasted in an evil cause.

THE FINAL ALLIED VICTORY IN EUROPE

In 1945, Bomber Command and the Eighth Air Force began to willingly accept tactical assignments, but the massive Allied Air Forces continued to pound German cities even after most "lucrative" targets had been disposed of. When one of the less lucrative was turned to in February, the resulting attack became yet another symbol of an excessive use of airpower.

Dresden, a city of some 600,000, had been little touched by the war; like Lübeck and Rostock, its city center was a warren of timbered houses, ready to be burned. Oddly, Dresdeners had imputed both comfort and meaning from the fact that they had suffered so lightly thus far in the war, and many assumed that it was deliberate Allied policy to spare a city of such immense cultural value. Given the loss of so many other ancient and beautiful cities, this was naive, to say the least.

With remorseless efficiency, Bomber Command launched 855 planes against Dresden on the night of February 13–14, the 786 attacking planes dropping 2,600 tons of bombs. In a now-familiar scenario, the Eighth Air Force attacked on the following two days, February 14 and 15, with a total of 521 bombers. Massive fires similar to those in Hamburg erupted, and the German and neutral press commented indignantly on the extensive damage and loss of life. Initial estimates indicated more than 100,000 dead, but official German police records later revised this down to approximately 35,000 to 60,000 killed or missing. As in all the devastated German cities, there was no precise count of transient military personnel, displaced persons, migrant workers, or slave laborers.

Unaware of or insensitive to the brewing controversy, the Eighth Air Force raided Dresden twice more before the end of the war, focusing the attacks on the marshaling yards, unquestionably legitimate military targets. Eisenhower was perhaps unreasonably concerned about the establishment of an Alpine redoubt, but he cannot be censured for wanting to minimize the flow of troops from the eastern front to the area.

A second firestorm erupted from the February bombing of Dresden, this time among critics of Sir Arthur Harris's area-bombing policy. Since then, the bombing of Dresden has been retrospectively attacked by everyone from Kurt Vonnegut in his novel *Slaughterhouse Five* to a myriad of revisionist historians.

Harris, the scapegoat of choice, was quick to point out that the Combined Chiefs of Staff had notified his own Air Staff on January 27, 1945, that Berlin, Dresden, Leipzig, and Chemnitz were designated as priority targets for both the Eighth Air Force and Bomber Command, Dresden deriving its importance from being a key transportation center. Harris has further noted that the decision was *officially* supported by Stalin, Roosevelt, Churchill, and Eisenhower.

Before passing judgment on Harris, it is important to recall the psychology of the time. Germany was a dreaded enemy; the war that Hitler started had cost the lives of more than 30 million people, soldiers and civilians. Yet even though Germany lay in ruins, the Führer commanded the loyalty, respect, and even affection of his nation as well as the absolute obedience of his soldiers to the day he died—and beyond. If by February 1945 the issue of who would win the war was no longer in doubt, still no one knew how many more long hard months the war would go on, nor how many more thousands of people would be killed. Devoid of airpower, short of weapons, possessed of nothing but unlimited courage and a tactical skill never surpassed in the history of warfare, the German Army fought on, defending every inch of territory just as it had done for the past three years. Dresden was a military target because it had crucial rail, governmental, and industrial facilities; the Soviet Union wanted it bombed to facilitate the advance of its armies. The Allies had ample resources, and applied them. Only when Portal and Churchill sensed the public outrage did they attempt to distance themselves from the decision. It never occurred to Stalin to do so.

THE BOMBING FINALLY ENDS

The uproar over Dresden at last convinced Bomber Command that it had run out of targets, and area bombing was formally ended on April 16, 1945. The very last major attack by the Eighth Air Force occurred on April 25, 1945, in a raid on airfields, rail targets, and the famous Skoda armament works in Pilsen, Czechoslovakia. A warning notice had been sent ahead, allowing the workers to escape. In the days following, several leaflet-dropping and supply missions were flown, including three food-dropping missions to Holland. The Eighth then engaged in evacuating liberated prisoners of war before standing down to prepare itself to move to the Pacific for the assault on Japan. The Fifteenth Air Force continued tactical operations against German ground forces in Italy until May 2, 1945, and then also engaged in relief and evacuation operations, putting a final good face on an unhappy war.

The air war was over in Europe, and well won. In interrogations after the war, Göring, Galland, Field Marshals Sperrle, Milch, Koller, von Rundstedt, and Keitel, Grand Admiral Dönitz, and Minister Albert Speer all said unequivocally that Allied airpower was chiefly responsible for Germany's defeat.

This is not to say that many mistakes were not made, some obvious immediately and some only after considerable analysis. The Allies consistently underestimated German production capacity and overestimated damage to targets. There were too many attacks on too many different targets, and not enough return attacks on critical targets. The standard 500-pound bomb was too light to damage machine tools, but was often the only available bomb. Incendiaries should have been made a bigger part of the bomb mixture, for they were more effective in damaging tools.

All in all, however, the Allied Air Forces did well with what they had and, after the Luftwaffe was defeated, could have gone on to destroy Germany so completely that the invasion would have been a mere walkover. The time it would have taken to do this would have opened all Europe to the Soviet Union, and thus was not a viable strategy. It would be different with Japan.

11

TRUE AIRPOWER . . . AT LAST

NEW WEAPONS AGAINST THE RISING SUN

Airpower terminated the Pacific war in a manner beyond the imagination of the most visionary prewar strategists. None of the Japanese or American planning had been conducted with any idea of the two weapons that would bring it so suddenly and so completely to an end—the Boeing B-29 Superfortress and the atomic bomb.

Conventional airpower had gone a long way toward defeating the Japanese, but the terrible losses they suffered on Guadalcanal, Saipan, Iwo Jima, and Okinawa did not destroy their determination to resist an invasion with every weapon at their disposal; as they proclaimed in everything from elementary-school songs to war poetry, the homogenous Japanese were 100 million strong in their willingness to die for their country and their emperor. It was not until after the Allies had island bases in the Marianas, and the B-29 began to implement new tactics to destroy most of Japan's cities, that some realistic Japanese leaders considered what had previously been unthinkable: surrender.

THE BOEING B-29

The Boeing B-29 was the most expensive single project of World War II, costing more than $3 billion for design, development, production, and deployment; the Manhattan Project consumed only $2 billion. The two were almost equivalent in terms of risk, for the success of the B-29 was as problematic as that of controlled nuclear fission.

Of the two weapons, the B-29 was the more important tactically, for during the buildup of operations from April 1944 through the first half of August 1945, the B-29 had dropped 176,059 tons of bombs on Japan, laying it waste from end to end. Had the Japanese not surrendered, this total was projected to rise to 390,959 tons by the end of November 1945—had there been any targets left.

In addition, the atomic bomb could be delivered only by the B-29. Strategically, of course, the atomic bomb was far more important, dominating world politics for the rest of the century.

The B-29 was clearly the most outstanding bomber of the war by any standard of performance, as far ahead of the B-17 or the Lancaster as the Messerschmitt Me 262 jet fighter was ahead of the P-51. The Superfortress was the joint product of a few visionary Air Corps planners (aided by the courage of General Hap Arnold, who pushed the project through despite the many hazards) and the engineering strength and heavy-bomber experience of the Boeing Aircraft Corporation.

Work on what became the B-29 began in 1938, when Boeing was asked to submit a design for a pressurized version of the B-17. There followed a long series of design revisions that prepared Boeing to address the "Superbomber" specification R-40B issued on January 29, 1940. The Air Corps called for a speed of 400 mph, a range of 5,333 miles, and a 2,000-pound bomb load, for by 1940 it seemed entirely possible that England would be invaded and occupied, and that Nazi Germany would have to be bombed from U.S. bases. The audacity of this specification is better understood if one remembers that at the time of its issue there were fewer than forty early-model B-17s in service.

It was an audacious gamble on the part of Boeing and the Air Corps in terms of both finance and engineering. Boeing was perhaps taking the greater chance, for the Air Corps could hedge its bets with other manufacturers for less ambitious airplanes like the

Consolidated B-32. Boeing had to rely not only on its own capability but on that of vendors, many of whom were being asked to create components fully as advanced as the aircraft itself.

One of the greatest risks was the early production delivery required, which meant Boeing had to compress the normal procurement cycle from six years to three. Shortcuts had to be taken, each of which added to an already ambitious program, and while dollars were freely available, they were not always a solution.

Boeing knew from the start that the greatest question mark was the unproven engine it had to use to get the necessary power—the eighteen-cylinder Wright R-3350 engine that used two General Electric turbosuperchargers to develop almost one horsepower for each pound of engine weight. The R-3350 needed several years' more development time than was available; it would go into the field unready, a mechanic's nightmare and a constant worry to pilots taking off with too-heavy loads from too-short runways. In the course of time, it would become a more reliable engine, but not before many good crews would lose their lives to sudden failures.

Even with the R-3350's power, the speed and range requirements were attainable only by combining a highly streamlined design with a wing using the new Boeing Design No. 117 high-lift airfoil and a sophisticated flap system. Boeing engineers fought a continual weight problem, for each additional pound of weight required additional fuel, and the fuel added to the weight in a vicious cycle. The USAAF thought the Boeing approach was too radical, the wing loading was too high, and that pilots wouldn't be able to handle the airplane, citing the experience with the notorious Martin B-26 as an example. Boeing responded by analyzing the B-26, noting that it had a low-aspect-ratio wing mounted to the fuselage in a manner that induced drag. They explained the B-26's problems as stemming from bad design and said that the B-29's excellent design would avoid the difficulties.

At first, the pilots in training tended to agree with the USAAF viewpoint; when they became familiar with the B-29, they loved its flying characteristics.

To achieve the necessary performance, the B-29 had to operate at high altitudes, making pressurization mandatory. Boeing had experience with pressurization in the ten Model 307 Stratoliner passenger planes it had manufactured, but no production bomber had ever been pressurized. The B-29 adopted a new "three-bubble" system. The pilot, copilot, engineer, radio operator, and navigator were in the front pod. Three gunners were positioned in the midfuselage pressurized area and connected to the cockpit by a tunnel spanning the twin bomb bays. The tail gunner was crammed into a third pressurized compartment in the rear, isolated and very much alone.

Because of the pressurization system, standard gun turrets could not be used. The armament had to be remotely operated, requiring the creation of a General Electric central fire-control system using an early computer that compensated for speed, range, altitude, wind, temperature, and trajectory. The results were remarkably satisfactory; any gunner but the tail gunner could control more than one station, and the computer permitted firing at targets far beyond the range of conventional hand-operated guns.

The handsome, streamlined airframe was a radical departure from all previous Boeing practice, involving the use of new metals and new fabrication techniques. Where the B-17 had used a tubular truss structure to build its wings, a technique dating back to its 1930 Monomail, the B-29's thin wing and massive flaps required a new structure that would lay the foundation for jet-age developments.

After years of starving for government contracts and scrambling for small airline orders, Boeing's production capacity was entirely occupied with building the B-17, so much so that Douglas and Lockheed had been enlisted to build the Fortress. For the B-29, it was necessary to build entire new plants to manufacture the aircraft, and with them, a greater challenge, the creation of a new, highly skilled work force. Vast schools were established on the factory sites, and with ninety days of training or less, farmers, housewives, and young men and women just out of high school were taught how to buck rivets, heat-treat metal, run cranes, and do everything else necessary to build the most complex aircraft in history. By 1943, Boeing alone had 58,000 employees building B-29s. Miraculously, the new plants and the new work force melded quickly and airplanes suddenly took shape on the huge production lines.

To deliver on the ever-increasing demand for B-29s, rival firms—Bell Aircraft and the Glenn L. Martin Company—were tasked with building the airplane. The need to providing drawings, jigs, parts, and training to new companies was daunting, and not without its adverse commercial aspects—Boeing felt it was being asked to train competition for the postwar marketplace.

The USAAF helped by getting the mammoth project under way with an order for 1,664 aircraft by the time the XB-29 Superfortress made its first flight on September 21, 1942. Colonel Kenneth B. Wolfe orchestrated the entire process of design, manufacture, testing, and training, a long and pressure-laden task fraught with tremendous difficulties and many crashes. The first two prototypes caught fire in the air, and the second one crashed into the Frey meatpacking plant in Seattle. The entire crew was killed, including the dean of test pilots, Eddie Allen.

In spite of all the difficulties, Brigadier General LaVerne G. "Blondie" Saunders landed the first B-29 of the 58th Bombardment Wing (VH) (Very Heavy) in Kharagpur, India, on April 24, 1944, to begin Operation Matterhorn. Matterhorn was designed to knock out the Japanese steel industry, which the Committee of Operational Analysis (COA) determined to be both vital and vulnerable. The decision to operate from Indian bases but bomb from Chinese bases made possible the fulfillment of President Roosevelt's promise to Chiang Kai-shek to begin bombing operations against Japan by November 1944.

The idea of B-29s bombing Japan from Chinese bases was attractive in political terms only, but was in practice flawed by a wide variety of economic, logistic, and command reasons. Although Chiang Kai-shek avowed interest, his subordinates refused to get serious about the construction of the air bases until sufficient money had been paid to permit embezzlement on a massive scale. Army General "Vinegar Joe" Stilwell estimated that at least half of the $100 million in gold required by the Chinese to build the bases was siphoned off by corrupt officials. The bases themselves were a monument to the patience and industry of the Chinese people, who literally built them by hand, without power equipment of any sort, using the most primitive tools to move earth or chip stones.

The logistics plan was later described by Major General Haywood S. "Possum" Hansell—a pioneer logistician himself—as "horrendous," for it was predicated on the B-29s' supporting their own operations by flying gasoline and bombs over the Hump, assisted by a fleet of B-24s of the 308th Bombardment Group serving as tankers. The B-29 was a brand-new weapon that had not received sufficient testing; it was bad practice to subject it to the rigors of continuous flights over the Himalayas, primitive maintenance in the field, and a continual shortage of parts and labor. Yet the task had to be done, and there was no alternative.

The complexity of the logistics was implicit in the sheer size of the B-29 units. The Superfortress had a crew of eleven; 7 aircraft were assigned per squadron, 28 per group, and a total of 112 for the wing. Each B-29 was assigned two crews, and a fully manned wing had a total personnel of 11,112, including 3,045 officers. When all of its elements arrived overseas, XX Bomber Command had more than 20,000 officers and men, plunked down in brand-new bases in India and China, eager to go to war.

There were command problems from the start. Wolfe, now a brigadier general, was granted his well-earned wish to take the B-29 into combat as commander of XX Bomber Command. The XX became part of the Twentieth Air Force, which had been organized on April 4, 1944. It was, as a result of a suggestion by General Hansell, commanded by none other than General Hap Arnold. Hansell became his Chief of Staff for the Twentieth Air Force. It was the only numbered air force not under a theater commander, and this anomaly amplified the confusion of the command setup in the China-Burma-India theater. It was determined that Lieutenant General George Stratemeyer, Commanding General of the India-Burma Air Service Command, would be responsible for XX Bomber Command's administration and logistics, while General Chennault would be responsible for both the fighter defense and the complete ground support of the B-29 bases in China.

The obviously difficult situation was exacerbated by the tendency of the Joint Chiefs of Staff to micromanage; in other theaters, the Joint Chiefs only set the directives and the goals, leaving it to theater commanders to determine how best to execute an operation. With command centered in Washington, and with relatively good radio communications, the temptation to interfere at a lower level of detail was irresistible, just as it would be to Lyndon Johnson and Richard Nixon two wars later in Vietnam.

BOMBING OPERATIONS BEGIN

The B-29's very first combat raid was mounted on June 5, 1944, when General Wolfe led 98 aircraft against the railroad marshaling yards in Bangkok, Thailand. Five aircraft crashed en route, while 42 had to make emergency landings. Later reconnaissance revealed that fewer than twenty bombs had landed in the target area. It was an inauspicious start for a $3 billion program, for the commanders, veterans of European operations, were not yet aware of just how different the B-29 was from the B-17, nor how difficult Japanese targets, geography, and weather were compared to Germany's.

Hap Arnold's legendary impatience asserted itself in a demand for immediate better results, to be obtained in an attack on the Japanese homeland. On June 15, Wolfe launched 92 B-29s from India. Of these, only 79 reached their Chinese staging bases, where they were joined by 4 others. Five bombers were not ready to take off, so 78 were dispatched on a night raid against the steel mills in Yawata, in Kyushu, Japan. The B-29s were sent individually on the round-trip distance of 3,200 miles because formation flying increased fuel consumption drastically. Each plane carried two tons of 500-pound general-purpose bombs, which were considered adequate to damage the primary target, the relatively fragile coke ovens.

They might have been, had they hit the target, but the results were once again very disappointing. Only 47 aircraft made it to Yawata; 7 aircraft were lost, including one shot up by Japanese fighters after making an emergency landing on a friendly Chinese airfield. Only *one* bomb hit Yawata, damaging a power station more than half a mile from the coke ovens.

The Americans took comfort that the B-29s evoked memories of Doolittle's raid, and coupled with the simultaneous attack on Saipan, must have had a negative effect on Japanese morale. But Arnold was not after Japanese morale—he was after their industry.

The Yawata raid characterized the efforts of XX Bomber Command over the next six months. Wolfe, badly needed at home to smooth out a myriad of B-29 production problems, was replaced by Blondie Saunders, who was replaced in turn in September by the firebrand from Europe, Major General Curtis LeMay.

TWO-PRONGED STRATEGY

The dramatic acceleration of the Pacific war, which resulted in the capture of the Marianas in the summer of 1944, permitted a two-pronged strategy of attack. From bases in Chengtu, China, the 1,600-mile operating radius of the B-29 permitted it to hit targets from Mukden, Manchuria, through the southern portion of Japan, Okinawa, the Philippines, Formosa, all the way down to the tip of French Indochina. Superfortresses operating from Saipan could cover all of the important targets in the heartland of Japan.

To implement this strategy, XXI Bomber Command was established in November 1944, to operate from five new airfields being carved out of the Marianas. One of the USAAF's great planners, "Possum" Hansell, was now rewarded with an operational command, being made C.O. of the XXI. Hansell landed his B-29, *Joltin' Josie, the Pacific Pioneer*, on Saipan on October 12, 1944, eager to validate in battle the many plans he'd participated in creating. He took enormous satisfaction from the knowledge that B-29s were operating from Saipan by virtue of his having persuaded the Joint Chiefs of Staff to bypass Truk and seize the Marianas as a base.

Hansell felt a heavy responsibility, for he knew that even LeMay had not been able to turn things around in China, although he had adopted tactics proven to work in Europe. The difficulties in securing fuel supplies and the unreliability of the R-3350 engine severely hampered XX Bomber Command operations, and although good bombing results were obtained occasionally, the damage to the Japanese for the most part was not commensurate with the cost and effort involved in the B-29 program. This was underlined in April 1945 when the assets of the XX Bomber Command were transferred to Tinian and Guam and, in the words of the official Air Force history, XX Bomber Command "died quietly like an old man who had outlived his usefulness and his friends." It had failed in its essential task of sustained bombing of Japan; the courage and hard work of the personnel of XX Bomber Command were simply insufficient to overcome the impossible logistics, even with LeMay as their leader.

So much had been expected of the B-29 that its utility was now being questioned. Just as Great Britain had been unable to divorce itself from its area-bombing campaign because of the immense resources expended upon it, so now were the American commanders driven to prove that the B-29 was an excellent weapon. At the very highest levels of command, where people were aware of the Manhattan Project, the urgency was even greater. *Only* the B-29 could carry the atomic bomb; if the Superfortress failed, the Manhattan

Project became a complete waste. The pressure was felt and transmitted.

Yet in the months after his arrival, Hansell was able to do no better in operations from Saipan than had previously been done from Chengtu. The Committee of Operational Analysis had reconsidered the priorities in Japan and now suggested that the aviation industry, the USAAF's choice all along, was the most important. The Joint Chiefs of Staff, exerting authority in part because it was possible to do so, directed that the principal aircraft-engine manufacturers around Tokyo—Mitsubishi, Nakajima, and Kawasaki—become the primary targets.

The long series of attacks on Tokyo was facilitated by the incredible bravery and skill of the crew of an F-13, the unarmed reconnaissance version of the Superfortress. On October 30, 1944, Captain Ralph D. Steakley and his crew arrived on Saipan after a thirty-three-hour flight from the United States. Early on the morning of November 1, Steakley's F-13 became the first U.S. plane to fly over Tokyo since the Doolittle raid. The weather was clear, and Steakley took the first-ever reconnaissance photos of Tokyo; these subsequently became the basis for all U.S. attacks on the city, including Hansell's first strike, San Antonio I.

After much training and many postponements, San Antonio I began at 0615 on November 24, 1944. As an indication of the degree of experience and expertise now resident in U.S. combat units, the first plane to roll down Isley Field's runway was *Dauntless Dotty*, flown by the Commander of the 73rd Bombardment Wing (VH), Brigadier General Emmett "Rosey" O'Donnell. O'Donnell's satisfaction was intense, after all the humiliations he'd suffered during the first months of the war, flying B-17s in the Philippines. His copilot was an equally distinguished combat veteran, Major Robert K. Morgan, who had been a pilot on the famous B-17 *Memphis Belle*.

Dauntless Dotty was followed by 110 more B-29s, carrying some 278 tons of bombs. The splendid start quickly unraveled as 17 aircraft aborted and 6 more found themselves unable to bomb for mechanical reasons. The remainder of the formation were caught up in a 120 knot wind—the infamous jet stream, just being recognized—and swept over the target at a blistering 445 miles per hour, far too fast for accurate bombing. On the positive side, Japanese fighter resistance was light and the flak was ineffective. One Japanese pilot rammed his Tony into the tail of a B-29, which subsequently crashed.

Once again, reconnaissance photos showed the bombing results to be totally inadequate; only sixteen bombs were observed to hit within the target area. And just as the Yawata raid had come to characterize XX Bomber Command results, so did San Antonio I typify XXI Bomber Command's early efforts. By now, the B-29 was performing fairly well, because extensive modifications had improved the reliability of its engines, but bombs were still not hitting the targets. And while the Japanese civilian populace could draw its own conclusions about the ultimate fate of the war from the very presence of B-29s over Japan, the military assessment was quite different. The Japanese military analysis was liberally laced with wishful thinking. The early consensus was that the cost of the B-29 operation was so great, and its results so negligible, that not even a wealthy nation such as the United States would be able to persist: the B-29 attack would fall of its own weight.

Unknown to all of the Japanese and to most of the Americans, a change was in the wind. On December 18, 1944, 84 B-29s of LeMay's XX Bomber Command had dropped 500 tons of incendiary bombs in a daylight raid on Hankow, China. The city was destroyed as a major Japanese base. A requirement came down from Brigadier General Lauris Norstad, Arnold's Chief of Staff for the Twentieth Air Force, to make a test raid on the city of Nagoya, Japan, with at least 100 B-29s, all dropping incendiary bombs.

Hansell, adhering to doctrine, objected, saying that he wanted to continue precision bombing on the primary target, the aircraft industry. In doing so, he put his career on the skids; you can buck the brass in the military, but only if you succeed.

After further discussion, during which Norstad was tactful but firm, a test raid was run on Nagoya on January 3, 1945, with 97 B-29s carrying primarily incendiary bombs. Each aircraft had fourteen M18 1B clusters of 350 pounds and one 420-pound fragmentation cluster. It was not a good mission; only 57 aircraft bombed the designated target and the damage on the ground was slight. The Japanese again drew an erroneous conclusion from the attack, imputing a far greater efficiency to their fire-prevention system than it deserved.

Hansell reverted to his previous precision tactics but was unable to generate better results, with the exception of the January 19,

1945, attack on the Kawasaki aircraft plant near Kobe. Poststrike photos showed extensive damage, and after the war it was learned that production had been reduced by 90 percent.

The success didn't help Hansell, however, for when you worked for Hap Arnold, you delivered or you were relieved, as he was the following day by Major General Curtis E. LeMay. Hansell was offered the post of Vice Commander under LeMay but refused it graciously. In essence, the time for planning, Hansell's forte, was past; now it was time for direct action, LeMay's strength.

As a new commander, LeMay received more latitude from the Joint Chiefs than Hansell had and, after two preliminary attacks using Hansell's methods, he put 69 aircraft over Kobe to drop 159 tons of incendiary bombs against heavy fighter opposition. Two B-29s were lost and another 35 were damaged by the 200 aircraft that opposed them, but Kobe was badly hurt. Poststrike photos showed damage to more than 2.6 million square feet of factory in the city, with more than a thousand buildings destroyed.

Curiously, LeMay then reverted to precision attacks, the first of these an attack on February 19 on the Nakajima factory at Ota, where the excellent Ki-84 "Frank" fighter was manufactured. But the Japanese defenses were improving, and twelve B-29s were shot down and another twenty-nine damaged.

Japanese industry had combined an intense study of the American aircraft they faced with a rigorous evaluation of the types of planes they needed to defend the home islands. The result was a series of excellent designs, some of which made it into production, but only in moderate quantities. The aircraft manufacturers suffered from material shortages, poor quality control, and the lack of sufficiently powerful engines.

A few of the later versions of Japanese fighters—the Frank; the Kawasaki Ki-100, a radial-engine version of the Tony; the Kawanishi N1K2-J Shiden-kai (Violet Lightning); and the Mitsubishi JM2 Raiden (Thunderbolt)—had superlative performance, and in the hands of capable pilots, were deadly in combat. However, they were few in number and suffered from maintenance and parts problems that kept in-commission rates at unacceptably low levels. For the latter part of the war, their overwhelming advantage in numbers and quality usually allowed the Americans to brush any Japanese opposition aside.

LEMAY PLAYS HARDBALL

As the precision-bombing efforts continued, further tests were made with incendiary bombs, including a heavy attack on Tokyo on February 25, when almost 30,000 buildings were destroyed. In contrast, the *eighth* precision strike against the Nakajima works at Musashino-Tama was another total failure, as was, indeed, the entire daylight precision-bombing campaign. The B-29, the multi-billion-dollar bomber, had failed in its projected role; the remedy, however, was already in LeMay's mind.

Enemy fighter opposition had stiffened, and in the series of attacks through February, 29 B-29s were lost to fighters and ten to flak or fighters. Sadly, almost as many more were lost on the long overwater round trip between Saipan and Japan. Another 21 crashed because of operational problems such as engine fires, runaway propellers or fuel exhaustion. Fifteen were missing, lost to unknown causes. Seventy-five bombers, 825 crew members and massive amounts of effort had produced insignificant results.

Totally disappointed with operations so far, and aware that he was as vulnerable to Arnold's impatience as any other man, LeMay decided to try tactics he'd long considered and which had been carefully tested in the United States. It was the common opinion that the Japanese cities were much more vulnerable to firebombing than German cities. Further, although Japanese industry was spread out into residential areas, it was still far more concentrated than its German counterpart.

The B-29 had been designed from the start as a high-altitude bomber and would have had to remain so in the European theater. But conditions were different in Japan. The antiaircraft and searchlights were not radar-controlled and reportedly there were only two night-fighter units in the homeland. Japanese airborne radar was relatively primitive and not widely used. After extensive consultation with his staff—but without notifying General Arnold—LeMay decided to launch a series of maximum-effort low-level incendiary night attacks against Japan, putting his career on the line.

Night bombing offered many advantages, for the winds were not so strong and the B-29's Loran navigation system operated more efficiently. Flying at lower altitudes eased the strain on the engines, lowered fuel consumption, and, with the deletion of the armament and ammunition, permitted a much bigger bomb load—about 12,000 pounds per plane. Some were concerned about flying unarmed; others felt that it was a safety factor, that the B-29s were more likely to shoot each other than Japanese fighters. The whole concept of unarmed, low-level night bombing alarmed some and the word "murder" was quietly bruited about—but not to LeMay.

The first raid was set for the night of March 9–10, with 334 B-29s carrying almost 2,000 tons of bombs. The B-29 bomb loads were varied to obtain the maximum effect. The aircraft in the lead squadrons were to act as pathfinders, each one dropping 180 of the 70-pound M47 napalm bombs. These were intended to start major "appliance fires," which would require the mobilization of all of the Japanese fire-fighting equipment. The rest of the B-29s each carried 24 of the 500-pound cluster units, each one containing 38 of the 6.2-pound M69 bombs. These outwardly simple devices are in fact a better metaphor than even the atom bomb to demonstrate the tremendous disparity in strength and sophistication between the United States and Japan, and, as such, worthy of a slight digression.

America had entered the war with incendiary bombs derived from British practice, but the M69 was the product of a brainchild of President Franklin D. Roosevelt, the Office of Scientific Research and Development (OSRD). The former dean of engineering at the Massachusetts Institute of Technology, Vannevar Bush, was made Director, and he had as his deputy the president of Harvard University, the renowned Dr. James B. Conant. They gathered a host of intellectual giants, some of whom would be vitally important in the Manhattan Project, including Roger Adams, Karl Compton, and Richard C. Tolman. These were towering figures, academics and scientists of the first rank in an organization for which the Japanese had no equivalent. The Japanese, in general, made little use of the research and engineering capability of their scientific community.

The American scientists were buttressed by some of the finest engineering and research concerns in the country. Among their creations was an incendiary material, called napalm, from its constituent chemical compound of naphthenic and palmitic acids. However, existing napalm bombs lacked some of the characteristics desired in an incendiary bomb, and the scientists were called upon to create a new weapon that could be made small in size, so that a great number could be carried in a single bomb load, but dense enough in mass to be able to penetrate a residential roof before igniting.

The M69 was quickly developed to meet the specifications. It was a cylindrical unit, twenty inches long and three inches in diameter, weighing only 6.2 pounds and lacking the tail fins and fusing propeller of conventional bombs. Instead, it had a three-foot cloth strip that streamed behind it, slowing the descent and keeping the bomb from tumbling. When the bomb crashed through the roof of its target, a delayed-action fuse detonated, spewing the flaming gasoline gel out of the casing in a stream like a fire hose for as far as thirty yards. The gel stuck to whatever it hit—animate or inanimate—and burned with a hellish intensity.

The tiny M69s were brought to Tokyo by the great fleet of B-29s, each equipped with radar sets and bombsights, the entire bombing effort but the tip of a logistics and supply iceberg extending 12,000 miles back to the United States' scientific and industrial powerhouse. The only response available to the Japanese was the pathetic balloon bombs, unaimed paper weapons carrying a handful of incendiaries on a windblown journey.

MARCH 9–10

A fateful wind was blowing in Tokyo on the night of March 9, when it had required almost three hours for LeMay's entire force of B-29s to get airborne. The 19th and 29th groups took off from Guam at 1735, while the 73rd and 313th wings left from Saipan and Tinian forty minutes later.

The bombers approached Tokyo individually at altitudes that varied from 4,900 to 9,200 feet. The city lay clear in the bombardiers' sights, with only a slight cloud cover and visibility of ten miles or better. The pathfinder's M47 napalm bombs started fires that spread swiftly before a brisk and rising wind .

The initial attack was focused on a twelve-square-mile area of the most densely populated part of the city, where houses of wood, bamboo, and plaster crowded each other, and the population density averaged 103,000 persons per square mile. The fires spread rapidly and the results were devastating. The fire-fighting services were overwhelmed within thirty minutes of the first attack and a firestorm swept the city, destroying 267,171 buildings (more than six times the number destroyed in the great fires of London, Moscow, Chicago, and San Francisco combined). One quarter of the city's homes were gone, and more than a million people were homeless.

The dead were everywhere, heaped in grotesque piles, 83,793 of them, with a further 160,000 injured. Some people were able to save themselves by jumping into the deeper rivers and canals. In the smaller canals, the firestorm's intense heat sometimes boiled the water around the victims, then sucked them, helpless, from their refuge. More than 15.8 square miles of the city were completely burned out, the majority of the buildings reduced to ashes, the few fire-resistant ones turned into gutted shells.

The Japanese were horror-stricken; there was no way to comprehend a disaster of this magnitude, one that completely overrode ideas of national superiority, of the samurai spirit, of their nation's place in the sun.

The defenses of Tokyo had been weak; some 70 aircraft were seen trying to make interceptions, and as many as 40 succeeded, but with little effect. Forty-two B-29s received damage from anti-aircraft fire, which on the whole was aimed either too high or too low. The rampaging fire drove many soldiers from their gun positions.

On March 11, Nagoya became the target for 285 B-29s dropping 1,790 tons of incendiaries. There was little wind, and the city was spared a firestorm, but more than two square miles were totally destroyed. The reduced damage was in part attributed to a change in the use of the incendiaries. In the Tokyo raid, the incendiary clusters of M69s had been dropped at fifty-foot intervals; some crews thought that bombs were wasted because they were so closely spaced, and at Nagoya, the interval was increased to 100 feet, too far to achieve the critical mass necessary for a firestorm. For this raid, the tail gunners were provided ammunition for their guns, on the off chance that the Japanese would become aware that the B-29s were defenseless.

The bomb interval was changed back to fifty feet for the third raid, on Osaka on March 13. Of the 301 B-29s taking off, 274 reached their target, only to find it blanketed by cloud cover, forcing them to use radar bombing. Unexpectedly, the radar bombing gave more uniform results than visual bombing, and within three hours more than eight square miles of the city were totally destroyed. Casualties were low compared to the Tokyo raid, with just under 4,000 being killed and just over 9,000 wounded or missing.

Morale in the B-29 units kept climbing, for LeMay had found the magic formula, making maximum use of the B-29 in tactics that took advantage of the enemy's weaknesses. It was a sensible way to fight a war, and it converted the B-29 from a blunder to a war winner.

LeMay began a rampage, driving his crews hard; they were already flying sixty hours per month, higher than the average for the Eighth Air Force, but a shortage in replacements caused him to increase the monthly combat time to eighty hours. He had the scent of victory in his nostrils—and not only victory over Japan, but victory for the very concept of airpower. Given a list of thirty-three priority targets by the Joint Target Group in Washington, he sent Norstad a message saying, "I consider that for the first time strategic air bombardment faces a situation where its strength is proportionate to the magnitude of its task. I feel that the destruction of Japan's ability to wage war lies within the capacity of this command, provided its maximum effort is exerted unstintingly during the next six months. . . ."

In other words, LeMay knew that he had arrived at the point that Douhet, Mitchell, Trenchard, and even Spaatz and Harris had only dreamed of. He had the decisive weapon at his disposal—and knew that there was more to come.

The B-29 effort was diverted temporarily to support the attack on Okinawa, to suppress the kamikaze sorties originating in Kanoya, and also to begin a massive mining campaign that would bottle up the Inland Sea. With the strength of XXI Bomber Command growing every day, LeMay, now with five hundred or more aircraft at his disposal, reverted to attacks on Japanese cities three days after V-E Day, on May 11, 1945. His goal was to create such havoc that the terrible cost of invading Okinawa would not be repeated in Japan.

By June 15, he had destroyed 112.7 square miles of Tokyo, Nagoya, Kobe, Osaka, Yokohama, and Kawasaki. His B-29s now had the benefit of long-range escort fighters, P-51s based on Iwo Jima, an island that served as a haven for damaged B-29s.

With 6,690 B-29 sorties, dropping 41,592 tons of bombs, LeMay had destroyed the six principal industrial cities of Japan at a cost of

136 aircraft, an acceptable 1.9 percent loss rate. Japan's leaders should have sued for peace, for it was abundantly clear that the country was not prepared to stop this destruction. It lacked the antiaircraft guns, radar, and fighters to repel the invaders, as well as the fire engines, bomb shelters, and hospitals to help its citizens. Yet, held captive by a martial spirit that had served it ill on almost every battlefield, the government vowed to fight on.

XX Bomber Command flew 124 incendiary missions against secondary cities, from Fukuoka, population 323,200, to Tsuruga, population 31,350. The level of destruction ranged from the 99.5 percent of Toyama to the less than 1 percent of Ichinomiya. In the process, the B-29s dropped millions of leaflets, trying to convince the Japanese public that the war was lost and urging them to surrender before they were killed by bombs or starved to death. Mines, submarines, and air attack had virtually eliminated the Japanese merchant marine, and, as if fate was intervening to halt the slaughter, a massive failure in 1945 cut the rice crop almost in half. On other occasions, leaflets were dropped on a series of eleven cities, warning the population that a bombing attack was scheduled for the following day and advising them to evacuate.

LeMay and XXI Bomber Command had brought Japan to its knees—but it would not surrender.

SEMANTICS, CULTURE, AND THE ATOMIC BOMB

The initial disappointment in the B-29's performance as a precision bomber was washed away in a tide of relief over its success in area bombing. Few people were aware of the Manhattan Project; fewer still were aware that its ultimate success depended upon the success of the B-29 as a delivery system. (The Germans, whose atomic-bomb effort was both low-key and abortive, had modified one of their Heinkel He 177s with a cavernous bomb bay to accept their bomb—when and if it ever materialized.)

The project milestone dates on the B-29 and the atomic weapon were surprisingly synchronous. The atomic weapon project began in 1939, with Albert Einstein's August 2 letter to Roosevelt indicating that an atomic bomb might be possible—and that the Germans might be working on one. By July 1941, a decision had been reached to create an atomic bomb before the Germans did, and before the end of the war. In what was thought to be the tightest security possible, marred only by several Soviet spies working at its very center, the Manhattan Project eventually employed more than 120,000 people, including the country's top engineers and scientists. The mammoth $2 billion effort had its first success at Alamogordo, New Mexico. On July 16, 1945, an experimental bomb was detonated with results that were incredible even to the scientists who had created it.

Word of the successful test was immediately transmitted to the new President, Harry S Truman, who, as a novice, was plunged into the Potsdam Conference with Winston Churchill (for a time) and Josef Stalin. The atomic bomb not only buoyed Truman's confidence; it gave him a stronger hand in dealing with the Soviet Union. The latter, though still badly wounded by the war with Germany, was now preparing to settle old scores with Japan. Truman casually mentioned to Stalin that a powerful new weapon had been tested, and the Soviet leader responded that he hoped it would be used to good effect against the Japanese. Truman, pleased that Stalin did not press for more information, would have been dismayed to know that traitors had already provided Stalin all he needed to know.

Japan, too, was indirectly warned, by the Potsdam Declaration of July 26, a thirteen-point ultimatum that called for a Japanese surrender. Making no reference to the Emperor, it warned that the only alternative for Japan was "prompt and utter destruction."

Badly wounded by the B-29 raids, cut off from food and industrial imports by the destruction of its merchant marine, Japanese leaders were fully aware that the war was lost, but as yet had not found a way to acknowledge it. With the Potsdam Declaration, another cultural phenomenon emerged, one as totally foreign to Westerners as *gekokujo*, permissible insubordination, or *gyokusai*, the mystic willingness to die for one's country. This was *mokusatsu*, a time-honored technique by which a Japanese officer would take refuge in lofty silence if he did not agree with, or did not understand, an order. When the new Prime Minister, Suzuki Kantaro, announced his response to the Potsdam Declaration, he used the term *mokusatsu*, intending to say, in essence, "No comment." However, his remarks were translated as meaning that Japan was contemptuously ignoring the Potsdam Declaration. It was a fatal error.

AIRPOWER'S ULTIMATE COMBINATION—THE B-29 AND
THE ATOMIC BOMB

General Hap Arnold had advised President Roosevelt in September 1943 that the Boeing B-29 was the only bomber capable of executing the atomic-bomb mission. In early 1944, plans for modifying fifteen B-29s were formulated; the modifications were not extensive, for the bombs were being designed concurrently, and were adapted as much as possible to fit the B-29's bomb bay. The following summer, Arnold authorized a top-secret team of experts to create the first combat unit to use the new weapon. Colonel Paul W. Tibbets, Jr., who had a distinguished record as pilot with the 97th Bombardment Group, was selected as commander of what would on December 17, 1944, become the 509th Composite Group. The remainder of the unit was handpicked to get the best possible people, many of them personally known to Tibbets. For a long period of time, Tibbets was the only person in the 509th to know the true nature of the mission; the rest accepted on faith that they were being trained to do something special and that they would find out what it was at the appropriate time.

The 393rd Bombardment Squadron (VH), in training at Fairmount Army Air Field in Nebraska and commanded by Major Charles W. Sweeney, became the operational element of the 509th. Intensive training at Wendover Field, Utah, included a series of drops of dummy bombs; this was followed by specialized training in Cuba in long-distance over-water flight.

The special facilities required for handling and loading the atomic bomb were prepared on Tinian in the spring of 1945, and by July, the 509th and its specially modified B-29s were in place. Further training began immediately with six specialized missions, some involving harassment-bombing of isolated garrisons on Truk or Marcus. After July 20, the 509th crews executed thirty-eight sorties, gaining experience in the precise tactics to be used when the atomic bomb was actually dropped, and also making the sight of small formations of B-29s seem both customary and innocuous to the Japanese.

While the practice runs were being made, there was already gathering concern as to how best to use the weapon. Secretary of War Henry L. Stimson, who with Manhattan Project manager Major General Leslie Groves, was directly responsible to the President for the success of the project, had appointed an ad hoc Interim Committee to advise the President on matters related to the atomic bomb. This committee had agreed—though hardly unanimously—that the bomb be used against a civilian-military target in Japan as soon as possible and without warning. In the meantime, a group of sixty-four scientists, whose knowledge stemmed from their own involvement in the Manhattan Project, felt differently, giving Stimson a petition for President Roosevelt which asked that the bomb not be used until the Japanese had been given a demonstration of its power by detonating one in the desert or on a deserted island.

Somewhat nonplussed, Stimson turned for advice to the scientific panel advising the Interim Committee. The panel was comprised of the most distinguished men in their profession, all of whom were fully aware of the implications of the bomb and who had participated extensively in its creation—Arthur Holly Compton, Enrico Fermi, Ernest O. Lawrence, and J. Robert Oppenheimer. It was their opinion that the test proposed for Japan's benefit was not feasible and that there was no alternative to direct military use.

A list of target cities was drawn up that included Kyoto, Hiroshima, Niigata, and Kokura, the largest cities with the least damage remaining in Japan. Because of its cultural significance, and thinking of Dresden, President Truman and Secretary Stimson insisted that Kyoto be deleted from the target list, feeling that the city was so important to the Japanese psyche that its destruction might drive them into the Russian camp after the war. Hiroshima thus moved to the front of the line. Later, Nagasaki was added to the list, although its geography, as events were to prove, made it less than optimal as a target.

Soon after all the necessary elements of the strike were prepared on Tinian, Field Order No. 13 was signed on August 2, 1945, by Lieutenant General Nathan Twining, Twentieth Air Force, directing the 509th Group to make a visual attack on Hiroshima.

The war had already diminished Hiroshima. At one time a busy naval port, the mining campaign had reduced its importance, and a series of mass evacuations had reduced its population by one-third, to 245,000. There were many military installations, and the entire economy was geared to the Japanese war effort. It was also an important consideration that there were no Allied prisoner-of-war camps in the area.

Seven aircraft were assigned to the mission. The principal force consisted of Tibbets in his soon-to-be-famous *Enola Gay*, named for his mother, and two escort planes carrying observers. One of these, *The Great Artiste*, was flown by Major Charles W. Sweeney, while the second, an unnamed B-29, was commanded by Captain George W. Marquardt. Both escort aircraft were crammed with observers and cameras to record the historic event. Three aircraft were assigned duty as weather planes, and one was designated a spare.

The crews involved were not informed of the exact nature of their mission, or of the bomb's predicted 20,000-tons-of-TNT power until August 4, and even then they were not told that it was an atomic bomb.

The *Enola Gay* took off on its fateful mission at 0245 on August 6. Five and a half hours later, Tibbets received word that the weather and visibility at Hiroshima were good. At exactly 0915, bombardier Major Thomas W. Ferebee dropped the bomb from an altitude of 31,600 feet and an airspeed of 328 mph. Tibbets then executed what later became known as a "breakaway maneuver", a steeply banked turn of 150 degrees to avoid the expected blast.

By the time the bomb exploded fifty seconds later, 1,900 feet over Hiroshima, the *Enola Gay* was fifteen miles away. At detonation, there occurred the fireball, followed by the swiftly rising mass of smoke that turned into the notorious mushroom cloud that still casts its symbolic shadow.

President Truman immediately announced the event to the world, amazing even many of the members of the 509th Composite Group. The Japanese reaction was confused, but officially they diminished the results of the attack, saying only that it was a new bomb "which should not be made light of."

Certainly not, for 4.7 square miles of Hiroshima's city center had been obliterated; damage varied in the rest of the city in proportion to the distance from ground zero, but 40,653 buildings were destroyed and another 8,396 badly damaged, 97.8 percent of the total. Almost 80,000 people had been killed, and an equal number injured, while 171,000 were made homeless.

Even after it had begun to assess the damage, the Japanese government did not provide its citizens with the information necessary to protect them, advising them only to wear clothing that covered the entire body and to take shelter at the sight of even one or two B-29s approaching. (Reconnaissance flights of B-29s were so common that the Japanese had reached the point that they could make up songs and jokes about them.)

LeMay's B-29s and the U.S. Navy carrier forces maintained pressure against Japan while the sole remaining atomic weapon in the world was prepared for use.

The second and last atomic mission of the war began at 0349 on August 9, again with a flight of three aircraft. Major Sweeney and his crew now flew *Bock's Car,* trading their aircraft *The Great Artiste* to Captain Frederick C. Bock.

Sweeney's mission was as troublesome as Tibbets's had been trouble-free. The primary target, Kokura, was weathered in; Sweeney made three bomb runs, but the bombardier was unable to see the target visually, and some Japanese fighter planes were in the area. Sweeney then diverted to the secondary target, Nagasaki, which was also cloud-covered.

Bock's Car used radar for its run in (and would have dropped on radar, too), but at the last moment the bombardier, Captain Kermit K. Beahan, saw the target and at 1058 hit the bomb release.

Nagasaki conformed to its terrain, with hills rising up to surround the harbor. Numerous air-raid shelters were dug into the hills, and if the Japanese government had been honest enough to warn the population of the true nature of an atomic attack, thousands of lives might have been saved. Instead, most people were either at work or at home when the bomb detonated within one mile of two huge Mitsubishi arms factories.

Nagasaki's bowl-shaped terrain confined the effects of the bomb to a relatively small 1.45-square-mile area and prevented a fire similar to that at Hiroshima. Approximately 35,000 persons were killed and 60,000 injured.

On August 8, the Soviet Union declared war on Japan, in a single stroke fulfilling its promises to its Allies, gaining revenge against Japan, and acquiring a vast new sphere of influence. Incredibly, Emperor Hirohito's advisors on the Supreme Council for the Direction of the War still debated whether or not to surrender. As Adolf Hitler had done, the military faction still wanted to resist in the hope of somehow obtaining better terms. On August 10, the Japanese announced not their surrender but their willingness to accept the Potsdam Declaration, as long as it did not prejudice the prerogatives of the Emperor as sovereign.

In the days preceding the Japanese statement, routine B-29 at-

tacks had continued. On August 11, they were suspended to give
negotiations a chance to mature. In the meantime, the B-29s had
dropped millions of leaflets telling the Japanese people of the Potsdam Declaration, the Soviet Union's declaration of war, and the
true nature of the atomic bomb.

The United States responded to the August 10 Japanese statement by advising that from the moment of surrender, the authority
of the Emperor and the Japanese government were subject to the
Supreme Commander of the Allied powers, but that "the ultimate
form of the Government of Japan shall be established by the freely
expressed will of the Japanese people." The full text of the Japanese
statement and the U.S. reply were delivered to the Japanese people
by propaganda leaflets on August 14.

When no word came from the Japanese government, LeMay's B-
29s were authorized to resume attacks. General Arnold had long
wanted his own Tokyo "Millennium," while General Spaatz would
have preferred to use a third atomic bomb—if one had been available. LeMay was able to meet Arnold's wish, putting up a total of
828 bombers and 186 fighters over Tokyo on August 14–15. Before
the last aircraft had landed, Japan had surrendered. As the American crews celebrated that night, *gekokujo* asserted itself in Tokyo in
an abortive revolt by fanatic army officers who wished to seize the
Emperor and force the continuance of the war. The coup was
Grand Guignol in its assassination attempts, but merely comic-
opera in its execution, and was quickly put down.

The American forces continued to make a display of airpower
over Japan, reaching a highlight on September 2, when 462 B-29s
cruised over Tokyo Bay while the surrender was signed aboard the
USS *Missouri*. In the meantime, 900 B-29s had dropped almost
5,000 tons of supplies to more than 63,000 prisoners of war in
camps in Japan, China, and Korea. The initial drops concentrated
on medicine, vitamins, food, and clothing; they were followed by
regular weekly drops until the prisoners could be evacuated to Allied bases. As in Europe, it was perhaps the only humane way to
end a vicious war.

APPENDIX 1
AIRCRAFT TYPES

KEY: (A) = American (U.S.); (D) = Dutch; (E) = English; (F) = French; (G) = German; (I) = Italian; (J) = Japanese; (P) = Polish; (R) = Russian (Soviet Union).

Aichi D3A Val (J) — Single-engine, low-wing, monoplane dive-bomber used at Pearl Harbor.

Aichi E13J Jake (J) — Single low-wing monoplane; recce floatplane.

Armstrong Whitworth Whitley (E) — Twin-engine monoplane bomber.

Arado Ar 240 (G) — Canceled entrant of "B" bomber contest.

Arado Ar 234 Blitz (G) — First jet bomber; twin jets, single-seat high-speed reconnaissance bomber.

Auster (E) — British version of Taylorcraft liaison plane.

Avro Anson (E) — Twin-engine, mixed-construction utility plane, roughly comparable to Beech D-18.

Avro Lancaster (E) — Best British bomber of World War II; four-Merlin-engine night bomber; versatile.

Avro Manchester (E) — Ill-fated twin-engine Lancaster forerunner.

B.E.2c (E) — World War I observation plane.

Beechcraft D-18 (A) — All-metal twin-engine light transport; aka C-45, "Bugsmasher."

Bell P-39 Airacobra (A) — Tri-gear, in-line engine fighter with poor high-altitude performance, but excelled as ground strafer with 37-mm cannon.

Bell P-400 (A) — Export version of P-39, used by USAAF in Pacific.

Blackburn Roc (E) — Two-seat, single-engine, turret-equipped fleet fighter developed from Skua.

Blackburn Skua (E) — First metal-cantilever monoplane, with retractable gear to be used on British carriers. Served well as dive-bomber at Dunkirk.

Bloch MB.174 (F) — Elegant twin-engine, twin-tail reconnaissance plane by forerunner of Dassault.

Bloch MB.151 (F) — Low-wing all-metal monoplane, comparable to Curtiss P-36; excellent combat plane; served also with Greek and Rumanian air forces.

Boeing B-17 Flying Fortress (A) — Classic four-engine low-wing monoplane bomber, famous for rugged reliability, easy flying characteristics; served in all theaters.

Boeing B-29 Superfortress (A) — Best bomber of World War II; four-engine,

	pressurized, central fire control; permitted attainment of true airpower at last.
Boeing B-47 Stratojet (A)	Six-engine swept-wing jet bomber; most important multiengine jet in history; direct ancestor of B-52, KC-135, 707 to 777.
Boeing B-52 Stratofortress (A)	"SAC's Long Rifle"; versatile eight-engine strategic nuclear bomber; first flight, 1952; still in service.
Boeing F-13 (A)	Reconnaissance version of B-29.
Boeing P-26 Peashooter (A)	Transitional fighter; first low-wing, all-metal fighter; last fixed-gear, open-cockpit fighter.
Boeing 307 Stratoliner (A)	Low-wing, four-engine pressurized transport.
Boeing 737 "Fat Albert" (A)	Twin-engine jet transport.
Boulton-Paul Defiant (E)	Ill-starred two-seat, low-wing, powered-turret fighter. No forward guns.
Brewster F2A Buffalo (A)	Low-wing retractable-gear carrier fighter; unsuccessful with U.S. and RAF; successful with Finns.
Bristol Blenheim (E)	First British twin-engine, all-metal, "high-speed" bomber; underarmed and under-armored; many lost in combat.
Bristol Beaufort (E)	Effective bomber–torpedo bomber develop-ment of Blenheim; twin-engine, low-wing, all-metal.
Bristol Beaufighter (E)	Highly successful fighter version of Beaufort; used as night fighter, intruder.
Consolidated PBY Catalina (A)	Beloved high-pylon mounted-wing, twin-engine amphibian; patrol plane/bomber/torpedo plane; sighted the *Bismarck*.
Consolidated B-24 Liberator (A)	Four-engine heavy bomber; slim Davis wing gave long range; more produced than any other American plane; helped win Battle of the Atlantic.
Curtiss C-46 Commando (A)	Heavy twin-engine, low-wing cargo plane. Used to "fly the Hump."
Curtiss P-36 Hawk (A)	Low-wing, radial-engine fighter; used by French, English, Finns; forerunner of P-40 series.
Curtiss SB2C-1 Helldiver (A)	Portly, trouble-prone heavy dive-bomber; long maturation process.
Curtiss Hydroplane (A)	Early floatplane sold to Japanese.
Curtiss Triad (A)	Amphibious version of biplane pusher.
Curtiss flying boat (A)	Antisub patrol planes of World War I.
Curtiss P-40 Warhawk, Kittyhawk (A)	In-line engine version of P-36; used exten-sively in all theaters; rugged, low-wing, all-metal; most famous use by Flying Tigers.
de Havilland Tiger Moth (E)	Wood and fabric biplane trainer.
de Havilland Mosquito (E)	All-wood, twin-engine; most versatile war-

	plane of World War II; fighter-bomber pathfinder, reconnaissance, etc.
DFS 230A Glider (G)	High-wing, mixed-construction troop carrier; starred at Eben-Emael.
Dornier Do 17 Flying Pencil (G)	Slim-fuselaged, twin-engine, high-speed-for-the-time bomber.
Dornier Do 18 (G)	Twin-push-pull-engine flying boat; long-range recce and air-sea rescue.
Dornier Do 217 (G)	Development of Do 17.
Douglas A-20 Havoc (Boston) (A)	Twin-engine, all-metal, high-speed light bomber; night fighter version designated P-70.
Douglas A-26 Invader (A)	Sophisticated development of A-20.
Douglas B-18 Bolo (A)	Portly bomber version of Douglas DC-2.
Douglas C-47 Dakota, Gooney Bird, Skytrain (A)	Military version of DC-3; over 13,000 built; invaluable to war effort, rugged, reliable, beloved by crews.
Douglas C-54 Skymaster (A)	Four-engine transport, à la DC-4.
Douglas SBD Dauntless (A)	Low-wing, all-metal, Ed Heinemann–designed dive-bomber; won Battle of Midway, and with it, Pacific war.
Douglas TBD Devastator (A)	Ill-fated low-wing, all-metal torpedo plane withdrawn from operations after catastrophic losses at Midway.
Fairey Battle (E)	Streamlined low-wing, all-metal monoplane; totally inadequate performance, armor, weaponry.
Fairey Swordfish (E)	Gallant victor of Taranto and many other battles; obsolete fabric-covered biplane.
Fairey Fulmar (E)	Two-seat shipboard fighter; effective development of Battle.
Farman, Henri (F)	Early French biplane.
Fiat CR.42 Falco (I)	Beautiful if obsolete biplane fighter, highly maneuverable.
Fiat G.50 Freccia (I)	First-generation all-metal monoplane fighter; radial engine, underpowered.
Fiat G.55, Fiat G.56 Centauro (I)	Elegant Daimler-Benz–DB–605A-1–powered G-50; probably best Italian fighter of World War II.
Fieseler Fi 156 Storch (G)	High-wing liaison plane.
Focke-Wulf Fw 189 The Flying Eye (G)	Twin-boom, twin-engine recce plane.
Focke-Wulf Fw 190 Wurger (G)	Only radial-engine–powered German fighter; low-wing, all-metal, high rate of roll; used as fighter bomber.
Focke-Wulf Fw 200 Condor (G)	Elegant all-metal, four-engine transport converted to recce/bomber.
Fokker D XXI (D)	Single-engine, fixed-gear monoplane fighter

	used by Dutch, Finns.
Fokker Triplane (G)	Famous World War I fighter flown by von Richthofen.
Fritz X (G)	Radio controlled "smart bomb"; sank Italian battleship *Roma* in 1943.
FSX (J)	Modern fighter project.
Gloster Gladiator (E)	Biplane fighter, last of line; direct descendant of World War I S.E.5a.
Gloster Sea Gladiator (E)	Shipboard version of Gladiator.
Gotha G.V (G)	World War I biplane pusher-engine bomber.
Gotha Go 229 (G)	Flying-wing jet fighter.
Grade (G)	Pre–World War I German aircraft.
Grumman F4F Wildcat (A)	Rugged, rotund mid-wing–retractable–gear fighter; Marine-Navy mainstay.
Grumman F6F Hellcat (A)	Designed specifically to meet Zero threat; first combat eighteen months after first flight; shot down 5,156 enemy aircraft.
Grumman TBF Avenger (A)	Effective torpedo bomber; low-wing, single radial engine.
Handley Page Hampden (E)	First-generation all-metal, twin-engine bomber.
Handley Page Halifax (E)	Four-engine heavy bomber; all-metal mono-plane.
Hawker Hurricane (E)	Single-engine, low-wing, mixed-construction interceptor; most important fighter in Battle of Britain.
Hawker Sea Hurricane (E)	Shipboard version of Hurricane.
Hawker Typhoon (E)	Low-wing, all-metal, thick-airfoil fighter-bomber; 24-cylinder in-line engine; initial high accident rate.
Hawker Tempest (E)	Thin-wing development of Typhoon.
Heinkel He 59 (G)	Twin-float biplane; air-sea rescue.
Heinkel He 111 (G)	All-metal, twin-engine, long-lived bomber; twin liquid-cooled engines.
Heinkel He 177 Greif (G)	Trouble-prone coupled–power-plant (four engines, two propellers) all-metal monoplane.
Heinkel He 219 Uhu (G)	Twin-engine monoplane; best German radar night fighter; fast; ejection seats for pilot, radar operator.
Henschel Hs 123 (G)	Pretty single-engine ground-attack biplane and dive-bomber.
Henschel Hs 129 (G)	Twin-engine armored ground-attack plane, significantly underpowered.
Horten Ho IX (G)	Prototype for Gotha Go 229.
Ilyushin Il-2 Shturmovik (R)	Low-wing, heavily armored antitank plane—"bread and air" to Russian soldiers, according to Stalin.
Junkers F 13 (G)	Successful early single-engine, all-metal

	transport.
Junkers G 38 (G)	Tentative step toward flying wing; four-engine passenger transport.
Junkers Ju 52/3m Tante Ju (G)	Three-engine, all-metal transport vital to German war effort.
Junkers Ju 86 (G)	Unsuccessful transport conversion to bomber; twin-engine, all-metal retractable gear; some used diesel engines.
Junkers Ju 87 Stuka (G)	Infamous all-metal, gull-wing, single-engine dive-bomber.
Junkers Ju 88 (G)	Most versatile German bomber/recce/night fighter/torpedo plane; twin-engine, all-metal.
Junkers Ju 90 (G)	Four-engine, all-metal transport.
Kawanishi H6K Mavis (J)	Four-engine flying-boat patrol bomber.
Kawanishi H8K Emily (J)	Best four-engine flying-boat patrol bomber of war.
Kawanishi N1K1-J George (J)	Formidable radial-engine, all-metal fighter, troubled by mechanical faults.
Kawasaki Ki-48 Lily (J)	Twin-engine, all-metal bomber.
Kawasaki Ki-61 Tony (J)	In-line–engine, all-metal fighter.
Kawasaki Ki-100 (J)	Radial-engine version of Tony; equal to P-51 in some respects.
Lavochkin LaGG-3 (R)	Mixed-construction, plywood-covered, strong, lightweight, low-wing fighter; in-line engine, retractable gear.
Lavochkin La-5 (R)	Development of LaGG-3 with radial air-cooled engine; good close-support weapon.
Lioré et Oliver LeO 45 (F)	Shapely series of twin-engine, all-metal bombers; numerically most important in French inventory.
Lockheed Hudson (A)	All-metal, twin-engine development of Lockheed Electra, used extensively by RAF Coastal Command.
Lockheed Ventura (A)	Development of Hudson.
Lockheed Harpoon (A)	Further development of Hudson.
Lockheed F-4 Lightning (A)	Photoreconnaissance version of P-38.
Lockheed P-38 Lightning (A)	Twin-boom, twin-engine, all-metal long-range fighter.
Macchi-Castoldi MC.72 (I)	Tandem-engine, twin-float speed-record setter at 440.4 mph in 1934. Record still stands.
Macchi-Castoldi MC.200 Saetta (I)	Single radial-engine, low-wing monoplane fighter; exceptionally maneuverable, lightly armed.
Macchi-Castoldi MC.202 Folgore (I)	Most successful Italian fighter; in-line engine development of Saetta.
Macchi-Castoldi MC.205 Veltro (I)	Development of Folgore.
McDonnell Douglas F-15 (A)	Modern air-superiority fighter.
Martin Maryland (A)	Twin-engine, all-metal light bomber used by

	French and English.
Martin Baltimore (A)	Development of Maryland.
Martin B-26 Marauder (A)	All-metal, twin-engine medium bomber; early crashes gave bad reputation, overcome by combat success.
Messerschmitt Bf 108 Taifun (G)	Four-seat, low-wing, all-metal touring plane, comparable to later Beech Bonanza.
Messerschmitt Bf 109 (G)	Single-engine, all-metal fighter; principal German fighter; more than 30,000 produced.
Messerschmitt Bf 110 Zerstörer (G)	Twin-engine, all-metal monoplane; successful night fighter.
Messerschmitt Me 163 Komet (G)	Radical delta-wing, rocket-powered interceptor.
Messerschmitt Me 210 (G)	Disastrous twin-engine fighter; numerous crashes in tests and on operations.
Messerschmitt Me 410 Hornisse (G)	Improved version of Me 210.
Messerschmitt Me 262 Schwalbe (G)	First operational jet fighter; twin jets, swept wings, four cannons.
Messerschmitt Me 323 Gigant (G)	Huge six-engine transport glider.
Mikoyan-Gurevich MiG-3 (R)	In-line-engine, low-wing fighter.
Mitsubishi A5M Claude (J)	Radial-engine, fixed-gear, low-wing monoplane, highly maneuverable.
Mitsubishi A6M Zero (J)	Lightweight, beautiful, all-metal, low-wing fighter, supreme in early years of war.
Mitsubishi G3M2 Nell (J)	Twin-engine, all-metal bomber.
Mitsubishi G4M1 Betty (J)	Portly twin-engine medium bomber, lightly armored.
Mitsubishi JM2 Jack (J)	Radial-engine interceptor; low-wing, stubby fuselage.
Mitsubishi Ki-21 Sally (J)	Twin-engine, all-metal bomber.
Morane-Saulnier MS. 406 (F)	In-line-engine, low-wing monoplane. Most numerous French fighter in 1940; outclassed by enemy planes.
Nakajima A6M2-N Zero (J)	Floatplane version of Zero.
Nakajima B5N Kate (J)	Handsome low-wing, radial-engine torpedo and level bomber.
Nakajima B6N Jill (J)	Improved version of Kate.
Nakajima E8N2 Dave (J)	Fabric-covered biplane; radial-engine catapult floatplane.
Nakajima Ki-27 Nate (J)	Radial-engine, fixed-gear fighter.
Nakajima Ki-43 Oscar (J)	Maneuverable radial-engine, all-metal army fighter; similar in performance and appearance to Zero.
Nakajima Ki-84 Frank (J)	Excellent radial-engine, highly maneuverable, low-wing, all-metal fighter.
North American B-25 Mitchell (A)	All-metal, twin-radial-engine medium bomber; fought in all theaters, including first raid on Tokyo.

North American P-51 Mustang (A) — All-metal, low-wing, in-line engine; probably best piston-engine fighter of the war.

North American F-86 (A) — Single-engine jet used in Korea.

Northrop B-2 (A) — Flying-wing stealth bomber.

Northrop P-61 Black Widow (A) — Twin-engine, twin-boom night fighter.

Petlyakov Pe-2 (R) — Graceful twin-engine bomber.

Piper Cub (A) — Classic American lightplane.

Polikarpov I-15 (R) — Radial-engine biplane fighter.

Polikarpov I-16 (R) — First cantilever low-wing monoplane with retractable gear to enter squadron service.

Polikarpov Po-2 (R) — Fabric-covered biplane; most-manufactured aircraft in history; perhaps 40,000 built.

Potez 63 (F) — Delicate-looking all-metal, twin-engine series of fighters, recce, bombers; more than 1,300 built.

Potez 633 (F) — Light bomber version of Potez 63.

P.Z.L. P.7 (P) — Gull-wing, radial-engine monoplane fighter.

P.Z.L. P.11 (P) — Improved version of P.7.

P.Z.L. P.23 Karas (P) — Single–radial-engine bomber.

P.Z.L. P.24 (P) — Improved version of P.11.

P.Z.L. P.37 Los (P) — Twin-engine, all-metal bomber.

Republic P-47 Thunderbolt (A) — Rugged single–radial-engine, all-metal fighter-bomber.

Savoia-Marchetti SM.79 Sparviero (I) — Trimotor, low-wing bomber.

Savoia-Marchetti SM.81 (I) — Trimotor bomber-transport.

Savoia-Marchetti SM.55 (I) — Tandem-engine, twin-hull flying boat used in mass-formation flights.

Seversky P-35 (A) — First Air Corps single-engine, retractable-gear enclosed-cockpit fighter; ancestor of P-47.

Short Stirling (E) — Four-engine heavy bomber.

Short Sunderland (E) — Four-engine patrol flying boat.

Sikorsky S-42 (A) — Four-engine flying-boat transport.

Supermarine Spitfire (E) — Classic single-engine monoplane fighter.

Tupolev SB-2 (R) — Twin-engine medium bomber.

V-1 (Fieseler Fi 103) Buzz Bomb (G) — Pulse-jet, gyro-controlled, pilotless bomb.

V-2 (A4 rocket) (G) — Ballistic missile.

Vickers Wellington (E) — Twin-engine heavy bomber.

Vought SB2U-3 Vindicator (A) — Mixed-construction, low-wing scout bomber, single-radial engine.

Vought F4U Corsair (A) — Large gull-wing fighter-bomber; single-radial engine.

Waco CG-4 (A) — Troop- and cargo-carrying glider.

Westland Lysander (E) — Single–high-wing cooperation aircraft; radial engine; used in clandestine work.

Wright Flyer (A) — The first aircraft.

Yakovlev Yak-1, -3, -5, -7, -9 (R) — Single-seat, mixed-construction fighters; in-line engines, superlative handling, built in

	vast quantities.
Yokosuka D4Y Judy (J)	Single–in-line–engine, torpedo–dive bomber, recce, kamikaze plane.
Yokosuka MXY7 Baka (J)	Manned rocket bomb.
Zeppelins (G)	World War I dirigible bombers/scouts.

APPENDIX 2
STATISTICS ON
MAJOR AIRCRAFT*

AIRCRAFT TYPE	WING SPAN	HEIGHT	LENGTH	MAXIMUM WEIGHT (POUNDS)	MAXIMUM SPEED (MPH)	SERVICE CEILING (FEET)	RANGE (MILES)
U.S. Fighters							
Bell P-39D	34'0"	11'10"	29'9"	8,200	368	32,100	800
Brewster F2A	35'0"	12'0"	26'4"	7,150	321	33,200	965
Curtiss P-40N	37'3"	12'4"	33'4"	8,850	378	38,000	750
Grumman F4F-4	38'0"	11'10"	28'9"	7,952	318	34,900	770
Grumman F6F-5	41'10"	13'1"	33'7"	15,413	380	37,300	945
Lockheed P-38J	52'0"	9'10"	37'10'	21,600	414	44,000	450
North American P-51D	37'0"	12'2"	32'3"	11,600	437	41,800	950
Republic P-47D	40'9"	12'8"	36'1"	14,925	433	42,000	550
U.S. Bombers							
Boeing B-17G	103'0"	19'1"	74'4"	65,500	287	35,600	2,000
Boeing B-29A	141'3"	29'7"	99'0"	141,000	358	31,850	4,100
Consolidated B-24H	110'0"	18'0"	67'2"	65,000	290	28,000	2,100
Curtiss SB2C-4	49'9"	13'2"	36'8"	16,616	295	29,100	1,000
Douglas A-20G	61'4"	17'7"	47'7"	27,200	339	25,800	1,090
Douglas A-26C	70'0"	18'3"	51'3"	35,000	373	22,100	1,400
Douglas SBD-5	41'6"	12'11"	33'0"	24,300	245	24,300	1,100
Grumman TBF-1	54'2"	16'5"	40'0"	15,905	271	22,400	1,215
Martin B-26B	65'0"	19'10"	58'3"	34,000	317	23,500	1,150
North American B-25C	67'6"	15'9"	52'11"	33,500	284	21,200	1,500
U.S. Miscellaneous							
Consolidated PBY 5	104'0"	18'6"	63'10"	34,000	189	18,100	2,990
Curtiss C-46	108'1"	21'9"	76'4"	56,000	269	27,600	1,200
Douglas C-47A	95'6"	17'0"	63'9"	26,000	230	24,000	1,600
RAF Fighters							
Beaufighter VIF	57'10"	15'10"	41'8"	25,200	333	26,500	1,470
Gladiator	32'3"	10'4"	27'5"	4,750	253	33,000	420
Hurricane	40'0"	13'1.5"	31'5"	6,600	316	33,200	460

*These figures are typical.

AIRCRAFT TYPE	WING SPAN	HEIGHT	LENGTH	MAXIMUM WEIGHT (POUNDS)	MAXIMUM SPEED (MPH)	SERVICE CEILING (FEET)	RANGE (MILES)
Mosquito VI	54'2"	15'3"	40'6"	21,600	380	39,000	1,300
Spitfire V	36'10"	11'5"	30'2"	6,615	376	37,000	470
Typhoon	41'7"	15'3.5"	31'11"	11,400	412	35,200	510

RAF Bombers

AIRCRAFT TYPE	WING SPAN	HEIGHT	LENGTH	MAXIMUM WEIGHT (POUNDS)	MAXIMUM SPEED (MPH)	SERVICE CEILING (FEET)	RANGE (MILES)
Battle	54'0"	15'6"	52'1.75"	10,792	241	23,500	1,050
Baltimore	61'4"	17'9"	48'6"	23,000	302	24,000	950
Beaufort	57'10"	12'5"	44'7"	21,228	265	16,500	1,035
Blenheim I	56'4"	9'10"	39'9"	12,500	260	27,280	1,200
Halifax I	98'10"	20'9"	71'7"	68,000	265	22,800	1,260
Hampden	69'2"	14'11"	53'7"	18,756	254	19,000	1,885
Hudson	65'6"	11'10"	44'4"	18,500	284	24,500	2,160
Lancaster	102'0"	20'0"	69'6"	68,000	287	24,500	1,660
Stirling III	99'1"	22'9"	87'3"	70,000	270	17,000	2,010
Swordfish*	45'6"	12'10"	36'4"	9,250	139	10,700	1,030
Wellington	86'2"	17'5"	64'7"	29,500	235	19,000	2,200
Whitley	84'0"	15'0"	69'3"	28,200	192	17,600	1,650

*Fleet Air Arm.

RAF Miscellaneous

AIRCRAFT TYPE	WING SPAN	HEIGHT	LENGTH	MAXIMUM WEIGHT (POUNDS)	MAXIMUM SPEED (MPH)	SERVICE CEILING (FEET)	RANGE (MILES)
Lysander	50'0"	11'6"	30'6"	5,920	219	26,000	600
Sunderland	112'9"	32'10"	85'4"	60,000	213	17,900	2,980

German Fighters

AIRCRAFT TYPE	WING SPAN	HEIGHT	LENGTH	MAXIMUM WEIGHT (POUNDS)	MAXIMUM SPEED (MPH)	SERVICE CEILING (FEET)	RANGE (MILES)
Focke-Wulf Fw 190 A-8	34'5"	12'11"	28'10'"	8,770	418	34,775	497
Heinkel He 219	60'8"	13'5"	50'12"	33,730	416	41,660	960
Mess. Bf 109G	32'6"	8'2"	29'0"	7,055	406	39,370	340
Mess. Bf 110	53'4"	13'6"	39'7"	15,873	352	35,760	745
Mess. Me 163	30'8"	9'0"	19'2"	9,500	596	39,500	75
Mess. Me 262	40'11"	12'7"	34'9"	9,742	540	37,000	652
Mess. Me 410	53'8"	14'1"	40'11"	21,276	373	33,000	1,050

German Bombers

AIRCRAFT TYPE	WING SPAN	HEIGHT	LENGTH	MAXIMUM WEIGHT (POUNDS)	MAXIMUM SPEED (MPH)	SERVICE CEILING (FEET)	RANGE (MILES)
Arado Ar 234B	46'3"	14'1"	41'5"	21,715	461	32,810	1,013
Dornier Do 17E	59'1"	14'2"	53'1"	15,520	220	16,730	932
Dornier Do 217E	62'4"	16'6"	59'8"	33,070	320	29,530	1,430
Focke-Wulf Fw 200	107'9"	20'8"	76'11"	50,045	224	19,000	2,210
Heinkel He 111H	74'2"	13'1"	53'9"	30,865	270	21,980	1,200
Heinkel He 177	103'2"	20'12"	72'2"	68,343	303	26,250	3,417
Henschel Hs 123A	34'5"	10'6"	27'4"	4,888	212	29,525	534
Henschel Hs 129B	46'7"	10'8"	31'12"	8,860	253	29,530	428
Junkers Ju 87D	45'3"	12'9"	37'9"	14,550	255	23,905	945
Junkers Ju 88A	65'7"	15'11"	47'3"	30,865	292	26,900	1,112

AIRCRAFT TYPE	WING SPAN	HEIGHT	LENGTH	MAXIMUM WEIGHT (POUNDS)	MAXIMUM SPEED (MPH)	SERVICE CEILING (FEET)	RANGE (MILES)
German Miscellaneous							
Junkers Ju 52/3m	95'11"	18'2"	62'0"	23,416	172	19,360	620
Italian Fighters							
Fiat C.R. 42	31'10"	10'10"	27'3"	5,302	266	33,300	488
Fiat G.50	36'1"	9'2"	27'2"	5,560	293	32,840	620
Fiat G.55	38'10"	10'3"	30'9"	8,179	385	42,650	745
Macchi-Castoldi MC.200	34'8"	11'6"	26'10"	5,715	312	29,200	354
Macchi-Castoldi MC.202	34'8"	9'11"	29'1"	6,459	370	37,730	475
Italian Bombers							
Savoia-Marchetti SM.79	69'7"	13'5"	53'2"	24,912	270	22,960	1,242
Russian Fighters							
Lavochkin La-5	32'3"	9'3"	27'11"	7,405	402	36,090	475
Lavochkin La-7	32'3"	9'2"	27'11"	7,495	413	33,300	395
MiG-3	33'9"	8'7"	26'9"	7,695	407	39,370	510
Polikarpov I-15	33'6"	9'10"	20'9"	3,827	230	26,245	280
Polikarpov I-16	29'6"	8'5"	20'1"	4,520	326	29,530	250
Yak-1	32'10"	8'8"	27'10"	6,217	364	32,800	435
Yak-3	30'2"	7'10"	27'11"	5,864	403	35,475	506
Russian Bombers							
Ilyushin Il-2	47'11"	11'1"	38'1"	12,947	275	19,000	480
Petlyakov Pe-2	56'4"	11'3"	41'11"	16,614	360	28,870	817
Japanese Fighters							
Frank	36'10"	11'1"	32'6"	8,576	392	34,550	1,050
George	39'4"	13'4"	29'2"	9,526	363	41,000	770
Oscar	37'6"	10'9"	28'12"	5,695	308	38,500	1,100
Tony	39'5"	12'2"	28'8"	6,504	368	37,730	373
Zero	39'4"	10'0"	29'9"	6,164	331	32,810	1,010
Japanese Bombers							
Betty	82'0"	19'8"	65'7"	20,944	266	28,000	3,256
Emily	124'8"	30'0"	92'4"	68,343	269	25,035	4,475
Kate	50'11"	12'2"	33'9"	8,852	229	24,280	679
Lily	57'4"	12'5"	41'4"	13,340	298	31,170	1,490
Mavis	131'3"	20'7"	84'1"	35,274	206	24,950	2,567

AIRCRAFT TYPE	WING SPAN	HEIGHT	LENGTH	MAXIMUM WEIGHT (POUNDS)	MAXIMUM SPEED (MPH)	SERVICE CEILING (FEET)	RANGE (MILES)
Nell	82'0"	12'1"	53'11"	16,848	216	24,540	2,500
Val	47'2"	12'7"	33'5"	8,047	240	30,000	915
Polish Fighters							
P.Z.L. P.11	35'2"	9'4"	24'9"	3,960	242	36,080	530
Polish Bombers							
P.Z.L. P.23	45'9"	10'10"	31'9"	3,857	193	24,000	800
P.Z.L. P.37	58'10"	16'8"	42'5"	18,872	276	19,680	930
French Fighters							
Bloch MB.152	34'8"	9'11"	29'11"	5,935	320	32,900	385
Dewoitine D.520	33'5"	8'5"	28'8"	6,129	329	36,000	620
Morane-Saulnier MS.406	34'10"	9'3"	26'9"	6,000	302	30,840	500
Potez 631	51'8"	11'10"	36'5"	9,930	276	29,600	760
French Bombers							
Bloch MB.174	58'9"	11'8"	40'1"	15,784	329	36,000	800
LeO 451	56'4"	17'2"	56'4"	25,133	307	29,500	1,430
Martin Maryland	61'4"	14'12"	46'8"	16,809	278	26,000	1,080

SELECTED READING

Agawa, Hirouki. *The Reluctant Admiral: Yamamoto and the Imperial Navy*. Tokyo and New York: Kodansha International, 1979.

Anderton, David A. *History of the U.S. Air Force*. New York: Military Press, 1989.

Arnold, Henry H. *Global Mission*. New York: Harper & Bros., 1949.

Baumbach, Werner. *The Life and Death of the Luftwaffe*. Reprinted as *Broken Swastika*. New York: Ballantine, 1967.

Boyle, Andrew. *Trenchard: Man of Vision*. New York: Norton, 1962.

Boyne, Walter J. *The Smithsonian Book of Flight*. Washington, D.C.: Smithsonian Institution Press, 1987.

————. *The Leading Edge*. New York: Stewart, Tabori & Chang, 1986.

Campbell, Christy. *Air War Pacific*. New York: Crescent, 1990.

Christienne, Charles, and Pierre Lissarrague. *A History of French Military Aviation*. Washington, D.C.: Smithsonian Institution Press, 1986.

Coffey, Thomas M. *Hap*. New York: Viking Press, 1982.

————. *Iron Eagle: the Turbulent Life of General Curtis LeMay*. New York: Crown, 1986.

Copp, DeWitt S. *Forged in Fire*. Garden City, N.Y.: Doubleday, 1982.

————. *A Few Great Captains*. Garden City, N.Y.: Doubleday, 1980.

Craven, Wesley Frank, and James L. Cate, eds. *The Army Air Forces in World War II*. 7 vols. Washington, D.C.: Office of Air Force History, 1983.

Douglas, Sholto. *Combat and Command*. New York: Simon & Schuster, 1963.

Francillon, René J. *Japanese Aircraft of the Pacific War*. Annapolis, Md.: Naval Institute Press, 1988.

Fuchida, Mitsuo, and Masatke Okumiya. *Midway*. Annapolis, Md.: U.S. Naval Institute Press, 1955.

Galland, Adolf. *The First and the Last*. New York: Holt, 1954.

Gilbert, Martin. *Churchill: A Life*. New York: Holt, 1991.

Glines, C. V. *Attack on Yamamoto*. New York: Orion Books, 1990.

Goldberg, Alfred, ed. *A History of the United States Air Force, 1907–1957*. Princeton, N.J.: Van Nostrand, 1957.

Green, William. *Warplanes of the Third Reich*. New York: Galahad Books, 1990.

Gunston, Bill. *Aircraft of the Soviet Union*. London: Osprey, 1983.

Hammel, Eric. *Guadalcanal*. New York: Crown, 1988.

Hansell, Haywood S. *The Air Plan That Defeated Hitler*. Atlanta: Hansell, 1972.

Hardesty, Von. *Red Phoenix*. Washington: Smithsonian Institution Press, 1982.

Harries, Meirion, and Susie Harries. *Soldiers of the Sun*. New York: Random House, 1991.

Hastings, Max. *Bomber Command*. New York: Dial Press/James Wade, 1979.

Hata, Ikuhiko, and Izawa Yasuho. *Japanese Naval Aces and Fighter Units in World War II*. Annapolis, Md.: Naval Institute Press, 1989.

Her Majesty's Stationery Office: *The Rise and Fall of the German Air Force, 1939–1945*. London: Arms & Armour, 1983.

Homze, Edward L. *Arming the Luftwaffe*. Lincoln: University of Nebraska Press, 1976.

Hough, Richard, and Denis Richards. *The Battle of Britain*. New York: Norton, 1989.

Ienaga, Saburo. *The Pacific War, 1931–1945*. New York: Pantheon, 1978.

Irving, David. *The Rise and Fall of the Luftwaffe*. Boston: Little, Brown, 1973.

———. *Goering*. New York: Morrow, 1989.

Jones, R. V. *Most Secret War*. London: Hamish Hamilton, 1978.

Kenney, George C. *General Kenney Reports*. New York: Duell, Sloan & Pearce, 1949.

Kimball, Warren F. *The Most Unsordid Act: Lend Lease, 1939–1941*. Baltimore: Johns Hopkins University Press, 1969.

Larabee, Eric. *Commander in Chief*. New York: Harper & Row, 1987.

Lee, Asher. *The Soviet Air Force*. New York: John Day, 1962.

Mason, Herbert M., Jr. *The Rise of the Luftwaffe, 1918–1940*. New York: Dial Press, 1973.

Mitcham, Samuel W., Jr. *Men of the Luftwaffe*. Novato, Calif.: Presidio Press, 1988.

Momyer, William W. *Air Power in Three Wars (World War II, Korea, Vietnam)*. Washington, D.C.: Office of Air Force History, 1985.

Morison, Samuel Eliot. *History of U.S. Naval Operations in World War II*. Boston: Little, Brown, 1975.

Murray, Williamson. *Luftwaffe*. Baltimore: Nautical & Aviation Publishing Co., 1985.

Nielsen, Andreas. *The German Air Force General Staff*. Montgomery, Ala.: USAF Historical Division, 1968.

Padfield, Peter. *Doenitz, the Last Fuehrer*. London: Panther, 1985.

Prange, Gordon W. *At Dawn We Slept: The Untold Story of Pearl Harbor*. New York: McGraw Hill, 1981.

Richards, Denis, and Hilary St. G. Saunders. *Royal Air Force. 1939-45*. 3 vols. London: Her Majesty's Stationery Office, 1953, 1954, 1955.

Roskill, S. W. *The War at Sea 1939–1945*. London: Her Majesty's Stationery Office, 1954.

Saward, Dudley. *Bomber Harris*. Garden City, N.Y.: Doubleday, 1985.

Shores, Christopher, and Brian Cull, with Nicola Malizia. *Air War for Yugoslavia, Greece and Crete, 1940–1941*. Carrolton, Tex.: Squadron/Signal Publishers, 1987.

———. *Malta: The Hurricane Years, 1940–1941*. Carrolton, Tex.: Squadron/Signal Publishers, 1987.

Shores, Christopher, et al. *Fledgling Eagles*. London: Grub Street, 1990.

Spector, Ronald H. *Eagles Against the Sun*. New York: Vintage, 1985.

Suchenwirth, Richard. *The Development of the German Air Force, 1919–1939*. Montgomery, Ala.: USAF Historical Division, 1968.

Swanborough, Gordon and Peter Bowers. *United States Military Aircraft Since 1909*. Washington, D.C.: Smithsonian Institution Press, 1989.

———. *United States Navy Aircraft Since 1911*. New York: Funk & Wagnalls, 1968.

Terraine, John. *A Time for Courage*. New York: Macmillan, 1985.

Thompson, Jonathan. *Italian Civil and Military Aircraft, 1930–1945*. Los Angeles: Aero Publishers, 1963.

Townsend, Peter. *Duel of Eagles*. New York: Simon & Schuster, 1971.

United States Strategic Bombing Survey (Pacific). *The Campaigns of the Pacific War*. New York: Greenwood Press, 1969.

Wagner, Ray, ed. *The Soviet Air Force in World War II: The Official History*. Translated by Leland Fetzer. Garden City, N.Y.: Doubleday, 1973.

Werth, Alexander. *Russia at War, 1941–1945*. New York: Dutton, 1964.

Wood, Derek, and Derek Dempster. *The Narrow Margin*. New York: McGraw-Hill, 1963.

Youngblood, W. T. *Red Sun Setting: The Battle of Leyte Gulf*. Annapolis, Md.: Naval Institute Press, 1981.

INDEX

Abe Hiroaki, 229
Adams, Roger, 370
Adlertag, 69, 77, 78, 83
Aeronautica Nazionale
    Repubblicana (ANR), 171, 172
Agello, Francesco, 169
A-Go plan, 254, 255
Aichi D3A (VAL), 96, 97, 107, 108,
    109, 110, 122, 124, 129, 136,
    214, 221, 225–26, 273, 381,
    392
Aichi E13 (Jake), 130, 381
airpower:
    air superiority and, 22–23, 188
    British development of, 22–23
    Churchill's view of, 166–67
    defined, 16
    excessive use of, 354–56
    in Field Manual 100–20, 187–88
    German development of, 19–21
    and onset of World War II, 12–13
    propaganda and, 17–20
    scale of, 13–14
    strategic, 16–22, 23
    tactical, 21–22
    Ten-Year Rule and, 19
Akagi, 104, 108, 126, 129, 134,
    135–37
Akebono Maru, 129
Alam Halfa, Battle of, 181–82
Albacore, 257
Albania, 12, 89, 173
Aleutian campaign, 278
Alexander, Harold, 180
Allen, Eddie, 362
Allied bombing campaign, 282–320
    aircrews lost in, 284
    Anglo-U.S. relationship and, 288
    assessment of, 356–57
    Big Week in, 336–38

British aircraft and equipment in,
    292–95
Churchill and, 284, 288, 289,
    290, 291–92, 303, 308
combined bomber offensive in,
    312
early British campaign in, 289–90
efficacy of, 286–88, 310
Eighth Air Force and, 303–6
fighter escort issue and, 322, 327,
    328, 333, 337, 338
German defensive systems in,
    296–302, 314, 321–22, 329–30
German propaganda and, 308–9
Hamburg bombing in, 316–20
loss rate in, 306–8
Luftwaffe and, 297, 314–15, 322
Millennium Operation in, 308–12
morality of, 284–85, 310
oil offensive in, 345–46
opposition to, 292
Pathfinder Force and, 316, 317
personalities and, 283–84
Pointblank Operation in, 313–15
political influences on, 288
precision vs. area bombing and,
    285–86, 307–8
radar and, 290, 295–96
RAF and, 288, 289–90, 297, 301,
    313–14
Ruhr operations in, 313–14
technology and, 295–96
weather and, 305–6
    see also bombing
Altmark, 43
Amari Hiroshi, 130
America First, 111
American Volunteer Group (Flying
    Tigers), 119–20, 275
Amerine, Richard R., 222–23

Anderson, Orvil A., 336
Anglo-French Purchasing Commission, 333
"anvil tactics," 229
appeasement policy, 18, 19, 24, 25
Arado Ar 234 Blitz, 349, 381, 390
Arado Ar 240, 34, 381
Arashi, 130–31, 133
area bombing, precision bombing
    vs., 285–86, 307–8
Argument, Operation, 335–36, 338
Arizona, 109
Ark Royal, 47
Armstrong, Frank, Jr., 323
Armstrong Whitworth Whitley, 52,
    53, 83, 293, 381, 390
Army Air Force, U.S., 166, 234,
    240–41, 242, 335
    Air War Plan of, 235
    aviators' psychology in, 331–32
    in Berlin Battle, 331–33
    bomb tonnage dropped by, 282
    equipment of, 187
    first Berlin raid of, 338
    Frantic Operation of, 351–52
    Hamburg bombing and, 317, 318
    oil offensive and, 346
    organizational differences in,
        339–40
    precision bombing favored by,
        285–86
    shuttle bombing by, 351–52
    Torch Operation and, 184–85
    Transportation Plan of, 341
    see also Eighth Air Force, U.S.
Arnim, Jürgen von, 184
Arnold, Henry H. "Hap," 209, 277,
    303–5, 308, 322–23, 328, 336,
    359, 363–64, 368–69, 376, 380
Ashigara, 117
Athenia, 197
Atlantic, Battle of, 14, 189–202
    Coastal Command and, 294–97
    Fw 200 in, 192–93
    radar and, 200–202
    tonnage sunk in, 190, 192, 197,
        198

"Wizard War" and, 196–97,
    200–202
atomic bomb, 14, 15, 349, 358,
    365–66, 374–79
    development of, 374–77
    dropping of, 378–79
Atwater, W. B., 94–95
Auchinleck, Claude, 177, 290
Australia, 121, 180, 211, 212, 214,
    234
Austria, 18, 24, 30, 41, 327
Avro Anson, 195, 196, 381
Avro Lancaster, 88, 293, 309, 330,
    331, 332, 359, 381, 390
    development of, 294–95
Avro Manchester, 294, 381

Bader, Douglas, 71
Baer, Heinz, 353
Baktin, I. P., 157
Balbo, Italo, 169
Baldwin, Stanley, 17, 83
Balkan campaign, 89, 90–91, 93
Banquet plan, 74
Barbarossa, Operation, 139–65
    defense of Moscow in, 149–50
    delayed by Balkan campaign, 90
    Demyansk airlift in, 150
    early German successes in, 144–48
    German air forces in, 143–44
    Kharkov Battle in, 159
    Kuban campaign in, 160–61
    Kursk Battle in, 161–64
    1942 summer offensive in, 150–52
    Soviet air forces in, 141–42
    Soviet purges and, 140–41
    Stalin and, 139, 144, 145, 148,
        154
    Stalingrad Battle in, 152–58
    Typhoon Operation in, 148
Barber, Rex, 239
Barkhorn, Gerhard, 146, 353
Barnwell, Frank, 53
Barratt, Arthur "Ugly," 52, 60, 66
Bataan, 255
Baumbach, Werner, 143
Bayerlein, Fritz, 344

Beahan, Kermit K., 379
Beaverbrook, Maxwell Aitken, Lord, 52, 288
Beda Fomm, Battle of, 176
Beech Bonanza, 31
Beechcraft D-18, 235–36
Belgium, 54, 55, 58, 61, 63
Belleau Wood, 255
Bell P-39 Airacobra, 116, 160, 187, 216, 223, 246, 381, 389
Bell P-400, 216, 220, 222, 224, 381
Benes, Eduard, 24
Bennett, D. C. T., 316
Berlin, Battle of, 283, 328–33, 337, 341–42
Best, Dick, 135
Big Week, 336–38
Birmingham, 264
Bismarck, 190, 196
Bismarck Sea, Battle of, 241–43, 275
Blackburn Roc, 64, 381
Blackburn Skua, 46–47, 64, 381
Blackett, P. M. S., 196
"Blitz," London, 83–84, 87–88
Blitzkrieg, 37, 53–54, 86, 139, 143, 159
"Blitz Week," Eighth Air Force, 323
Bloch MB.151, 381
Bloch MB.152, 392
Bloch MB.174, 51, 381, 392
Bloody Ridge, Battle of, 221–22
Bock, Fedor von, 54
Bock, Frederic C., 379
Bock's Car, 379
Bodenplatte, Operation, 352
Boeing 307 Stratoliner, 382
Boeing 737, 348, 382
Boeing B-17 Flying Fortress, 21, 128, 199, 236, 242, 244, 294, 359, 361, 364, 366, 381, 389
   bombing of Germany and, 304, 306, 307, 318, 324, 326, 327, 329, 343, 352
   Pearl Harbor attack and, 105, 106, 108, 109
   Philippines attack and, 113, 114, 115, 116–17

Boeing B-29 Superfortress, 14, 15, 254, 259, 261, 262, 269, 270, 277, 380, 381, 389
   atomic bomb and, 374, 378–79
   design and development of, 358–61
   first combat raid by, 363–64
   initial deployment of, 362
   in Japanese bombing campaign, 365–74
Boeing B-47 Stratojet, 348, 381
Boeing B-52 Strato Fortress, 31, 382
Boeing F-13, 366, 382
Boeing P-26 Peashooter, 106, 382
Boeman, John, 241
bombing:
   area, 285–86, 307–8
   carpet, 343–44
   combat box and, 307, 314
   G-H system of, 296
   Luftwaffe techniques of, 87
   radar, 246–47, 372–73
   shuttle, 351–52
   skip, 236
   strategic, 18, 20, 21, 23, 27, 39, 345–46
   see also precision bombing; terror bombing
Bong, Richard, 238
Bose, Subhas Chandra, 276
Bouchard report, 50
Bougainville, 243, 245–50
Boulton Paul Defiant, 71, 382
Bowhill, Frederick, 195, 196
Brand, Christopher, 71
Brannon, Dale D., 216
Brauchitsch, Walther von, 35
Braun, Wernher von, 351
Breguet 693, 61
Brereton, Lewis Hyde, 113
Brett, George H., 234
Brewster F2A Buffalo, 128, 129, 382, 389
Bristol Beaufighter, 88, 242, 245, 382, 389
Bristol Beaufort, 194, 242, 382, 390
Bristol Blenheim, 46, 51, 52, 53, 58,

Bristol Blenheim *(cont.)*
    61, 71, 72, 89, 91, 169, 176,
    178, 292, 382, 390
Britain, Battle of, 33, 67–85, 100,
    335
    Adlertag in, 78
    Black Thursday in, 79–80
    Blitz in, 83–84, 87–88
    British defense system in, 71–72
    comparative strengths in, 72–75
    Coventry bombing in, 88
    effects of, 84–85
    Hitler and, 68–69, 70, 81, 83, 85
    Luftwaffe in, 69, 70, 72–75,
        77–79, 80, 81, 82, 83–84
    overview of, 68–70
    Phase One of, 75–77
    Phase Two of, 77–79
    Phase Three of, 81–82
    Phase Four of, 82–84
    Phase Five of, 84
    radar and, 73–74, 79, 84, 87–88
    RAF in, 72–75, 76, 78, 79, 80,
        81, 82, 83–84
British Admiralty, 63, 203, 204
British Commonwealth Air Training
    Plan, 85
British Expeditionary Force (BEF),
    39, 51, 52
Broadhurst, Harry, 185
Brown, Ben, 115
Buckner, Simon Bolivar, 272
Bulgaria, 90, 91
Bunker Hill, 249, 256
Burma, 100, 118, 252, 276, 277
Buscaglia, Carlo Emanuele, 171
Bush, George, 128
Bush, Vannevar, 370
Butt, D. M. B., 291

Cactus Air Force, 216, 222, 223,
    227, 229, 231
California, 109
Cape Engaño, Battle of, 266
Carl, Marion, 216–17
carpet bombing, 343–44
Casablanca Conference (1943), 184,

    198, 313
Cavella, 257
Cavour, 90
Ceylon, 120–21
Chamberlain, Neville, 18, 19, 24,
    25–26, 44
Chennault, Claire, 96, 119, 277, 363
Cherwell, Frederick Lindemann,
    Lord, 290–91
Chiang Kai-shek, 276, 277, 362
Chicago, 230–31
Chikuma, 104, 265
China, Republic of, 16, 18, 21, 95,
    99, 100, 119, 120, 211, 252,
    276, 277, 278, 279, 365
China-Burma-India theater, 275–77,
    362–63
Chinese Air Force, 96
Chitose, 219, 266
Chiyoda, 257, 266
Chokai, 224, 265
Christian X, King of Denmark, 45
Churchill, Winston, 11, 19, 55, 118,
    183, 203, 205, 340, 344, 355,
    375
    airpower as seen by, 166–67
    Allied bombing campaign and,
        284, 288, 289, 290, 291–92,
        303, 308
    Battle of Berlin and, 329, 330
    Battle of Britain and, 68, 82–85
    Battle of France and, 51, 61–63,
        65
    Battle of the Atlantic and, 189,
        193, 195
    Europe first policy and, 209–10
    North Africa campaign and, 177,
        179–80
    Scandinavia campaign and, 42, 43
Ciano, Galeazzo, 89
Citadel, Operation, 161
Clark, J. J. "Jocko," 255, 257
Clark, Virginius, 333
Coastwatchers, 214–15, 220
Cobra, Operation, 343
Coffin, Al, 229
Collins, James F., Jr., 129

Combat and Command (Douglas), 50

combat box, 307, 314

Combined Chiefs of Staff, 183, 341, 355

Command of the Air, The (Douhet), 14

Committee of Operational Analysis (COA), 362, 366

Compass, Operation, 176

Compton, Arthur Holly, 377

Compton, Karl, 370

Conant, James B., 370

Condor Legion, 75

Congress, U.S., 111

Coningham, Arthur "Mary," 177, 178, 179, 181, 182, 184, 185, 339

Consolidated B-24 Liberator, 199, 242, 244, 245, 246, 251, 252, 253, 277, 278, 305, 307, 343, 362, 382, 389

Consolidated Vultee PBY Catalina, 112, 137, 196, 219, 271, 382, 389

Consolidated Vultee PBY Privateer, 105, 106, 128, 129

Copahee, 223

Coral Sea, Battle of, 120–25

Cossack, 43

Cowpens, 256

Crete, 86, 91–93, 172, 202

Cripps, Stafford, 292

Crossbow operations, 336, 338

Crusader, Operation, 177–78

Cunningham, Alan, 177

Curtiss C-46, 276–77, 382, 389

Curtiss P-36 Hawk, 50, 61, 106, 110, 382

Curtiss P-40 Warhawk, 98, 106, 110, 114, 115, 119, 170, 178, 186, 242, 246, 277, 333, 382, 389

Curtiss SB2C Helldiver, 249, 255, 266, 272, 382, 389

Curtiss Triad, 95

Cyprus, 92

Czechoslovakia, 18, 23–26, 29, 41

Daladier, Édouard, 25–26

"Dam Buster" raids, 313, 329

Dauntless Dotty, 366

D-Day, 342

de Havilland Mosquito, 296, 318, 325, 329, 330, 332, 382, 390

de Havilland Tiger Moth, 74, 382, 389

Demyansk airlift, 150

Denmark, 42, 45

Deutsche Lufthansa, 33, 192

Dewoitine D.520, 392

DFS 230A, 58, 383

Dietrich, Josef "Sepp," 342

Dilley, Bruno, 34–35

Dippy, R. J., 295

Dixon, Robert, 123

Donalson, Jack, 115

Dönitz, Karl, 190, 191–92, 193, 197–98, 201, 356

Doolittle, James H., 16, 120, 184, 185, 323, 335–36, 364, 366

Dornier Do 17 Flying Pencil, 30, 33, 64, 144, 146, 383, 390

Dornier Do 18, 195, 383

Dornier Do 217, 205, 300, 302, 383, 390

Douglas, Sholto, 50–51, 85, 297–99

Douglas A-20 Boston, 181, 242, 304, 383

Douglas A-20 Havoc, 106, 160, 236, 242, 253, 339, 383, 389

Douglas A-26 Invader, 383, 389

Douglas B-18 Bolo, 106, 383

Douglas C-47, 185, 237, 244, 276–77, 339, 383, 389

Douglas C-54 Skymaster, 383

Douglas DC-2, 106

Douglas SBD Dauntless, 16, 96–97, 106, 109, 123, 124, 127, 128, 131–36, 215, 216, 219–20, 224, 226, 246, 249, 255, 383, 389

Douglas TBD Devastator, 107, 123, 124, 127, 132, 133, 383

Douhet, Giulio, 14, 17, 282, 373
Dowding, Hugh "Stuffy," 62, 63,
    66, 67, 70, 72, 73–74, 79, 82,
    84, 85, 191, 192, 290, 297
Dresden, bombing of, 283, 284,
    290, 292, 354–55, 356
Duilio, 90
Dunkirk evacuation, 63–65, 66
Dynamo, Operation, 63–67

Eaker, Ira C., 284, 303–5, 313, 315,
    322–23, 326, 328, 336, 344
Egypt, 89, 90, 167, 168, 176
Eighth Air Force, U.S., 315, 341,
    343, 345
    Allied bombing campaign and,
        303–6
    Big Week and, 336–38
    Doolittle in command of, 335–36
    Dresden bombing and, 354–55,
        356
    fighter escort issue and, 322, 327,
        328, 333, 337, 338
    in Frantic Operation, 352
    growth of, 303–4, 312
    LeMay's innovations and, 307–8
    Schweinfurt and Regensburg raids
        and, 323–27
Einstein, Albert, 374
Eisenhower, Dwight D., 332, 339,
    340–41, 355
El Alamein, Battles of, 67–68,
    179–81, 182–83
Emmons, 273
Enigma cypher, 44, 191, 192
Enola Gay, 378
Enterprise, 106, 109, 121, 127, 130,
    132, 133, 136, 137, 207–8,
    214, 215, 219, 225–27, 228,
    229, 250
Essex, 249, 256, 271
Ethiopia, 12, 18
Everett, R. W. H., 199
Evers, W. H., 333

Fairey Battle, 52, 53, 60–61, 89,
    142, 173, 383, 390

Fairey Fulmar, 173, 383
Fairey Swordfish, 90, 107, 173, 383,
    390
Falaise-Argentan pocket, 344–45
Falck, Wolfgang, 300
Falkenhorst, Nikolaus von, 44–45
Fall Gelb, 53–55
Faure, Jacques, 95
Ferebee, Thomas W., 378
Fermi, Enrico, 377
Fiat CR.42 Falco, 383, 391
Fiat G.50 Freccia, 89, 170, 383, 391
Fiat G.55 Centauro, 170, 383, 391
Fiat G.56 Centauro, 170, 383
Fieberling, Langdon K., 129
Field Manual 100-20, 187–88
Fieseler Fi 156 Storch, 37, 383
Finland, 42–43, 47–48
Fitch, Aubrey W., 122
Flax, Operation, 186
Fleet, Reuben, 196
Fletcher, Frank J., 121–23, 127,
    129, 132, 214–19
Flight to Arras (Saint-Exupéry), 51
Flying Tigers, 119–20, 275
Focke-Wulf Fw 189 Flying Eye, 383
Focke-Wulf Fw 190 Wurger, 162,
    170, 298, 315, 321, 327, 334,
    344, 348, 383, 390
Focke-Wulf Fw 200 Condor, 155,
    192–93, 198, 199, 383, 390
Fokker D XXI, 57, 383
Fokker Dr. I Triplane, 98, 384
Forager, Operation, 253–55
Fort Eben-Emael, 56, 58
Foss, Joe, 223
France, 21, 43, 48, 183
    Blitzkrieg's effect on, 61–62
    fall of, 65–66
    Munich Pact and, 25–26
    "phony war" and, 35, 39
    Rhineland crisis and, 17–18
    strategic bombing policy of, 18,
        23, 27
    Sudeten crisis and, 23, 24
France, Battle of, 49–67
    airborne operations in, 56–59

Allied air campaign in, 60–61
Dunkirk evacuation in, 63–65, 66
French failure in, 61–62
French surrender in, 65–66
Hitler and, 54, 55, 56
Luftwaffe in, 53, 54–55, 59, 60, 62, 67
Plan D in, 55–56, 59
RAF in, 52–53, 57–58, 62, 66, 67
Franklin, 271
Frantic, Operation, 351–52
Freeman, Wilfred, 52
French, James, 274
French Air Force (Armée de l'Air), 49, 50–51, 66, 328
Freya radar, 73, 299, 301, 318
Friedman, William F., 105
Fritz X, 384
FSX, 384
Fuchida Mitsuo, 103, 108, 110, 111, 135
Fukudome Shigeru, 262
Furious, 47

Gabszewicz, Aleksander, 36
Gallaher, Wilmer Earl, 134, 136–37
Galland, Adolf, 81, 284, 352–53, 354, 356
Galvanic, Operation, 250–52
Gamelin, Maurice, 61
Gassner, Alfred, 333
Gay, George "Tex," 133
Gee radar, 295, 296, 316, 331
Geiger, Roy, 222, 223
Geisler, Hans Ferdinand, 45, 174
Genda Minoru, 102, 103, 109, 111, 135, 262
German Air Force, *see* Luftwaffe
Germany, Nazi, 13, 27, 28, 43
aircraft production of, 40–41, 150, 160–61, 297, 314, 327, 335, 347–51, 354
airpower development in, 19–21
atomic bomb effort of, 374
aviation industry reorganized in, 150, 160–61
Cologne bombing and, 310

declares war on U.S., 111
exotic weapons produced by, 348–50
failure of leadership in, 354
Hamburg firestorm and, 319
Japan's strategic goals compared with, 100–101
oil industry of, 344–45
strategic bombing policy of, 18
Sudeten crisis and, 23–24
G-H bombing system, 296
Glorious, 47
Gloster Gladiator, 19, 46, 47, 51, 71, 72, 91, 170, 384, 389
Gloster Sea Gladiator, 172–73
Gneisenau, 194
Goebbels, Joseph, 18, 308–9
"Golden Comb" attack, 204
Gomorrah, Operation, 315–20
Göring, Hermann, 20, 29, 34, 45, 54, 66, 88, 92, 144, 154, 335, 348, 353, 354, 356
Battle of Britain and, 70, 77, 78, 79, 80–81, 83, 85
and bombing of Germany, 287, 297, 299, 300, 310, 325, 326
interservice rivalries and, 202–3
Gotha Go 229, 350, 384
Gotha G.V, 21, 71, 83, 384
Grade, 384
Graf Spee, 43
"Grand Slam" bomb, 294
Grattan, Joseph, 96
Great Artiste, The, 378, 379
Great Britain, 13, 24, 27, 68–69
aircraft production of, 41, 51–52, 292, 294–95, 310, 347
airpower development in, 22–23
in Japanese strategy, 100, 101, 252
Munich Pact and, 25–26
"phony war" and, 39
Polish campaign and, 28–29
Rhineland crisis and, 17–18
Scandinavian campaign and, 44, 46–47
Soviet-Finnish conflict and, 43, 48

Great Britain *(cont.)*
  strategic bombing policy of, 18,
    20, 39
  Ten-Year Rule and, 19
Greater East Asia Co-Prosperity
    Sphere, 100, 211
Greece, 89–90, 91, 202
Grohé, Josef, 310
Groves, Leslie, 376–77
Grumman F4F Wildcat, 98, 106,
    127–29, 132, 136, 215–16,
    219–24, 230, 246, 265–66,
    384, 389
Grumman F6F Hellcat, 246,
    255–57, 263–64, 268, 271–74,
    384, 389
Grumman TBF Avenger, 128, 129,
    219, 224, 229, 230, 249, 255,
    257, 265, 266, 272, 384, 389
Guadalcanal, Battle of, 208–32
  Bloody Ridge Battle in, 221–22
  Cactus Air Force in, 216, 222,
    223, 227, 229–30, 231
  Coastwatchers and, 214–15, 220
  Japanese dissension and, 210–11
  KA operation in, 218–19
  Santa Cruz Battle and, 225–27
  Tassafaronga Battle in, 230
  Tokyo Express and, 217, 222
  U.S. air forces in, 216
  U.S. command structure and,
    209–10
Guam, 103, 118, 254, 255, 258,
    365, 371
Guderian, Heinz, 59–60
Gunn, Paul I. "Pappy," 235–36, 242
Gymnast, Operation, 303

H2S radar, 296, 302, 331
Haakon VII, King of Norway, 46
Hácha, Emil, 25
Halder, Franz, 147
Halsey, William F. "Bull," 121, 127,
    228, 231, 248, 249, 261, 264,
    266
Hamburg, bombing of, 283, 313,
    315–20, 329, 330

Hamilton, Weldon L. "Ham," 123
Handley Page Halifax, 88, 293, 294,
    309, 331, 384, 390
Handley Page Hampden, 83, 293,
    384, 390
Hansell, Haywood S., 362, 365–68
Hara Chuichi, 123, 124, 218–19
Hardison, Osborne B., 226
Harlinghausen, Martin, 203, 204
Harris, Arthur, 190–95, 284,
    290–95, 303, 308–13, 315–17,
    321, 329, 339–41, 355, 373
Hartmann, Erich, 146
Haruna, 132, 223–24
Hawker Hurricane, 19, 31, 47,
    51–52, 57–58, 61–67, 71–72,
    74, 79, 82, 91, 118, 170, 173,
    176, 178, 185, 384, 389
Hawker Sea Hurricane, 198–99, 384
Hawker Tempest, 384
Hawker Typhoon, 178, 345, 384,
    390
Heinemann, Ed, 96–97
Heinkel He 59, 46, 57, 79, 384
Heinkel He 111, 30, 32–33, 36, 56,
    79, 87, 144, 155, 158, 169,
    203, 204, 384, 390
Heinkel He 115, 203
Heinkel He 177 Greif, 34, 155, 352,
    374, 384, 390
Heinkel He 219 Uhu, 330, 384, 390
Helena, 109
Henderson, Lofton R., 131–32
Henri Farman biplane, 383
Henschel Hs 123, 30, 38, 384, 390
Henschel Hs 129, 162, 384, 390
Hercules, Operation, 175, 179
Herrmann, Hajo, 205, 321, 329
Hiei, 104, 229
Himmelbett radar system, 318, 321
Hindenburg, 46
Hino Kumazo, 94
Hirohito, Emperor of Japan, 259,
    279, 375, 379
Hiryu, 104, 108, 126, 129, 136, 137
Hitchcock, Thomas, 334
Hitler, Adolf, 11, 12, 15–16, 18, 22,

30, 35, 89, 143, 172, 175, 205, 279, 282, 297, 302, 308, 310, 325, 348, 353, 379
aircraft production and, 40–41
Barbarossa and, 145–54, 163, 165
Battle of Britain and, 68–69, 70, 81, 83, 85
Battle of France and, 54, 55, 56
and declaration of war on U.S., 111
French surrender and, 66–67
Hamburg firestorm and, 319
Me 262 and, 349
as military gambler, 41–42
Munich Pact and, 25–26
"no retreat" rule of, 150
North Africa campaign and, 176, 179, 182, 183
Polish campaign and, 28, 38–40
Scandinavian campaign and, 43, 44
Sudeten crisis and, 23, 24
Hodgkin, Alan, 295
Hohagen, Erich, 353
Horii Tomitaro, 234
Hornet, 16, 120, 127, 132, 136, 137, 222, 225–26, 227, 255, 257
Horten, Reimar, 350
Horten, Walter, 350
Horten Ho IX, 350, 384
Horthy, Miklós, 24
Hosho, 95
Hughes, Howard, 195–96, 333
Hull, Cordell, 105
Hülsmeyer, Christian, 200
Humphreys, Frederic E., 299
Hump, Operation, 277
Hungary, 24, 25, 90
Hunter, Frank O'Donnell "Monk," 303, 323
Hyakutake Harukichi, 223, 224–25, 233–34, 249–50

I–16, 222
I–19, 222
I–26, 219, 229

Ichiki Kiyano, 217
Illustrious, 90, 173, 174, 273
Iluyshin Il-2 Shturmovik, 142–43, 149, 153–57, 162–64, 384, 391
Iluyshin Il-10 Shturmovik, 142
Indefatigable, 273
Independence, 249
India, 167, 276, 277
Indochina, 100, 277, 365
Indomitable, 273
Indonesia, 100
Inouye Shigeyoshi, 122
Iran, 203
Irvine, Charles B., 225
Israeli Air Force, 26
Italia, 204–5
Italian Air Force (Regia Aeronautica), 89, 91, 169–76
Italian CoBelligerent Air Force, 171
Italian Navy, 89–90
Italy, 13, 18, 167, 183, 186, 202, 327
declares war on Allies, 66, 168, 172
Greece invaded by, 89–90, 91
Itaya Shigeru, 108
Iwo Jima, 269–70

Japan, 12, 13, 20, 21, 100–101, 207
aircraft production in, 98–99, 347
army-navy conflict and, 210–11, 221, 280
atomic bombing of, 14, 15, 375, 378–80
aviation development in, 23, 94–96
B-29 bombing campaign against, 364–74
defensive strategy of, 251–52
Doolittle raid on, 16, 120
failure of leadership in, 279–81
Panay incident and, 18
samurai concept and, 232
Soviet Union declares war on, 379, 380
surrender of, 380
war plans of, 103–4

Japanese Army, 101, 210–11, 217, 221, 230, 280
Japanese Army Air Force, 114, 208
Japanese Naval Air Force, 96–98, 112, 215, 245
Japanese Navy, 96–98, 101, 210–11, 217–19, 221, 280
Jeschonnek, Hans, 29, 70, 325–26, 354
Johnson, Lyndon B., 363
Joint Chiefs of Staff, 243, 269, 363, 365, 366, 368
Joint Target Group, 373
Joltin' Josie, the Pacific Pioneer, 365
Jones, R. V., 87
Joubert, Philip, 196
Juneau, 229
Junkers F 13, 34, 384
Junkers G 38, 46, 385
Junkers Ju 52, 18, 30–31, 34, 46, 56–58, 67, 92, 150, 153–58, 186, 385, 391
Junkers Ju 86, 30, 33, 155, 385
Junkers Ju 87 Stuka, 15, 30, 34–35, 38, 56, 59–61, 64, 67, 78–80, 144, 146, 174, 179–81, 385, 390
Junkers Ju 88, 34, 56, 78, 79–80, 84, 144, 146, 203, 204, 302, 322, 330, 333, 348, 385, 390
Junkers Ju 90, 155, 385
Junyo, 225, 257
Jyo Eiichiro, 261, 266

KA, Operation, 218
Kaga, 104, 108, 126, 129, 133–35
Kalinin, K. A., 140
Kalinin Bay, 265
Kamikaze strategy, 259–75, 373
    debut of, 263–66
    defensive tactics against, 266–68
    Japanese psychology and, 259–60
    at Okinawa, 273–74
    picket ships and, 273–74
Kammhuber, Joseph, 284, 300–302, 321
Kasserine Pass, Battle of, 184

Kaufmann, Karl, 318
Kawaguchi Kiyotake, 221–22, 224
Kawanishi H6K (Mavis), 215, 221, 385, 391
Kawanishi H8K (Emily), 385, 391
Kawanishi N1K1-J Shiden (George), 263, 385, 391
Kawanishi N1K2-J Shiden-kai, 368
Kawasaki Ki-48 (Lily), 112–13, 385, 391
Kawasaki Ki-61 Hien (Tony), 248, 252, 367, 368, 385, 391
Kawasaki Ki-100, 368, 385
Keator, Randall B., 115
Keitel, Wilhelm, 356
Keller, Alfred, 144
Kelly, Colin Purdie, Jr., 116–17
Kenney, George Churchill, 234–37, 241, 242–43, 244, 245, 249, 252
Kepner, William, 323, 335
Kesselring, Albert, 30, 54, 56, 70, 144, 175
Kharkov, Battle of, 159
Kikusui air campaign, 270
Kimmel, Husband E., 106
Kincaid, Thomas "Fighting Tom," 225, 229
Kindleberger, James Howard, 333
King, Ernest J., 199, 209, 210
Kinugasa, 224, 229
Kirishima, 104, 229, 230
Kluge, Günther von, 343–44
Knickebein radar system, 87, 295
Koenig, Marie Pierre, 179, 341
Koller, Karl, 326, 356
Kondo Nobukate, 218
Kongo, 223–24
Königsberg, 47
Korean War, 35
Korten, Günther, 326
Kozhedub, Ivan, 160
Kreipe, Werner, 326
Krogmann, Carl, 318
Krupinski, Walter, 353
Kuban campaign, 160–61
Kurita Takeo, 264, 265

Kursk, Battle of, 161–64
Kuter, Laurence S., 307
Kwajalein, 251

Lanphier, Thomas G., 239
Lavochkin La-5, 153, 154, 163, 385, 391
Lavochkin La-7, 391
Lavochkin LaGG-3, 142, 385
Lawrence, Ernest O., 377
League of Nations, 18
Leeb, Wilhelm von, 54, 55
Leigh, H. de V., 201
Leigh-Mallory, Trafford, 71, 72, 73, 85, 298–99, 339, 340
LeMay, Curtis E., 306–7, 324, 325, 364–65, 367–71, 373–74
Lend-Lease, 160, 161, 203
Le Roux, Chris, 343
Leslie, Maxwell, 135, 136
Lexington, 106, 121–25, 135, 250
Leyte Gulf, Battle of, 259–66
    Halsey and, 261, 264, 266
    Kamikaze attacks in, 263–66
Libya, 89, 176, 185
Lichtenstein radar, 301, 302, 318
Lindsey, Eugene, 133
Lindsey, Robin M., 226–27
Lioré et Olivier LeO 45, 50, 385
Lioré et Olivier LeO 451, 61, 392
Lippisch, Alexander M., 349
Littorio, 90
Lloyd, Hugh P., 173, 184
Locarno Treaty, 17
Lockheed F-4 Lightning, 241, 385
Lockheed Harpoon, 196, 385
Lockheed Hudson, 64, 195–96, 199, 200, 246, 385, 390
Lockheed P-38 Lightning, 186–87, 230, 237–39, 242, 244–46, 252, 269, 305, 322, 339, 385, 389
Lockheed Ventura, 196, 246, 385
Löhr, Alexander, 30, 144
Longfellow, Newton, 323
Lörzer, Bruno, 76
Lovell, Bernard, 295
Lucchini, Franco, 171–72

Lufbery circle, 79
Luftwaffe, 12, 288
    aces of, 145–46, 353
    Adlertag and, 78
    airpower development and, 19–21
    air-sea rescue by, 76–77
    Allied bombing campaign and, 297, 314–15, 322
    antishipping operations of, 202–5
    attrition rate and, 86–87
    in Balkan campaign, 90–91
    Barbarossa Operation of, 139, 143–50, 159–60
    in Battle of Britain, 69–84
    in Battle of France, 53–62, 67
    Big Week and, 337–38
    Bodenplatte Operation of, 352
    bombers of, 32–34
    bombing techniques of, 87
    Crete invasion and, 91–92
    decline of, 159–60, 337–38, 342, 347–51, 352, 353, 354
    defensive innovations of, 314–15
    doctrine of, 36–37, 40
    Dunkirk evacuation and, 64–65
    elite units in, 353
    equipment of, 30–32, 54
    "Golden Comb" tactic used by, 204
    intelligence service of, 78, 143
    in Kuban campaign, 160–61
    in Kursk Battle, 162–64
    leadership turnover in, 326
    Malta operations and, 173–74
    mobility of, 86–87, 91, 147, 204
    in North Africa, 178–79, 184, 186–87
    organization of, 29–30, 54
    in Polish campaign, 29–30, 35–40
    Scandinavian campaign and, 42, 44–45
    Schweinfurt raids and, 324–27
    Soviet 1942 summer offensive and, 151–52
    Stalingrad Battle and, 153–58
    Torch Operation and, 184, 186–87

Lützow, Günther, 353
Luxembourg, 54, 55, 60

M69 incendiary bomb, 370–71
McAfee, Harry E., 258
MacArthur, Douglas, 250, 261, 269
  Guadalcanal and, 209, 210–12
  New Guinea and, 233, 234–35,
    241, 242, 244
  Nimitz's dispute with, 243
  Philippines attack and, 112, 113,
    115–16, 117, 209, 263, 269,
    275
Macchi-Castoldi MC.72, 169, 385
Macchi-Castoldi MC.200 Saetta, 89,
  170, 172, 385, 391
Macchi-Castoldi MC.202 Folgore,
  170, 171, 186, 385, 391
Macchi-Castoldi MC.205 Veltro,
  170, 385
McCampbell, David, 258
McClusky, Clarence "Wade,"
  130–31, 133–34, 135
McCoy, Frank T., Jr., 96
McDonnell Douglas F-15 Eagle, 31,
  385
McGuire, Thomas B., 238
McNair, Lesley J., 343
Maeda Kosei, 102
Maginot Line, 18, 24, 55, 61–62, 65
Mahoney, Grant, 114, 115
Makigumo, 137
Malaya, 103, 105, 117, 118
Malta, 86, 92, 168, 172–74, 177,
  179
Manchukuo, 21, 99
Mangrum, Richard, 216
Manhattan Project, 359, 365–66,
  370, 374–76
Manila Bay, 258
Mannert L. Abele, 273
Manstein, Fritz Erich von, 41–42,
  154, 159, 163
Marcel Bloch MB.151, 89
Mareth Line, Battle of, 185
Marita, Operation, 90
Marseille, Hans-Joachim, 179

Marshall, George C., 166, 183, 209,
  234, 277, 305
Martin B-26 Marauder, 128, 129,
  187, 339, 360, 386, 389
Martin Baltimore, 181, 386, 390
Martin Maryland, 113, 173, 385,
  392
Martin PBM Mariner, 271
Maryland, 109
Massey, Lance, 133
Matterhorn, Operation, 362
Maupin, 199
Mediterranean theater, 187–88
  Barbarossa Operation and, 148
  size of, 167–69
Mein Kampf (Hitler), 143
Meister, Rudolf, 352
Memphis Belle, 366
Merrill, A. S. "Tip," 249
Messe, Giovanni, 184
Messerschmitt Bf 108 Taifun, 31,
  386
Messerschmitt Bf 109, 30, 55, 67,
  77, 81, 82, 142, 144, 145, 153,
  179, 184–86, 298, 315, 321,
  324, 327, 334, 348, 386, 390
  bomb load of, 78
  development and production of,
    31–32
  limited range of, 80
  Spitfire compared with, 64
Messerschmitt Bf 110, 30, 36, 45,
  46, 55, 58, 67, 77, 79–80, 174,
  186, 300, 322, 326, 386, 390
  bomb load of, 78
  as night fighter, 301–2
Messerschmitt Me 163 Komet,
  349–50, 386, 390
Messerschmitt Me 210, 34, 386
Messerschmitt Me 262, 16, 54, 325,
  352, 359, 386, 390
  development of, 348–49
Messerschmitt Me 323 Gigant, 186,
  386
Messerschmitt Me 410 Hornisse,
  386, 390
Midway, Battle of, 67, 68, 125–38

Doolittle raid and, 120
Japanese forces and strategy in, 125–27
McClusky's exploit in, 130–31, 133–34, 135
U.S. forces and strategy in, 127–28
Mikawa Gunichi, 216
Mikoyan MiG-3, 142, 386, 391
Mikuma, 137
Milch, Erhard, 29, 30, 45, 54, 66, 147, 150, 160–61, 296–97, 327, 337, 354, 356
Millennium, Operation, 292, 308–12
Missouri, 232, 380
Mitchell, Billy, 14, 16, 17, 190, 282, 373
Mitchell, Harris E., 274
Mitchell, John W., 237, 238
Mitscher, Marc A., 237, 245, 251, 253, 255–57, 264, 266, 271
Mitsubishi A5M (Claude), 112, 115, 386
Mitsubishi A6M Zero, 98, 107–10, 114, 115, 129, 133, 136–37, 208, 214, 215, 216, 223, 225, 226, 233, 237–38, 246, 253, 265, 273, 274, 386, 391
    improved version of, 247
    Thach weave tactic used against, 220–21
Mitsubishi G3M (Nell), 95–96, 114, 247, 386, 392
Mitsubishi G4M1 (Betty), 97, 114, 208, 214, 220–24, 230–33, 237–39, 247, 268–69, 273, 386, 391
Mitsubishi JM2 Raiden (Jack), 368, 386
Mitsubishi Ki-21 (Sally), 113, 386
Mogami, 137
Mölders, Werner, 81, 146
"Monica" radar, 302
Montgomery, Bernard Law, 180–83, 184, 339
Moore, Joseph H., 115
Morane-Saulnier MS.406, 50, 386, 392

Morgan, Robert K., 366
Morison, Samuel Eliot, 265
Morocco, 183
Morotai (Boeman), 241
Morzik, Fritz, 150
Munich crisis, 19, 24–25
Murata Shigeharu, 226
Musashi, 254, 264
Mussolini, Benito, 11–12, 24–25, 28, 89, 167, 169, 175

Nagara, 135
Nagato, 264
Nagumo Chuichi, 104, 107, 111, 121, 129–35, 218–19, 225–27
Nakajima A6M2-N Zero, 386
Nakajima B5N (Kate), 107–10, 112, 122, 129, 131, 136, 225–27, 233, 255, 386, 391
Nakajima B6N Tenzan (Jill), 254, 255, 256, 257, 273, 386
Nakajima E8N2 (Dave), 130, 386
Nakajima Ki-27 (Nate), 114–16, 386
Nakajima Ki-43 Hayabusa (Oscar), 252, 253, 386, 391
Nakajima Ki-84 Hayate (Frank), 262–63, 368, 386, 391
Natoma Bay, 258
Nautilus, 135
Nazi-Soviet Pact (1939), 28
Neosho, 122–23
Netherlands, 54–55, 58, 61, 92, 100
Netherlands East Indies, 100, 103, 118
Nevada, 109
Newall, Cyril, 289
New Guinea, 121, 210, 211, 212, 233–37, 242, 244, 252–53
Nimitz, Chester W., 121, 122, 237, 240, 250, 275
    Guadalcanal and, 210, 211, 212, 214, 233
    MacArthur's dispute with, 243
    Midway and, 125–28, 130
Nishimura Shogi, 264
Nixon, Richard M., 363

Norden bombsight, 285, 286, 346
Norris, Benjamin W., 132
Norstad, Lauris, 367, 373
North African campaign, 111, 166,
    175–84
  Barbarossa and, 148
  Churchill and, 177, 179–80
  Compass Operation in, 176
  Crusader Operation in, 177–78
  El Alamein battles in, 67–68,
    179–81, 182–83
  Hitler and, 176, 179, 182, 183
  Luftwaffe in, 178–79, 184,
    186–87
  RAF in, 176–81
  Torch Operation in, 182–86
North American B-25 Mitchell, 16,
    97–98, 120, 181, 186, 187,
    242, 245, 253, 277, 386, 389
North American F-86 Sabre, 348,
    387
North American P-51 Mustang, 97,
    170, 187, 208, 269, 270, 283,
    314, 333–35, 337, 339, 344,
    359, 373, 387, 389
North Carolina, 222
Northrop, Jack, 350
Northrop B-2, 350, 387
Northrop P-61 Black Widow, 387
Norway, 42-47, 92, 202, 323
Novikov, A. A., 155
Nowaki, 136

Oboe blind-bombing radar system,
    295–96, 331
O'Brien, 222
O'Donnell, Emmett "Rosey," 366
Office of Scientific Research and
    Development (OSRD), 370
O'Hare, Edward "Butch," 122
Okamura Motoharu, 262
Okinawa, 270–75
Oklahoma, 109
Oldendorf, Jesse B., 264
Ommaney Bay, 275
Onishi Takijiro, 95, 102, 261, 262,
    263

Opitz, Rudy, 349
Oppenheimer, J. Robert, 377
Osmus, Wesley, 133
Osterkamp, Theo, 81
Overlord, Operation, 313, 328, 332,
    340
Ozawa Jisaburo, 254–58, 261–62,
    264, 266

Pacific theater, 208–13
  Guadalcanal's effect on, 231–33
  island-hopping strategy in,
    243–44, 250
  Japanese dissension and, 210–11
  U.S. aircraft in, 242
  U.S. command and, 209–10
"Pact of Steel," 28
Palm Sunday massacre, 186
Panay, 18, 101
Park, Keith, 71, 72, 85
Parks, Floyd B., 129
Patch, Alexander M., 231
Pathfinder Force, British, 316, 317
Pattle, Marmaduke St. John "Pat,"
    91
Patton, George, 60, 344
Paul, Prince Regent of Yugoslavia,
    90
Paulus, Friedrich von, 153–54, 158
Pearl Harbor attack, 102–12
  Japanese fleet and, 103–4
  Taranto's influence on, 102, 103,
    173
  U.S. dispositions and, 104–6
  Yamamoto and, 102–3, 109
Peden, Murray, 294
Peenemünde raids, 329
Peirse, R. E. C., 289, 290, 291
Pennsylvania, 110
Pétain, Henri Philippe, 66
Petlyakov Pe-2, 143, 157, 391
Petrof Bay, 265
Phelps, 124
Philippines, 100, 103, 105, 212,
    275, 365
  Japanese campaign in, 112–17
  U.S. recapture of, 263–64, 269

Philippine Sea, Battle of, 256–59
"phony war," 35, 39, 46, 49, 51
Pilsudski, Józef, 26–27
Piper Cub, 387
Pittsburgh, 271
Plan D, 55–56, 59
Plan Orange, 207
Plan 17, 59
Ploesti raid, 324
Podgorny, I. D., 157
Pointblank, Operation, 313–15, 327,
    330, 336, 338
Pokryshkin, A. I., 160
Poland, 12, 14, 15, 24
    Russo-Polish conflict and, 26, 28
Polikarpov I–15, 142, 391
Polikarpov I–16, 142, 145, 146,
    387, 391
Polikarpov Po-2, 157, 387
Polish Air Force, 26–27, 39
Polish campaign, 29–41
    Luftwaffe doctrine and, 31–37, 40
    Luftwaffe operations in, 29–30,
        35–40
Portal, Charles, 52, 289–90, 291,
    308, 330, 356
Potez 63, 51, 89, 387
Potez 631, 392
Potez 633, 50, 387
Potsdam Conference (1945), 375
Potsdam Declaration, 379–80
precision bombing, 326, 341, 346
    area bombing vs., 285–86, 307–8
    combat box and, 307, 314
    USAAF and, 285–86
Prince of Wales, 96, 117–18, 208
Princeton, 249, 256, 264
Program L, 293, 294
Punishment, Operation, 90–91
P.Z.L. P.7, 387
P.Z.L. P.11, 36, 37, 387, 392
P.Z.L. P.23 Karas, 387, 392
P.Z.L. P.24, 89, 387
P.Z.L. P.37, 387, 392

Quesada, Elwood, 344
Question Mark, 344

radar, radar systems, 78, 80, 329–30
    acoustic version of, 191
    airborne, 88, 296, 301
    Allied bombing campaign and,
        290, 295–96
    Battle of Britain and, 73–74, 79,
        84, 87–88
    bombing with, 246–47, 372–73
    development of, 200–202
    Freya, 73, 299, 301, 318
    Gee, 295, 296, 316, 331
    German defenses and, 300–302
    H2S, 296, 302, 331
    Himmelbett, 318, 321
    kamikazes and, 273
    Knickebein, 87, 295
    Lichtenstein, 301, 302, 318
    "Monica," 302
    stealth technology and, 350
    window (chaff) and, 317–18, 321
    Würzburg A, 300, 301, 318
Raeder, Erich, 42
Rainbow 5 plan, 113
Raleigh, 109
Rayski, Ludomil, 27, 28
Reichenau, Walter von, 37
Republic P–47 Thunderbolt, 115,
    178, 187, 244, 269, 305, 322,
    324, 326, 339, 345, 387, 389
Repulse, 96, 117–18, 208
Reynaud, Paul, 62
Rhineland, 17–18, 41
Ribbentrop, Joachim von, 28, 29,
    279
Richthofen, Manfred von, 37, 115
Richthofen, Wolfram von, 37, 38,
    39, 60, 92, 145, 154, 159, 354
Rickenbacker, Eddie, 223
Rochefort, Joseph J., 211
Roma, 204–5
Rommel, Erwin, 60, 148, 172, 175,
    176, 178–82, 184, 342–43
Roosevelt, Franklin D., 11, 41, 183,
    198, 277, 355, 362, 370, 374
    atomic bomb and, 376, 377
    Eighth Air Force and, 303, 305
    Europe first policy and, 209–10

Roosevelt, Franklin D. *(cont.)*
  Pearl Harbor and, 105
Rose, C. R., 46
Rosenberg, Alfred, 279
Rowehl, Theo, 144
Royal Air Force, 19, 20, 21, 27, 44,
      162, 286
  aircraft production and, 51–52
  airpower development and, 22–23
  air-sea rescue by, 77
  Allied bombing campaign and,
      288, 289–90, 297, 301, 313–14
  area defense system of, 70–74
  aviators' psychology in, 331–32
  Balkan campaign and, 89, 91
  in Battle of Britain, 72–84
  in Battle of France, 52–53, 57–58,
      62, 66, 67
  Berlin Battle and, 328–33, 341–42
  Big Week and, 336–37
  bomb tonnage dropped by, 282
  bureaucratic controversy in, 72,
      339–40
  Butt report and, 291
  Dunkirk evacuation and, 63–65
  Eighth Air Force and, 303, 304
  first aerial victory of, 195
  formations used by, 52, 76
  growth of, 88
  Hamburg bombing and, 317,
      318–19
  Malta defense and, 172–73, 174
  Millennium Operation and,
      309–10
  in North African campaign,
      176–81
  oil offensive and, 346
  Pathfinder Force of, 316, 317
  Peenemünde raids of, 325
  pilot shortage of, 67
  Pointblank Operation and, 315
  Ruhr operations of, 313–14
  in Scandinavian campaign, 46–47
  Torch Operation and, 184–85
Royal Australian Air Force, 242
Royal Navy, 89–90, 273
Royal Netherlands Air Force, 56, 57

Rubensdörffer, Walter, 77–78
Rudel, Hans-Ulrich, 146, 162–63
Rumania, 90
Rundstedt, Gerd von, 38, 54, 55, 59,
      151, 287, 344, 346, 356
Ryujo, 112, 113, 218, 219

Saint-Exupéry, Antoine de, 51
St. Lo, 265, 267, 275
Saipan, 254, 255, 258–59, 269
Sakai Saburo, 215
Sakamoto Akira, 108
Samurai (Sakai), 215
San Antonio I strike, 366–67
Sangamon, 265
San Juan, 226
Santa Cruz, Battle of, 225–27
Santee, 265
Saratoga, 106, 214, 215, 219, 222,
      249, 251
Sardinia, 202, 204
Saul, Richard, 71
Saunders, LaVerne G. "Blondie,"
      362, 364
Saur, Karl Otto, 347
Savoia-Marchetti SM.55, 169, 387
Savoia-Marchetti SM.79 Sparviero,
      89, 169, 171, 172, 387, 391
Savoia-Marchetti SM.81, 89, 387
Savoia-Marchetti SM.82, 186
Scandinavia campaign, 42–47
Schacht, Hjalmar, 25
Scharnhorst, 47, 194
Schlieffen plan, 41
Schmetz, Heinrich, 205
Schmid, Josef "Beppo," 78, 143, 302
Schmued, Edgar, 333, 334
Schweinfurt and Regensburg raids,
      283, 323–27, 330
Sea Lion, Operation, 69, 83
Second World War (Churchill), 193
Seki Mamoru, 225, 226
Seki Yukio, 263, 265
Serrate device, 329
Seversky P-35, 114–15, 387
Shape of Things to Come, The
      (Wells), 18

Sherman, Frederic C., 124
Shimazaki Shigekazu, 110
SHO-1, Operation, 261, 263–64
Shoho, 123, 124
Shokaku, 104, 108, 109, 124, 126,
    208, 218, 219, 225, 226, 257
Short, Walter C., 106
Short S.25 Sunderland, 173, 194,
    196, 199, 387, 390
Short Stirling, 88, 293–94, 309, 317,
    318, 331, 387, 390
shuttle bombing, 351–52
Siam, 100
Sibuyan Sea, Battle of, 263–64
Sicily, 148, 163, 174, 202, 204
Sikorsky S–42, 221, 387
Sims, 122–23
Singapore, 117, 118, 178
skip bombing, 236
Slaughterhouse Five (Vonnegut), 355
Slessor, John, 196, 201
Smith, Clinton O., 274
Smith, Herbert, 95
Smith, John, 216–17
Solomon Islands, 100, 211, 212
Somerville, James, 121
sonar, 191
Sorge, Richard, 145
Soryu, 104, 108, 126, 129, 132,
    133, 135
South African Air Force, 170
South Dakota, 225, 226, 230, 256
Soviet Air Force:
    defense of Moscow and, 149–50
    equipment of, 142–43
    formations used by, 160
    growth of, 141, 149–50, 158–59,
        164
    in Kuban campaign, 158–59
    in Kursk Battle, 162–64
    1942 summer offensive and,
        151–52
    Novikov's reorganization of, 155
    Stalingrad Battle and, 153,
        155–58
    Stalin's purges and, 140–41, 145
Soviet Union, 12, 13, 22, 23, 48, 85,

87, 356, 375
    aircraft production in, 147–48,
        157, 161, 347
    declares war on Japan, 379, 380
    Finland invaded by, 42–43
    German invasion of, *see*
        Barbarossa, Operation
    Polish campaign and, 38
    Russo-Polish conflict and, 26, 28
    Sudeten crisis and, 24
Spaatz, Carl, 184, 303, 328, 329,
    336, 339–42, 344–46, 373, 380
Spain, 21, 31, 87
Spanish Civil War, 12, 36, 75, 203
Speer, Albert, 13, 29, 287, 311, 319,
    325, 327, 337, 347, 356
Sperrle, Hugo, 54, 70, 356
Sprague, Clifton A. F., 264–65, 266
Spruance, Raymond A., 121, 127,
    129, 132, 253, 256, 257, 258
Stalin, Josef, 38, 111, 209, 288, 355,
    356, 375
    German invasion and, 139, 144,
        145, 148, 154
    purges of, 12, 140, 142
Stalingrad, Battle of, 67–68, 150,
    152–58
Steakley, Ralph D., 366
Steinhoff, Johannes, 353
Stilwell, Joseph "Vinegar Joe," 276,
    362
Stimson, Henry L., 376–77
Strangle, Operation, 187
strategic bombing, 18, 20, 21, 23,
    27, 39, 345–46
Stratemeyer, George, 276, 363
Streib, Werner, 330
Strong, Stockton Birney, 225
Student, Kurt, 56, 92
Stumpf, Hans-Jürgen, 71
Sudetenland, 23, 25
Sullivan brothers, 229
Supermarine Spitfire, 16, 19, 31, 51,
    64, 67, 71, 72, 74, 78, 79, 80,
    82, 160, 186, 298, 305, 322,
    324, 334, 387, 390
Sutherland, Richard K., 113, 235

Suwanee, 265
Suzuki Kantaro, 375
Suzuya, 265
Sweden, 43, 305, 325
Sweeney, Charles W., 376, 378, 379
Sweeney, Walter C., 128, 129–30
Switzerland, 55, 305

Taiho, 257
Takahashi Kakuichi, 108–9, 122
Tambor, 137
Tanaka Raizo, 218, 229, 230, 231
Taranto, Battle of, 89–90, 102, 173
Tarawa, 251
Tassafaronga, Battle of, 230
Tatsutakawa Maru, 255
Taylor, Kenneth M., 110
Tedder, Arthur W., 177, 182, 184,
    185, 186, 339, 341
Telecommunications Research
    Establishment (TRE), 295
Ten-go, Operation, 273
Tennessee, 109
Ten-Year Rule, 19
terror bombing, 12, 39
    in Battle of France, 61
    of Belgrade, 90–91
    in Polish campaign, 39
    of Rotterdam, 61
    see also Hamburg, bombing of
Thach, John S., 221
Thailand, 364
Thompson, J. H., 195
Thousand Shall Fall, A (Peden), 294
Tibbets, Paul W., Jr., 376, 379
Timoshenko, Semion, 145
Tirpitz, 126, 190, 204
Tizard, Henry, 200
Togo Heihachiro, 239
Tojo Hideki, 101, 230, 259, 279,
    281
Tokugawa Yoshitoshi, 94
Tokyo, bombing of, 371–72
Tokyo Express, 217, 222
Tokyo Rose, 262
Tolman, Richard C., 370
Tomonaga Joichi, 129, 131

Tone, 104, 130, 131, 135, 218–19
Torch, Operation, 182–86, 303, 328
Toyoda Soemu, 254, 256
Trenchard, Hugh, 27, 58, 282, 298,
    373
Trettner, Heinrich, 56
Trident Conference (1943), 313
Truman, Harry S, 375, 377, 378
Tsuji Masanobu, 228
Tsukahara Nishizo, 221
Tukhachevski, Mikhail, 140
Tunisia, 152, 182, 185–86
Tupolev, A. N., 140
Tupolev SB-2, 113, 142, 387
Turner, R. Kelly, 254
Twining, Nathan, 245–46, 377
Tyler, Kermit, 107–8
Typex code, 44
Typhoon, Operation, 148

U–570, 195
Udet, Ernst, 29, 34, 35, 348, 354
Ukraine, 26
Ultra intercepts, 161, 168, 181
United States, 13, 18, 21, 24
    aircraft production in, 99, 347
    Germany declares war on, 111
    in Japanese strategy, 100–101
    strategic airpower and, 20–23
Uranus, Operation, 154
U.S. Army Air Force, *see* Army Air
    Force, U.S.
U.S. Far Eastern Air Force, 114
Ushijima Mitsuru, 272
Utah, 109

V-1 rocket (buzz bomb), 325, 336,
    338, 348, 350–51, 387
V-2 (A4) rocket, 17, 325, 338, 348,
    350, 351, 387
Valencia, Eugene A., 274
Vandegrift, Alexander, 214
Vejtasa, Stanley W. "Swede," 226
Versailles Treaty, 17, 19
"Vic" formation, 52, 76
Vichy France, 100
Vickers-Armstrong Wellington, 83,

173, 185, 201, 289, 292–93,
300, 309, 316, 387, 390
Victorious, 273
Visconti, Adriano, 171–72
Vonnegut, Kurt, 355
Vose, James E. "Moe," 226, 249
Vraicu, Alex, 258
Vought F4U Corsair, 246, 255, 263,
269, 387
Vought SB2U-3 Vindicator, 128,
132, 387

Waco CG-4, 339, 387
Wagner, Boyd "Buzz," 116
Wainwright, Jonathan, 117
Wakamiya Maru, 95
Wake Island, 103, 106, 118, 279
Waldron, John, 132
Walker, Kenneth M., 235
Walter, Hellmuth, 349
Washington, 230
WASP, 214, 215, 222, 271
Watchtower, Operation, 210
Welch, George S., 110
Wells, H. G., 18
Welsh, William, 184
Weser, Operation, 44, 45
Westland Lysander, 52, 53, 387,
390
West Virginia, 109
Whitehead, Ennis C., 235
Williams, Francis, 96
Williams, Robert B., 324
Window (chaff), 317–18, 321
"Wizard War," 196–97
Wolfe, Kenneth B., 362, 363–64
World War I, 12, 13, 16, 18, 20, 21,
28, 284
Wright, Wilbur, 299
Wright Flyer, 387
Würzburg A radar, 300, 301, 318

X-Gerat, 88

Yahagi, 271–72
Yakovlev Yak-1, 142, 387, 391
Yakovlev Yak-3, 387, 391
Yakovlev Yak-5, 387
Yakovlev Yak-7, 387
Yakovlev Yak-9, 153–54, 163, 387
Yamada Sadayoshi, 214
Yamaguchi Maseo, 226
Yamaguchi Tamon, 136
Yamamoto Isoroku, 106, 120, 279
Coral Sea Battle and, 121, 122,
125
death of, 237–39
Guadalcanal and, 218, 221, 223,
230
Midway Battle and, 125, 126,
127, 135, 137–38
Pearl Harbor attack and, 101–3,
109
Yamashita Tomoyuki, 118–19, 261,
269
Yamato, 126, 135, 254, 264, 271–72
Yankee Doodle, 304–5
Yawata raid, 363–64
Yellow, Operation, 53–55
Y-Gerat, 88
Yokosuka D4Y Suisei (Judy),
254–55, 256, 257, 258, 264,
265, 388
Yokosuka MXY7 Okha, 268–69,
273, 274, 388
Yorktown, 121–24, 127, 129–36,
207–8, 228, 250, 255, 271, 274
Yugoslavia, 23, 90

Zagorski, Wlodzimierz, 27
Zeppelin airships, 21, 388
Zerstörer concept, 75, 79
Zhukov, Georgi K., 149, 153
Zuckerman, Solly, 340–41
Zuiho, 225, 266
Zuikaku, 104, 108, 110, 124, 126,
208, 218–19, 225–26, 257, 266